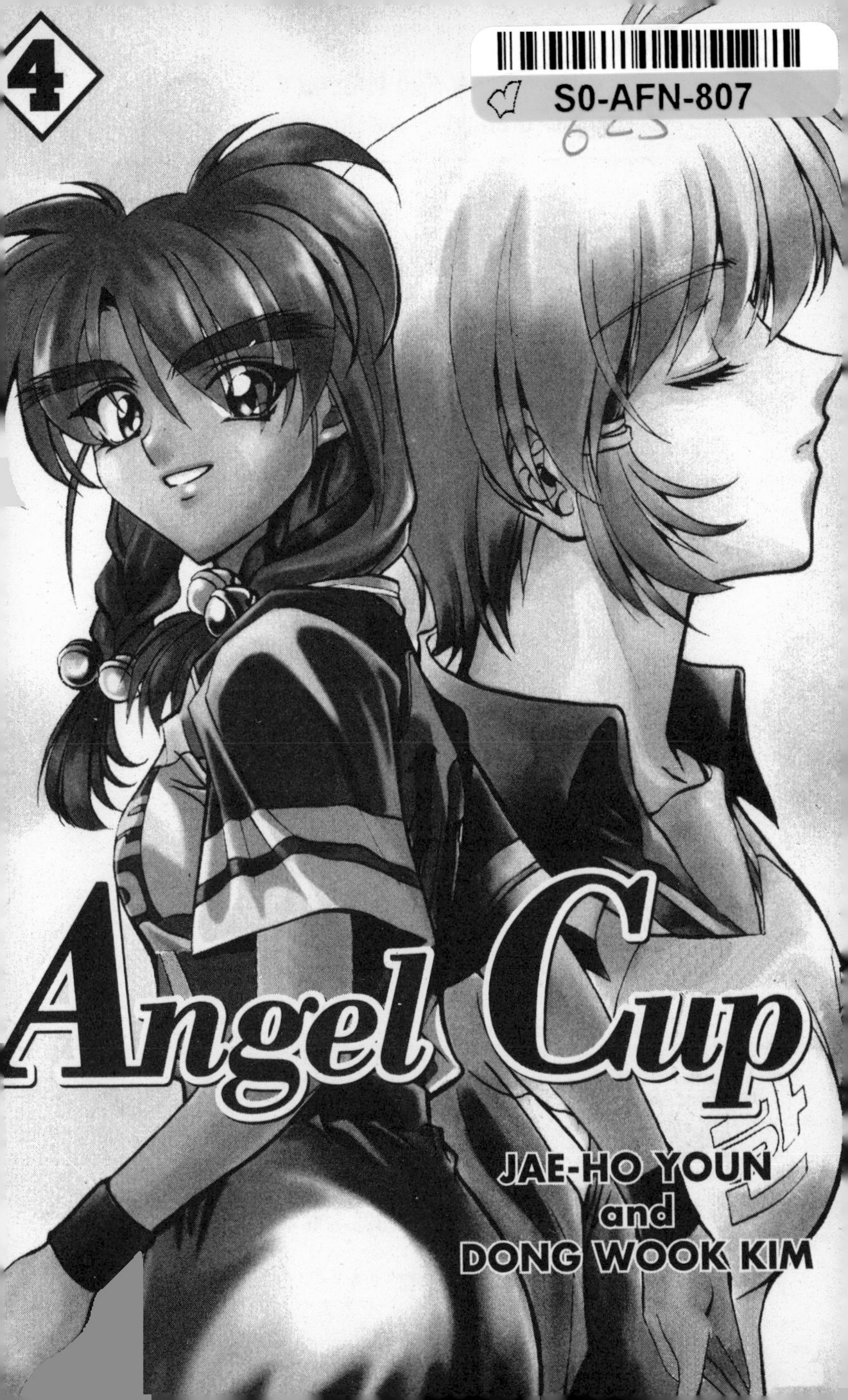
4
Angel Cup
JAE-HO YOUN
and
DONG WOOK KIM

Angel Cup Volume 4
Created by Jae-ho Youn

Translation - Jumi V. Yang
English Adaptation - Hope Donovan
Retouch and Lettering - Star Print Brokers
Production Artist - Courtney Geter
Graphic Designer - Fawn Lau

Editor - Katherine Schilling
Digital Imaging Manager - Chris Buford
Pre-Production Supervisor - Erika Terriquez
Art Director - Anne Marie Horne
Production Manager - Elisabeth Brizzi
Managing Editor - Vy Nguyen
VP of Production - Ron Klamert
Editor-in-Chief - Rob Tokar
Publisher - Mike Kiley
President and C.O.O. - John Parker
C.E.O. and Chief Creative Officer - Stuart Levy

A 🌐 TOKYOPOP Manga

TOKYOPOP and 🌐 are trademarks or registered trademarks of TOKYOPOP Inc.

TOKYOPOP Inc.
5900 Wilshire Blvd. Suite 2000
Los Angeles, CA 90036

E-mail: info@TOKYOPOP.com
Come visit us online at www.TOKYOPOP.com

ISBN: 978-1-59532-306-4

First TOKYOPOP printing: June 2007
10 9 8 7 6 5 4 3 2 1
Printed in the USA

Volume 4

written by Dong Wook Kim
illustrated by Jae-Ho Youn

HAMBURG // LONDON // LOS ANGELES // TOKYO

ANGEL CUP STORY SO FAR...

⚽ So-jin's boyfriend thinks he's got the perfect girl – funny, energetic, and cute! Little does he know that this girl's got a burning passion for soccer that puts the World Cup players to shame! And though the school she's just transferred to didn't have its own girls' soccer team, she made sure that all changed...

Just when So-jin got her team together, and the school finally recognized their abilities, Coach Chae-young had to borrow a little power from an old friend from the states—Chris! Deadly and precise as a panther, Chris whipped the girls into shape with her soccer boot camp. But when their first match just so happens to be against Gai Leung, who placed 2nd in the national level, the girls are going to have to learn to work as a team for once!

THE GIRLS

So-jin

An energetic and tough girl whose determination led to the creation of a girls' soccer team at her new high school. Though she represents the leader of the team, she's still got a lot to learn about teamwork..

Shin-bee

A quiet and passive girl who was known as the MVP during her soccer career in junior high. After years of running away from the sport, she's finally stepped on the field again—as a player on So-jin's team! A mysterious heart condition keeps her from showing her true potential...

Yee-ju

Cool and calm on the outside, but raging and tough on the inside, Yee-ju has a natural gift as goalie for the team with her experience in the sport of handball.

Soo-hee

Soft-spoken and faithful lapdog to Yee-ju, Soo-hee left the team after an injury, and took up pom-poms instead, as her team's cheerleader!

THE COACHES

Chris

A professional soccer coach from the United States, Chris lends her skills when training So-jin's team of beginners. Her tactics may seem harsh, but she knows it takes more than fancy footwork to win a game.

Chae-young

The kind-hearted but klutzy daughter of the rich Yoon Kang-ui, and coach for the girls' team. She sought out help from her friend, Chris, to run the team.

VS. THE BOYS...

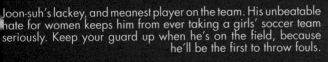

Joon-suh

Popular boy-hottie of the school and captain of the boys' soccer team. He's a fierce player, but has an honorable attitude for the sport.

In-hyuk

Joon-suh's lackey, and meanest player on the team. His unbeatable hate for women keeps him from ever taking a girls' soccer team seriously. Keep your guard up when he's on the field, because he'll be the first to throw fouls.

THE SIDELINES

Chairman Yoon Kang-ui

The dying chairman of the powerful Dae Hang group who donated a hefty portion of his money to forming a girls' soccer team. His reasons may go with him to his grave...

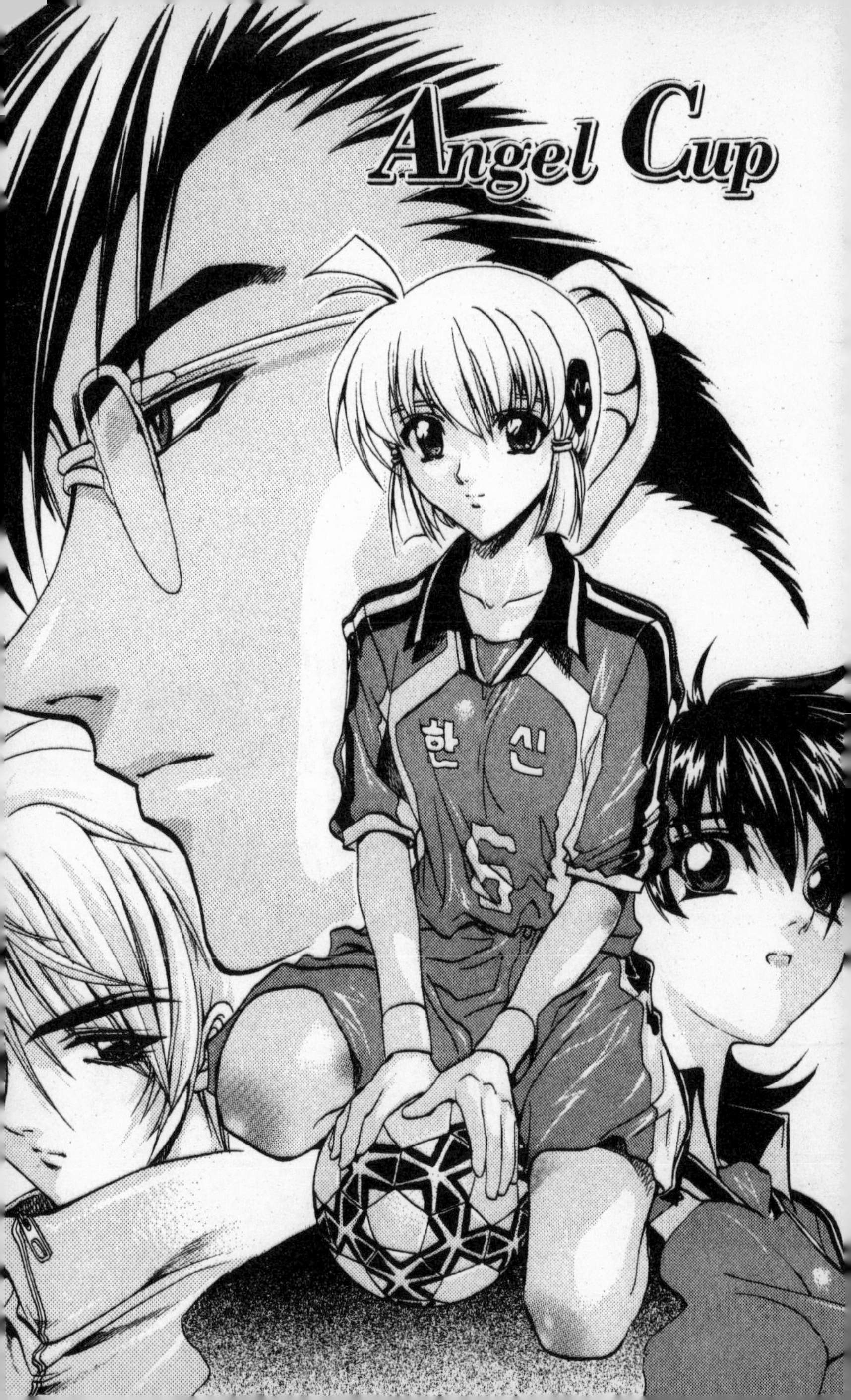
Angel Cup
한 신
5

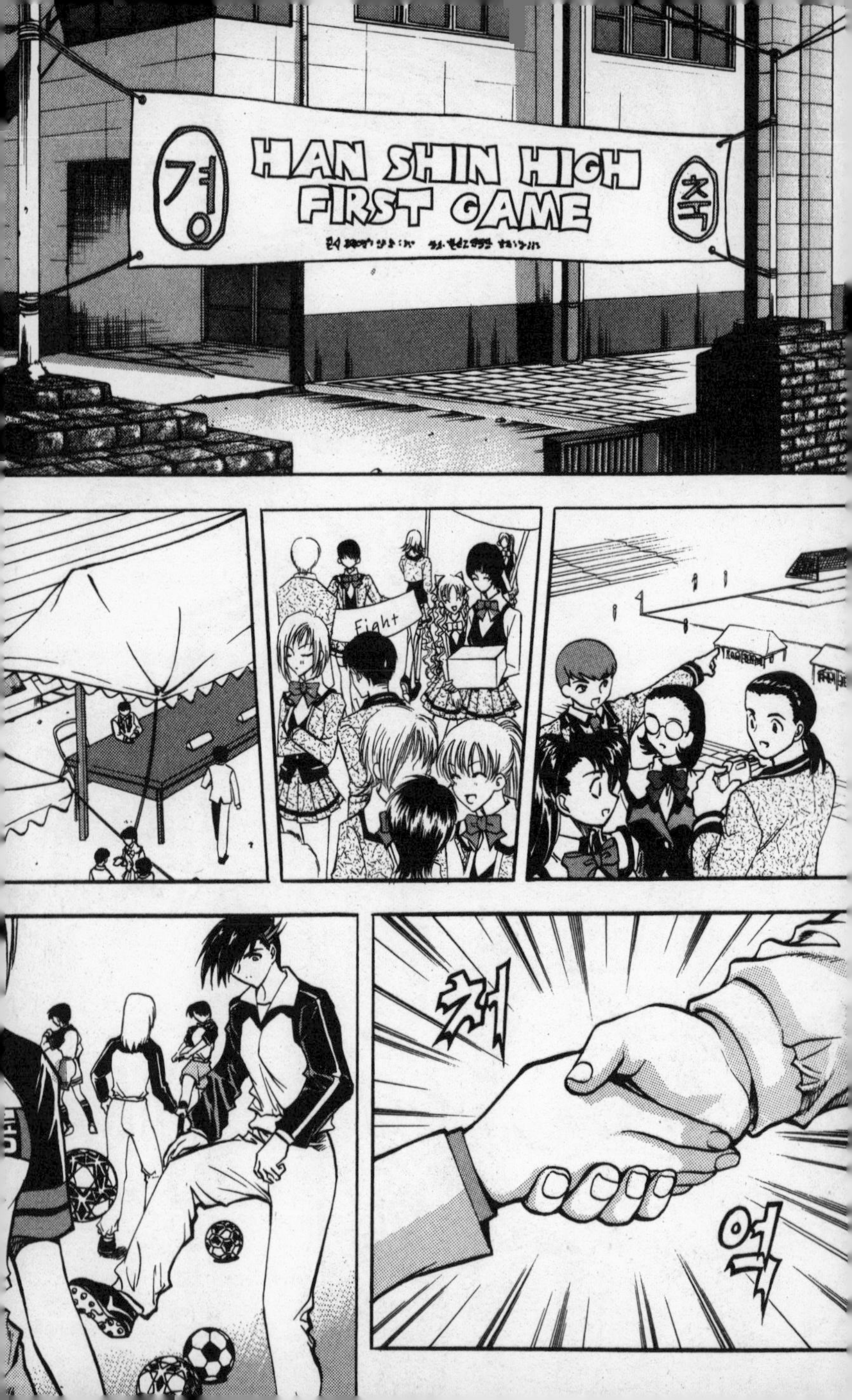
경
HAN SHIN HIGH
FIRST GAME
축
Fight
처
억

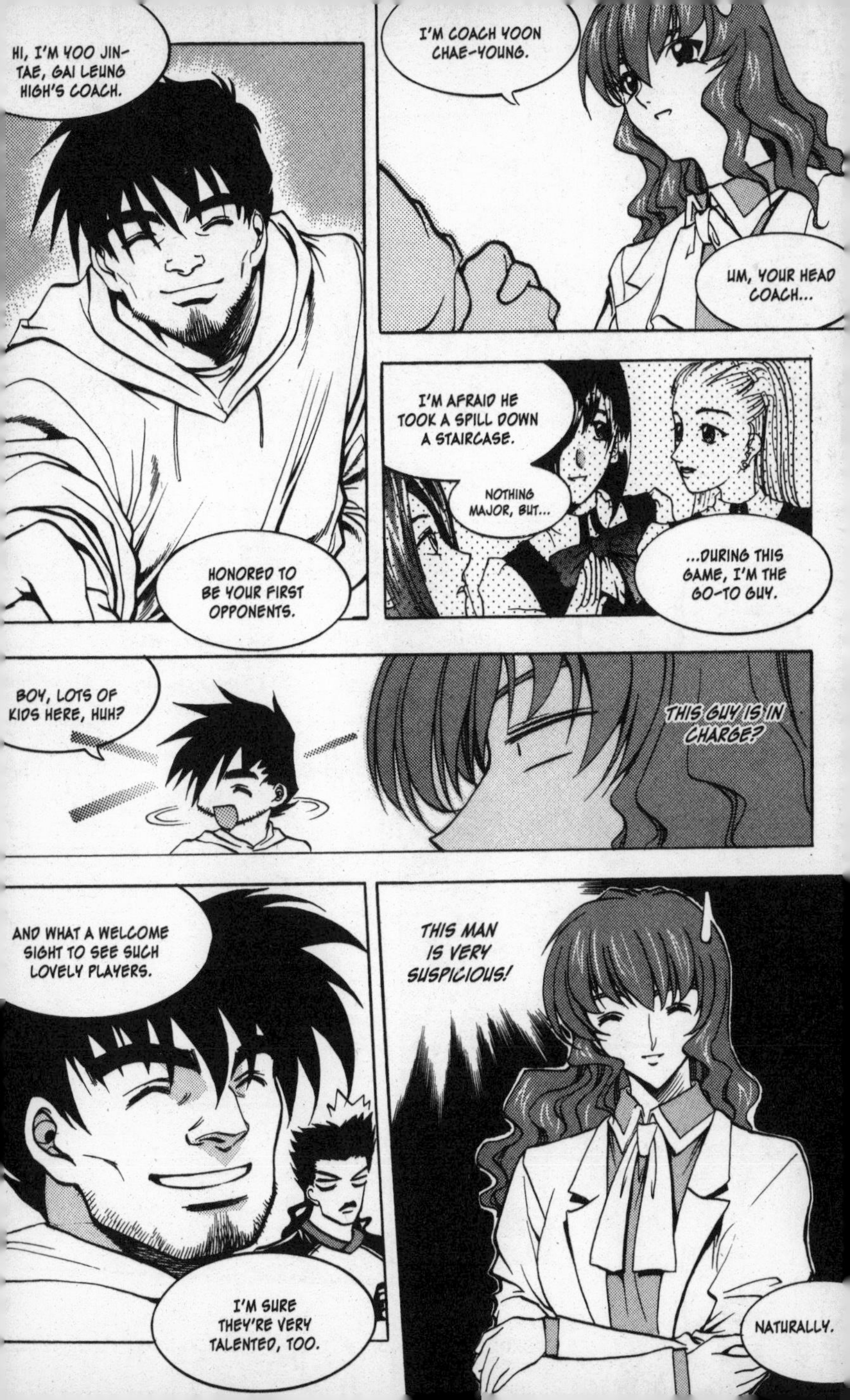
HI, I'M YOO JIN-TAE, GAI LEUNG HIGH'S COACH.
I'M COACH YOON CHAE-YOUNG.
UM, YOUR HEAD COACH...
HONORED TO BE YOUR FIRST OPPONENTS.
I'M AFRAID HE TOOK A SPILL DOWN A STAIRCASE.
NOTHING MAJOR, BUT...
...DURING THIS GAME, I'M THE GO-TO GUY.
BOY, LOTS OF KIDS HERE, HUH?
THIS GUY IS IN CHARGE?
AND WHAT A WELCOME SIGHT TO SEE SUCH LOVELY PLAYERS.
I'M SURE THEY'RE VERY TALENTED, TOO.
THIS MAN IS VERY SUSPICIOUS!
NATURALLY.

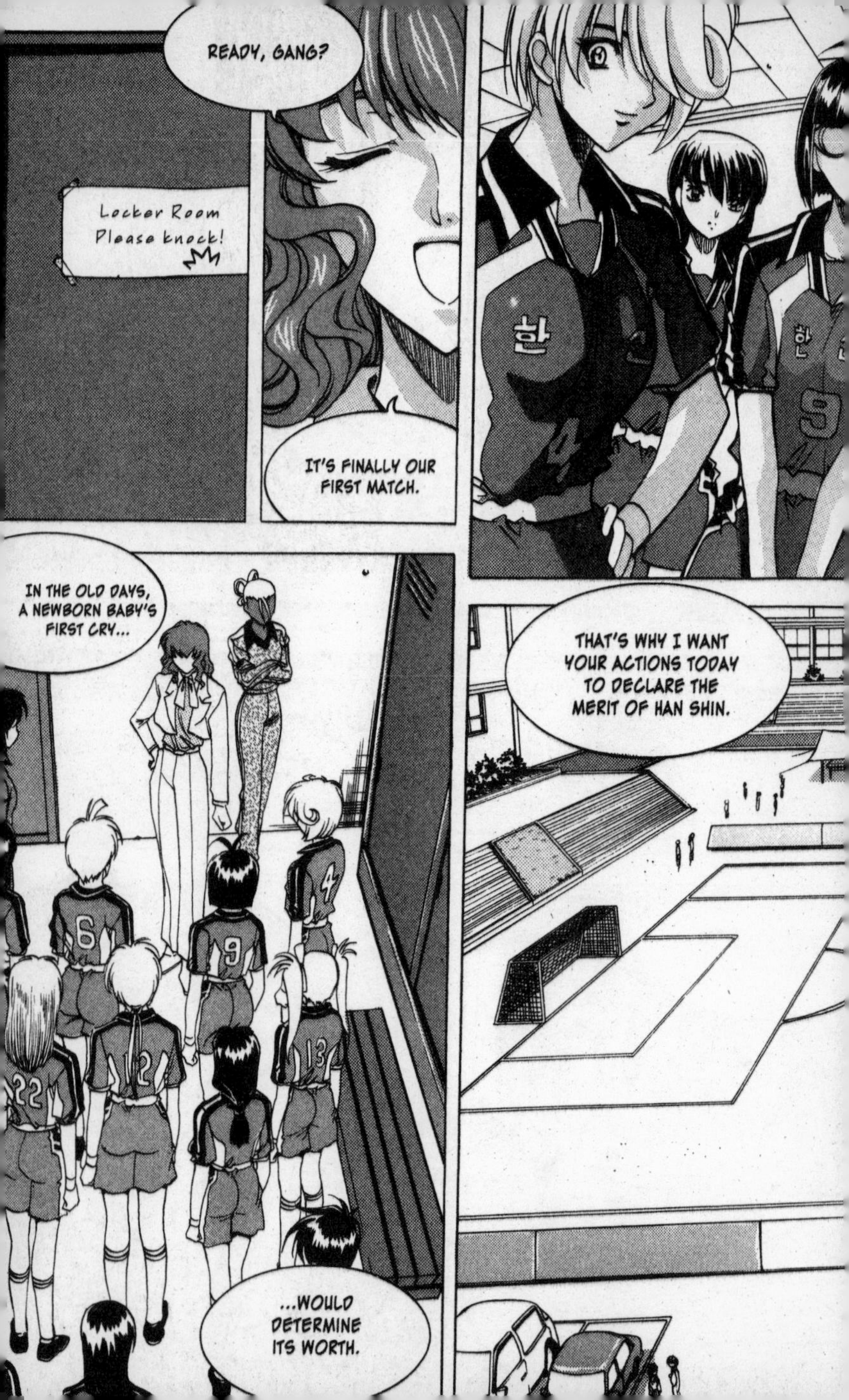
Locker Room
Please knock!
READY, GANG?
IT'S FINALLY OUR FIRST MATCH.
IN THE OLD DAYS, A NEWBORN BABY'S FIRST CRY...
...WOULD DETERMINE ITS WORTH.
THAT'S WHY I WANT YOUR ACTIONS TODAY TO DECLARE THE MERIT OF HAN SHIN.

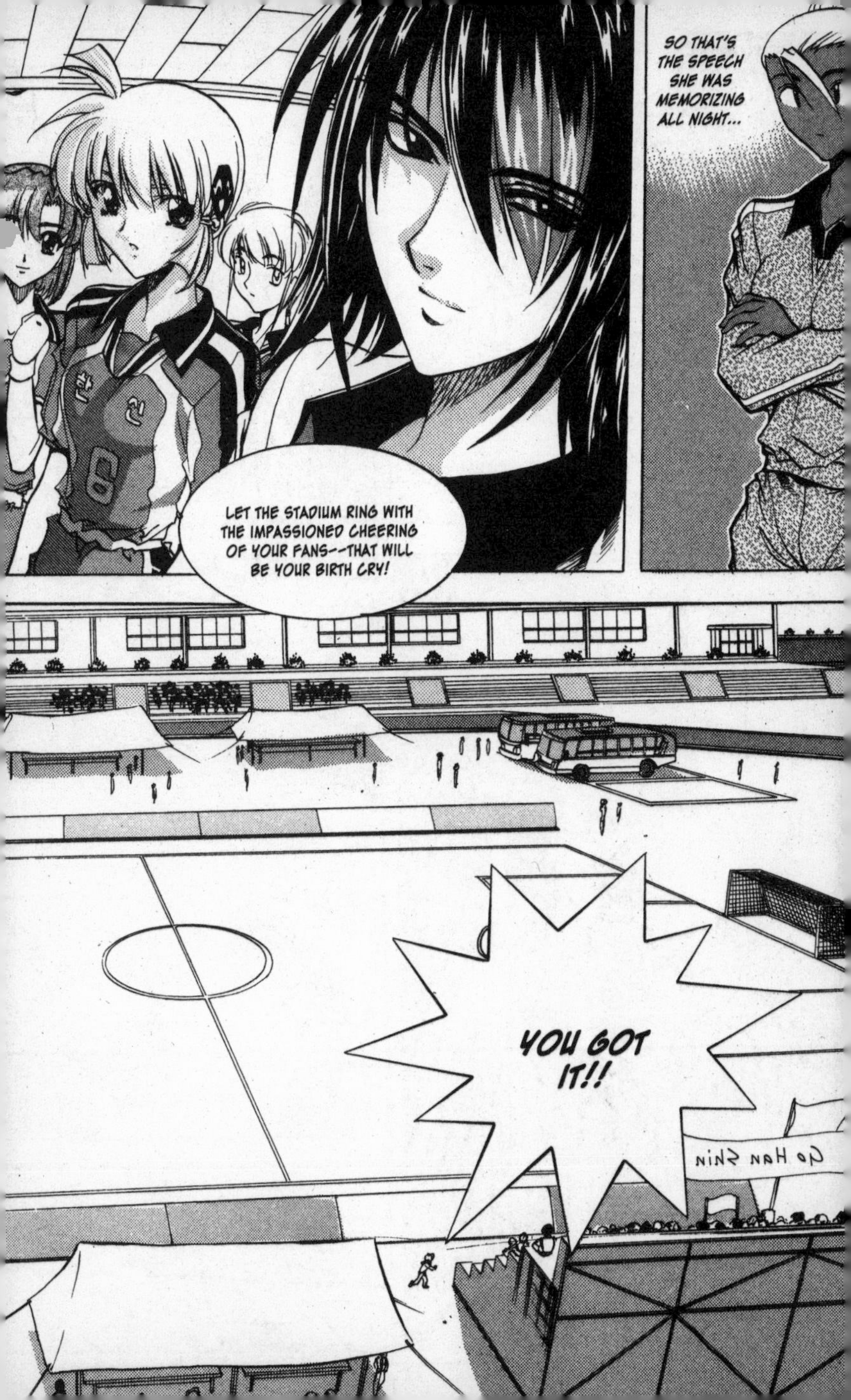
LET THE STADIUM RING WITH THE IMPASSIONED CHEERING OF YOUR FANS--THAT WILL BE YOUR BIRTH CRY!
SO THAT'S THE SPEECH SHE WAS MEMORIZING ALL NIGHT...
YOU GOT IT!!

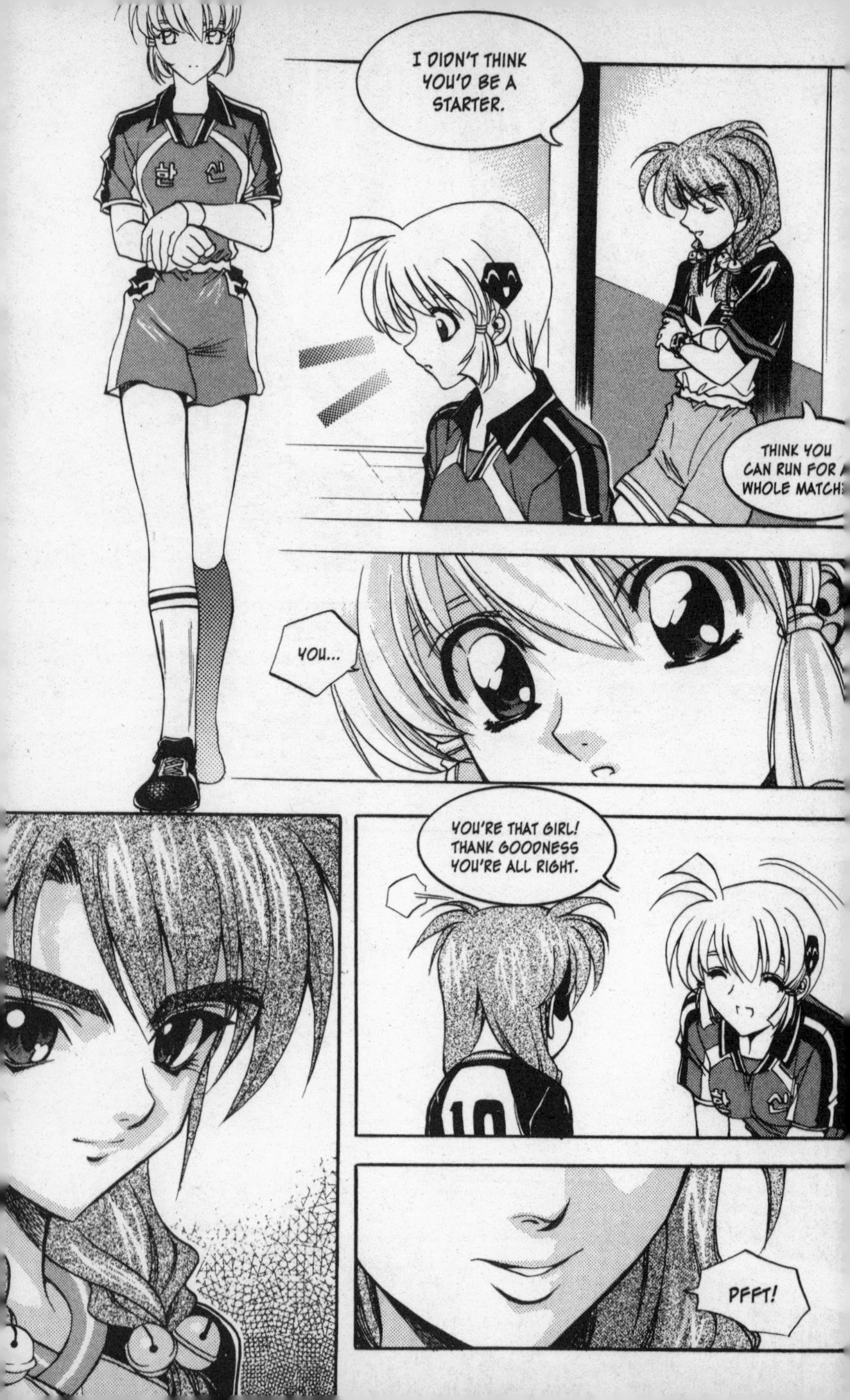
I DIDN'T THINK YOU'D BE A STARTER.
THINK YOU CAN RUN FOR WHOLE MATCH
YOU...
YOU'RE THAT GIRL! THANK GOODNESS YOU'RE ALL RIGHT.
PFFT!

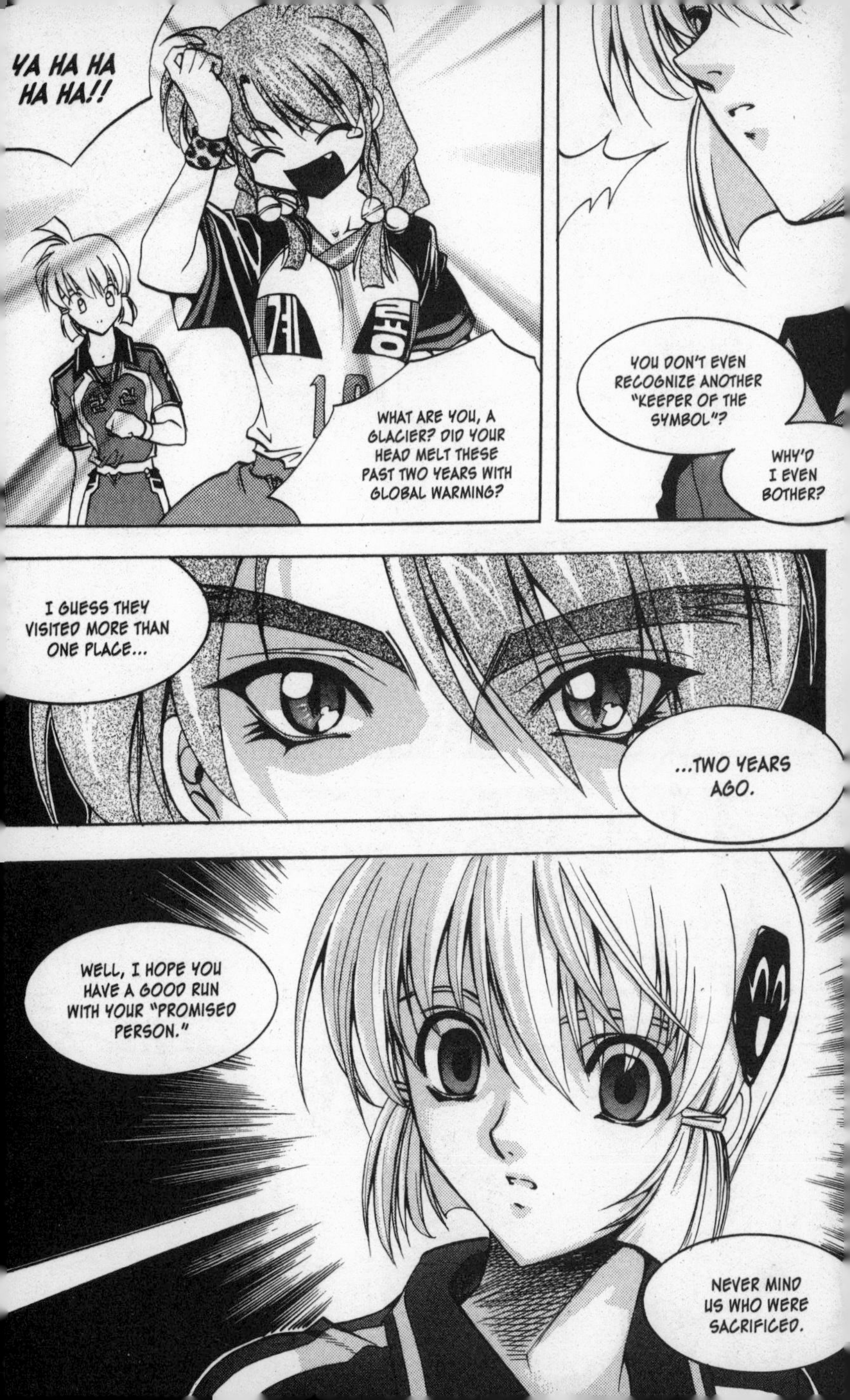
YA HA HA HA HA!!
WHAT ARE YOU, A GLACIER? DID YOUR HEAD MELT THESE PAST TWO YEARS WITH GLOBAL WARMING?
YOU DON'T EVEN RECOGNIZE ANOTHER "KEEPER OF THE SYMBOL"?
WHY'D I EVEN BOTHER?
I GUESS THEY VISITED MORE THAN ONE PLACE...
...TWO YEARS AGO.
WELL, I HOPE YOU HAVE A GOOD RUN WITH YOUR "PROMISED PERSON."
NEVER MIND US WHO WERE SACRIFICED.

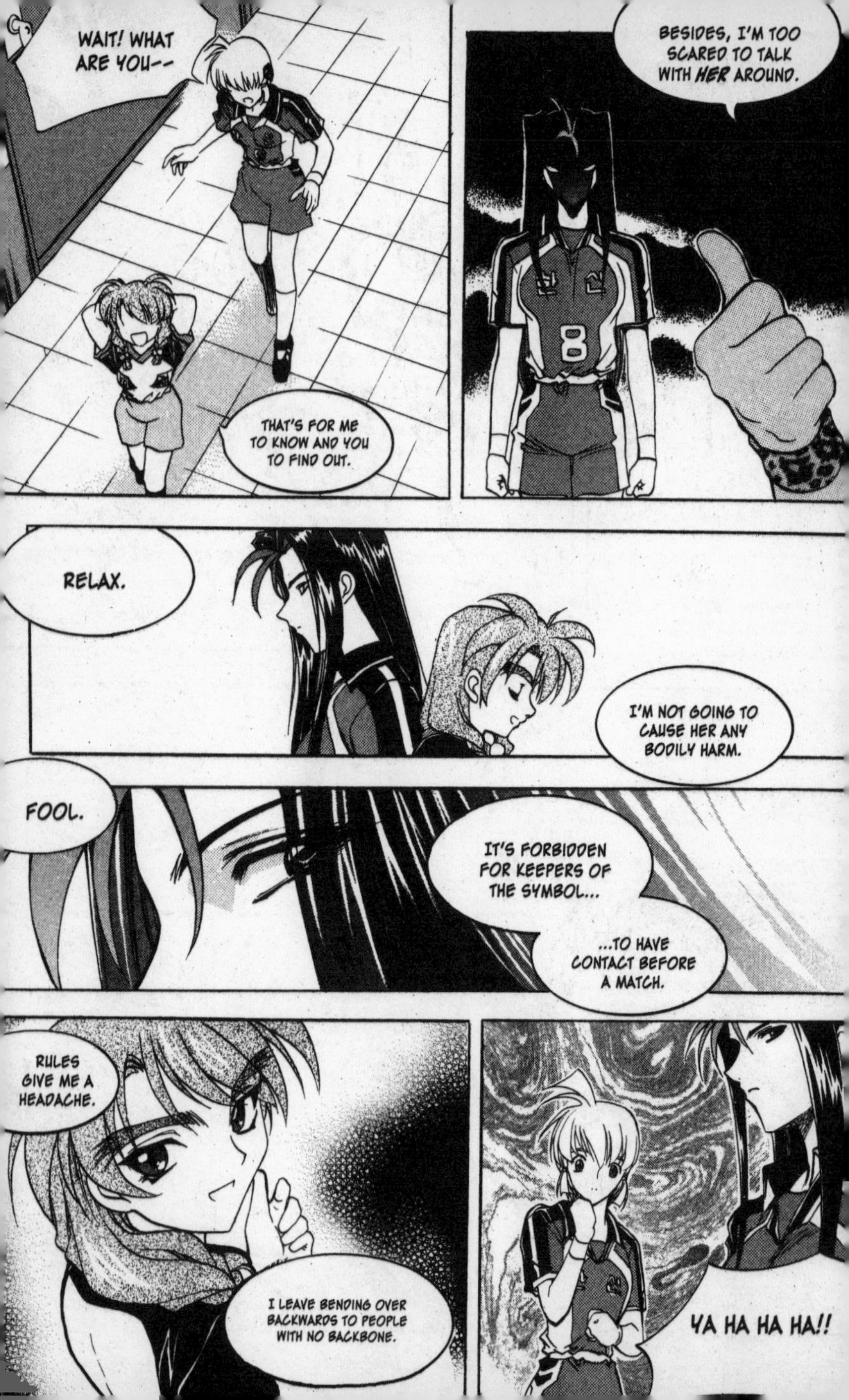
WAIT! WHAT ARE YOU--
THAT'S FOR ME TO KNOW AND YOU TO FIND OUT.
BESIDES, I'M TOO SCARED TO TALK WITH HER AROUND.
RELAX.
I'M NOT GOING TO CAUSE HER ANY BODILY HARM.
FOOL.
IT'S FORBIDDEN FOR KEEPERS OF THE SYMBOL...
...TO HAVE CONTACT BEFORE A MATCH.
RULES GIVE ME A HEADACHE.
I LEAVE BENDING OVER BACKWARDS TO PEOPLE WITH NO BACKBONE.
YA HA HA HA!!

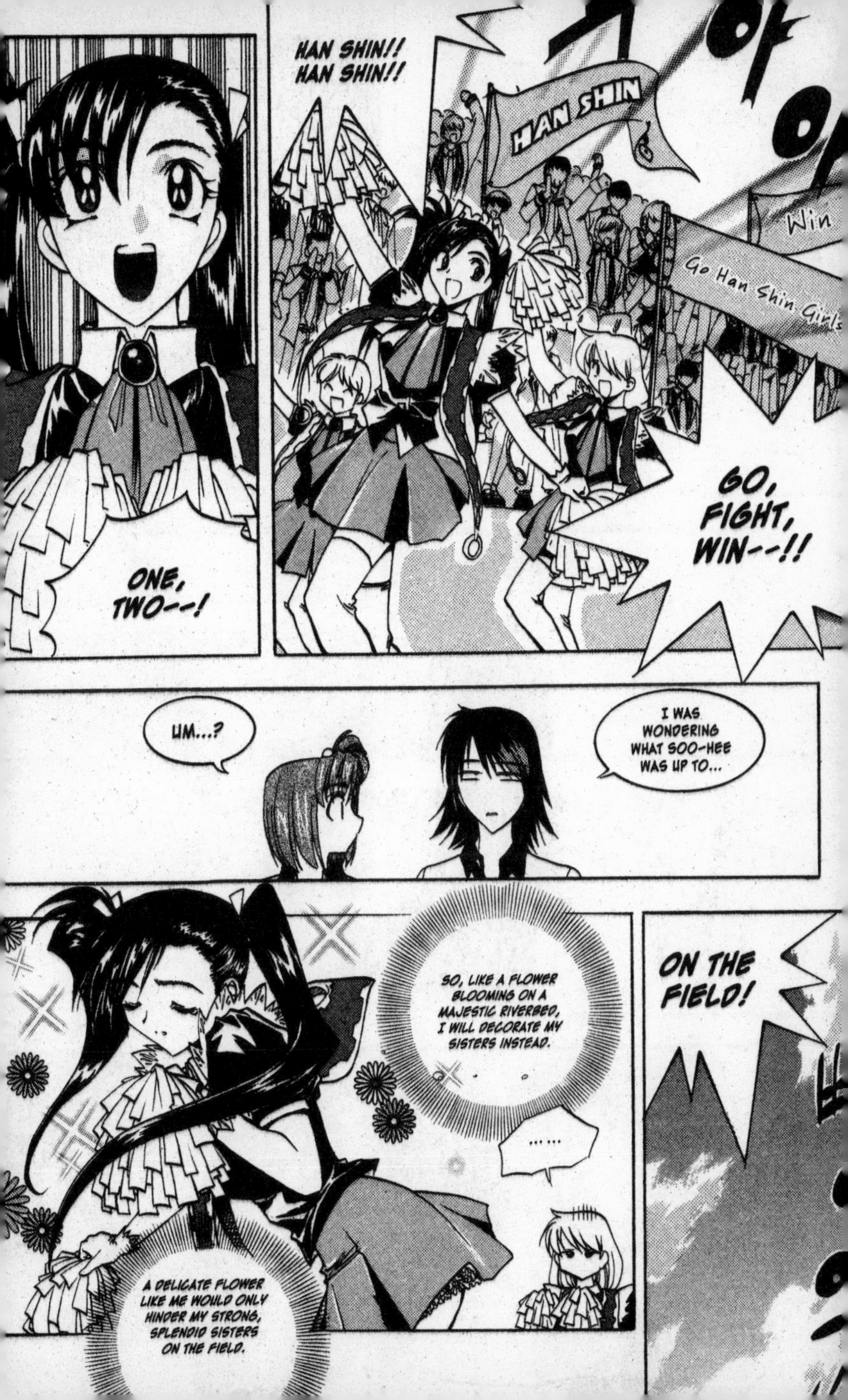
ONE, TWO--!
HAN SHIN!! HAN SHIN!!
HAN SHIN
Win
Go Han Shin Girls
GO, FIGHT, WIN--!!
UM...?
I WAS WONDERING WHAT SOO-HEE WAS UP TO...
A DELICATE FLOWER LIKE ME WOULD ONLY HINDER MY STRONG, SPLENDID SISTERS ON THE FIELD.
SO, LIKE A FLOWER BLOOMING ON A MAJESTIC RIVERBED, I WILL DECORATE MY SISTERS INSTEAD.
......
ON THE FIELD!

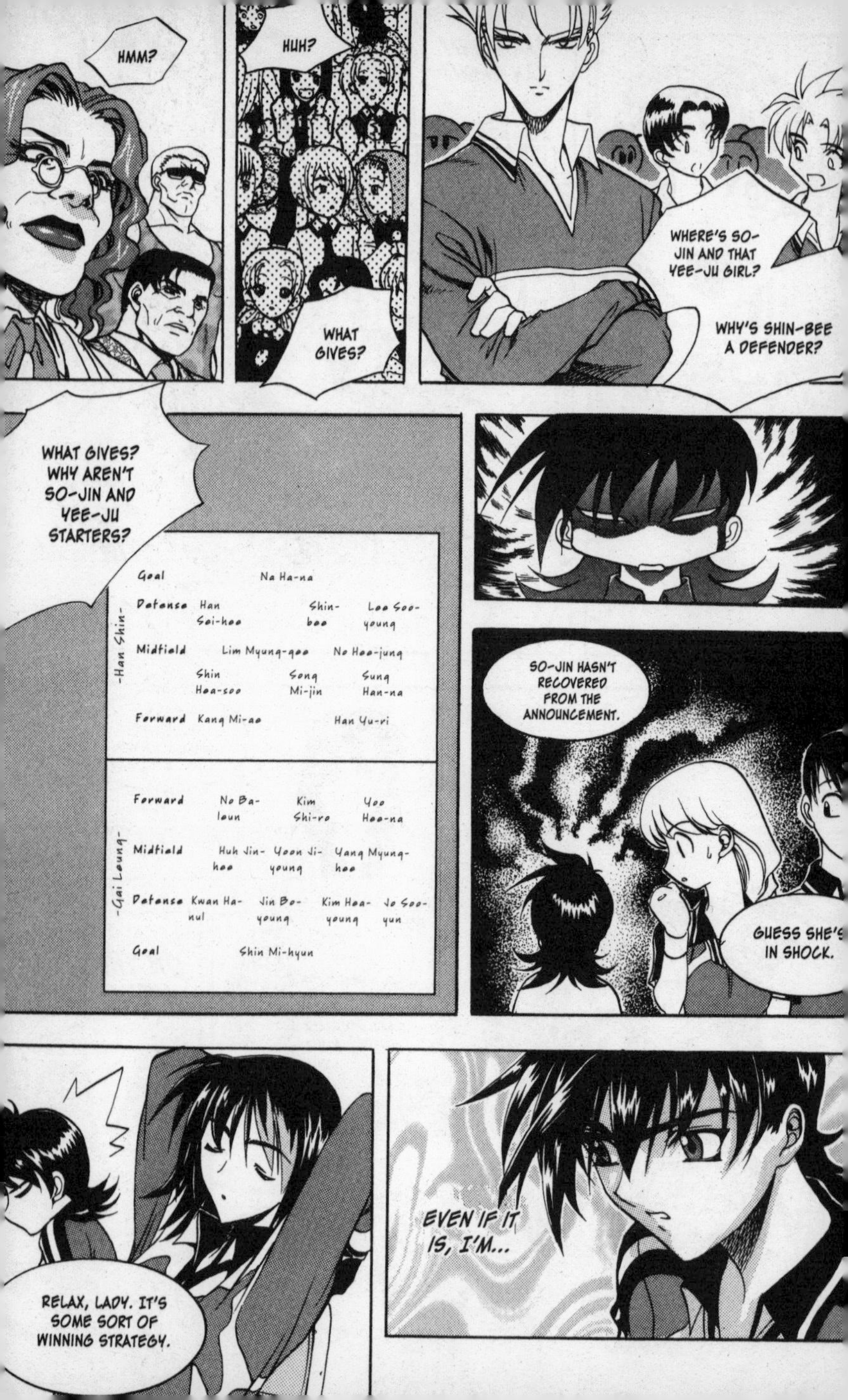
HMM?
HUH?
WHAT GIVES?
WHERE'S SO-JIN AND THAT YEE-JU GIRL?
WHY'S SHIN-BEE A DEFENDER?
WHAT GIVES? WHY AREN'T SO-JIN AND YEE-JU STARTERS?
-Han Shin-
Goal Na Ha-na
Defense Han Sei-hee Shin-bee Lee Soo-young
Midfield Lim Myung-gee No Hee-jung
Shin Hea-soo Song Mi-jin Sung Han-na
Forward Kang Mi-ae Han Yu-ri
-Gai Leung-
Forward No Ba-leun Kim Shi-ro Yoo Hee-na
Midfield Huh Jin-hee Yoon Ji-young Yang Myung-hee
Defense Kwan Ha-nul Jin Bo-young Kim Hea-young Jo Soo-yun
Goal Shin Mi-hyun
SO-JIN HASN'T RECOVERED FROM THE ANNOUNCEMENT.
GUESS SHE'S IN SHOCK.
RELAX, LADY. IT'S SOME SORT OF WINNING STRATEGY.
EVEN IF IT IS, I'M...

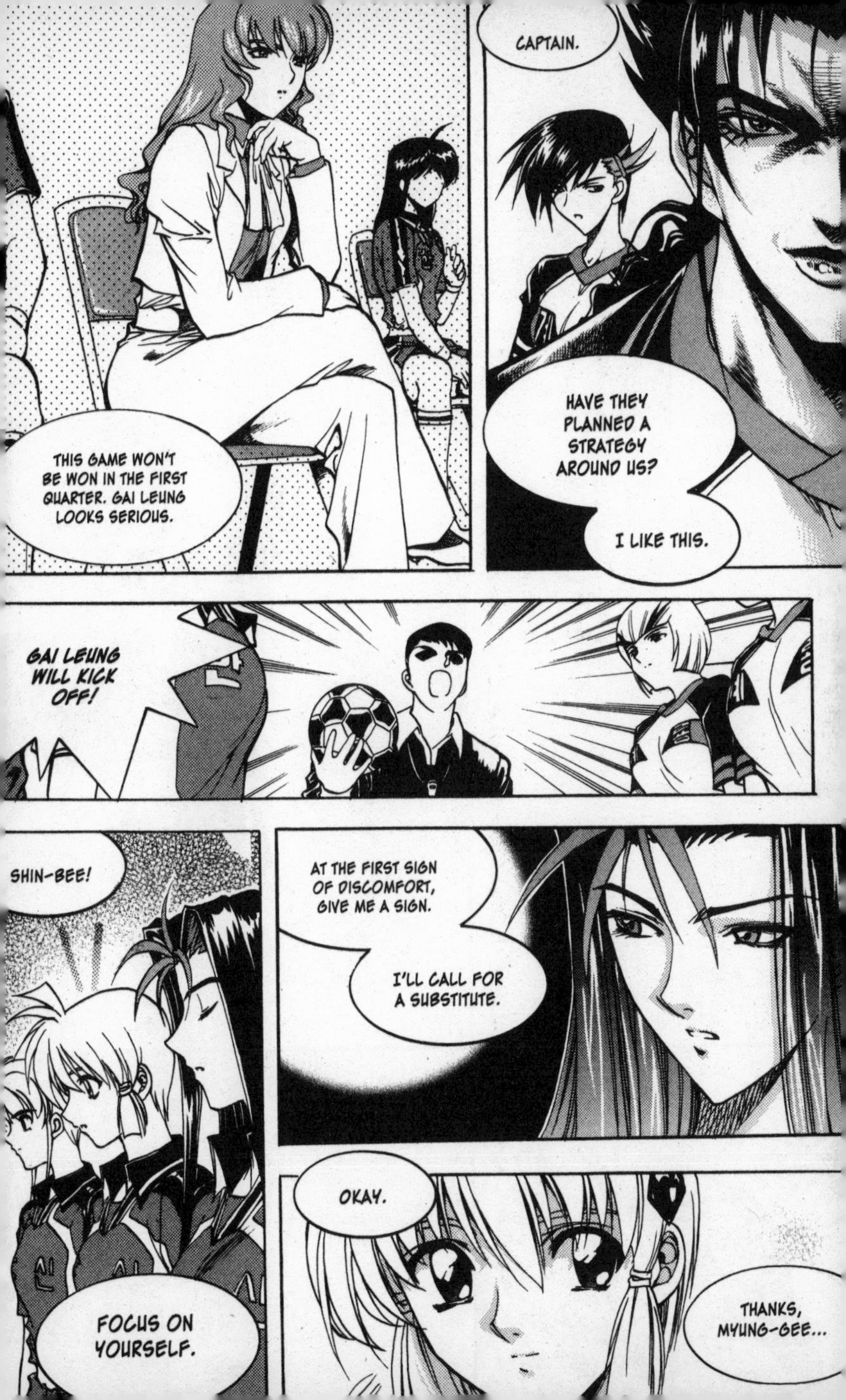
THIS GAME WON'T BE WON IN THE FIRST QUARTER. GAI LEUNG LOOKS SERIOUS.
CAPTAIN.
HAVE THEY PLANNED A STRATEGY AROUND US?
I LIKE THIS.
GAI LEUNG WILL KICK OFF!
SHIN-BEE!
FOCUS ON YOURSELF.
AT THE FIRST SIGN OF DISCOMFORT, GIVE ME A SIGN.
I'LL CALL FOR A SUBSTITUTE.
OKAY.
THANKS, MYUNG-GEE...

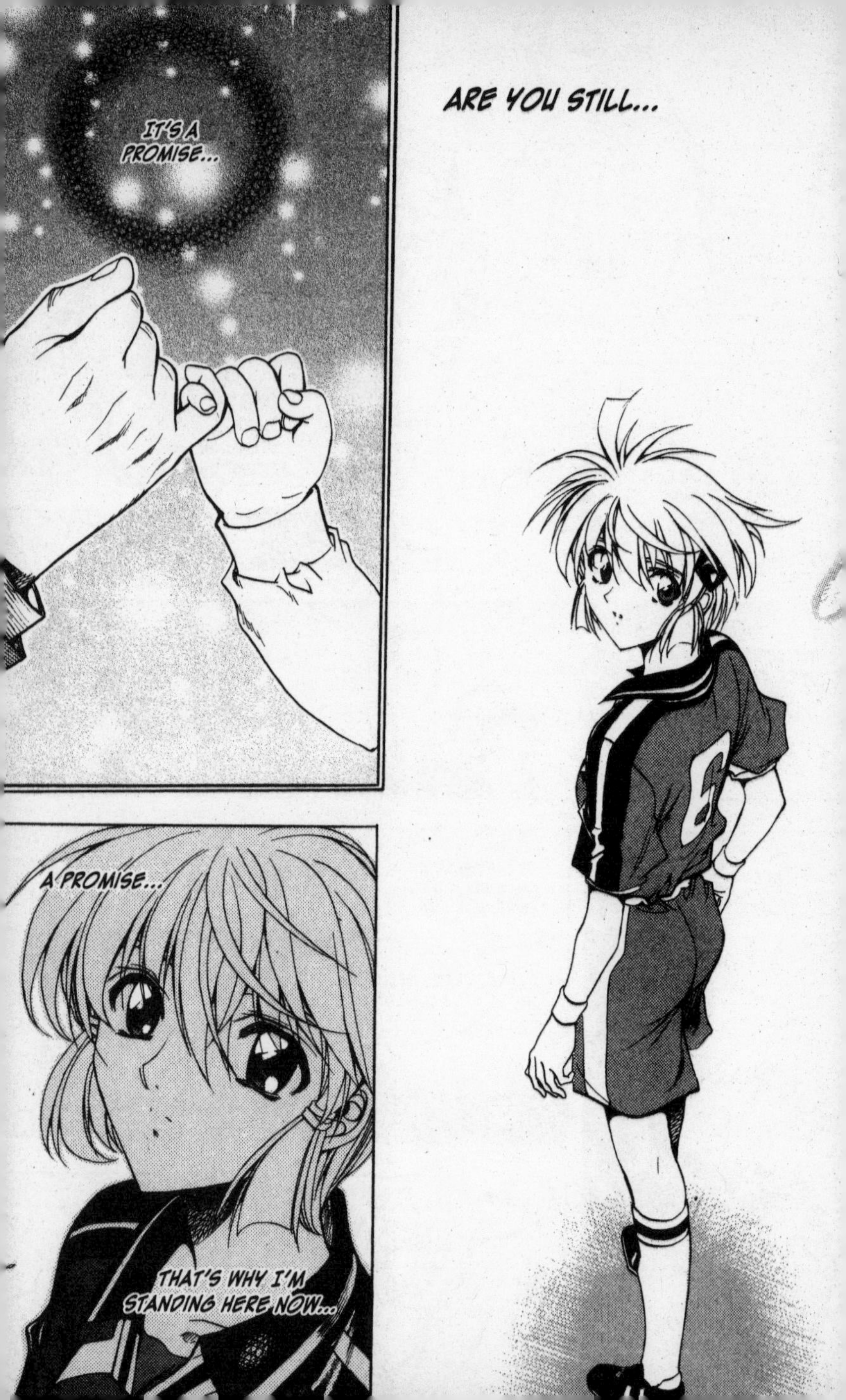
IT'S A PROMISE...
A PROMISE...
THAT'S WHY I'M STANDING HERE NOW...
ARE YOU STILL...

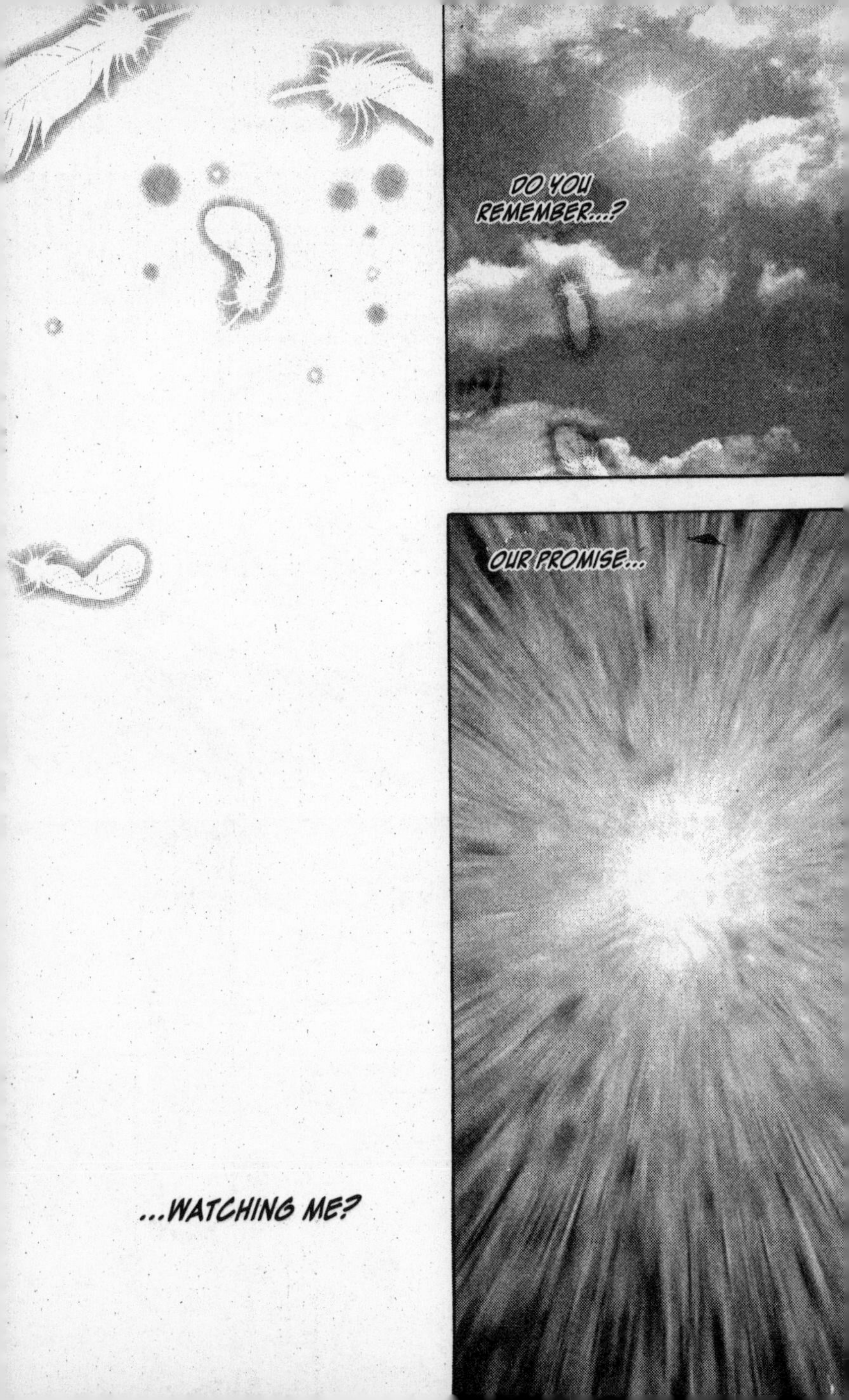
...WATCHING ME?
DO YOU REMEMBER...?
OUR PROMISE...

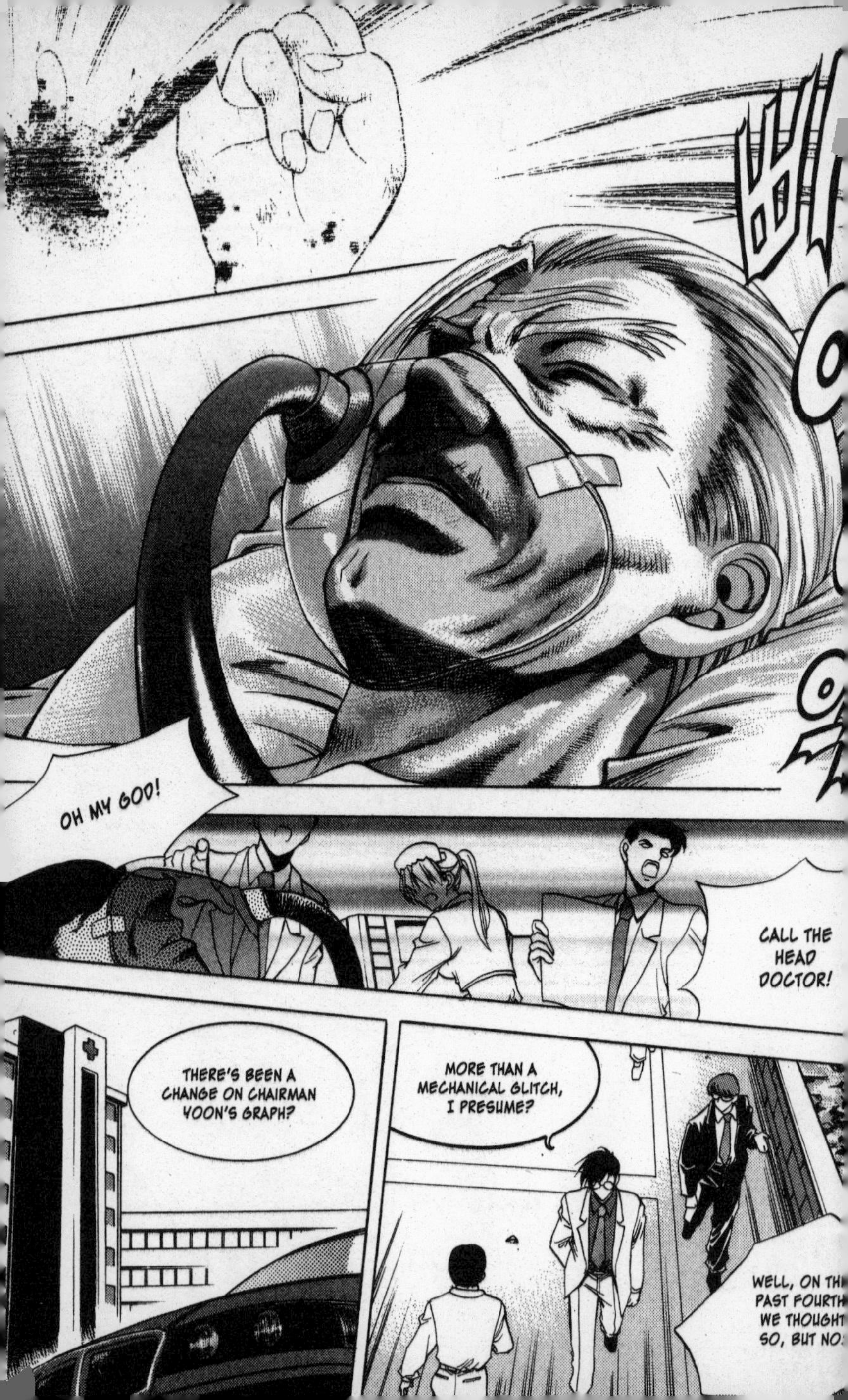
삐
OH MY GOD!
CALL THE HEAD DOCTOR!
THERE'S BEEN A CHANGE ON CHAIRMAN YOON'S GRAPH?
MORE THAN A MECHANICAL GLITCH, I PRESUME?
WELL, ON TH PAST FOURTH WE THOUGHT SO, BUT NO.

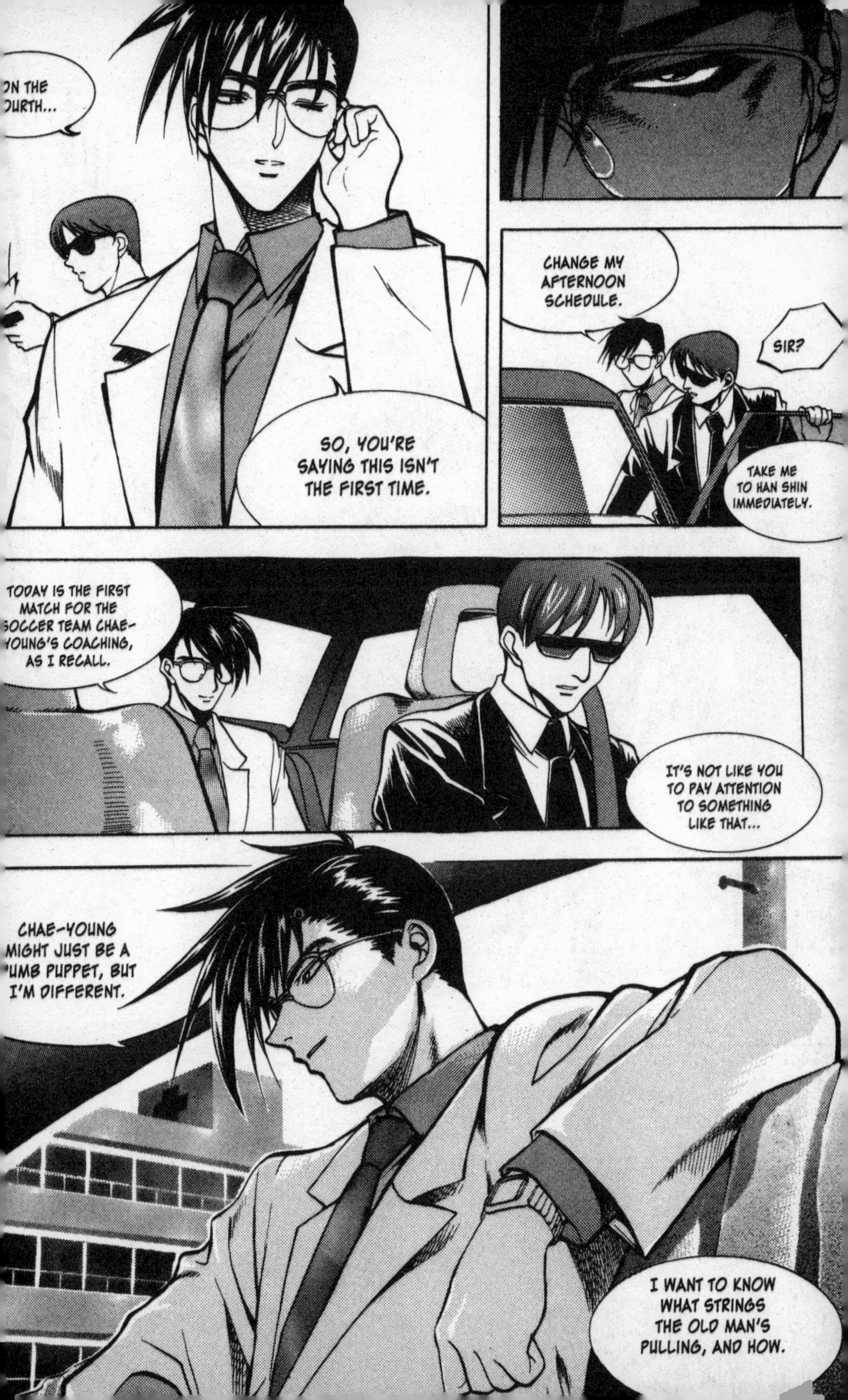
ON THE
OURTH...
SO, YOU'RE SAYING THIS ISN'T THE FIRST TIME.
CHANGE MY AFTERNOON SCHEDULE.
SIR?
TAKE ME TO HAN SHIN IMMEDIATELY.
TODAY IS THE FIRST MATCH FOR THE SOCCER TEAM CHAE-YOUNG'S COACHING, AS I RECALL.
IT'S NOT LIKE YOU TO PAY ATTENTION TO SOMETHING LIKE THAT...
CHAE-YOUNG MIGHT JUST BE A UMB PUPPET, BUT I'M DIFFERENT.
I WANT TO KNOW WHAT STRINGS THE OLD MAN'S PULLING, AND HOW.

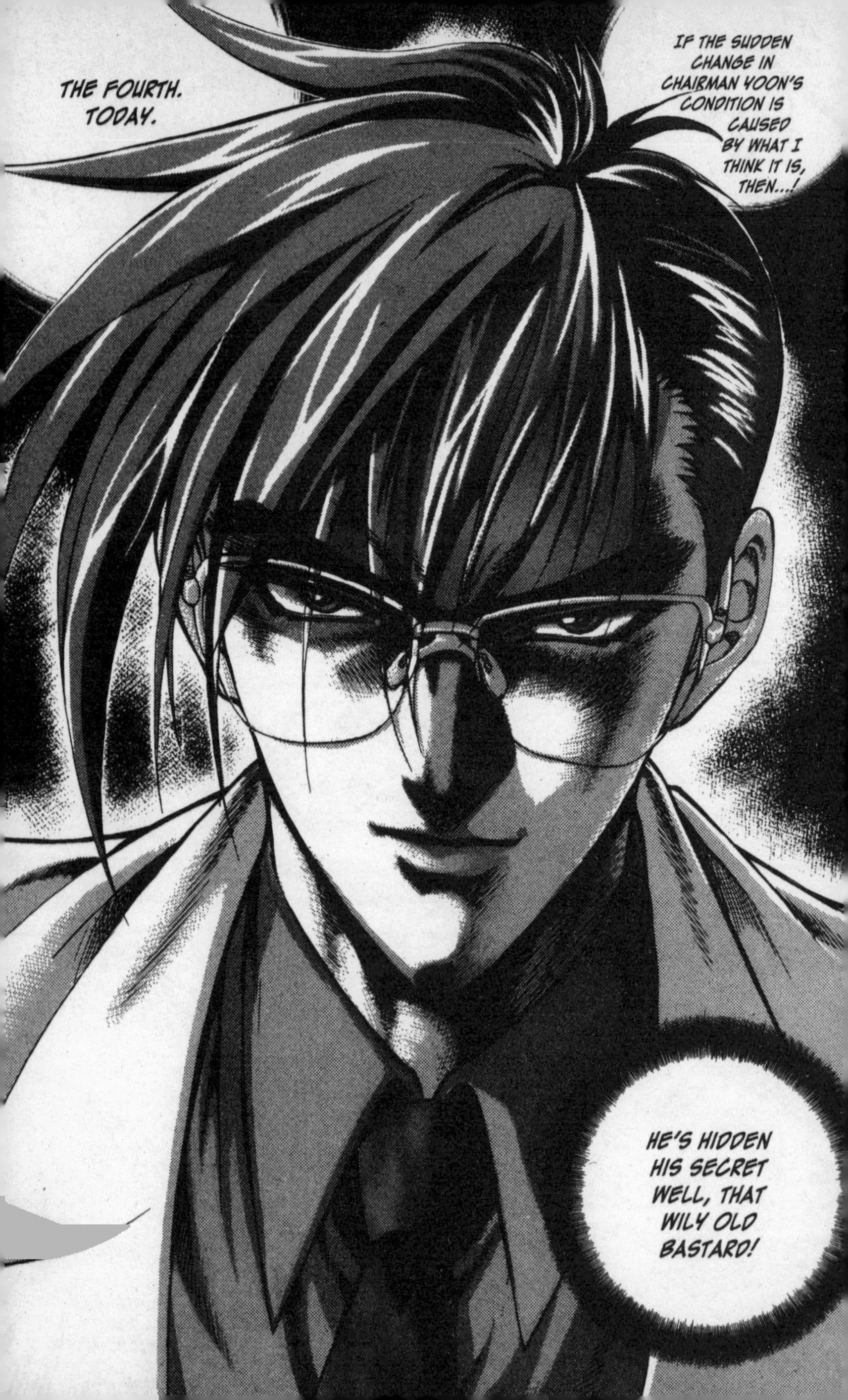
THE FOURTH. TODAY.
IF THE SUDDEN CHANGE IN CHAIRMAN YOON'S CONDITION IS CAUSED BY WHAT I THINK IT IS, THEN...!
HE'S HIDDEN HIS SECRET WELL, THAT WILY OLD BASTARD!

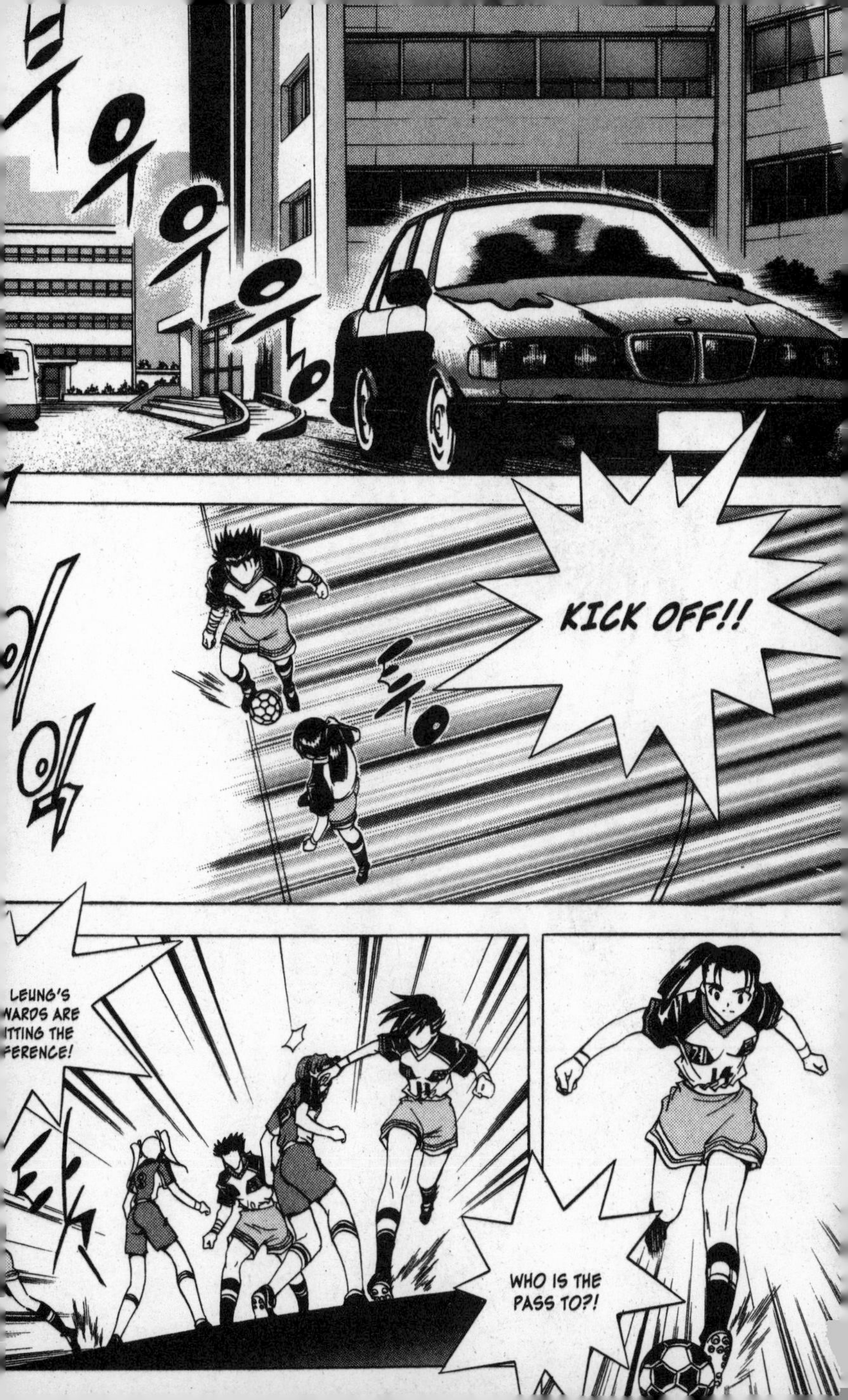
부우우웅
KICK OFF!!
LEUNG'S
WARDS ARE
ITTING THE
FERENCE!
WHO IS THE
PASS TO?!

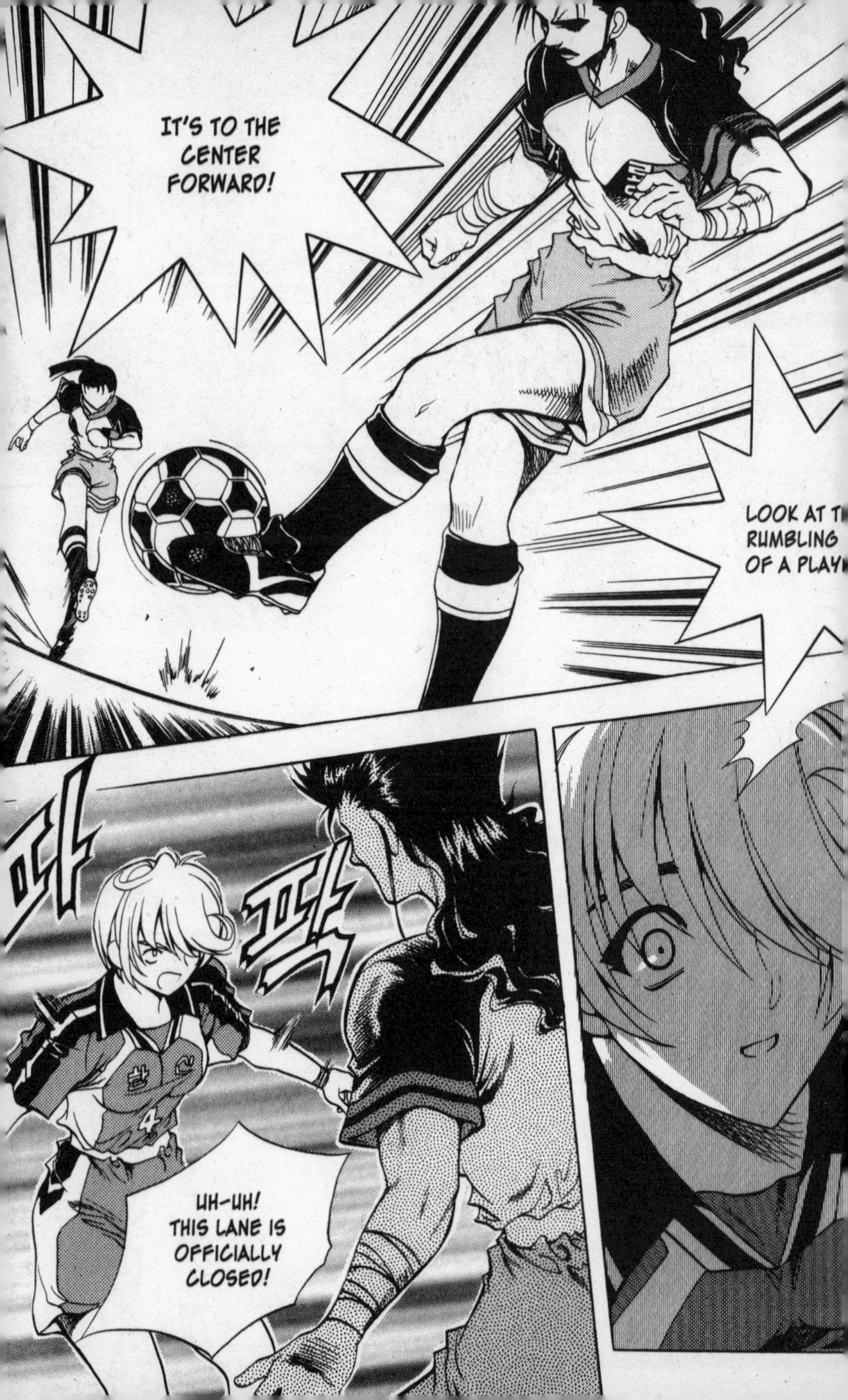
IT'S TO THE CENTER FORWARD!
LOOK AT T RUMBLING OF A PLAY
UH-UH! THIS LANE IS OFFICIALLY CLOSED!

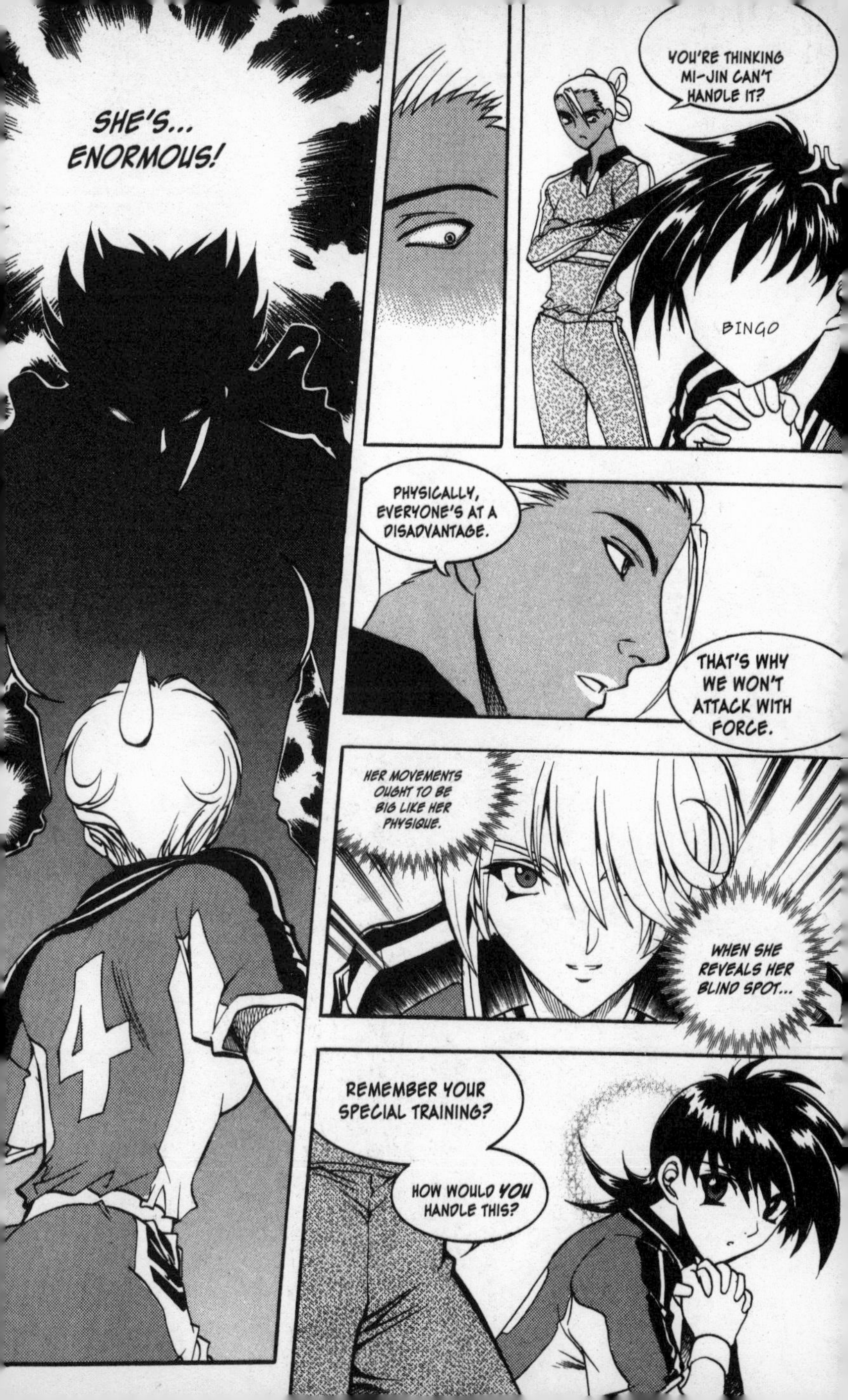
SHE'S... ENORMOUS!
YOU'RE THINKING MI-JIN CAN'T HANDLE IT?
BINGO
PHYSICALLY, EVERYONE'S AT A DISADVANTAGE.
THAT'S WHY WE WON'T ATTACK WITH FORCE.
HER MOVEMENTS OUGHT TO BE BIG LIKE HER PHYSIQUE.
WHEN SHE REVEALS HER BLIND SPOT...
REMEMBER YOUR SPECIAL TRAINING?
HOW WOULD *YOU* HANDLE THIS?

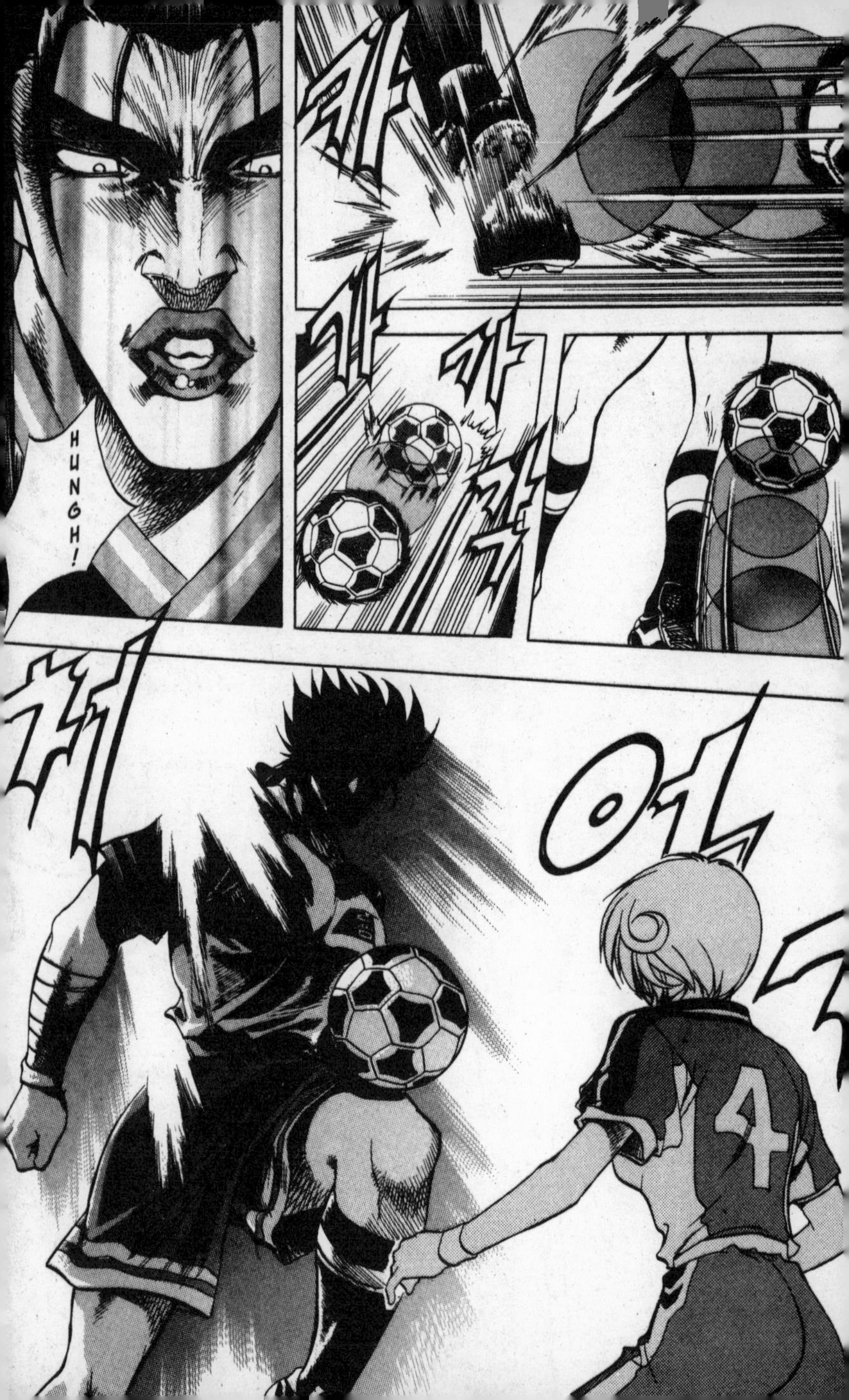
HUNGH!

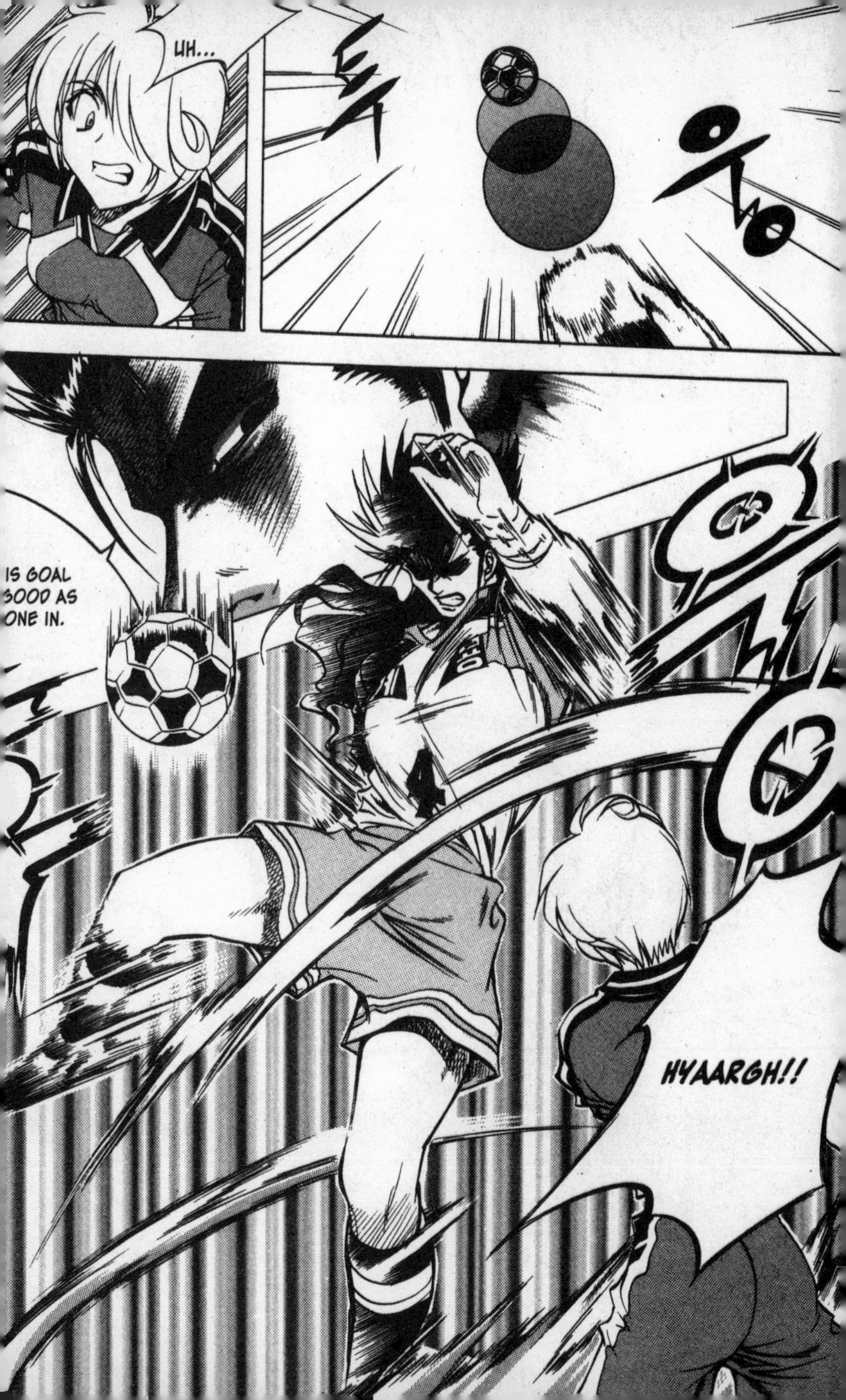
UH...
IS GOAL
OOD AS
ONE IN.
HYAARGH!!

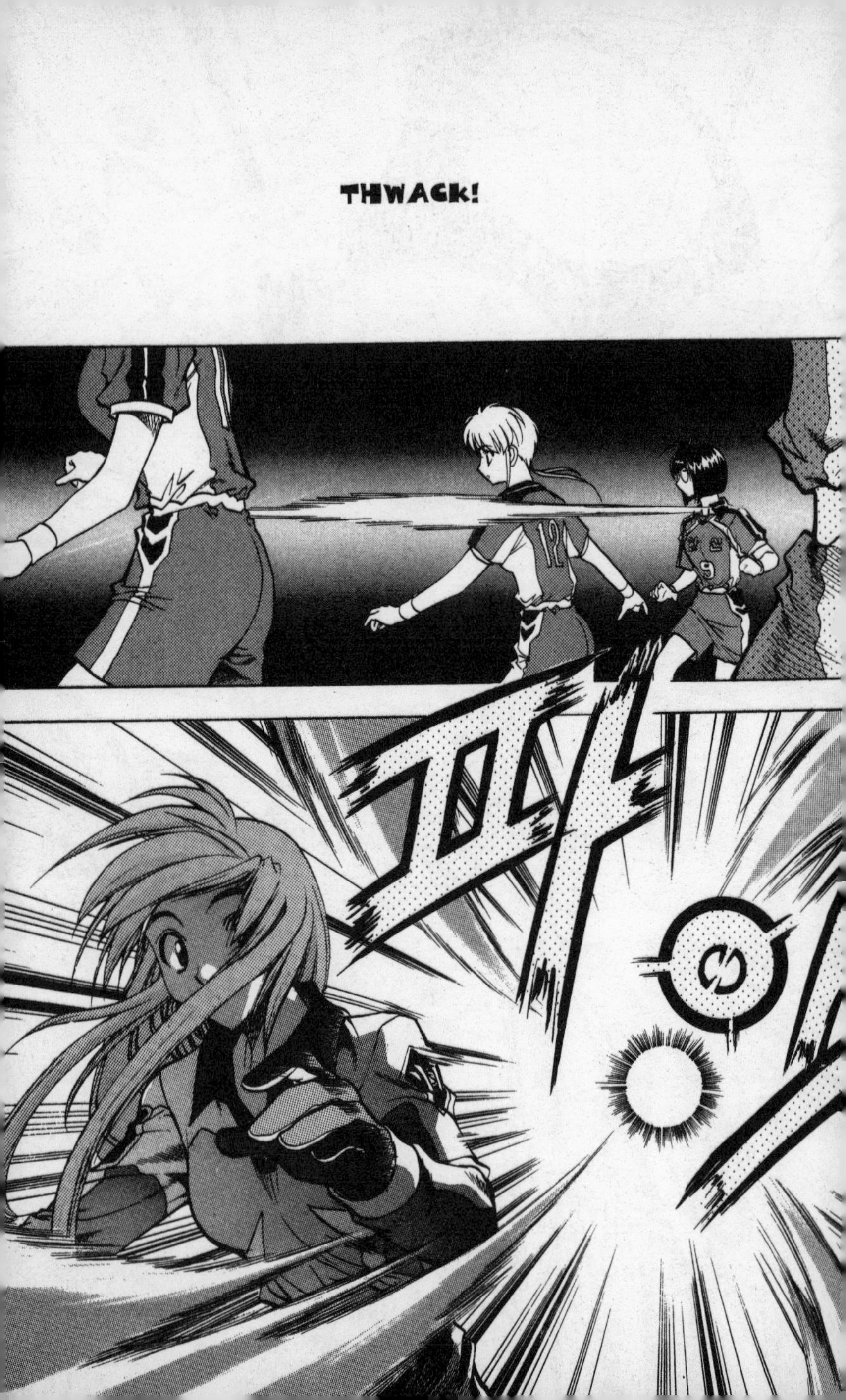
THWACK!

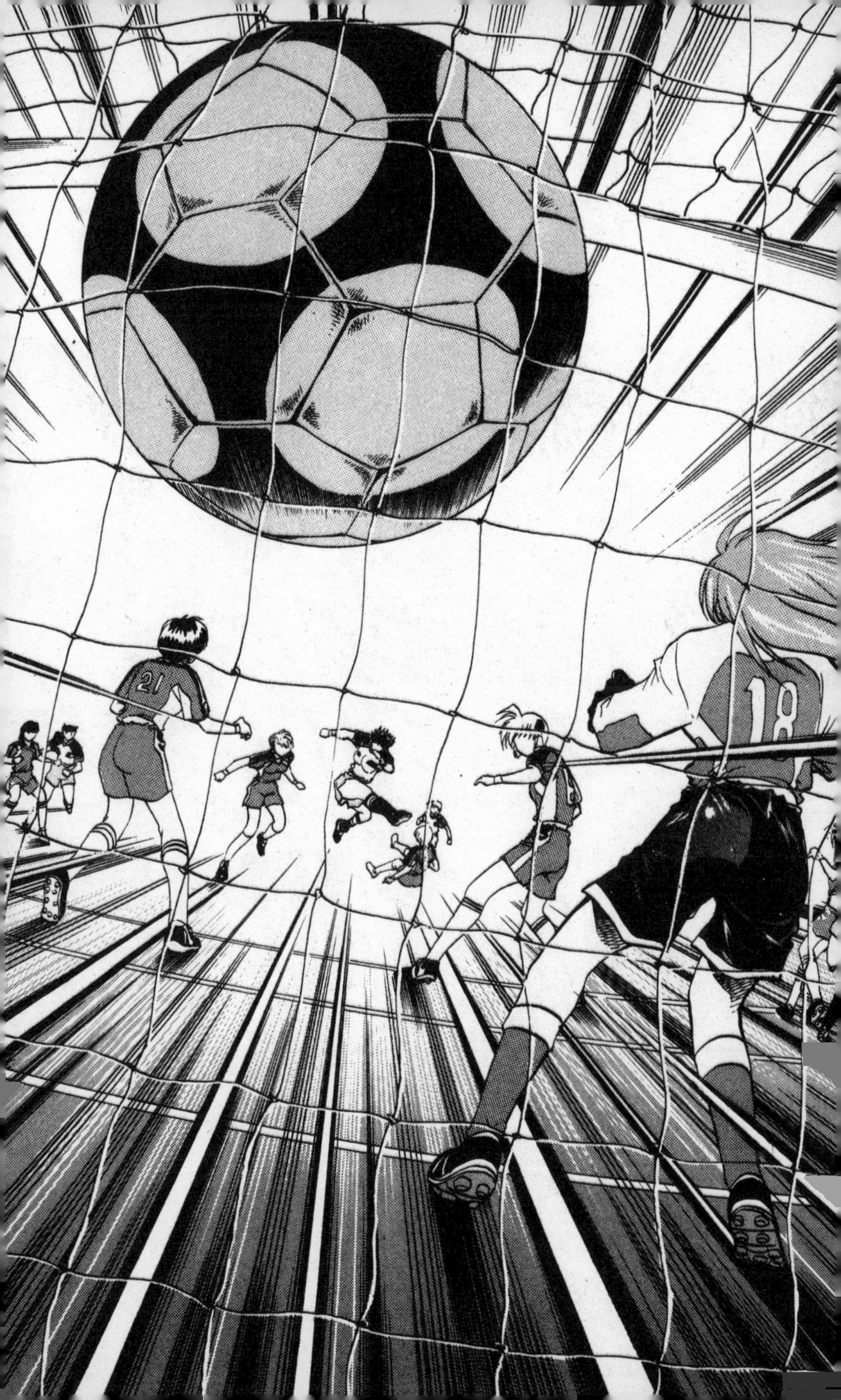

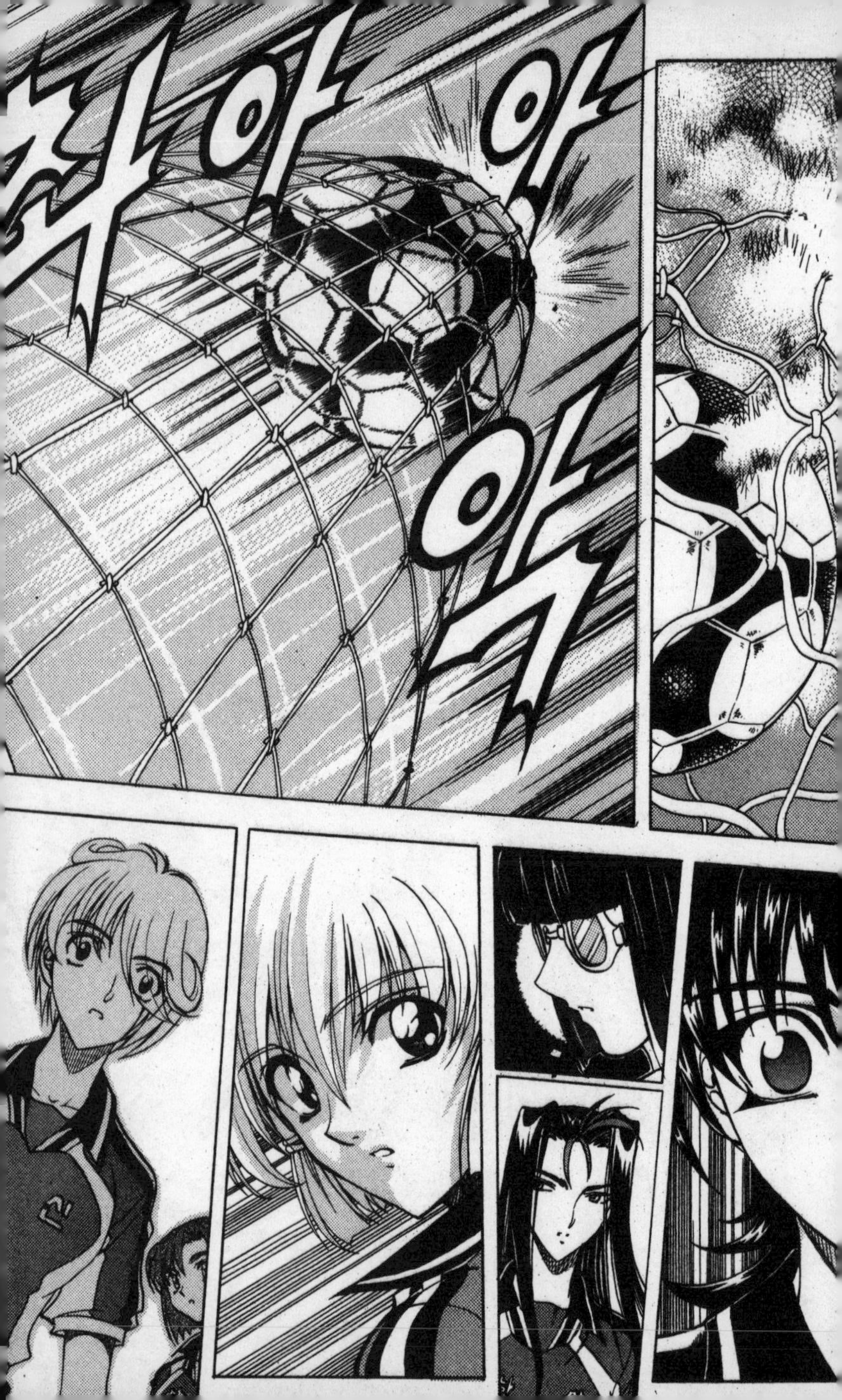
차아아앙

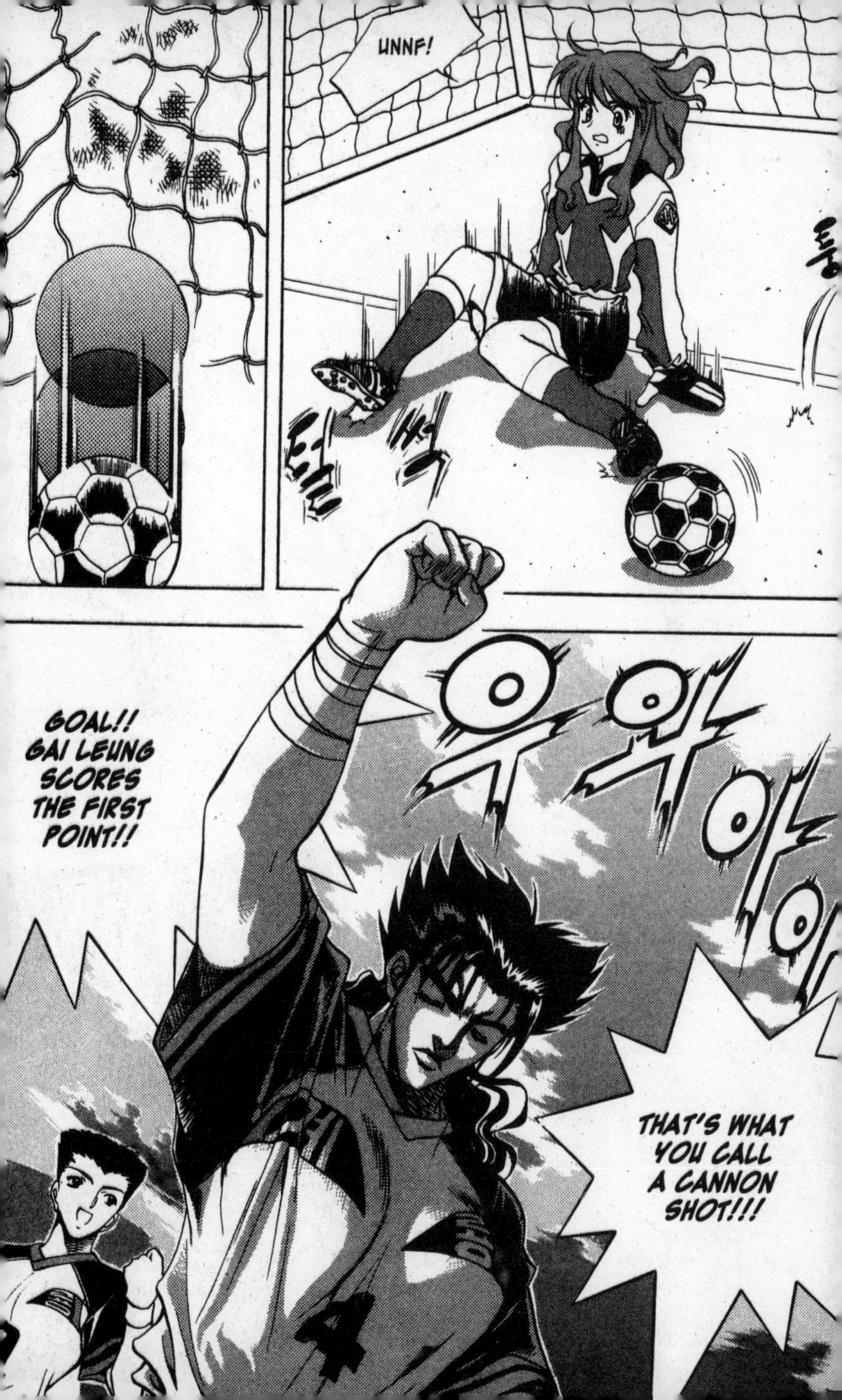
UNNF!
GOAL!! GAI LEUNG SCORES THE FIRST POINT!!
THAT'S WHAT YOU CALL A CANNON SHOT!!!

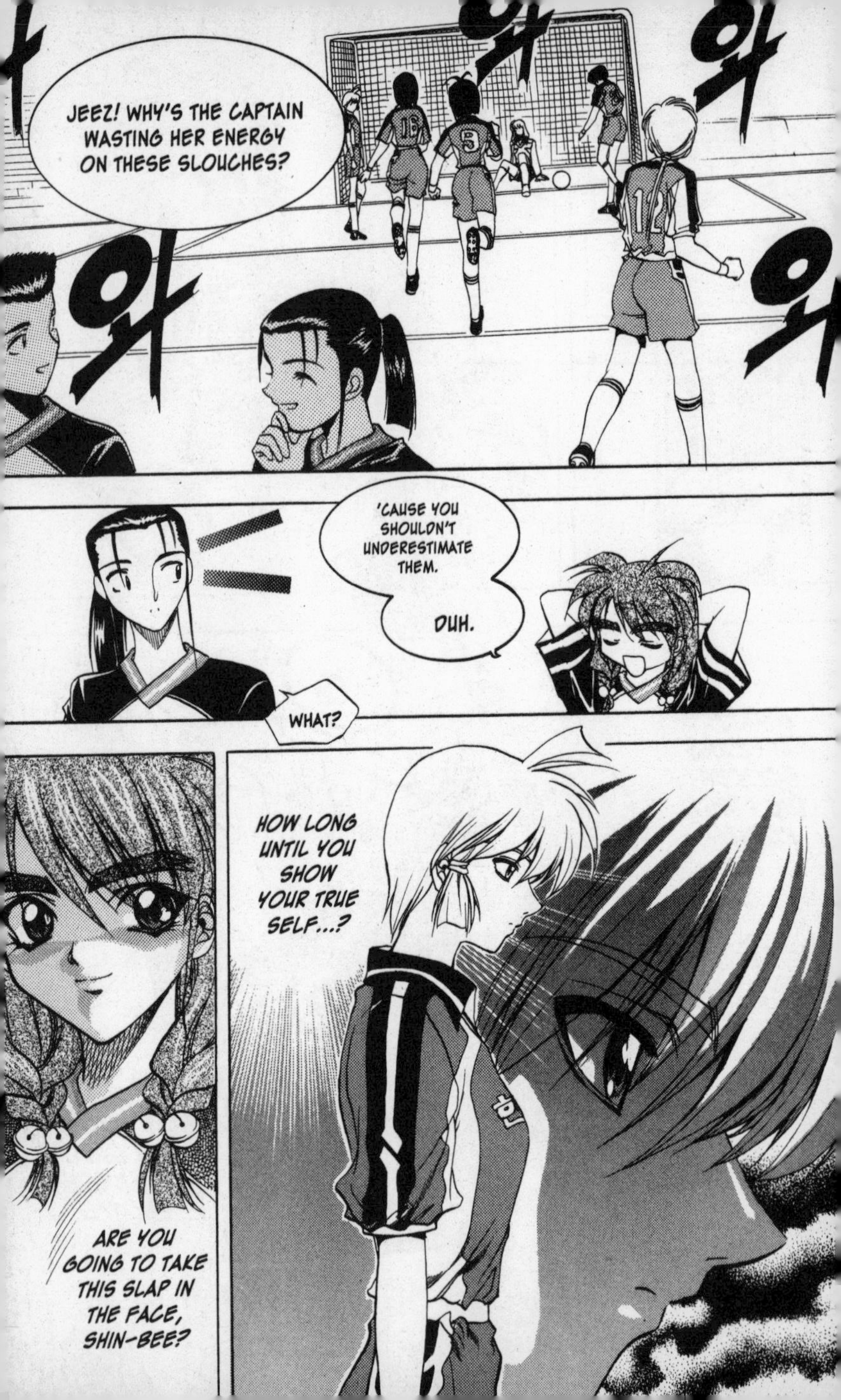
와
와
JEEZ! WHY'S THE CAPTAIN WASTING HER ENERGY ON THESE SLOUCHES?
와
와
'CAUSE YOU SHOULDN'T UNDERESTIMATE THEM.
DUH.
WHAT?
ARE YOU GOING TO TAKE THIS SLAP IN THE FACE, SHIN-BEE?
HOW LONG UNTIL YOU SHOW YOUR TRUE SELF...?

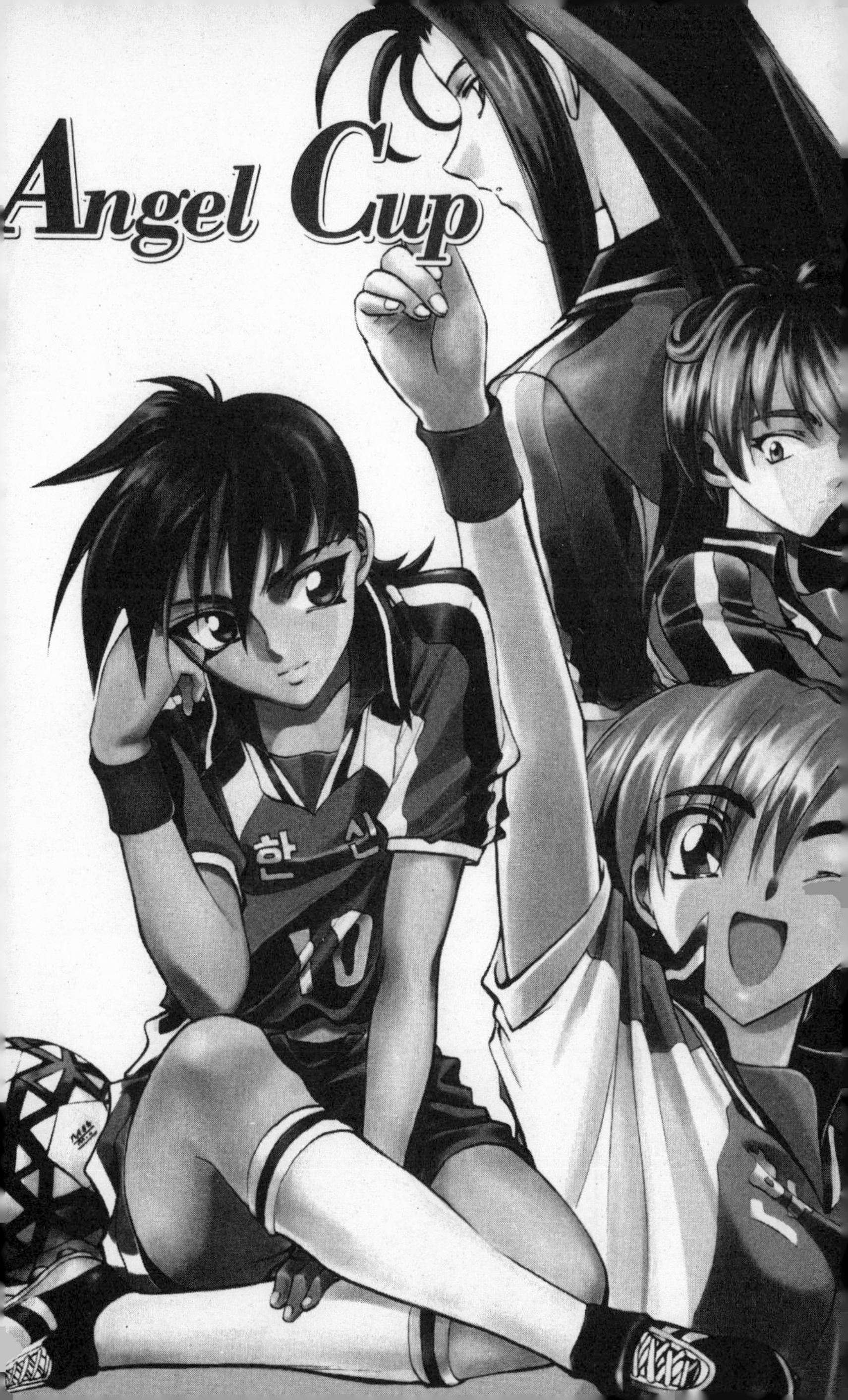
Angel Cup
한 신

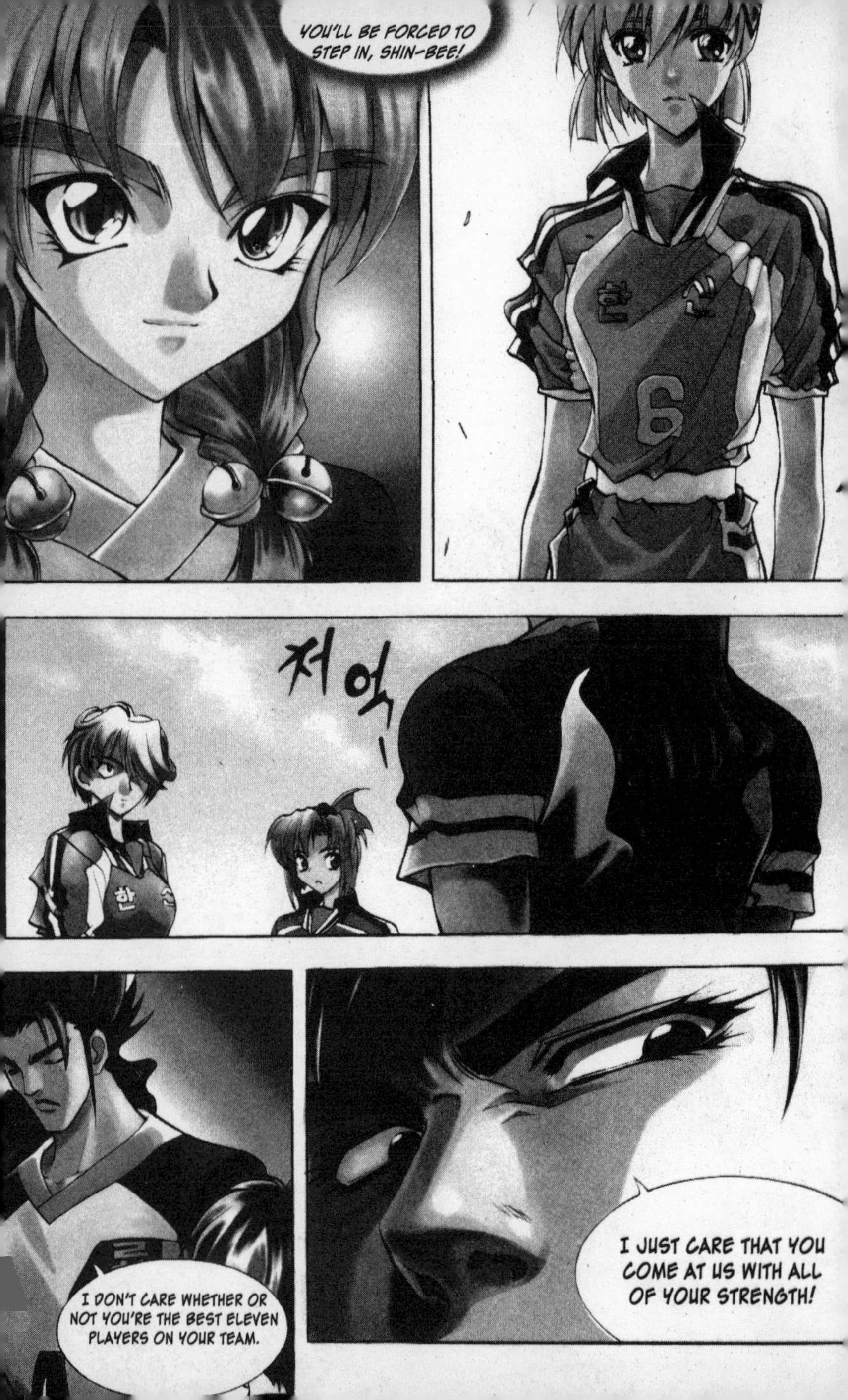
YOU'LL BE FORCED TO STEP IN, SHIN-BEE!
저억
I DON'T CARE WHETHER OR NOT YOU'RE THE BEST ELEVEN PLAYERS ON YOUR TEAM.
I JUST CARE THAT YOU COME AT US WITH ALL OF YOUR STRENGTH!

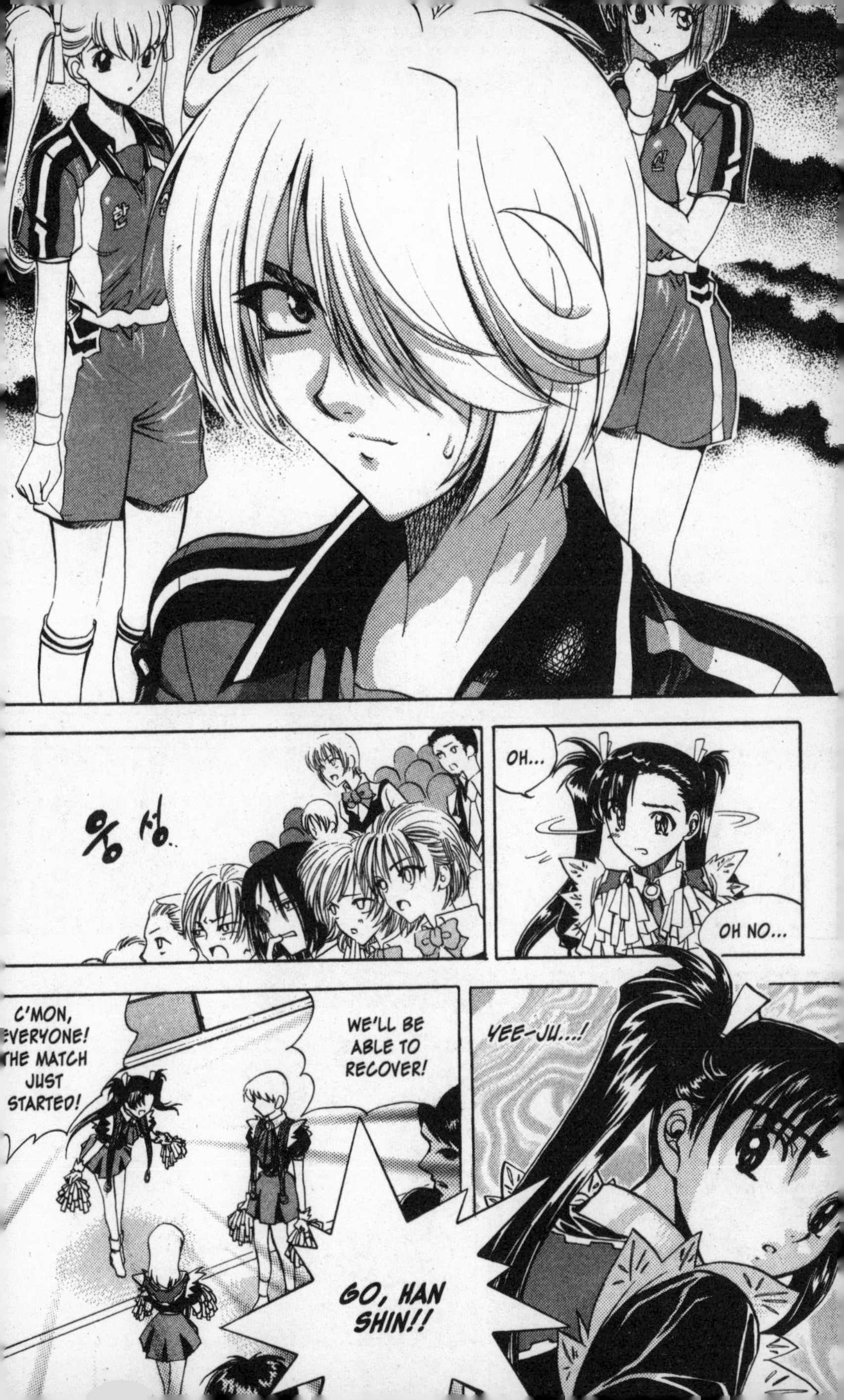
웅성..
OH...
OH NO...
C'MON, EVERYONE! THE MATCH JUST STARTED!
WE'LL BE ABLE TO RECOVER!
GO, HAN SHIN!!
YEE-JU...!

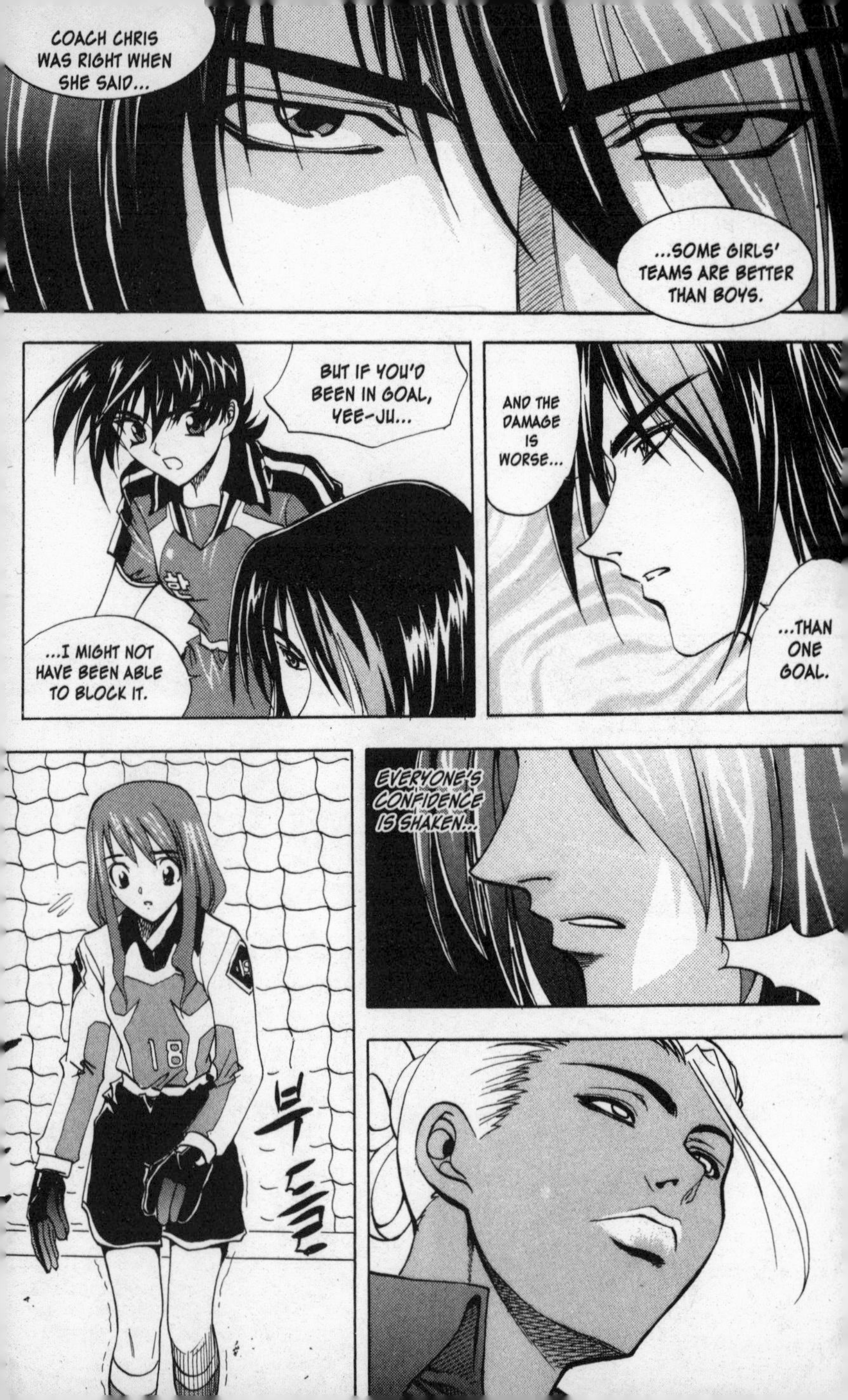
COACH CHRIS WAS RIGHT WHEN SHE SAID...
...SOME GIRLS' TEAMS ARE BETTER THAN BOYS.
BUT IF YOU'D BEEN IN GOAL, YEE-JU...
...I MIGHT NOT HAVE BEEN ABLE TO BLOCK IT.
AND THE DAMAGE IS WORSE...
...THAN ONE GOAL.
EVERYONE'S CONFIDENCE IS SHAKEN...

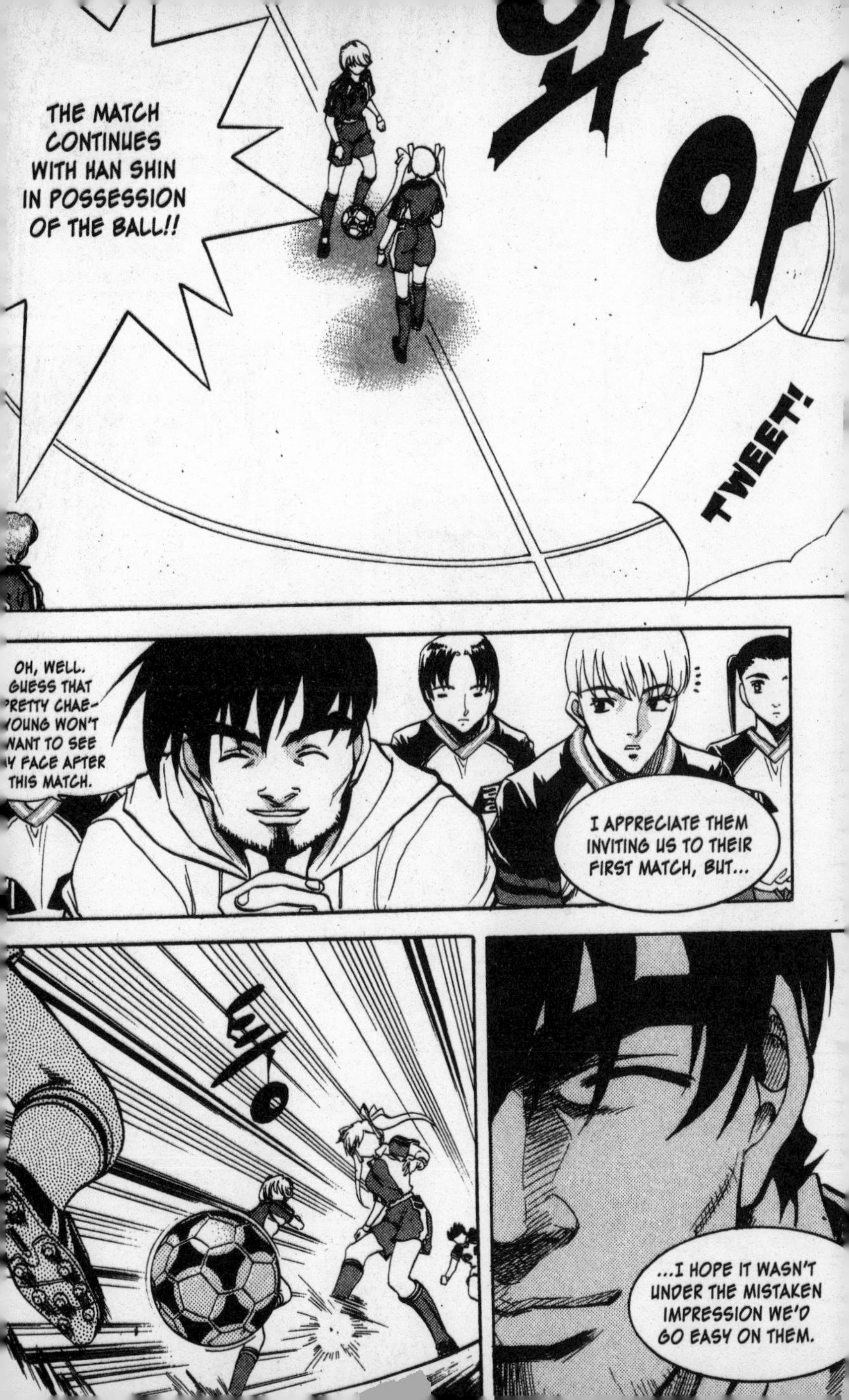
THE MATCH CONTINUES WITH HAN SHIN IN POSSESSION OF THE BALL!!
TWEET!
OH, WELL. GUESS THAT PRETTY CHAE-YOUNG WON'T WANT TO SEE MY FACE AFTER THIS MATCH.
I APPRECIATE THEM INVITING US TO THEIR FIRST MATCH, BUT...
...I HOPE IT WASN'T UNDER THE MISTAKEN IMPRESSION WE'D GO EASY ON THEM.

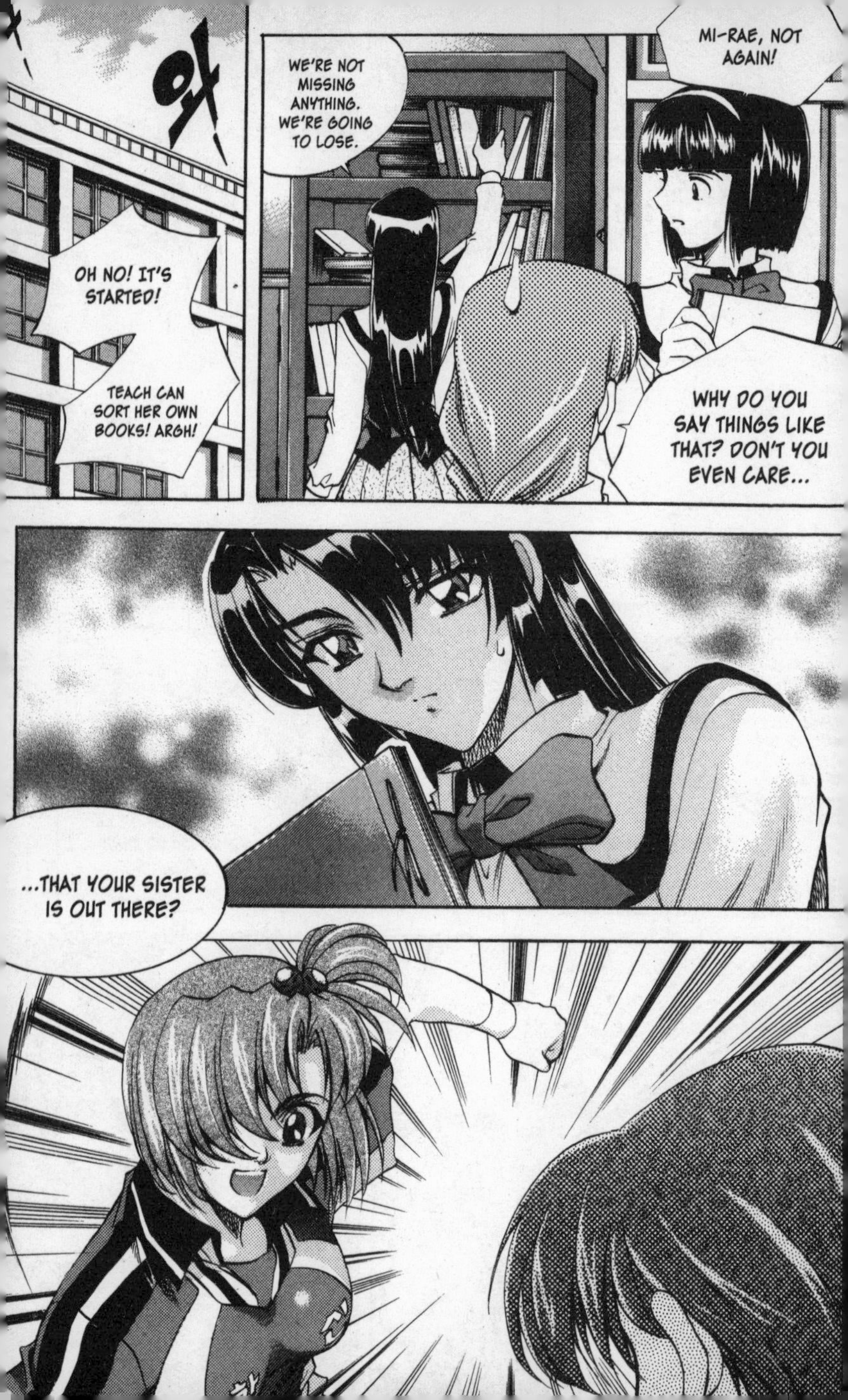
OH NO! IT'S STARTED!
TEACH CAN SORT HER OWN BOOKS! ARGH!
WE'RE NOT MISSING ANYTHING. WE'RE GOING TO LOSE.
MI-RAE, NOT AGAIN!
WHY DO YOU SAY THINGS LIKE THAT? DON'T YOU EVEN CARE...
...THAT YOUR SISTER IS OUT THERE?

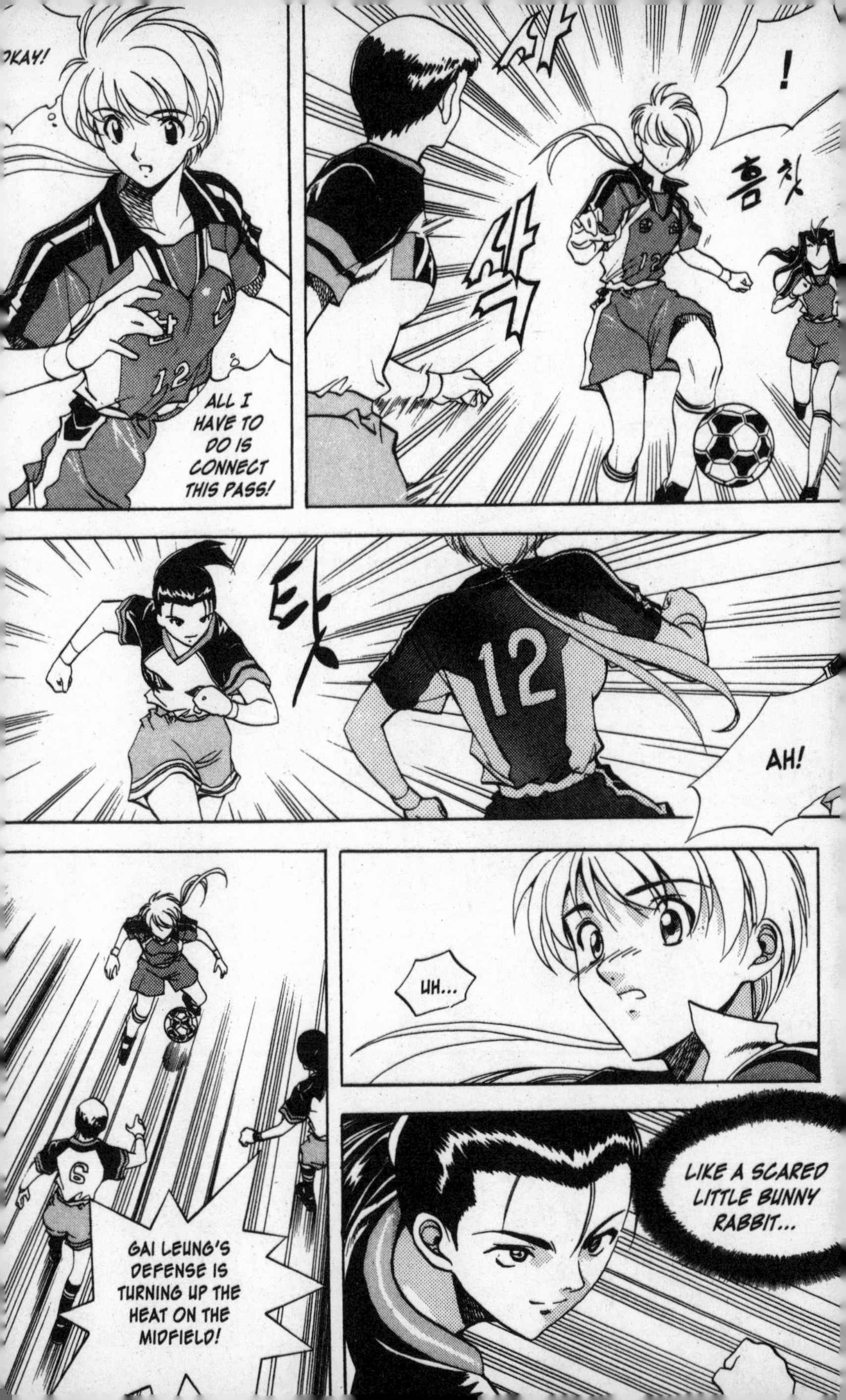
OKAY!
ALL I HAVE TO DO IS CONNECT THIS PASS!
삭
!
흠칫
삭
타
AH!
UH...
GAI LEUNG'S DEFENSE IS TURNING UP THE HEAT ON THE MIDFIELD!
LIKE A SCARED LITTLE BUNNY RABBIT...

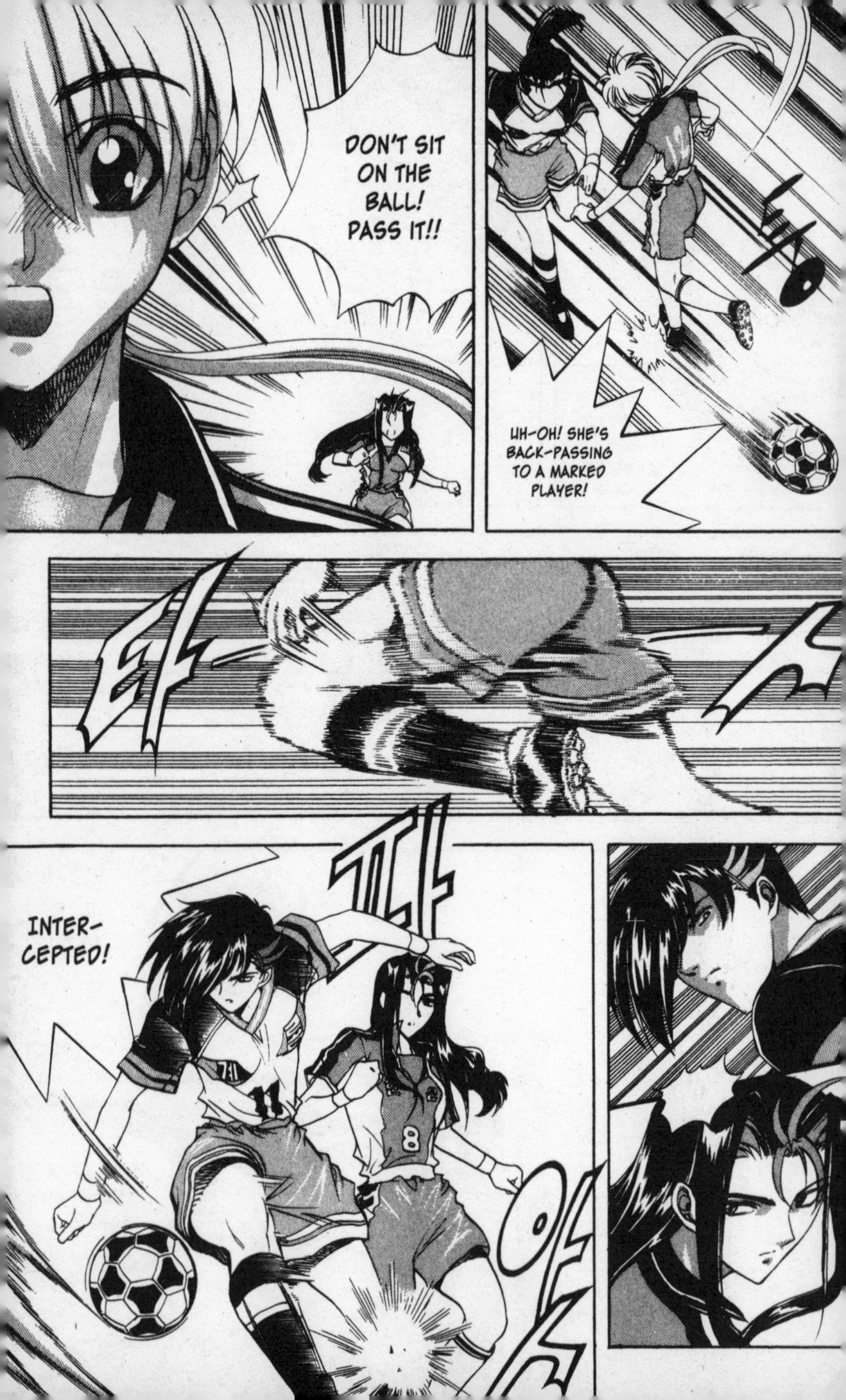
DON'T SIT ON THE BALL! PASS IT!!
UH-OH! SHE'S BACK-PASSING TO A MARKED PLAYER!
INTER-CEPTED!

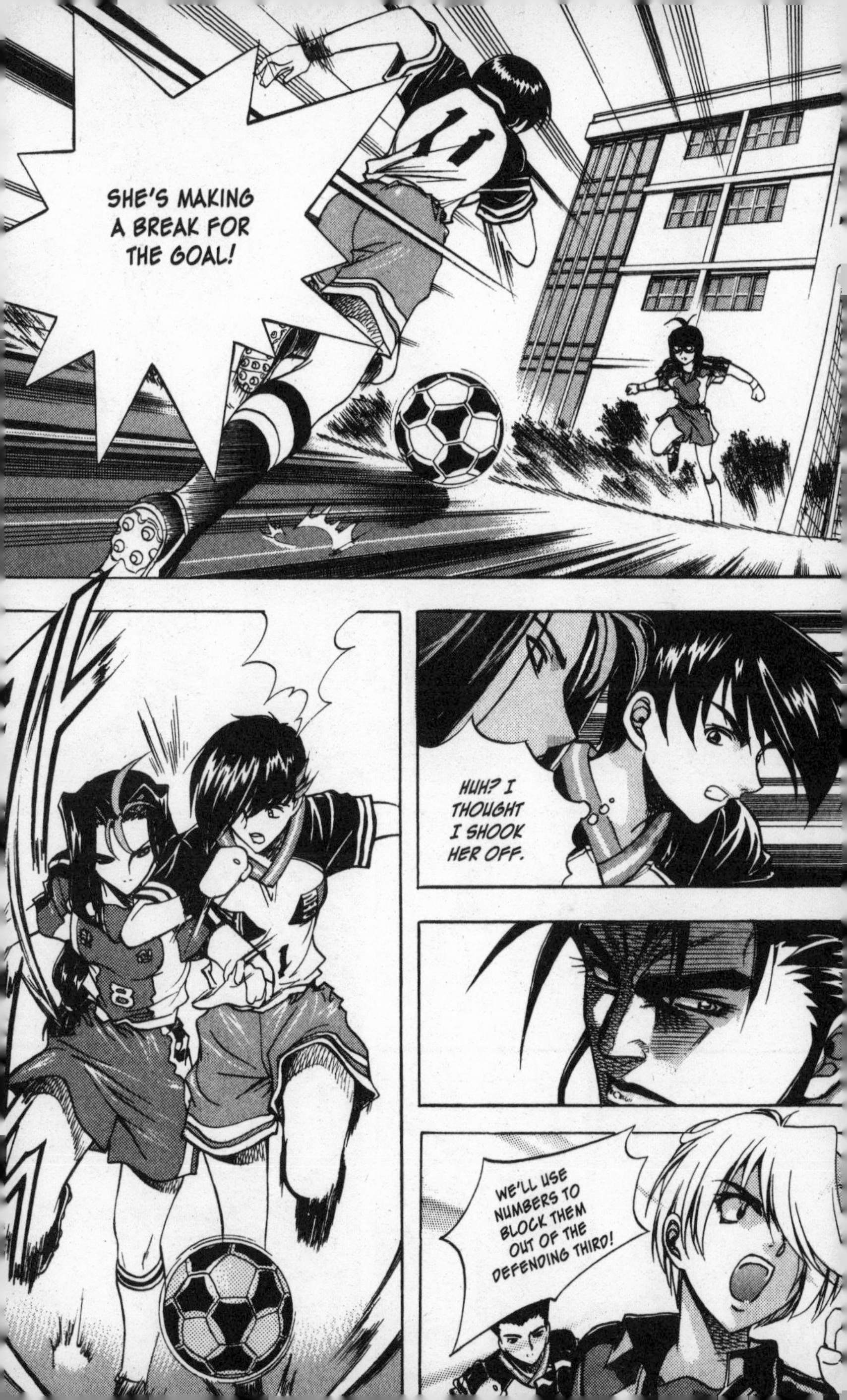
SHE'S MAKING A BREAK FOR THE GOAL!
HUH? I THOUGHT I SHOOK HER OFF.
WE'LL USE NUMBERS TO BLOCK THEM OUT OF THE DEFENDING THIRD!

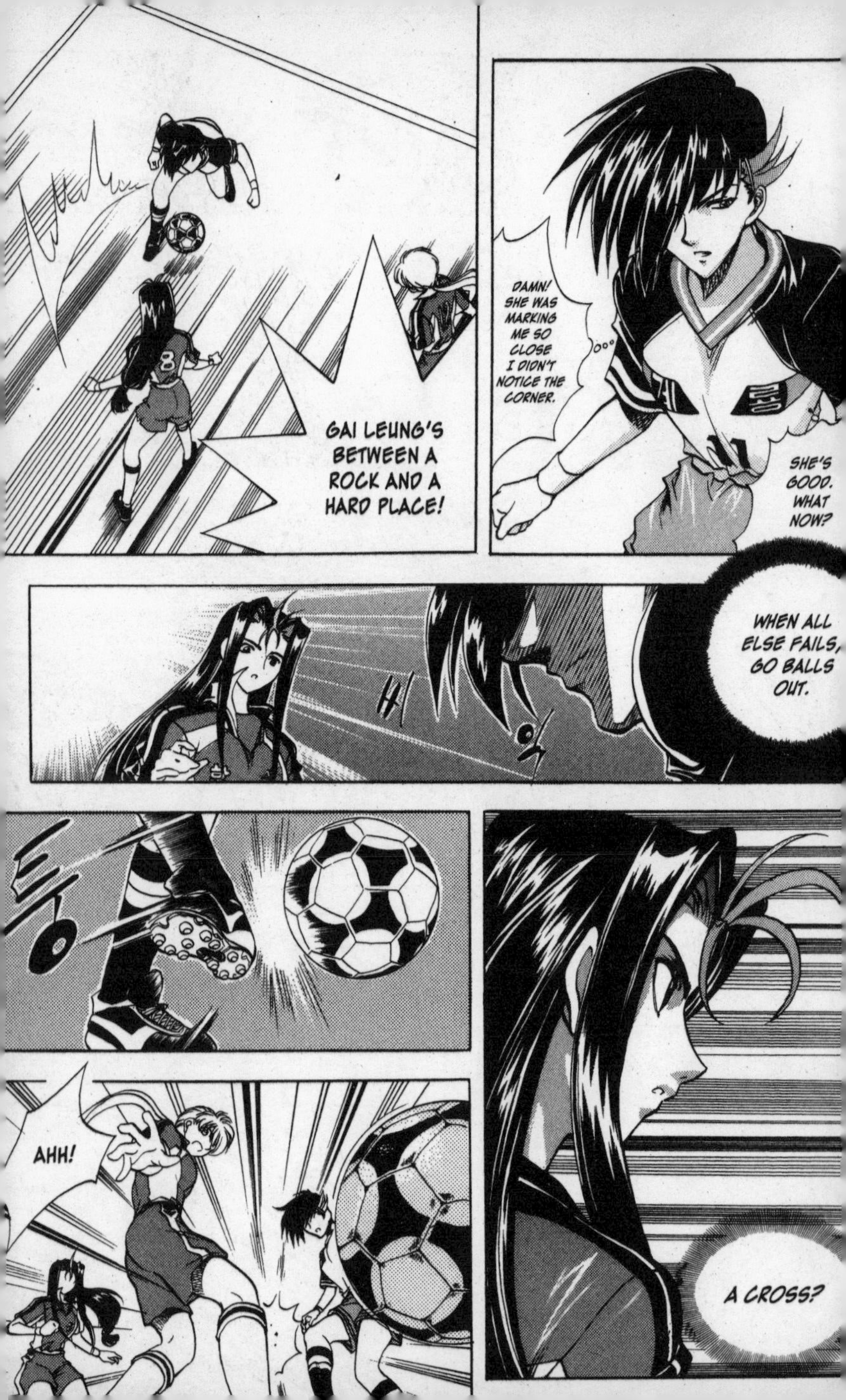
GAI LEUNG'S BETWEEN A ROCK AND A HARD PLACE!
DAMN! SHE WAS MARKING ME SO CLOSE I DIDN'T NOTICE THE CORNER.
SHE'S GOOD. WHAT NOW?
WHEN ALL ELSE FAILS, GO BALLS OUT.
AHH!
A CROSS?

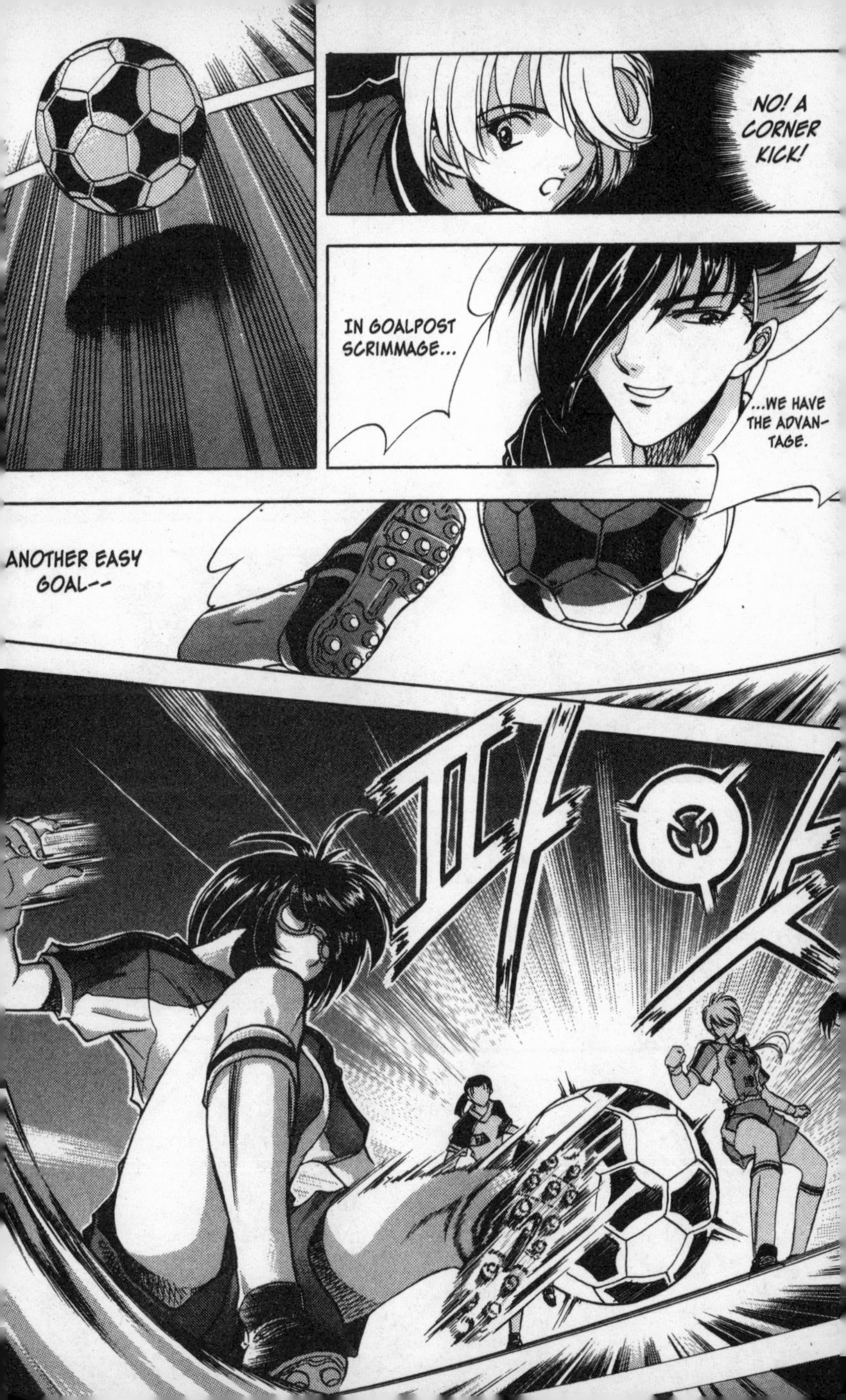
NO! A CORNER KICK!
IN GOALPOST SCRIMMAGE...
...WE HAVE THE ADVANTAGE.
ANOTHER EASY GOAL--

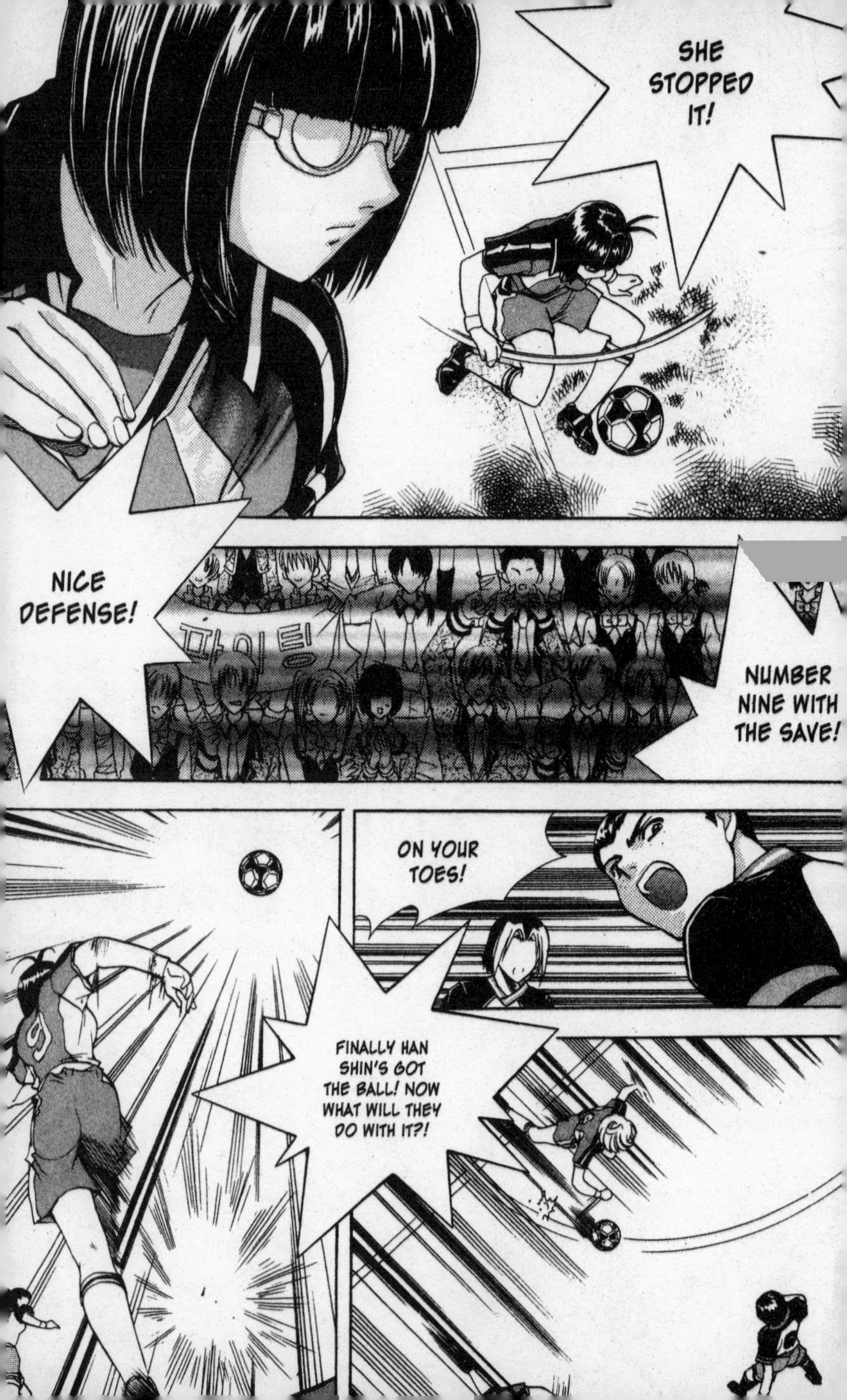
SHE STOPPED IT!
NICE DEFENSE!
파이팅
NUMBER NINE WITH THE SAVE!
ON YOUR TOES!
FINALLY HAN SHIN'S GOT THE BALL! NOW WHAT WILL THEY DO WITH IT?!

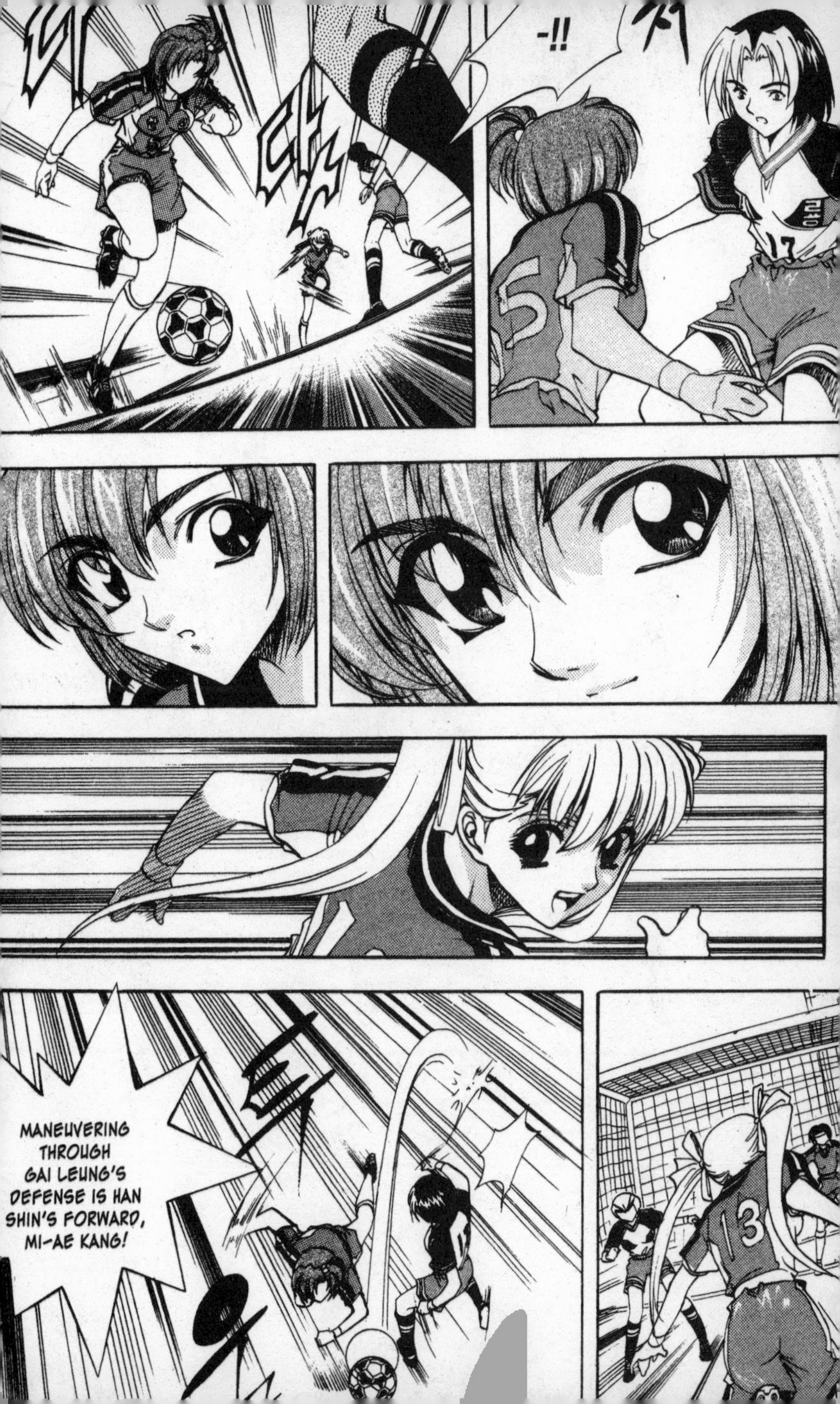
-!!
MANEUVERING THROUGH GAI LEUNG'S DEFENSE IS HAN SHIN'S FORWARD, MI-AE KANG!

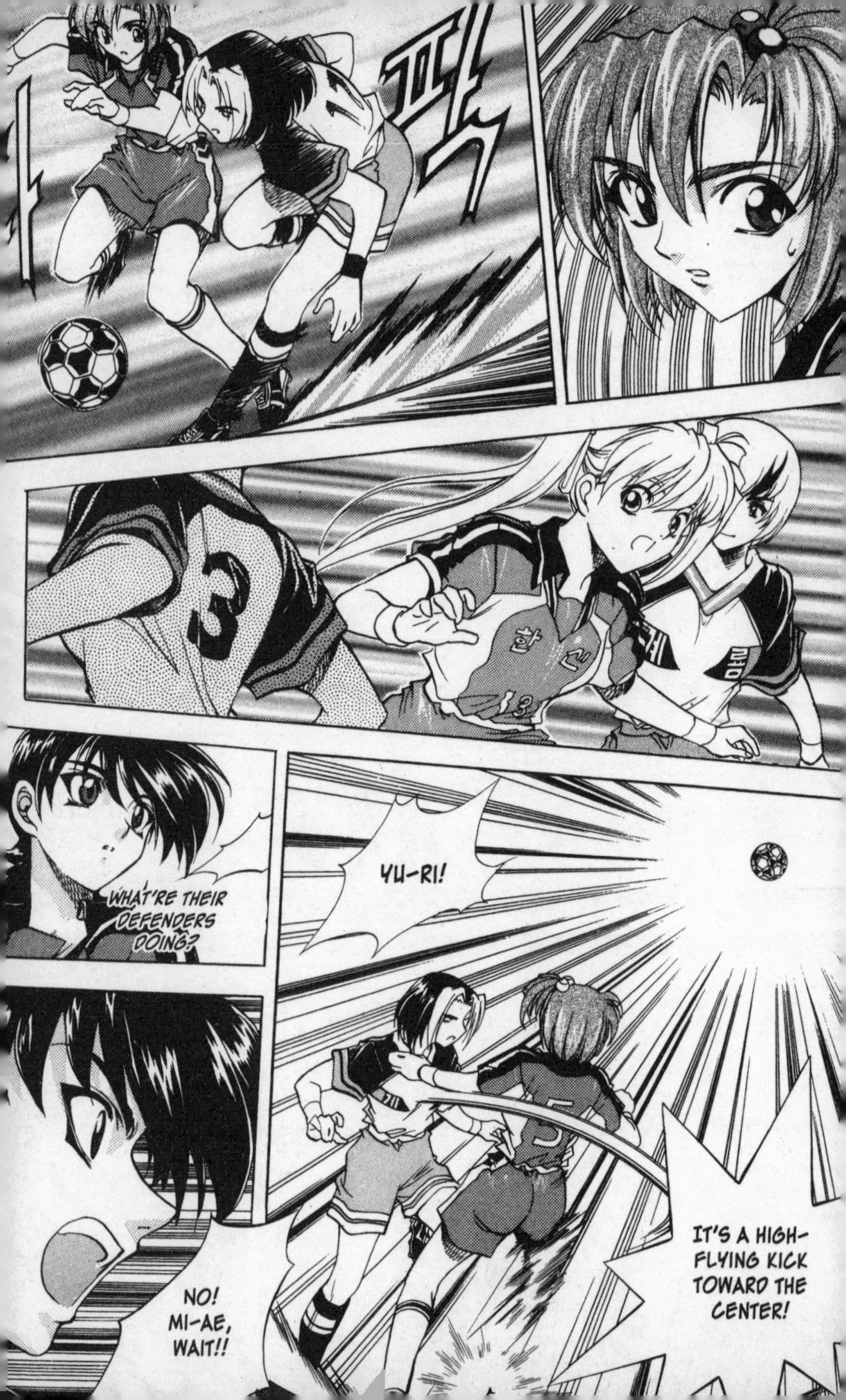
WHAT'RE THEIR DEFENDERS DOING?
NO! MI-AE, WAIT!!
YU-RI!
IT'S A HIGH-FLYING KICK TOWARD THE CENTER!

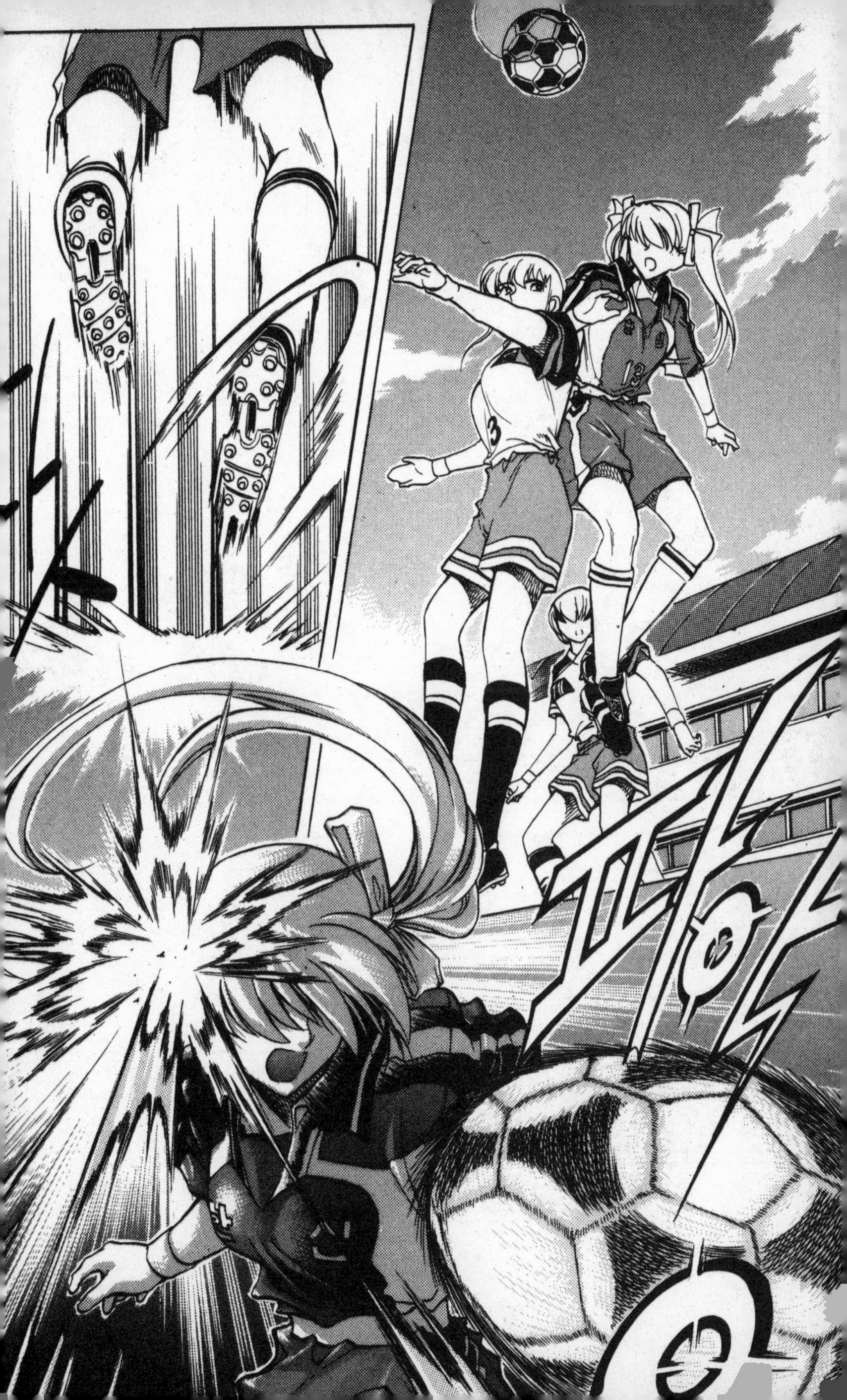

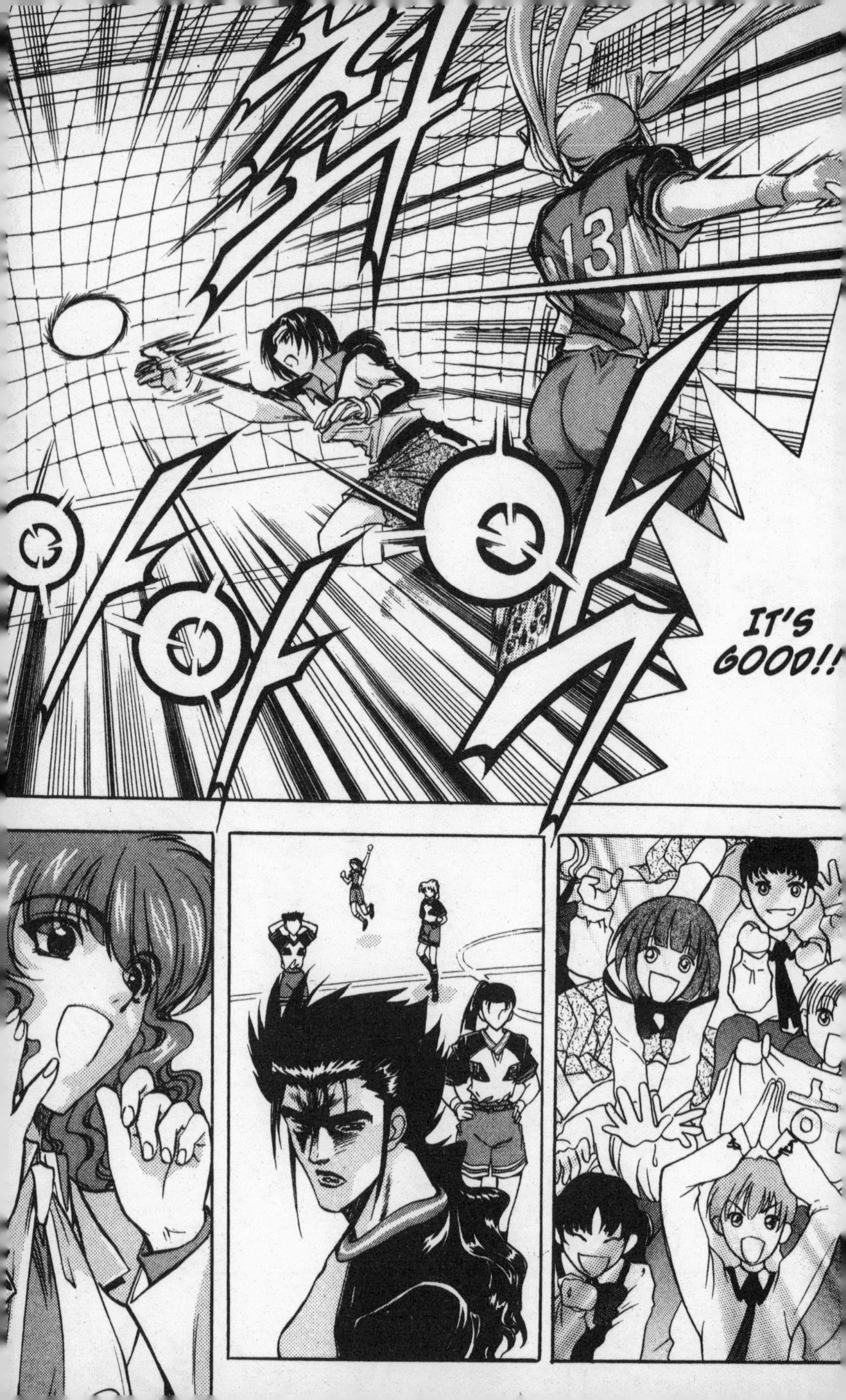
IT'S GOOD!!

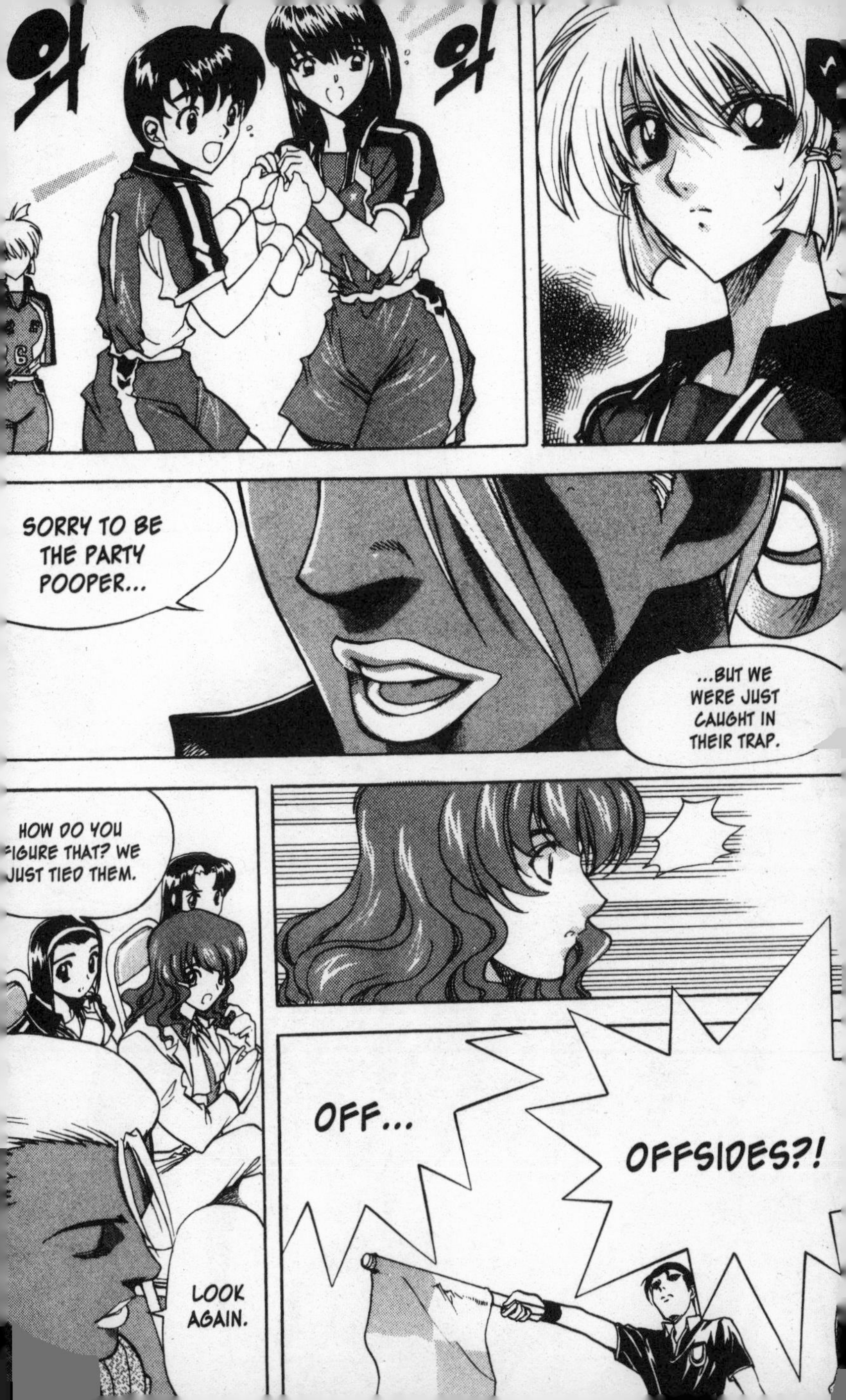

와
와
SORRY TO BE THE PARTY POOPER...
...BUT WE WERE JUST CAUGHT IN THEIR TRAP.
HOW DO YOU FIGURE THAT? WE JUST TIED THEM.
LOOK AGAIN.
OFF...
OFFSIDES?!

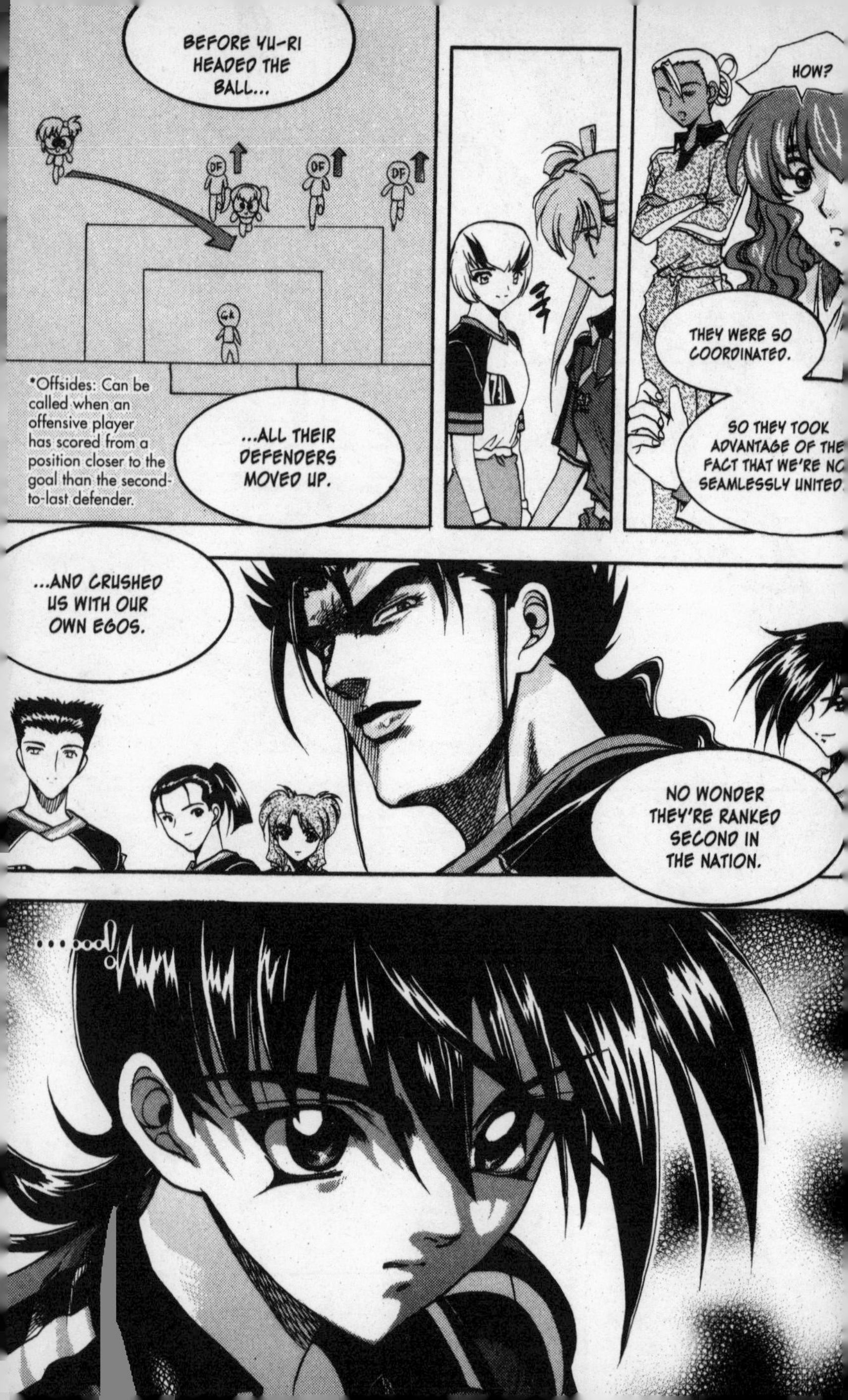

BEFORE YU-RI HEADED THE BALL...
DF
DF
DF
GK
*Offsides: Can be called when an offensive player has scored from a position closer to the goal than the second-to-last defender.
...ALL THEIR DEFENDERS MOVED UP.
HOW?
THEY WERE SO COORDINATED.
SO THEY TOOK ADVANTAGE OF THE FACT THAT WE'RE NO SEAMLESSLY UNITED.
...AND CRUSHED US WITH OUR OWN EGOS.
NO WONDER THEY'RE RANKED SECOND IN THE NATION.

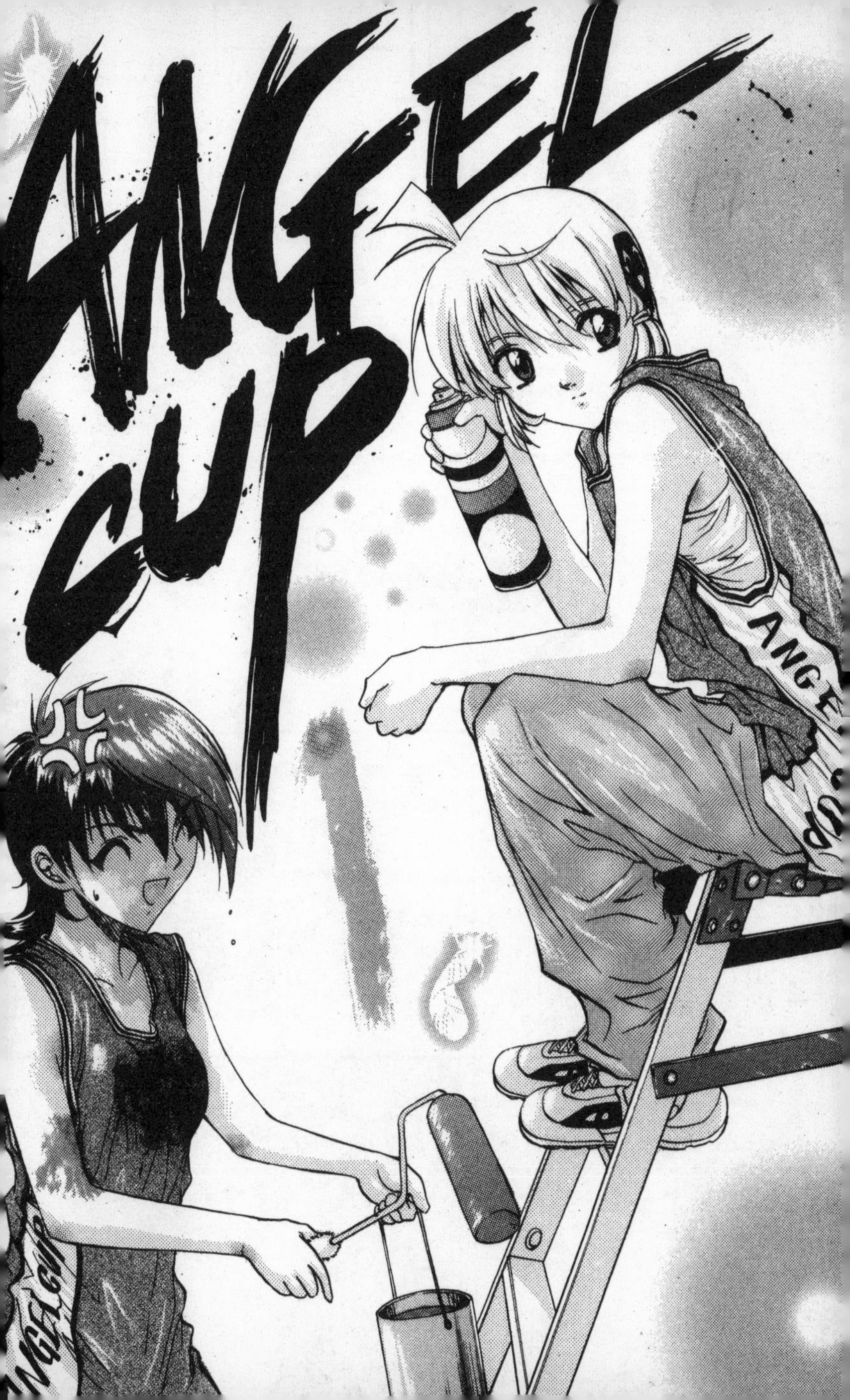
ANGEL CUP

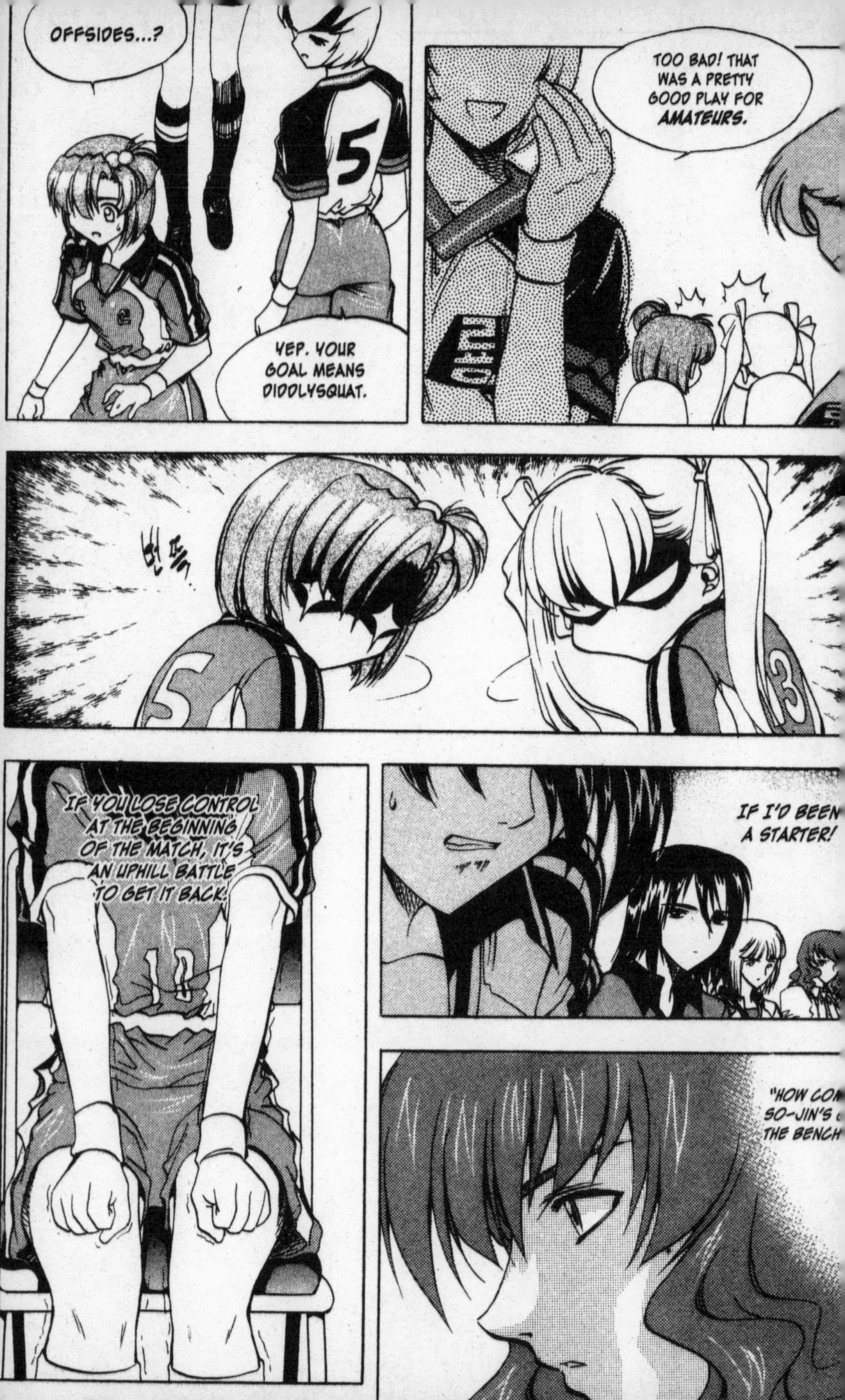
OFFSIDES...?
YEP. YOUR GOAL MEANS DIDDLYSQUAT.
TOO BAD! THAT WAS A PRETTY GOOD PLAY FOR AMATEURS.
번뜩..
IF YOU LOSE CONTROL AT THE BEGINNING OF THE MATCH, IT'S AN UPHILL BATTLE TO GET IT BACK.
IF I'D BEEN A STARTER!
"HOW COM
SO-JIN'S
THE BENCH

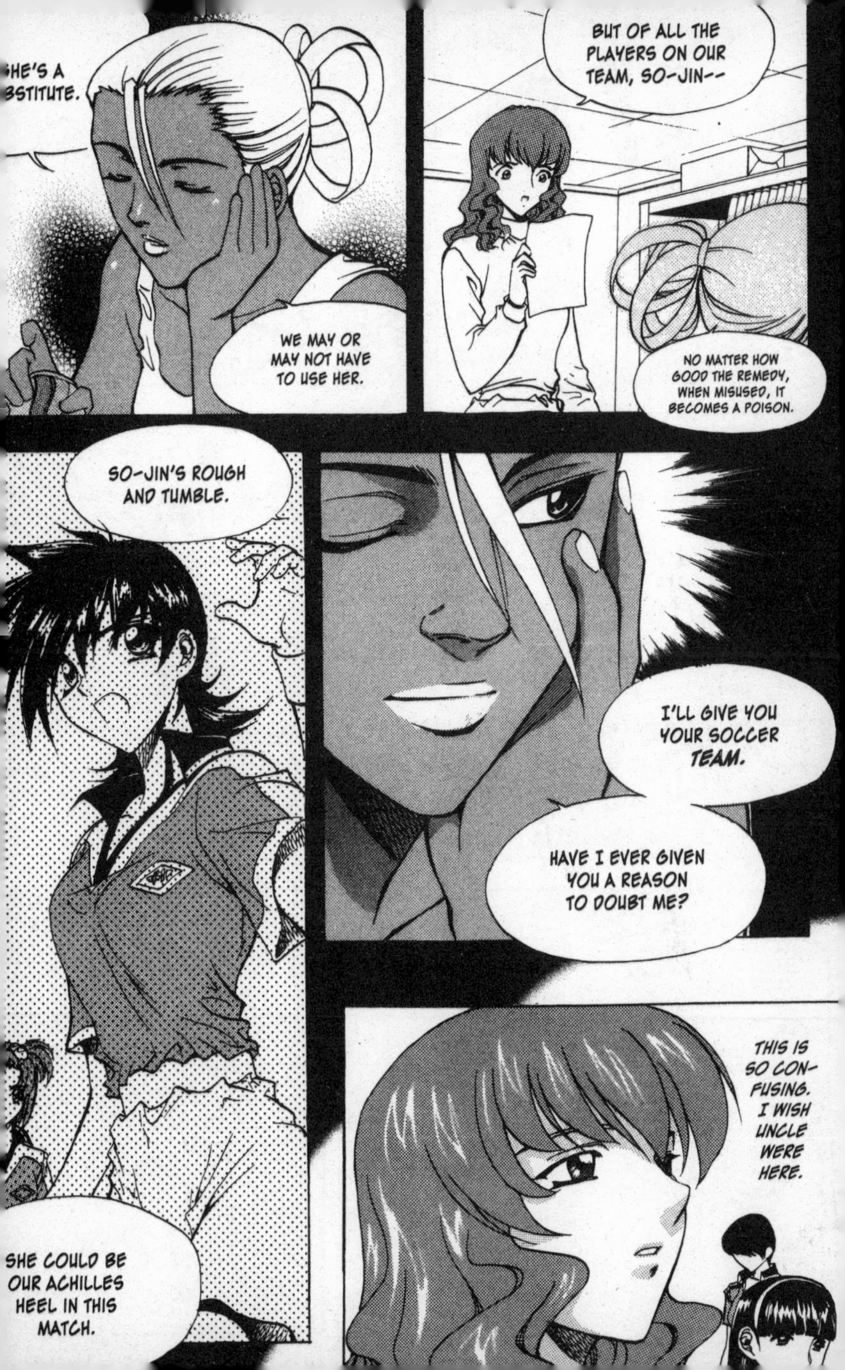
HE'S A
BSTITUTE.
WE MAY OR MAY NOT HAVE TO USE HER.
BUT OF ALL THE PLAYERS ON OUR TEAM, SO-JIN--
NO MATTER HOW GOOD THE REMEDY, WHEN MISUSED, IT BECOMES A POISON.
SO-JIN'S ROUGH AND TUMBLE.
SHE COULD BE OUR ACHILLES HEEL IN THIS MATCH.
I'LL GIVE YOU YOUR SOCCER TEAM.
HAVE I EVER GIVEN YOU A REASON TO DOUBT ME?
THIS IS SO CON-FUSING. I WISH UNCLE WERE HERE.

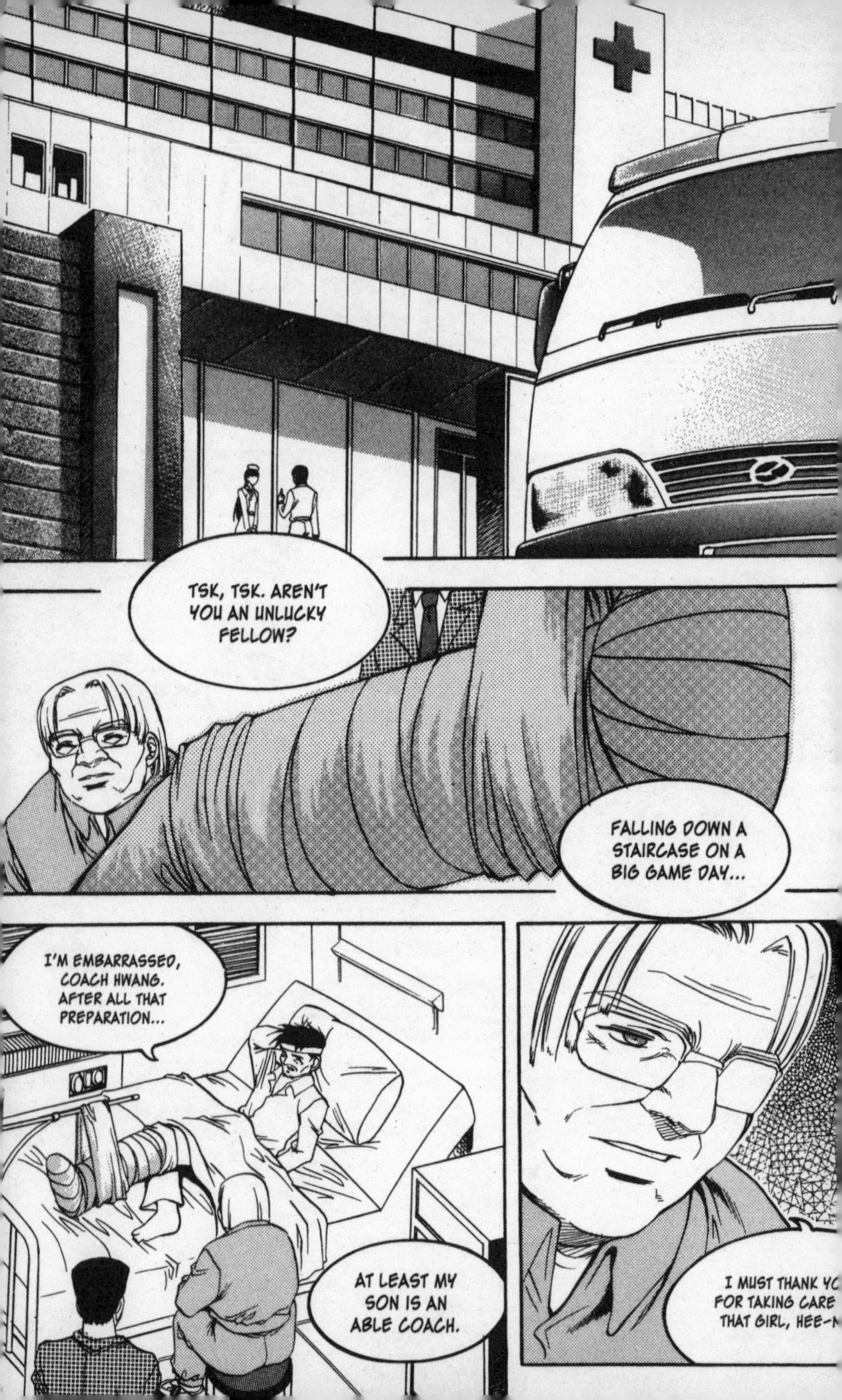
TSK, TSK. AREN'T YOU AN UNLUCKY FELLOW?
FALLING DOWN A STAIRCASE ON A BIG GAME DAY...
I'M EMBARRASSED, COACH HWANG. AFTER ALL THAT PREPARATION...
AT LEAST MY SON IS AN ABLE COACH.
I MUST THANK YO FOR TAKING CARE THAT GIRL, HEE-

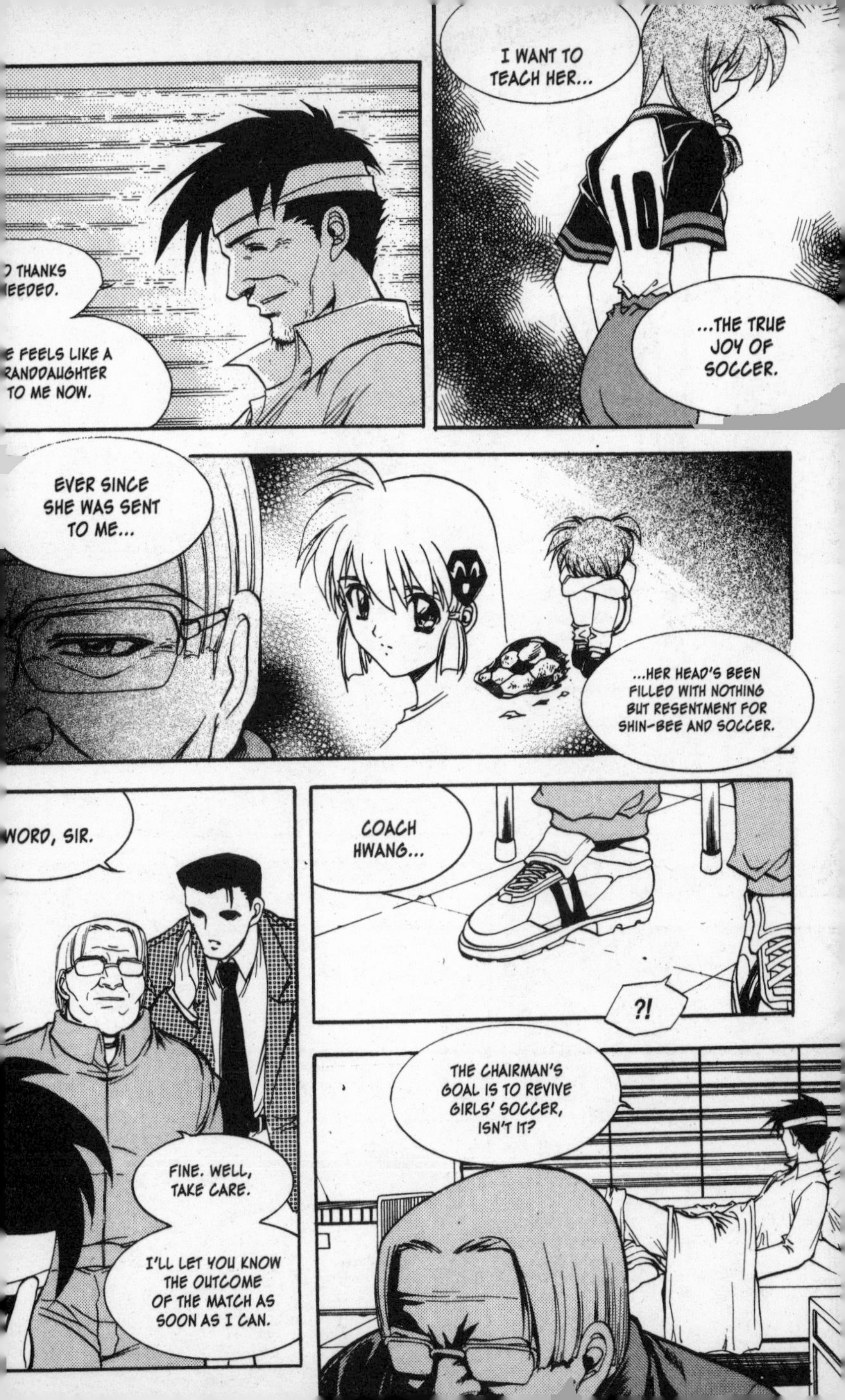

O THANKS
EEDED.
E FEELS LIKE A
RANDDAUGHTER
TO ME NOW.
I WANT TO TEACH HER...
...THE TRUE JOY OF SOCCER.
EVER SINCE SHE WAS SENT TO ME...
...HER HEAD'S BEEN FILLED WITH NOTHING BUT RESENTMENT FOR SHIN-BEE AND SOCCER.
WORD, SIR.
FINE. WELL, TAKE CARE.
I'LL LET YOU KNOW THE OUTCOME OF THE MATCH AS SOON AS I CAN.
COACH HWANG...
?!
THE CHAIRMAN'S GOAL IS TO REVIVE GIRLS' SOCCER, ISN'T IT?

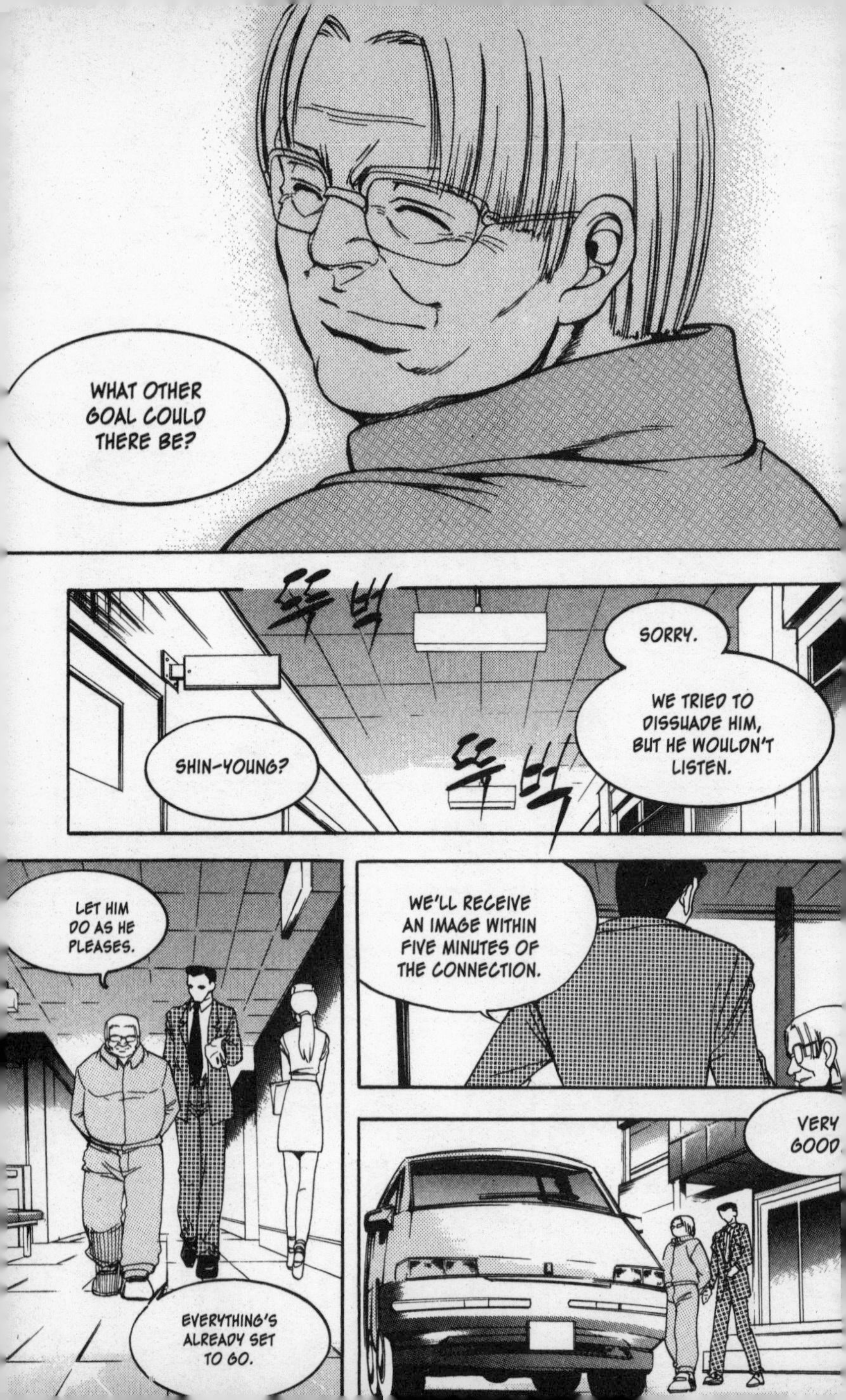
WHAT OTHER GOAL COULD THERE BE?
뚜벅
SHIN-YOUNG?
뚜벅
SORRY.
WE TRIED TO DISSUADE HIM, BUT HE WOULDN'T LISTEN.
LET HIM DO AS HE PLEASES.
EVERYTHING'S ALREADY SET TO GO.
WE'LL RECEIVE AN IMAGE WITHIN FIVE MINUTES OF THE CONNECTION.
VERY GOOD.

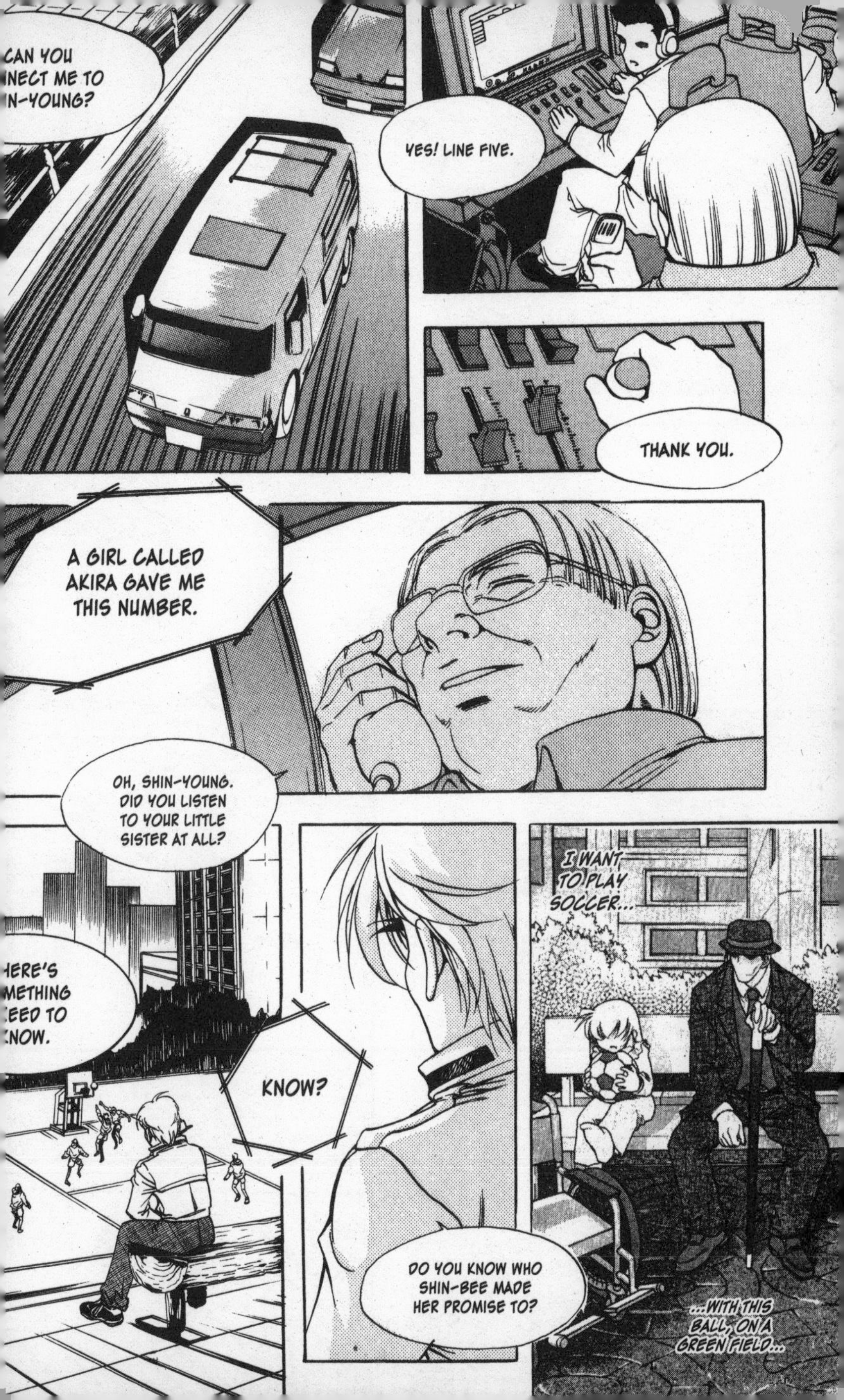
CAN YOU
NECT ME TO
N-YOUNG?
YES! LINE FIVE.
THANK YOU.
A GIRL CALLED AKIRA GAVE ME THIS NUMBER.
OH, SHIN-YOUNG. DID YOU LISTEN TO YOUR LITTLE SISTER AT ALL?
HERE'S
METHING
EED TO
NOW.
KNOW?
DO YOU KNOW WHO SHIN-BEE MADE HER PROMISE TO?
I WANT TO PLAY SOCCER...
...WITH THIS BALL, ON A GREEN FIELD...

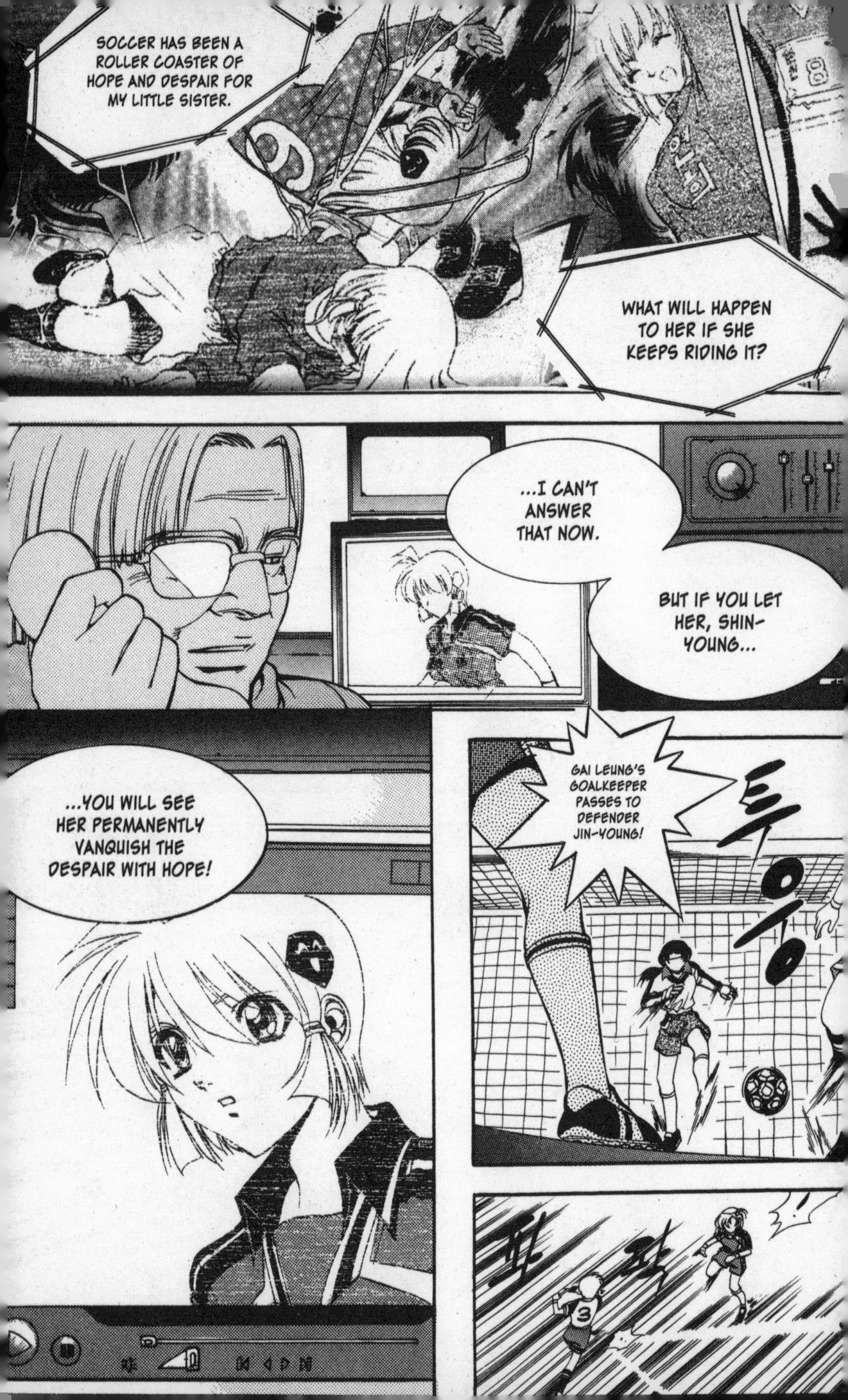
SOCCER HAS BEEN A ROLLER COASTER OF HOPE AND DESPAIR FOR MY LITTLE SISTER.
WHAT WILL HAPPEN TO HER IF SHE KEEPS RIDING IT?
...I CAN'T ANSWER THAT NOW.
BUT IF YOU LET HER, SHIN-YOUNG...
...YOU WILL SEE HER PERMANENTLY VANQUISH THE DESPAIR WITH HOPE!
GAI LEUNG'S GOALKEEPER PASSES TO DEFENDER JIN-YOUNG!

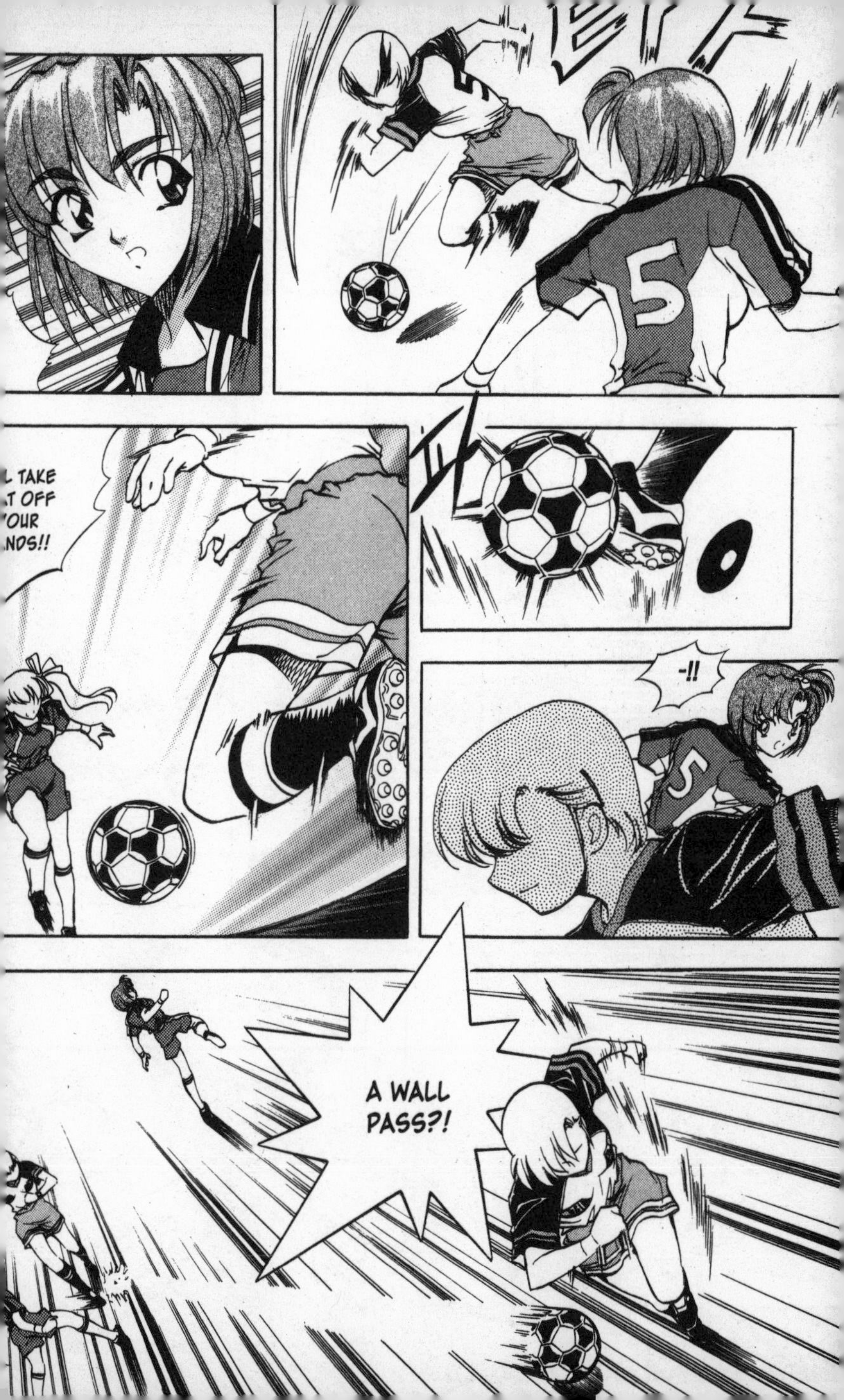
L TAKE
AT OFF
YOUR
ANDS!!
-!!
A WALL
PASS?!

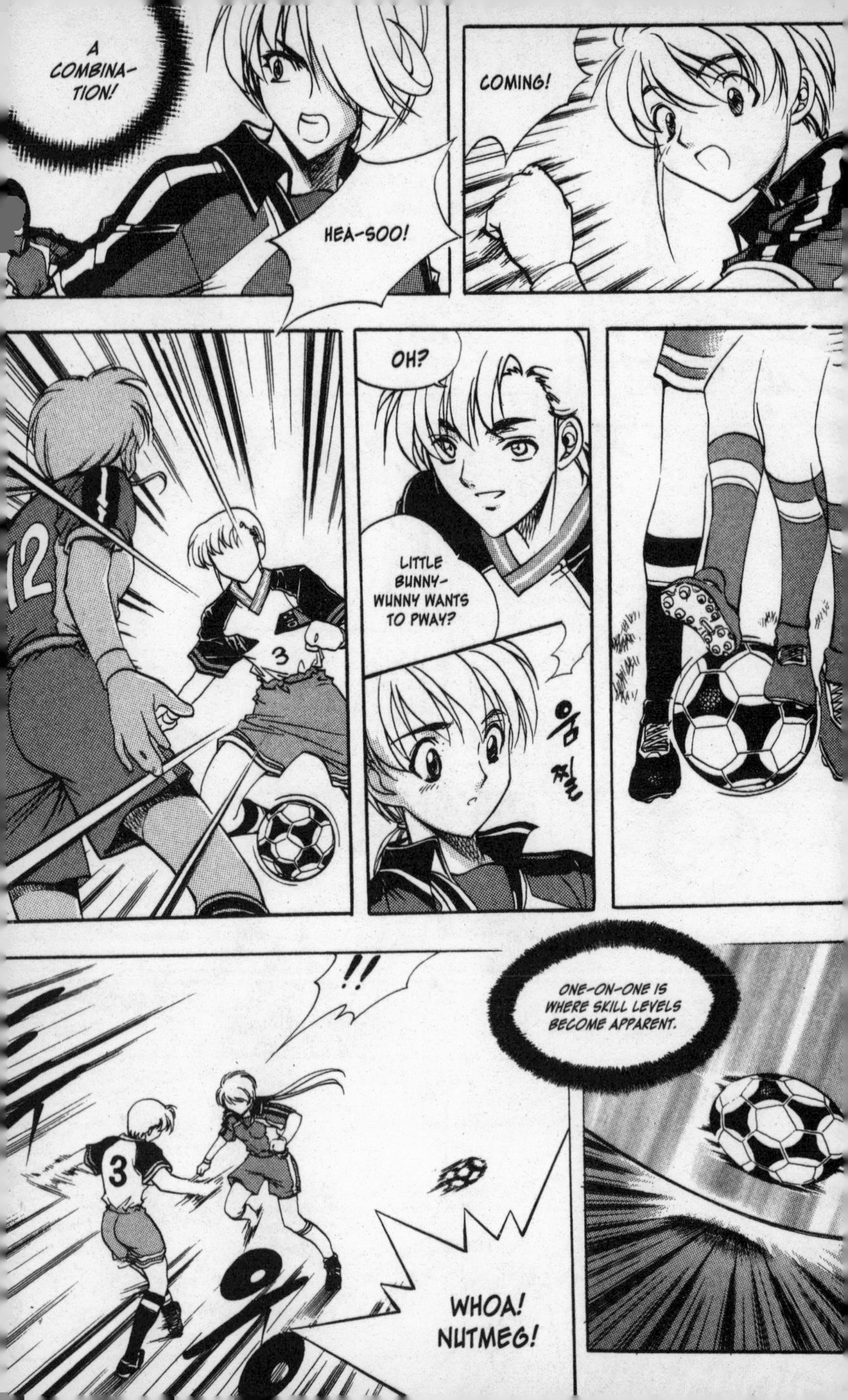

A COMBINATION!
HEA-SOO!
COMING!
OH?
LITTLE BUNNY-WUNNY WANTS TO PWAY?
움찔
!!
WHOA! NUTMEG!
ONE-ON-ONE IS WHERE SKILL LEVELS BECOME APPARENT.

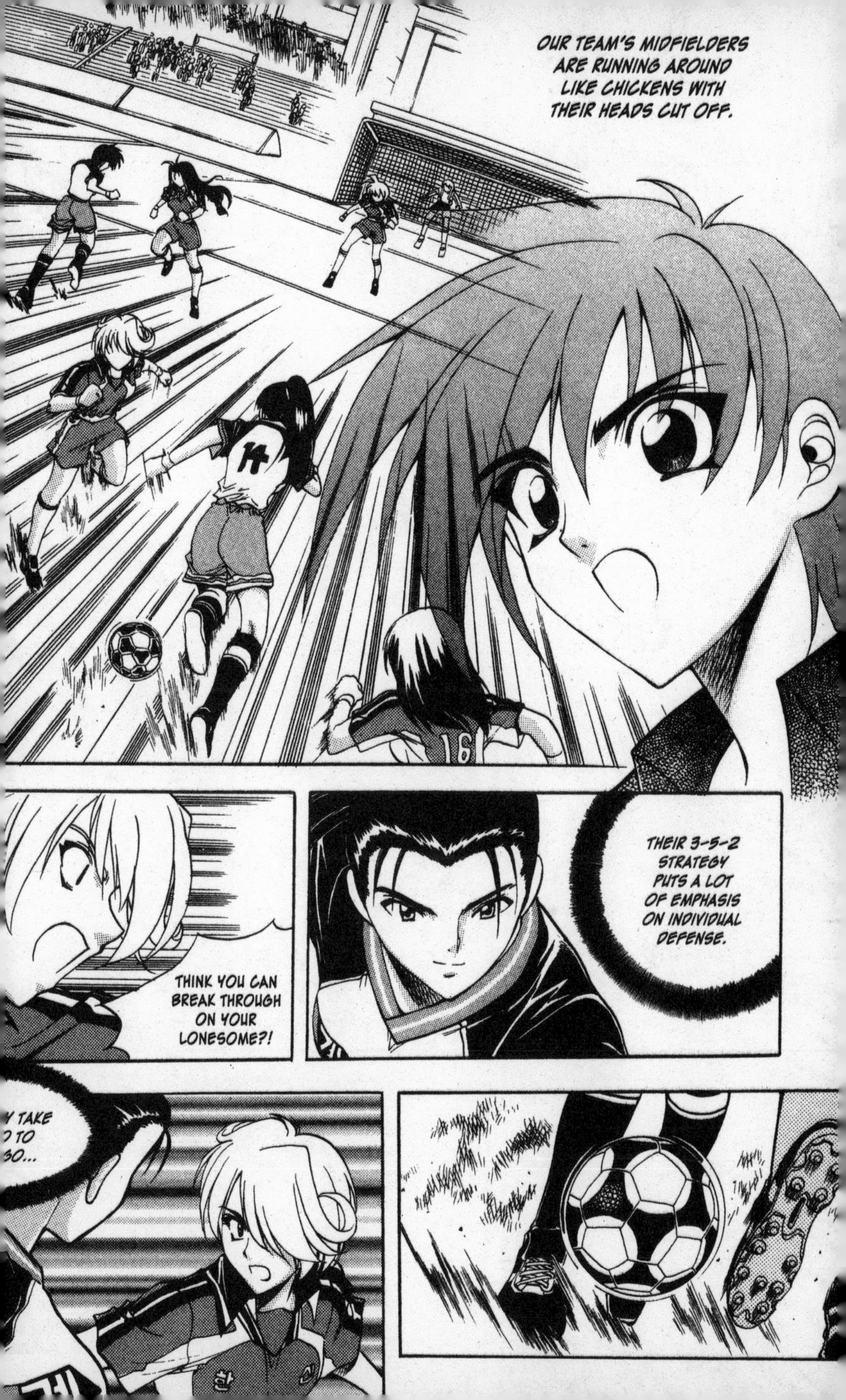
OUR TEAM'S MIDFIELDERS ARE RUNNING AROUND LIKE CHICKENS WITH THEIR HEADS CUT OFF.
THINK YOU CAN BREAK THROUGH ON YOUR LONESOME?!
THEIR 3-5-2 STRATEGY PUTS A LOT OF EMPHASIS ON INDIVIDUAL DEFENSE.

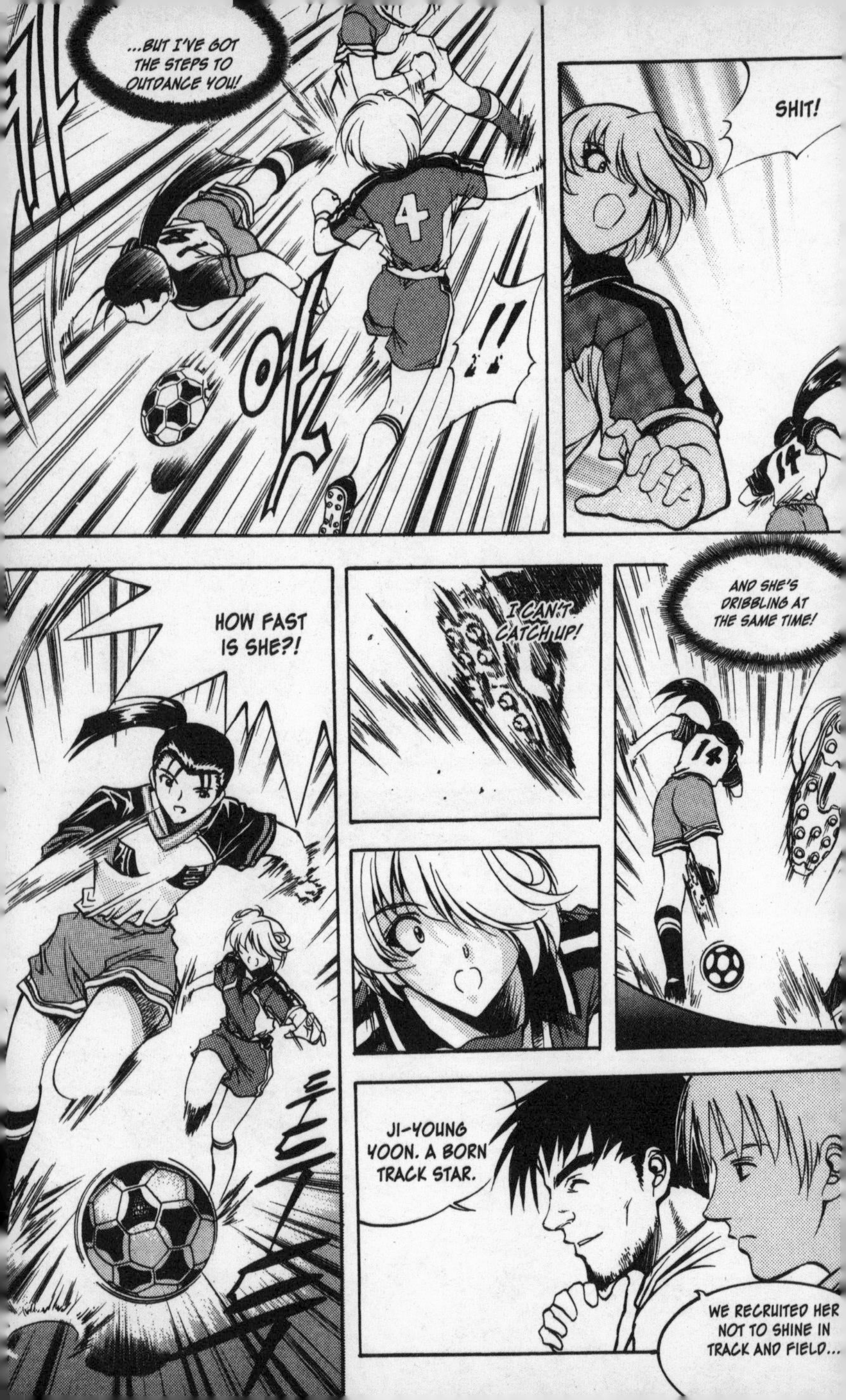
...BUT I'VE GOT THE STEPS TO OUTDANCE YOU!
!!
SHIT!
HOW FAST IS SHE?!
I CAN'T CATCH UP!
AND SHE'S DRIBBLING AT THE SAME TIME!
JI-YOUNG YOON. A BORN TRACK STAR.
WE RECRUITED HER NOT TO SHINE IN TRACK AND FIELD...

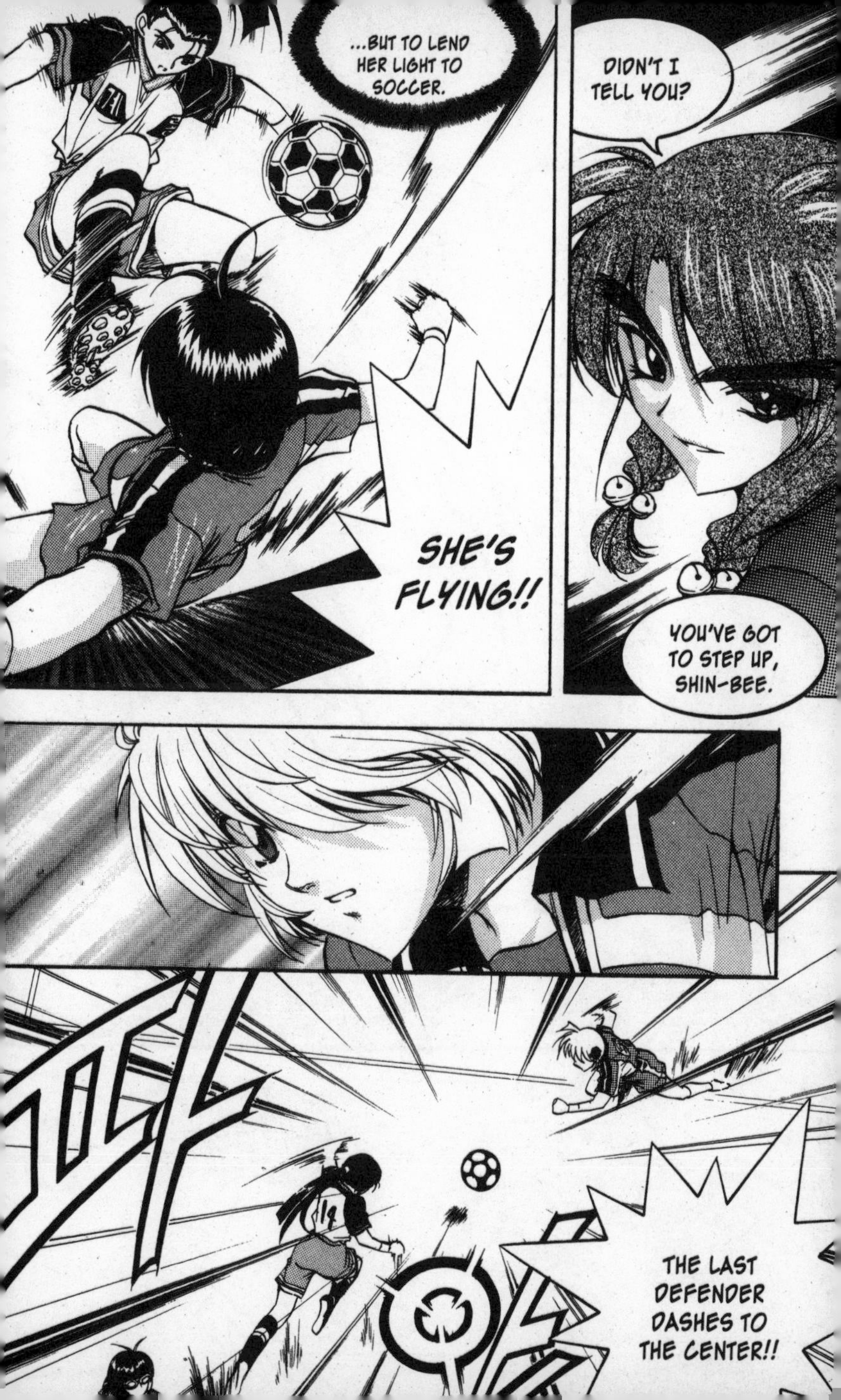
...BUT TO LEND HER LIGHT TO SOCCER.
SHE'S FLYING!!
DIDN'T I TELL YOU?
YOU'VE GOT TO STEP UP, SHIN-BEE.
THE LAST DEFENDER DASHES TO THE CENTER!!

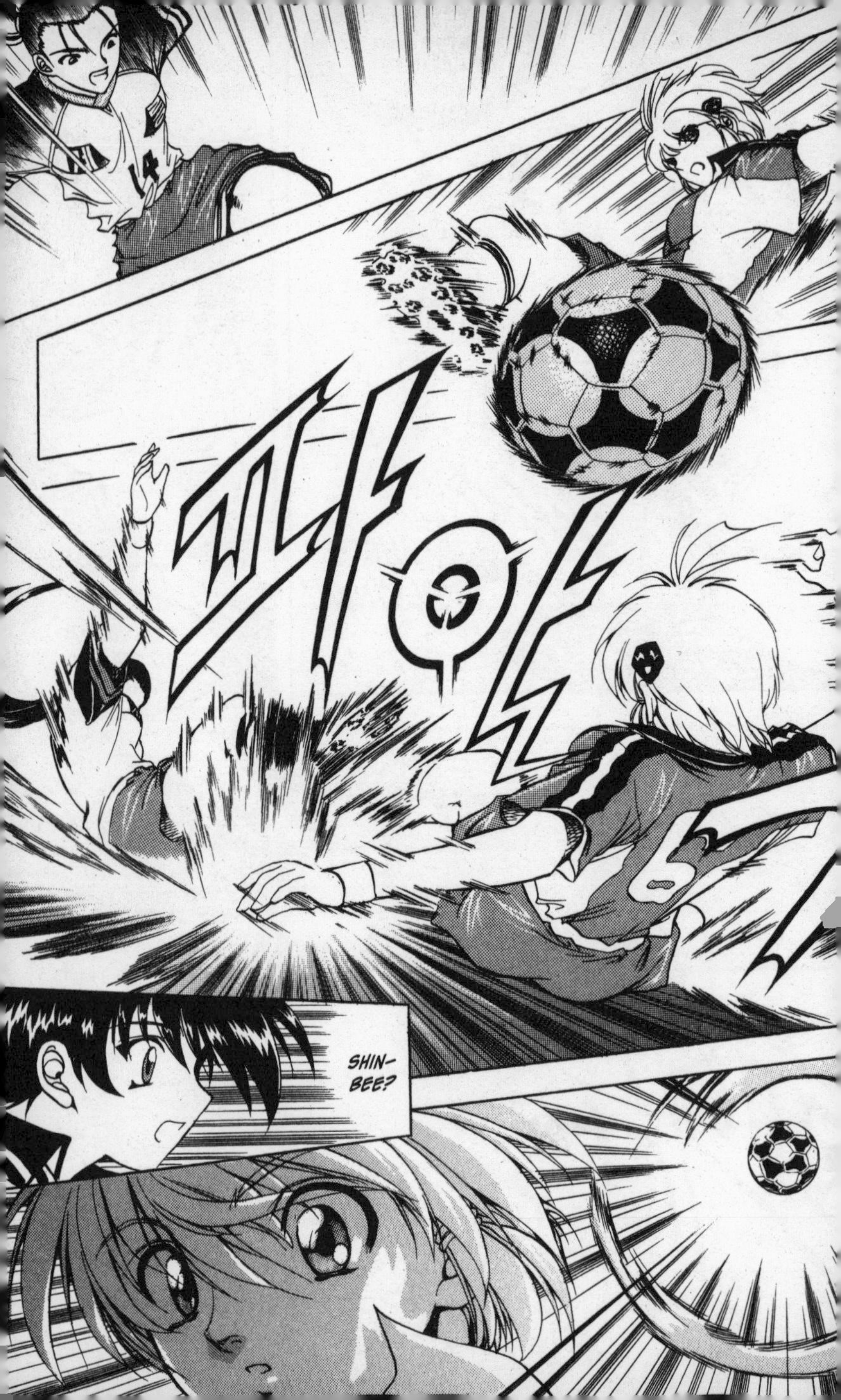
SHIN-BEE?

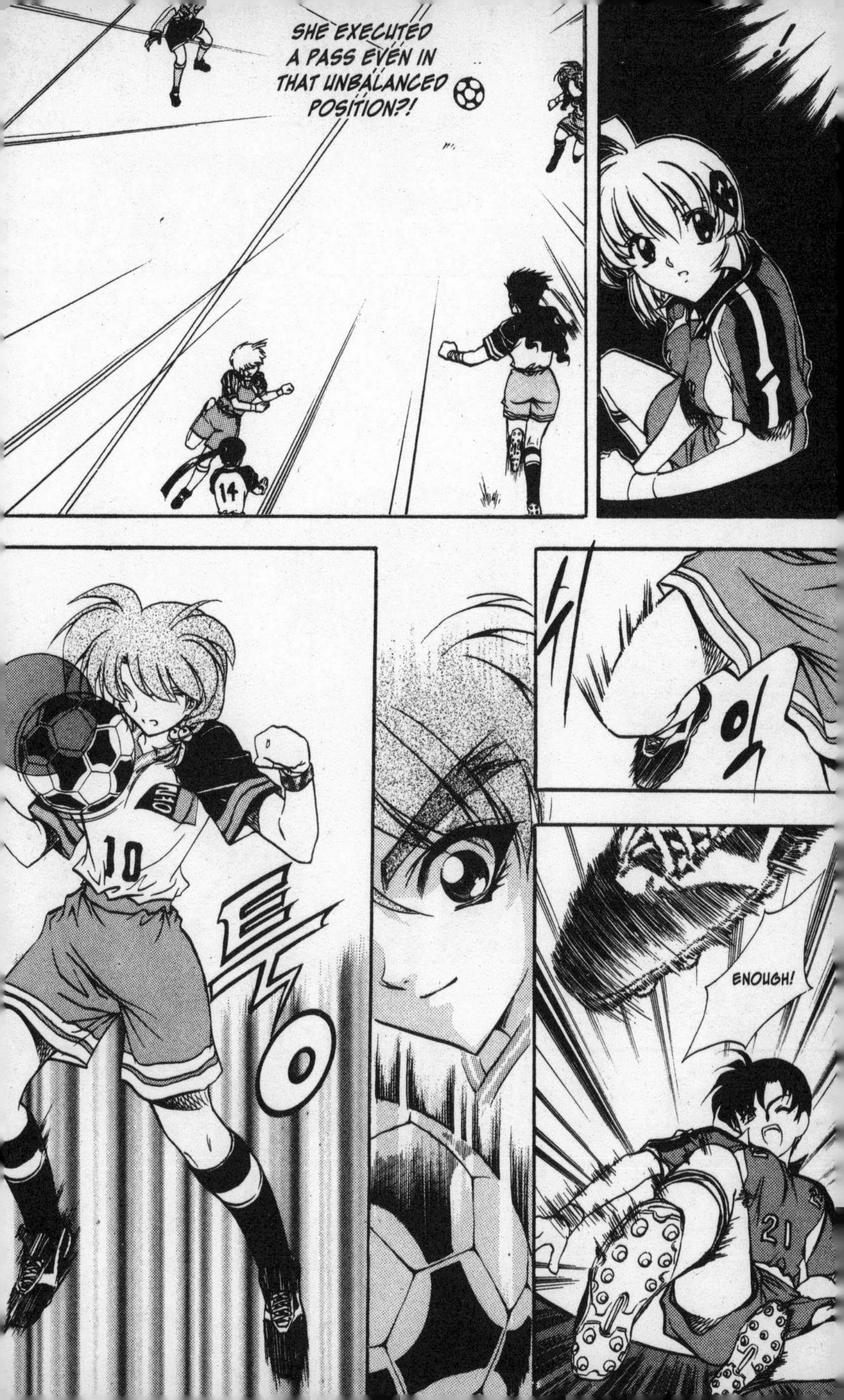

SHE EXECUTED A PASS EVEN IN THAT UNBALANCED POSITION?!
!
ENOUGH!

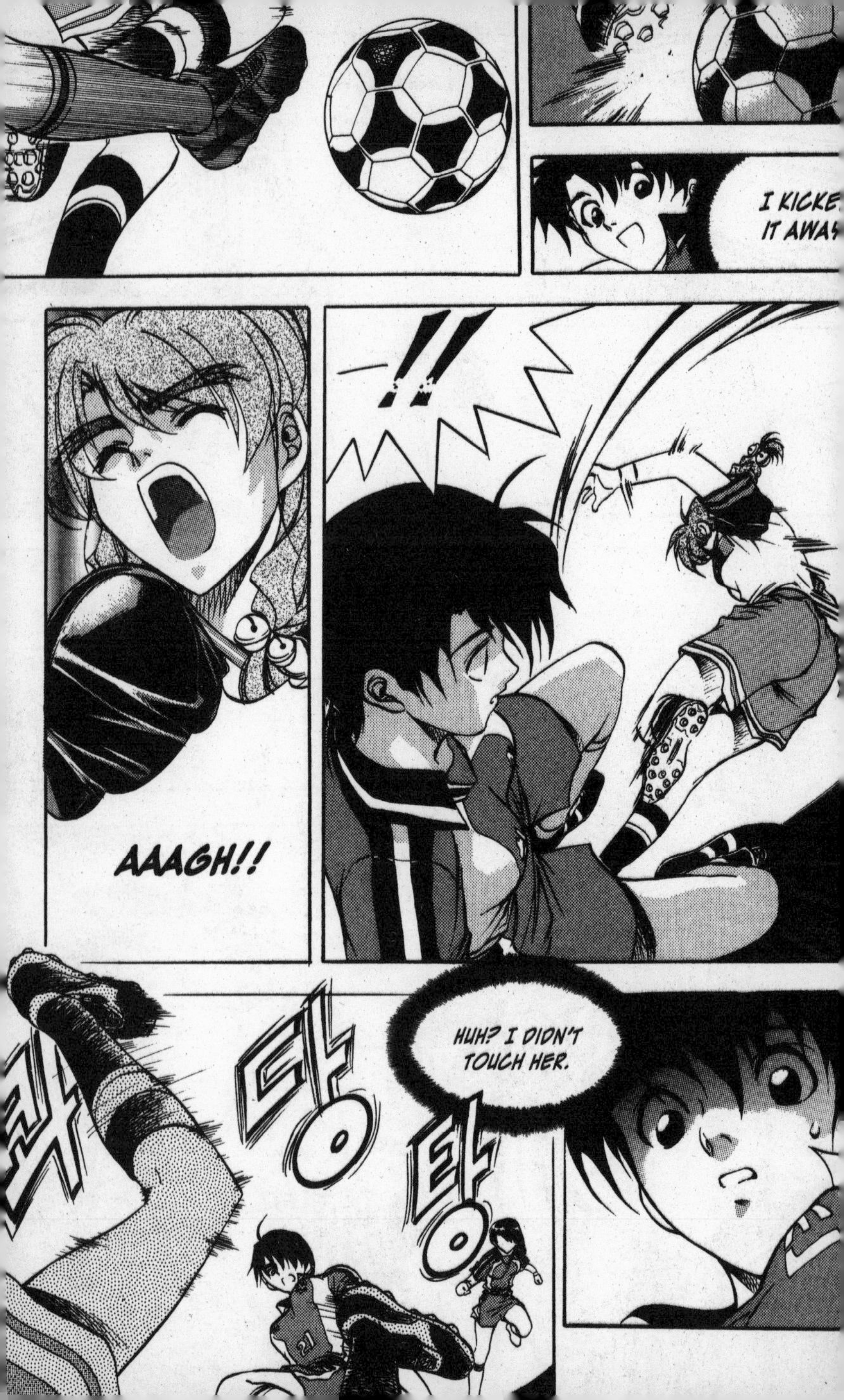
I KICKE
IT AWA
AAAGH!!
!!
HUH? I DIDN'T TOUCH HER.

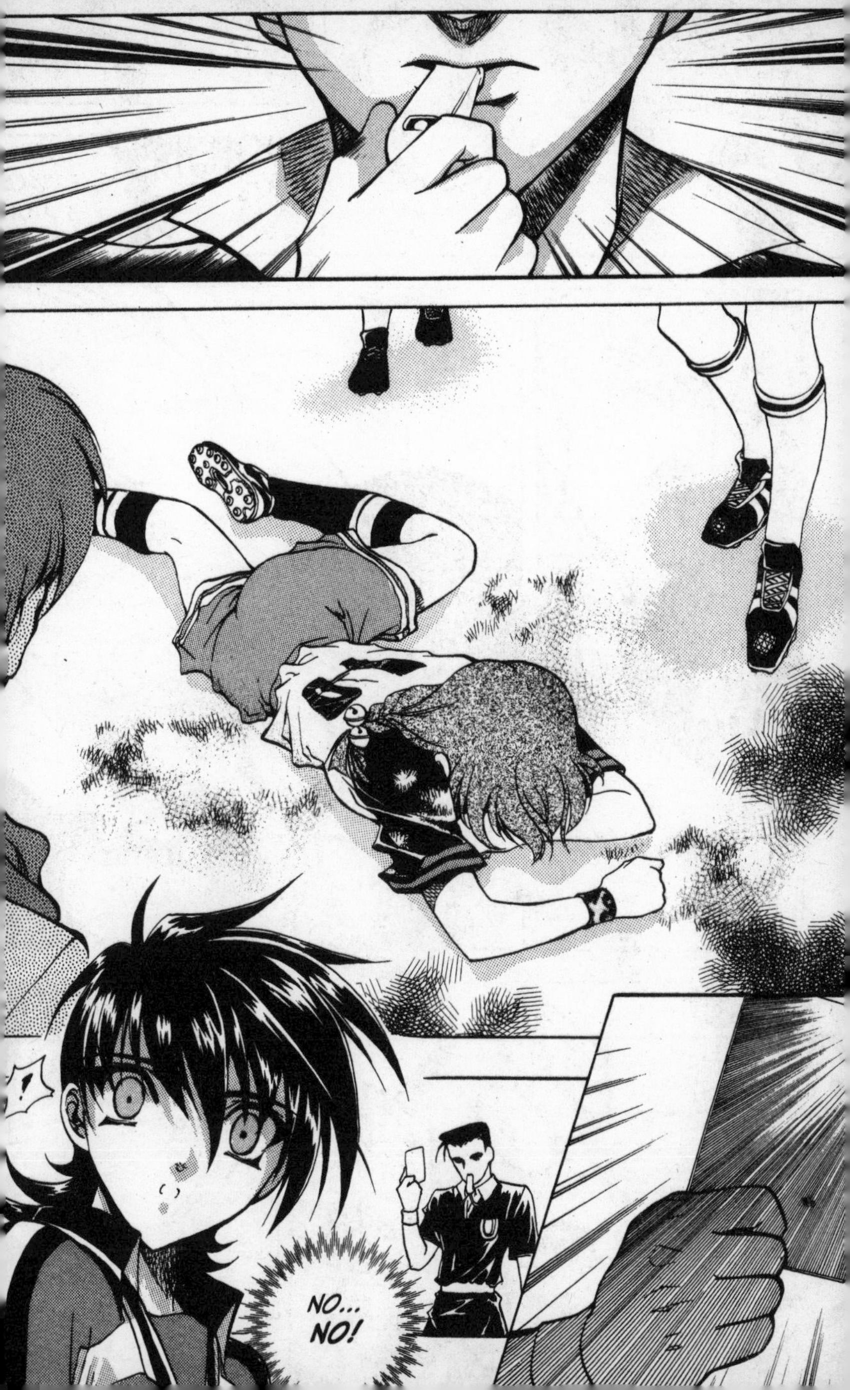
!
NO... NO!

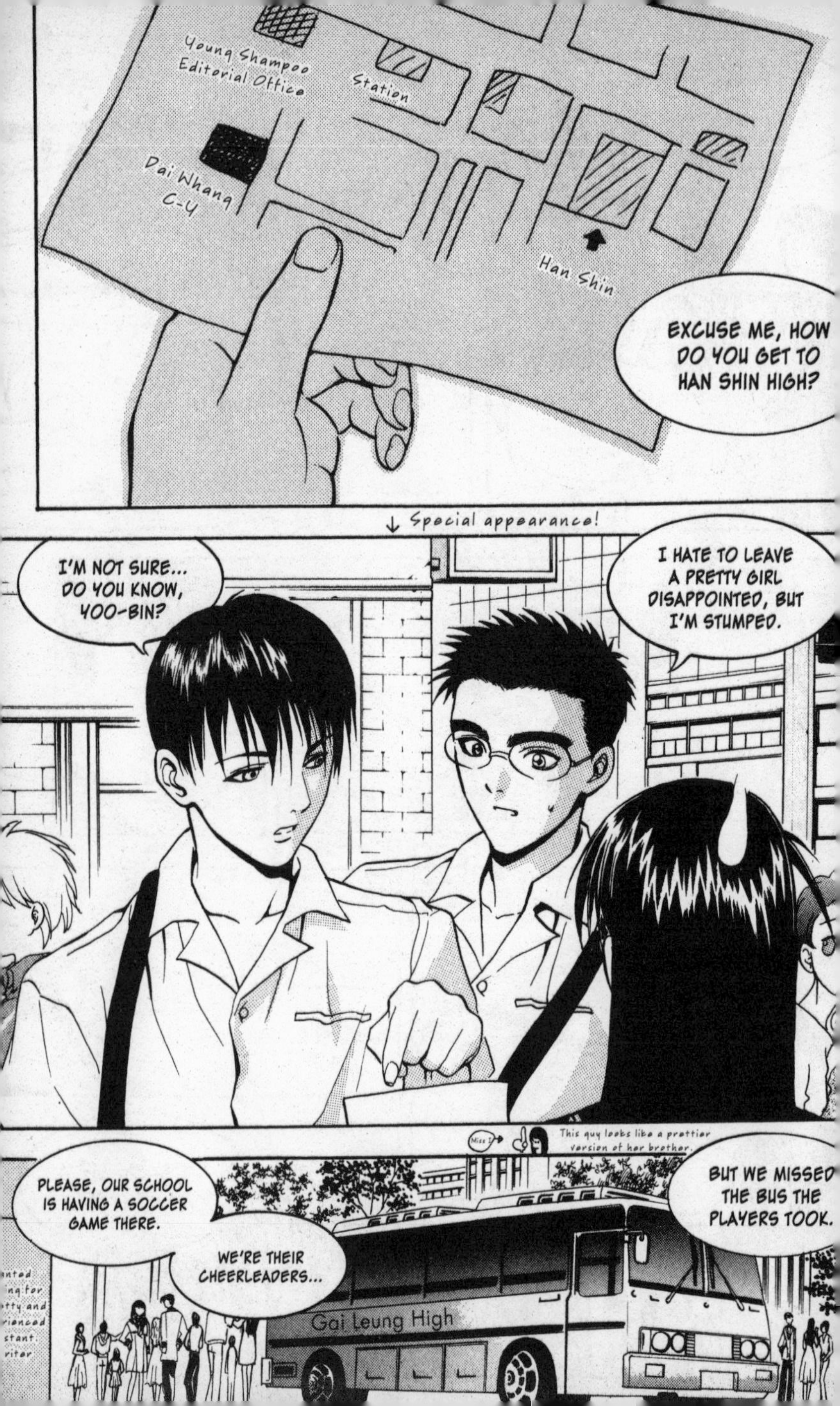
Young Shampoo Editorial Office
Station
Dai Whang C-U
Han Shin
EXCUSE ME, HOW DO YOU GET TO HAN SHIN HIGH?
↓ Special appearance!
I'M NOT SURE... DO YOU KNOW, YOO-BIN?
I HATE TO LEAVE A PRETTY GIRL DISAPPOINTED, BUT I'M STUMPED.
Miss I
This guy looks like a prettier version of her brother.
PLEASE, OUR SCHOOL IS HAVING A SOCCER GAME THERE.
WE'RE THEIR CHEERLEADERS...
BUT WE MISSED THE BUS THE PLAYERS TOOK.
Gai Leung High

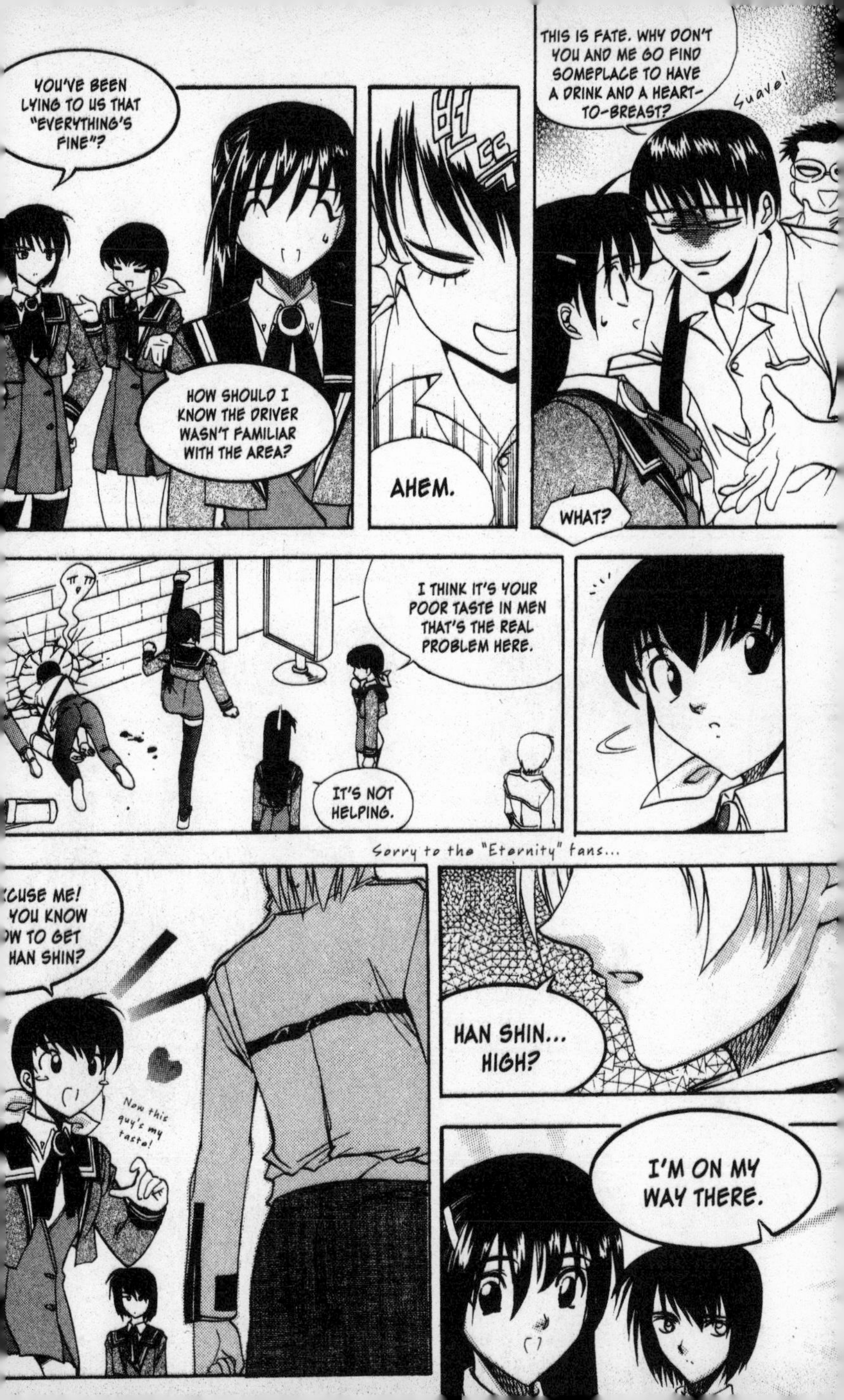
YOU'VE BEEN LYING TO US THAT "EVERYTHING'S FINE"?
HOW SHOULD I KNOW THE DRIVER WASN'T FAMILIAR WITH THE AREA?
AHEM.
THIS IS FATE. WHY DON'T YOU AND ME GO FIND SOMEPLACE TO HAVE A DRINK AND A HEART-TO-BREAST?
Suave!
WHAT?
I THINK IT'S YOUR POOR TASTE IN MEN THAT'S THE REAL PROBLEM HERE.
IT'S NOT HELPING.
Sorry to the "Eternity" fans...
CUSE ME! YOU KNOW W TO GET HAN SHIN?
Now this guy's my taste!
HAN SHIN... HIGH?
I'M ON MY WAY THERE.

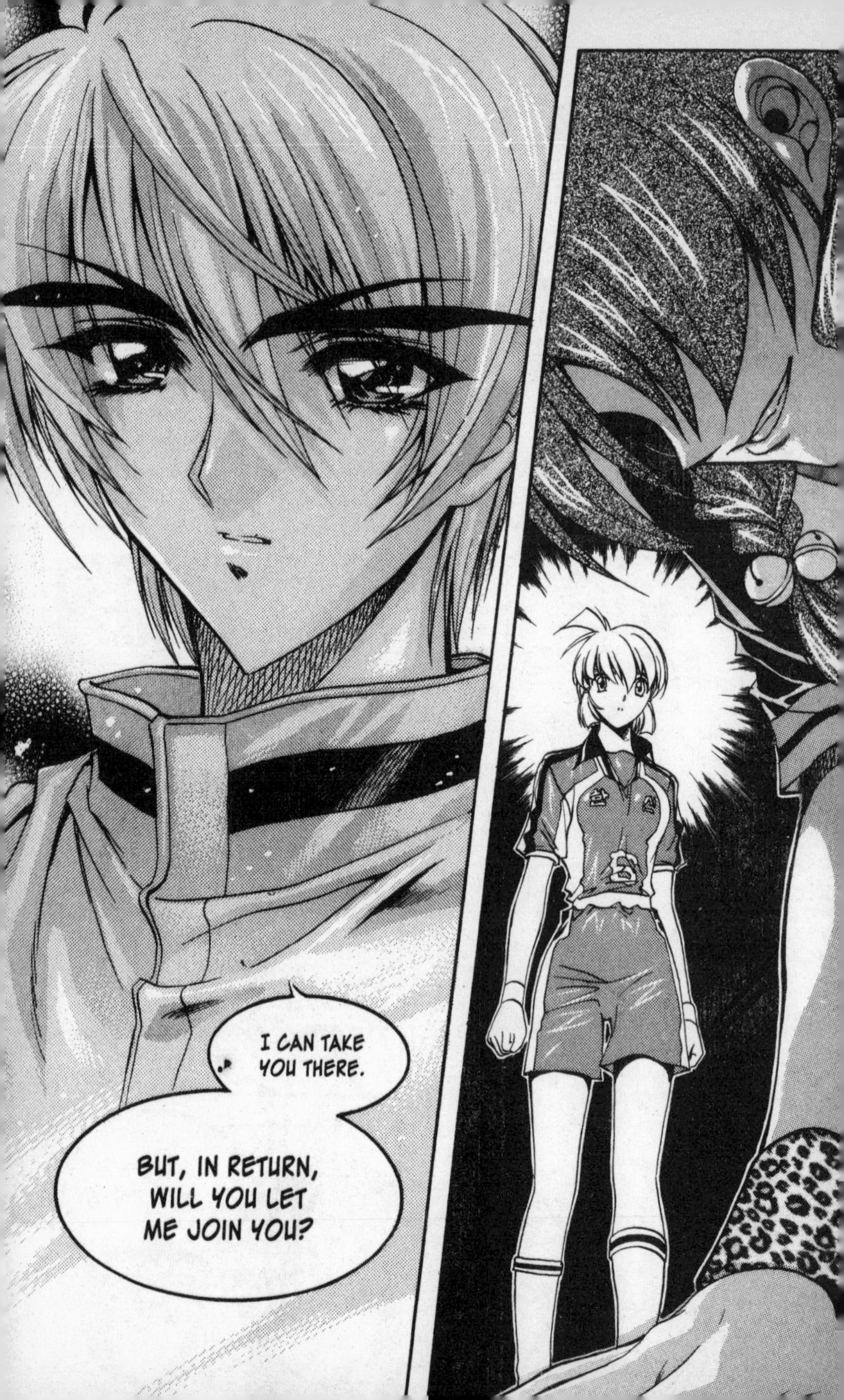
I CAN TAKE YOU THERE.
BUT, IN RETURN, WILL YOU LET ME JOIN YOU?

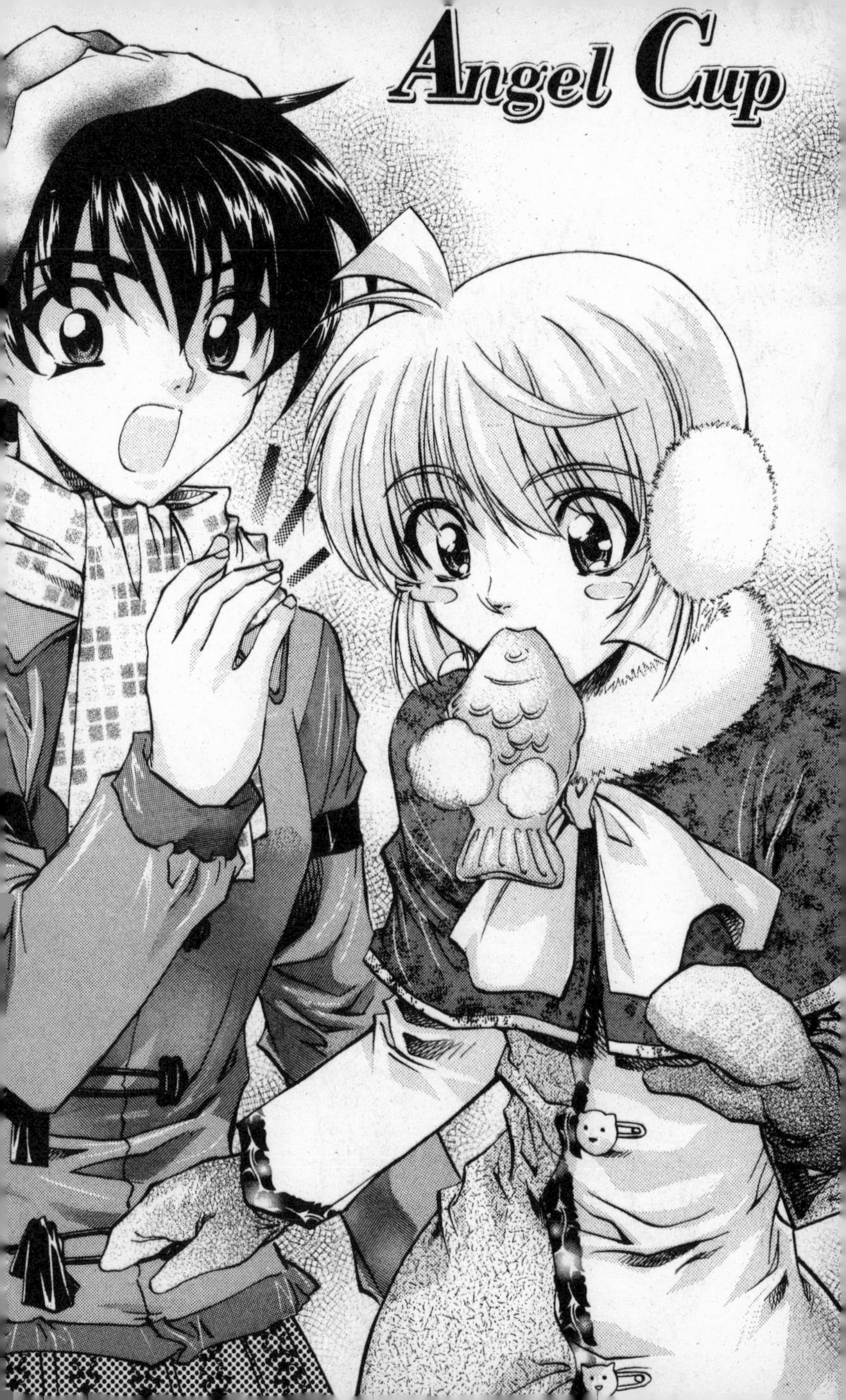
Angel Cup

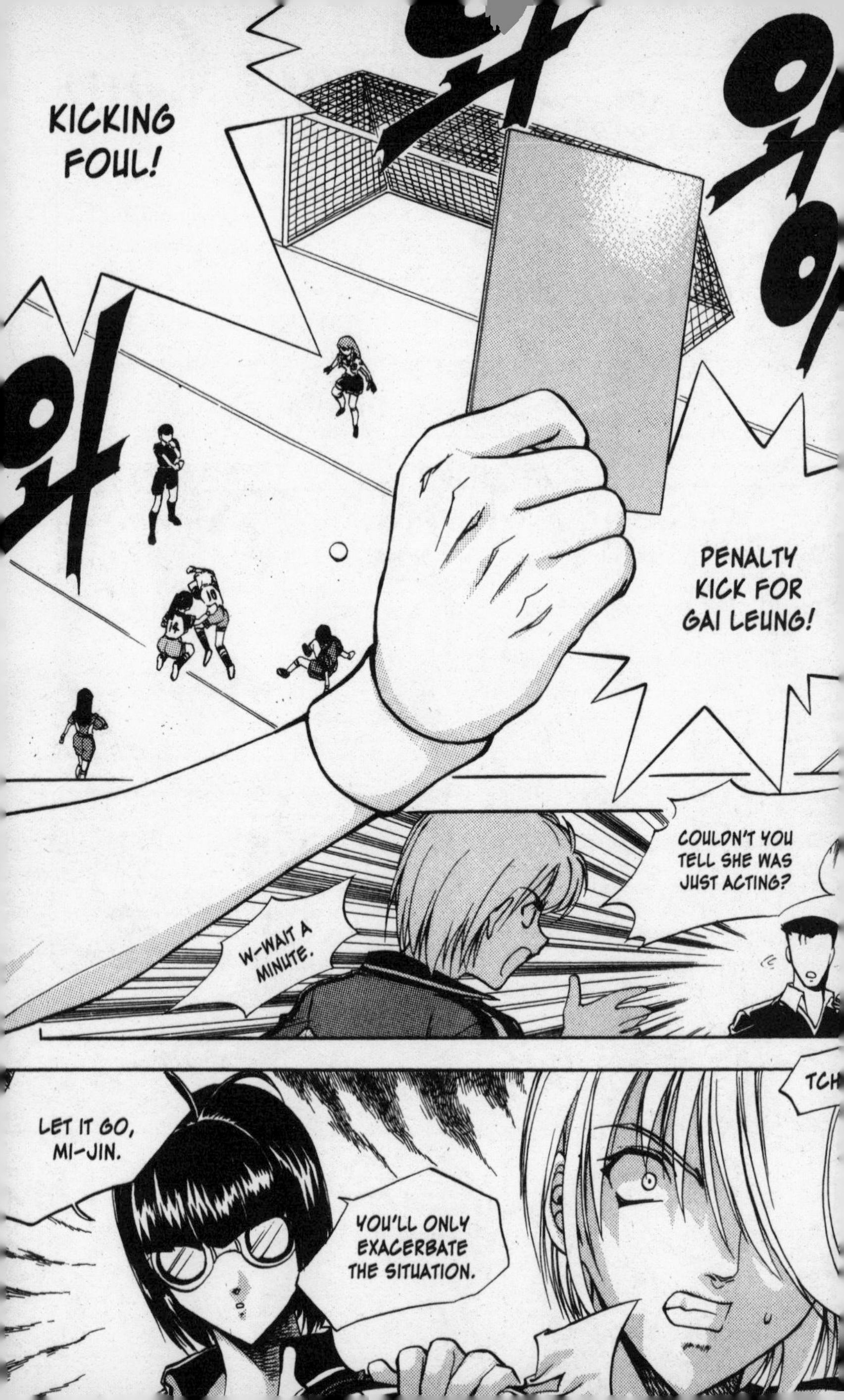
KICKING FOUL!
PENALTY KICK FOR GAI LEUNG!
W-WAIT A MINUTE.
COULDN'T YOU TELL SHE WAS JUST ACTING?
LET IT GO, MI-JIN.
YOU'LL ONLY EXACERBATE THE SITUATION.
TCH

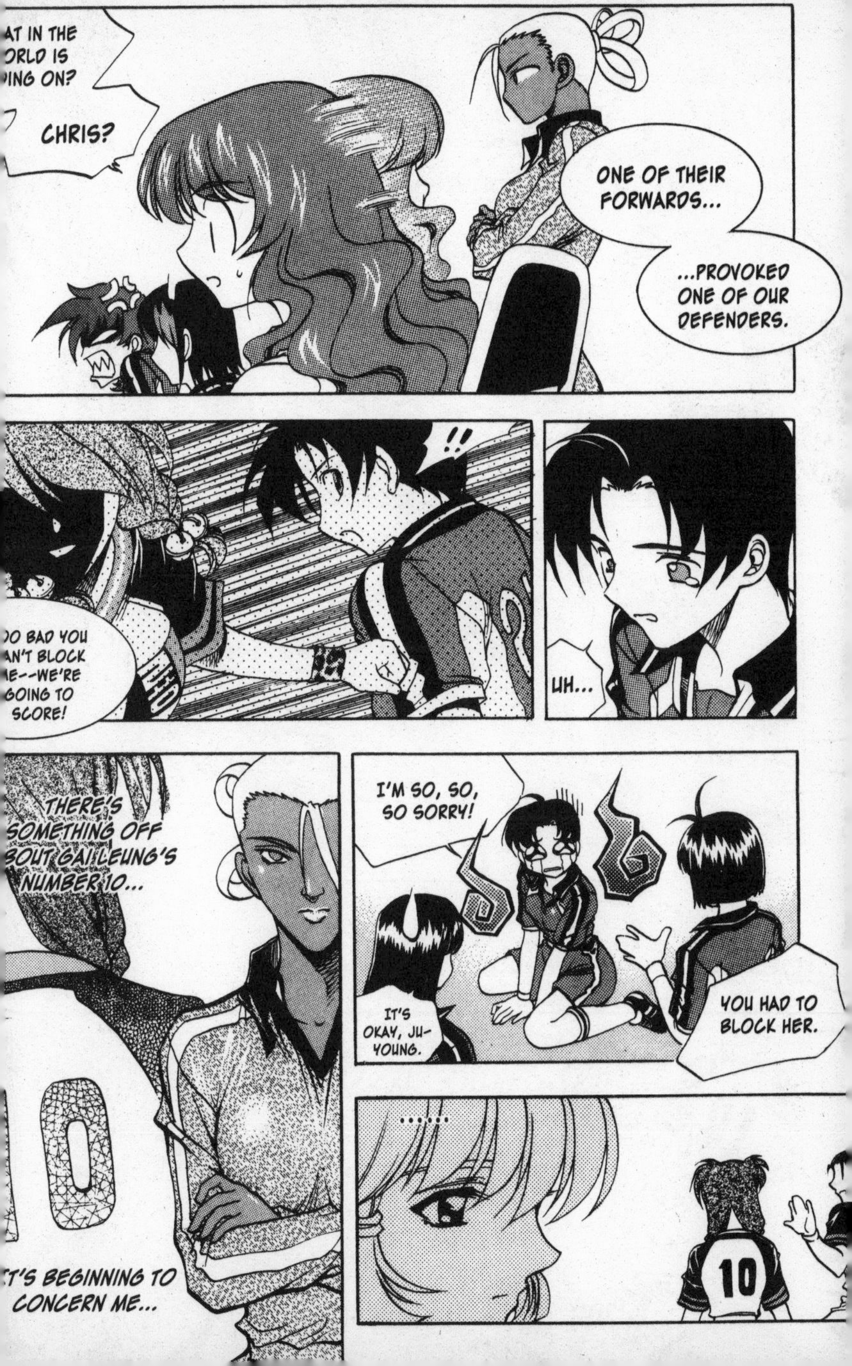
AT IN THE
ORLD IS
OING ON?
CHRIS?
ONE OF THEIR FORWARDS...
...PROVOKED ONE OF OUR DEFENDERS.
!!
OO BAD YOU AN'T BLOCK E--WE'RE GOING TO SCORE!
UH...
THERE'S SOMETHING OFF BOUT GAI LEUNG'S NUMBER 10...
T'S BEGINNING TO CONCERN ME...
I'M SO, SO, SO SORRY!
IT'S OKAY, JU-YOUNG.
YOU HAD TO BLOCK HER.
......
10

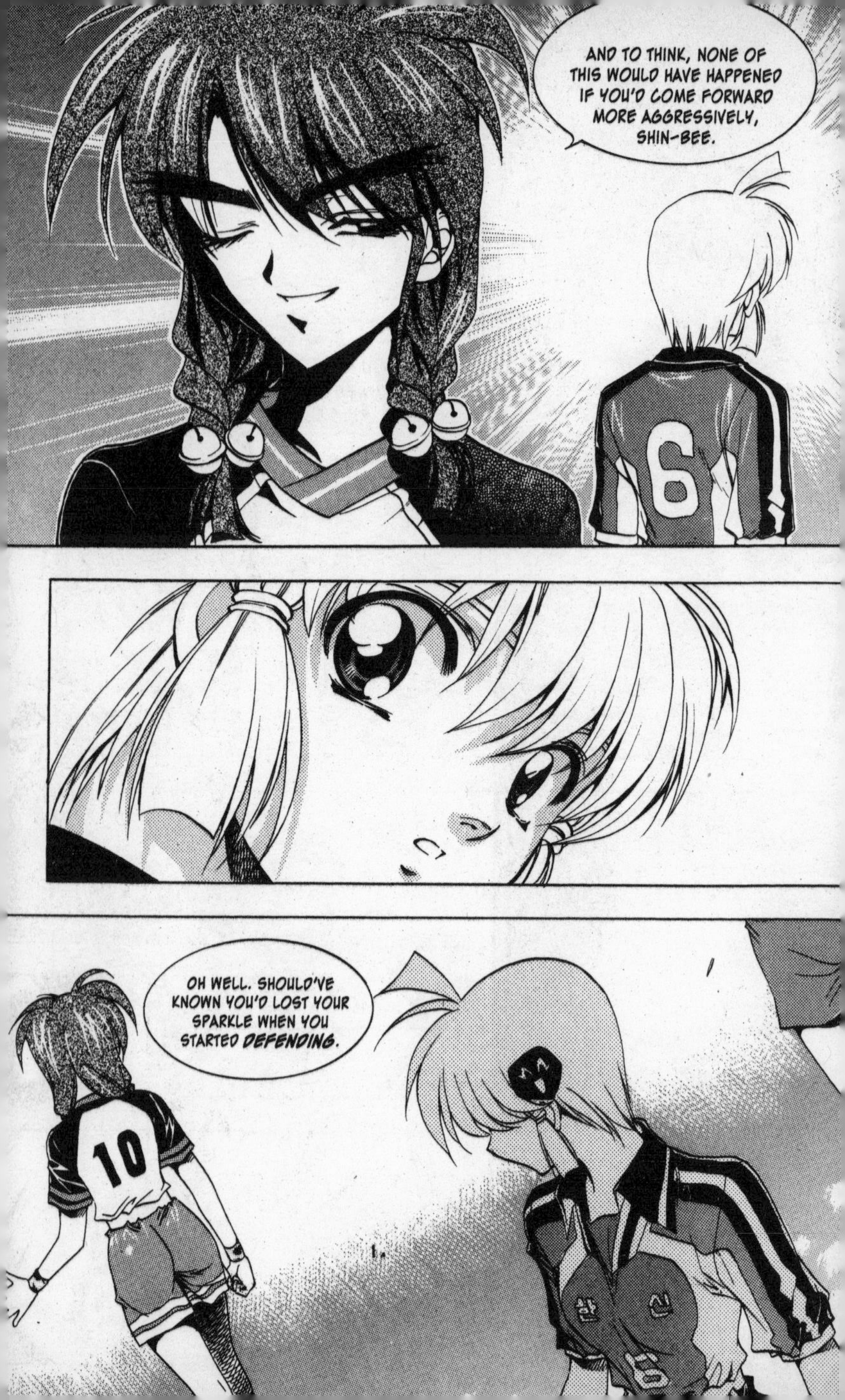
AND TO THINK, NONE OF THIS WOULD HAVE HAPPENED IF YOU'D COME FORWARD MORE AGGRESSIVELY, SHIN-BEE.
6
OH WELL. SHOULD'VE KNOWN YOU'D LOST YOUR SPARKLE WHEN YOU STARTED *DEFENDING*.
10

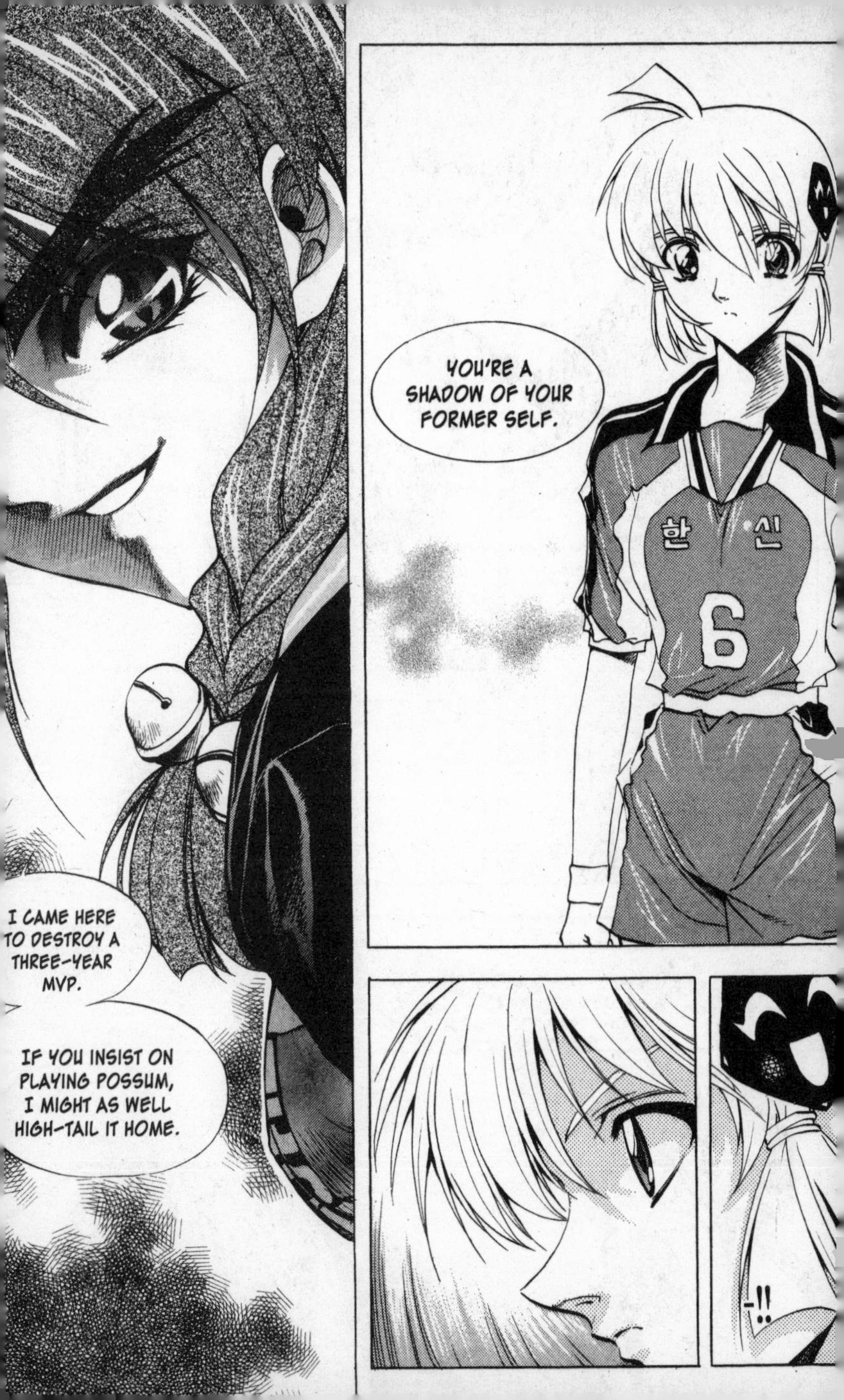
I CAME HERE TO DESTROY A THREE-YEAR MVP.
IF YOU INSIST ON PLAYING POSSUM, I MIGHT AS WELL HIGH-TAIL IT HOME.
YOU'RE A SHADOW OF YOUR FORMER SELF.
한 신
6
-!!

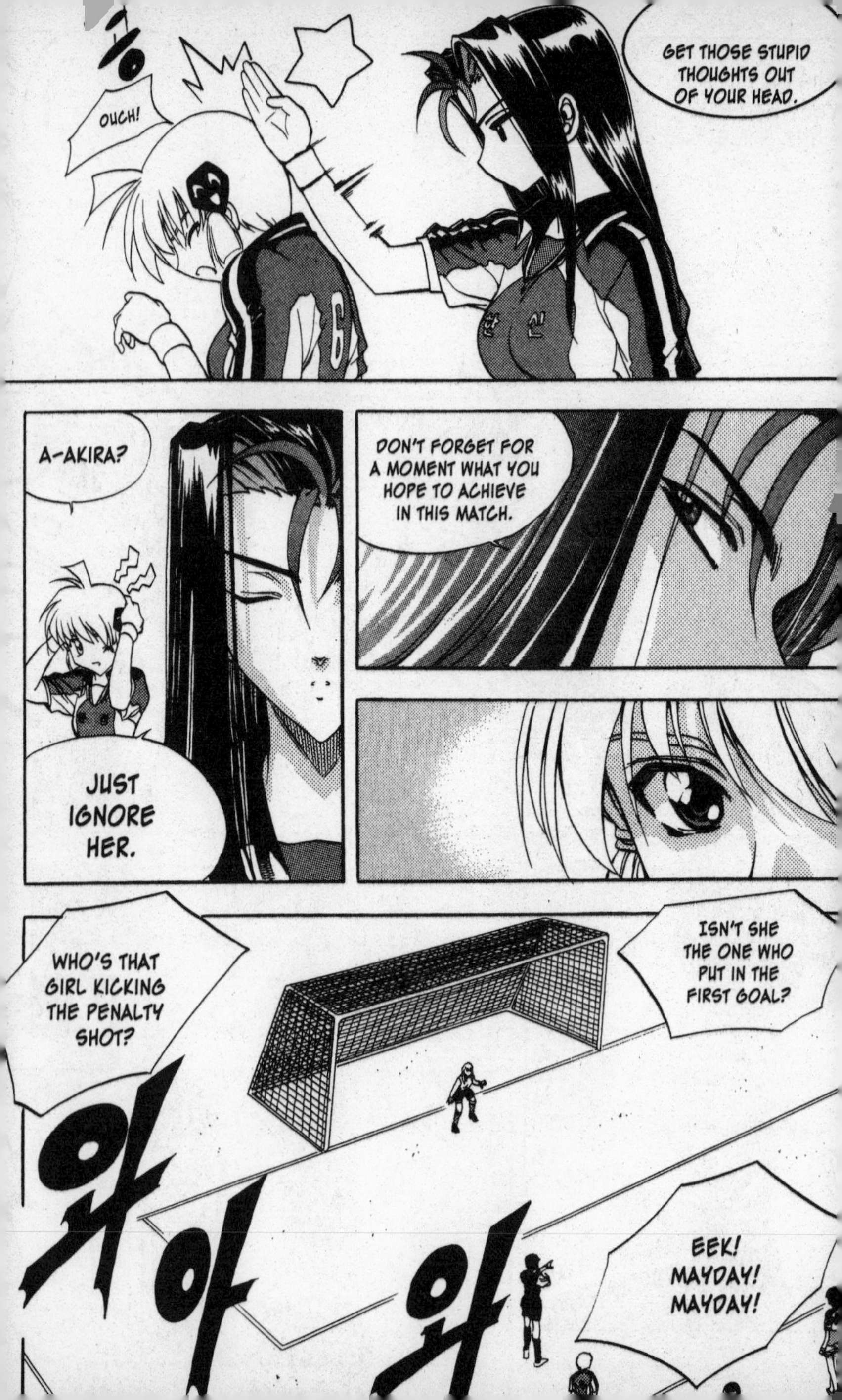
OUCH!
GET THOSE STUPID THOUGHTS OUT OF YOUR HEAD.
A-AKIRA?
JUST IGNORE HER.
DON'T FORGET FOR A MOMENT WHAT YOU HOPE TO ACHIEVE IN THIS MATCH.
WHO'S THAT GIRL KICKING THE PENALTY SHOT?
ISN'T SHE THE ONE WHO PUT IN THE FIRST GOAL?
와 아 와
EEK! MAYDAY! MAYDAY!

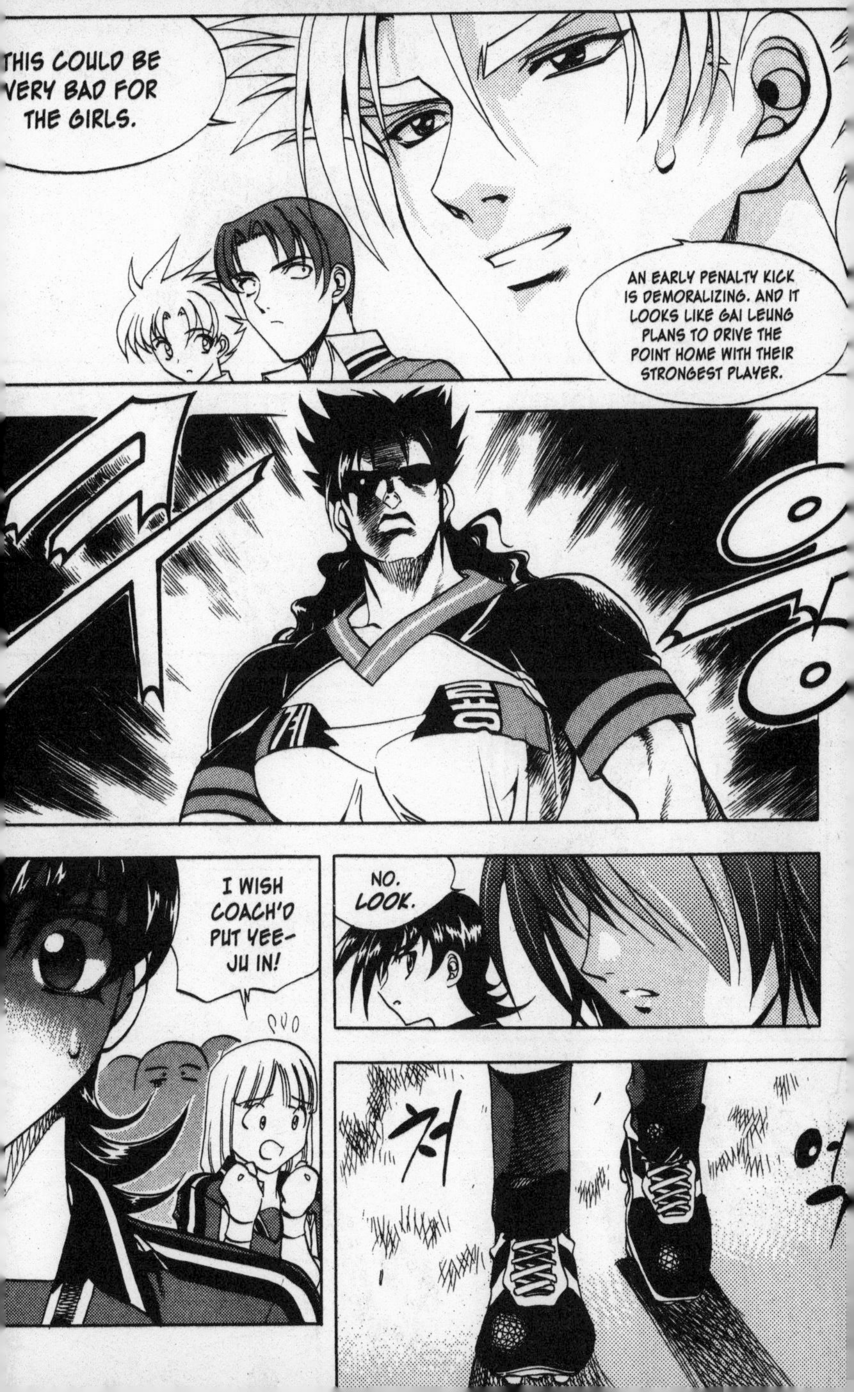
THIS COULD BE VERY BAD FOR THE GIRLS.
AN EARLY PENALTY KICK IS DEMORALIZING. AND IT LOOKS LIKE GAI LEUNG PLANS TO DRIVE THE POINT HOME WITH THEIR STRONGEST PLAYER.
I WISH COACH'D PUT YEE-JU IN!
NO. LOOK.

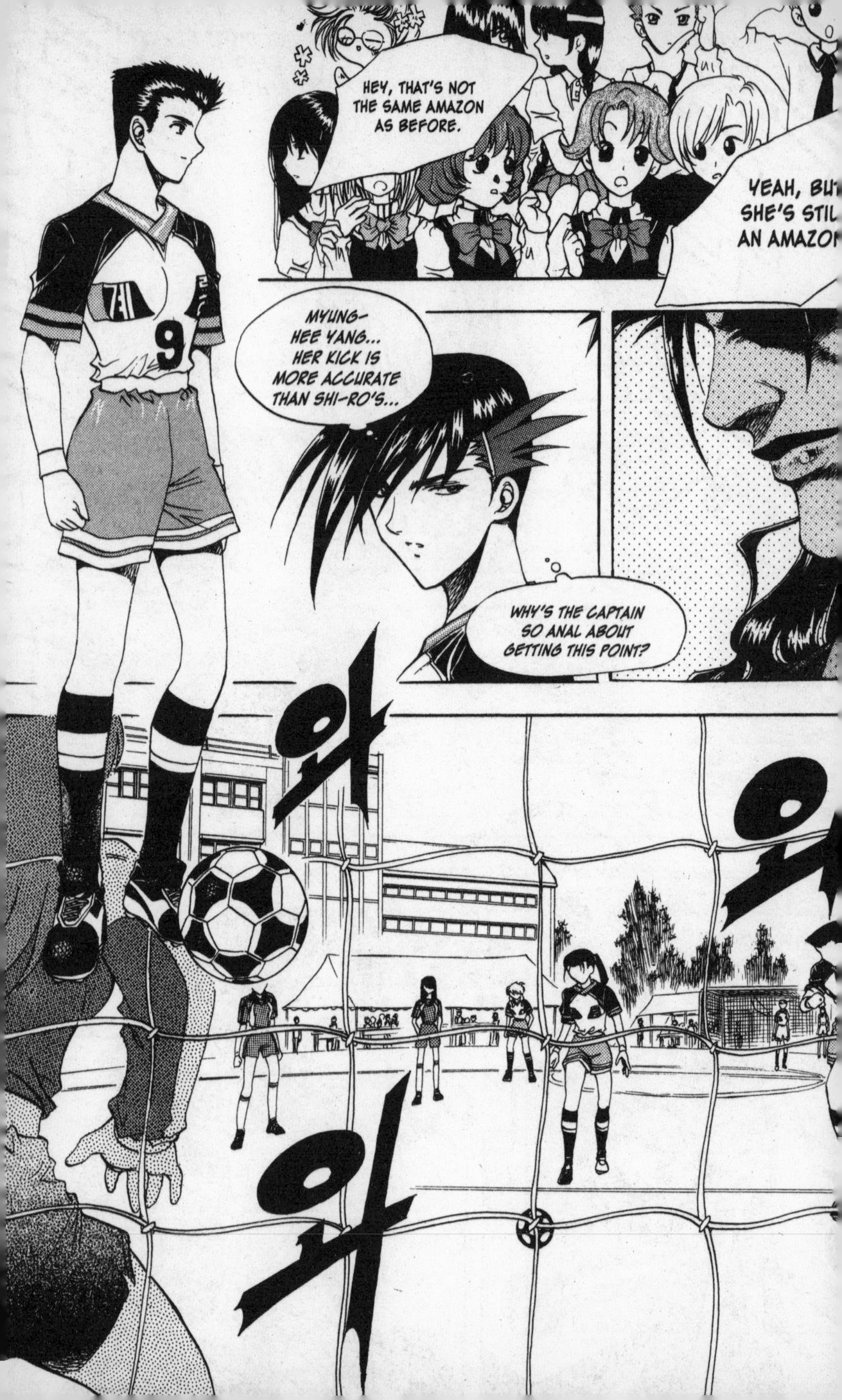
HEY, THAT'S NOT THE SAME AMAZON AS BEFORE.
YEAH, BU SHE'S STIL AN AMAZO
MYUNG-HEE YANG... HER KICK IS MORE ACCURATE THAN SHI-RO'S...
WHY'S THE CAPTAIN SO ANAL ABOUT GETTING THIS POINT?

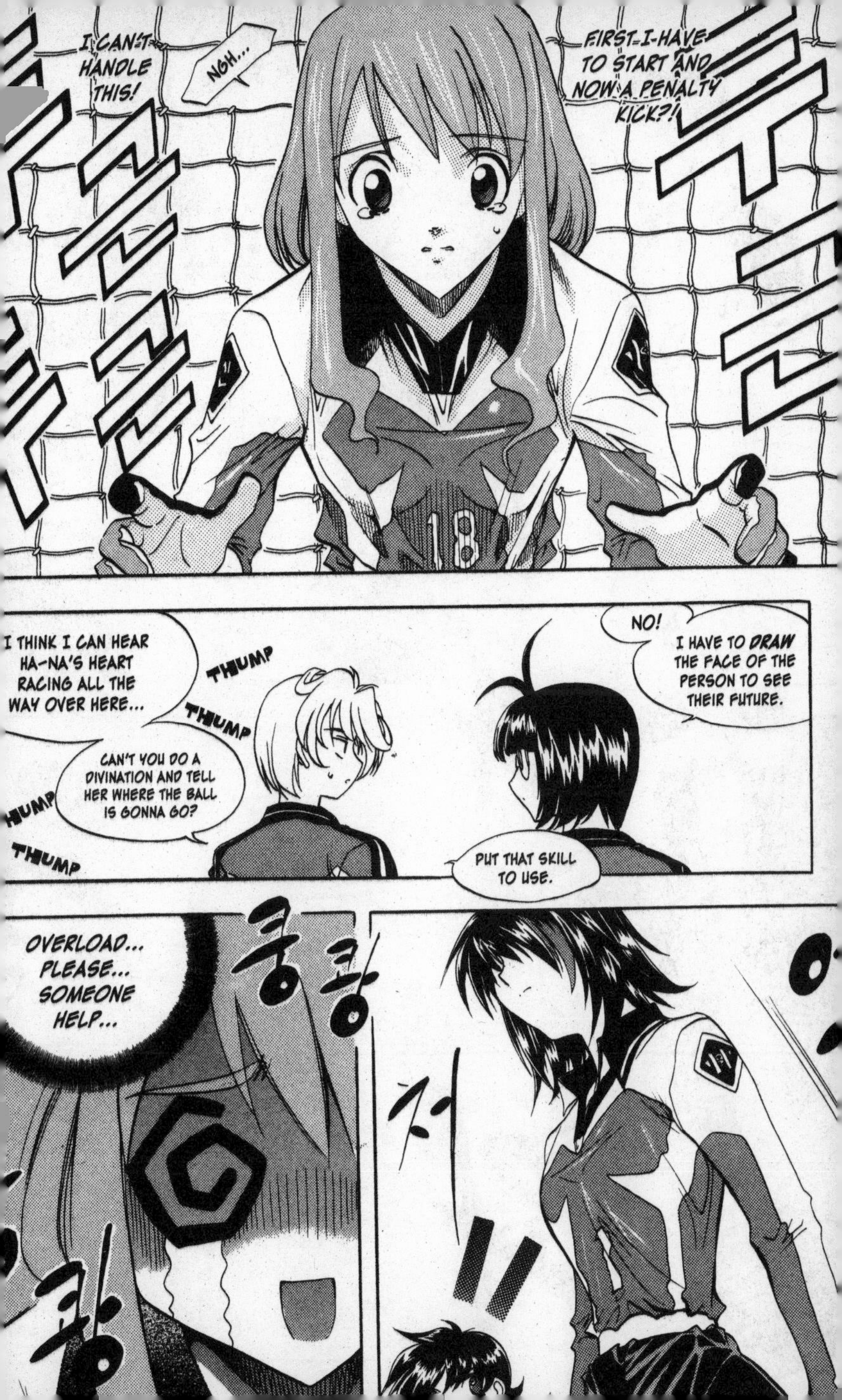
I CAN'T HANDLE THIS!
NGH...
FIRST I HAVE TO START AND NOW A PENALTY KICK?!
I THINK I CAN HEAR HA-NA'S HEART RACING ALL THE WAY OVER HERE...
THUMP
THUMP
CAN'T YOU DO A DIVINATION AND TELL HER WHERE THE BALL IS GONNA GO?
THUMP
THUMP
NO!
I HAVE TO DRAW THE FACE OF THE PERSON TO SEE THEIR FUTURE.
PUT THAT SKILL TO USE.
OVERLOAD... PLEASE... SOMEONE HELP...

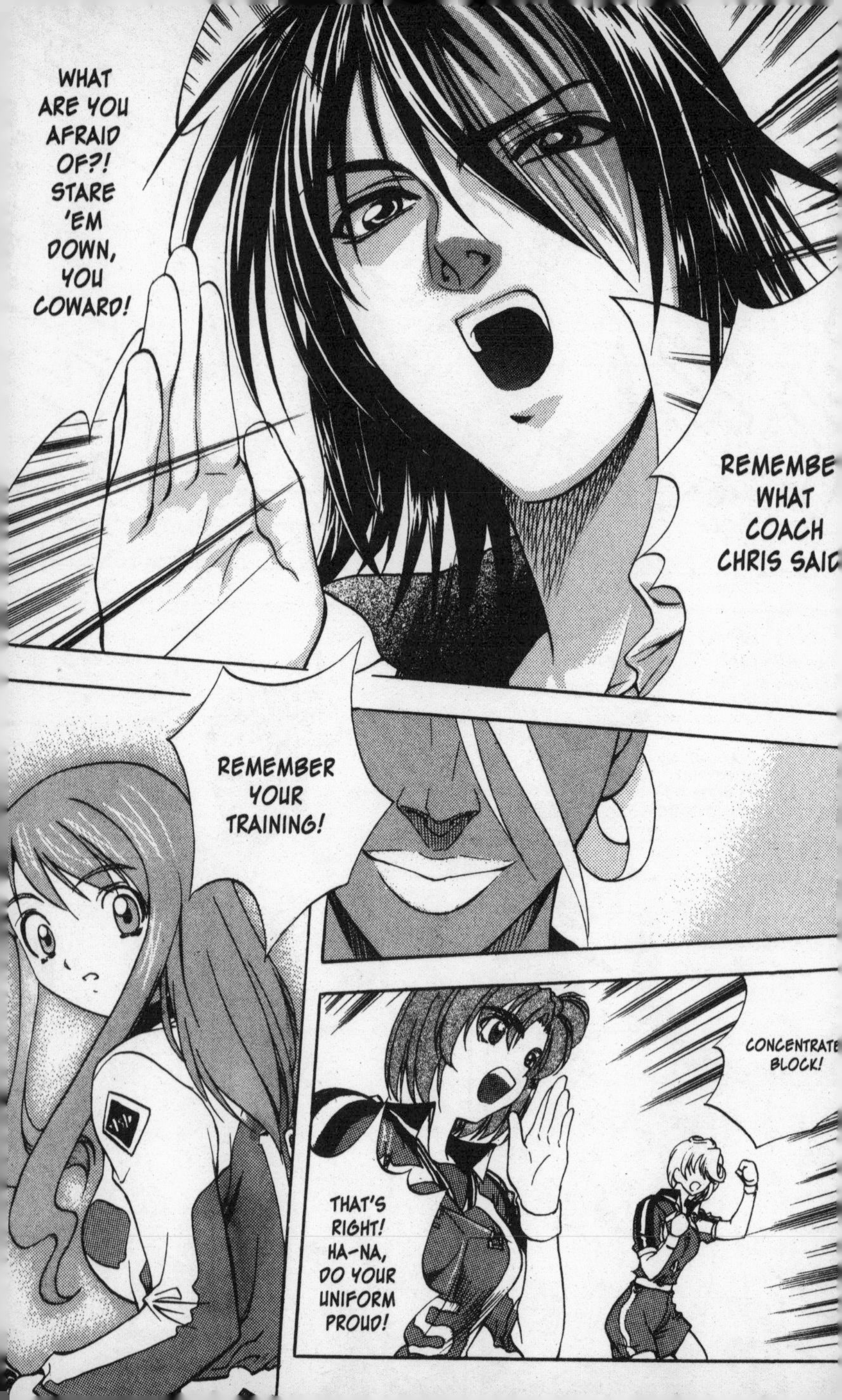
WHAT ARE YOU AFRAID OF?! STARE 'EM DOWN, YOU COWARD!
REMEMBE WHAT COACH CHRIS SAID
REMEMBER YOUR TRAINING!
CONCENTRATE BLOCK!
THAT'S RIGHT! HA-NA, DO YOUR UNIFORM PROUD!

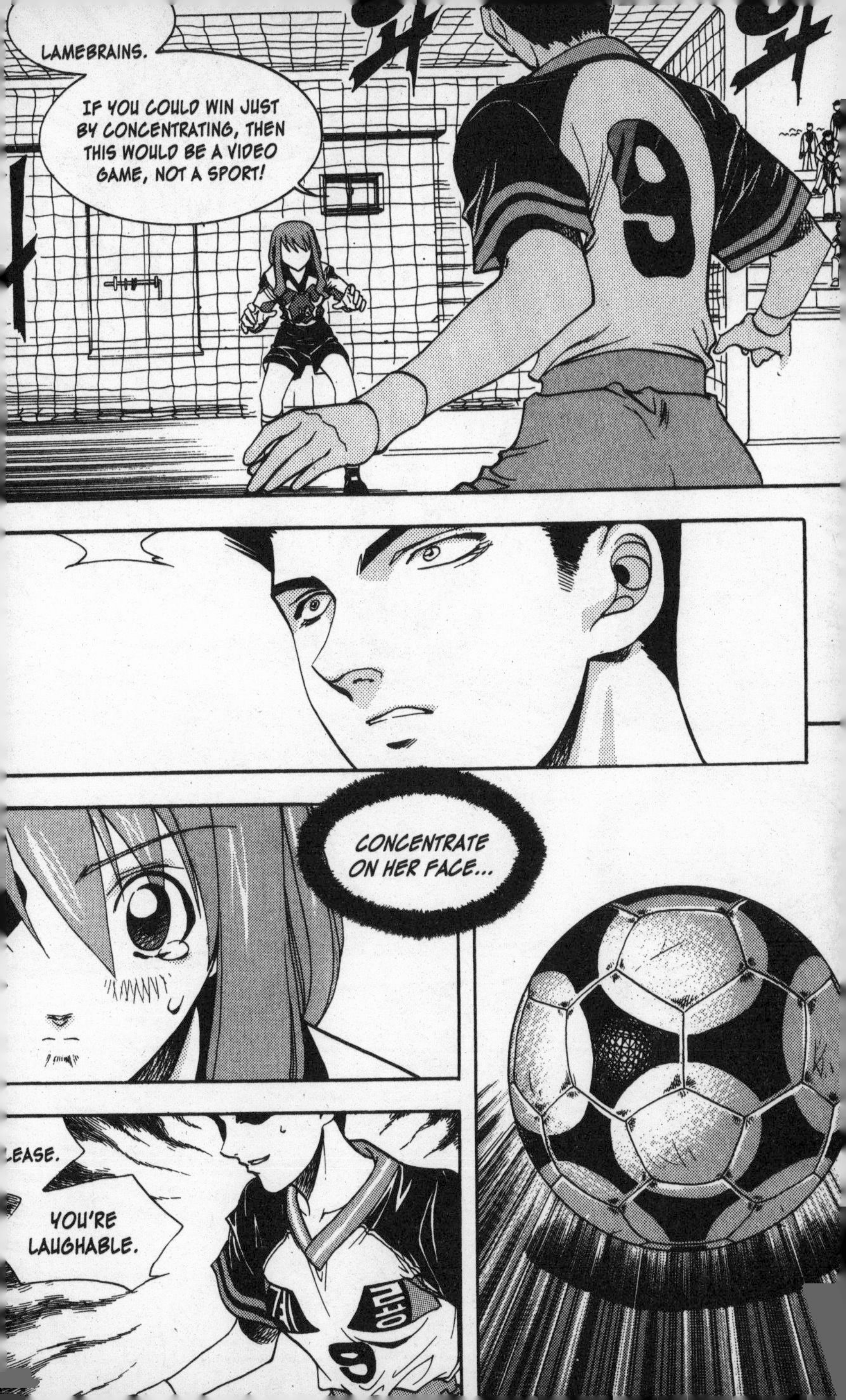
LAMEBRAINS.
IF YOU COULD WIN JUST BY CONCENTRATING, THEN THIS WOULD BE A VIDEO GAME, NOT A SPORT!
CONCENTRATE ON HER FACE...
LEASE.
YOU'RE LAUGHABLE.

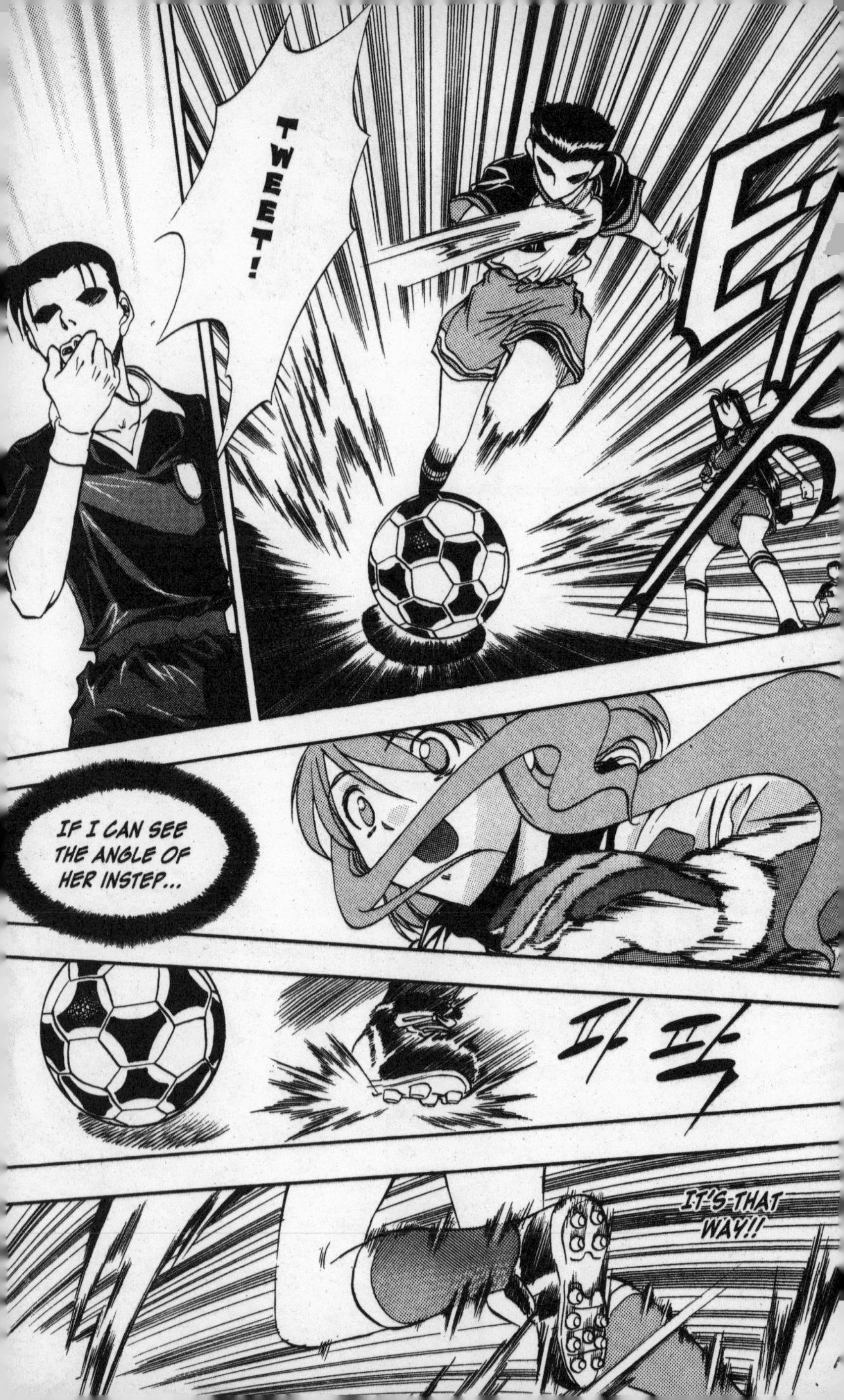
TWEET!
IF I CAN SEE THE ANGLE OF HER INSTEP...
파팍
IT'S THAT WAY!!

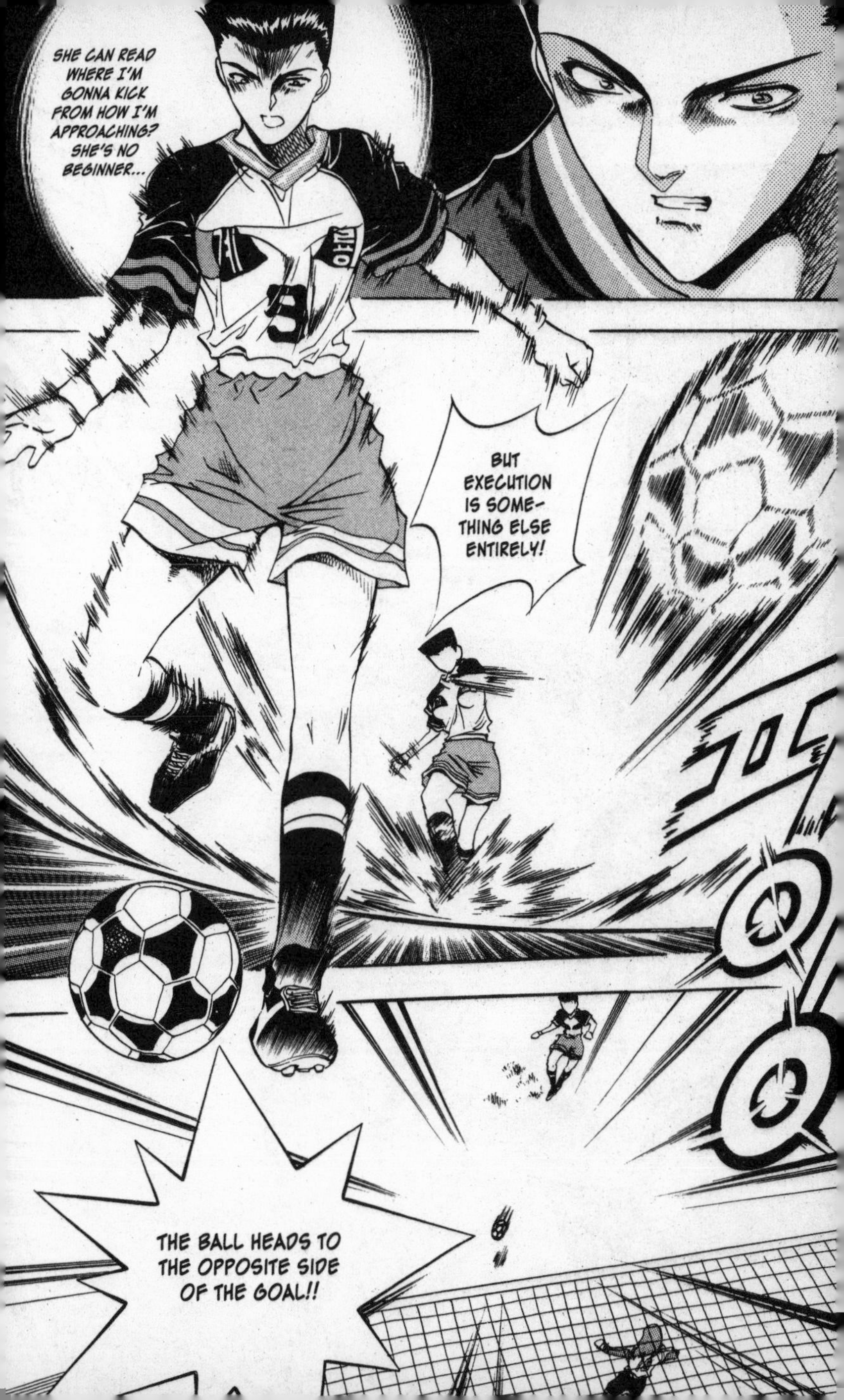
SHE CAN READ WHERE I'M GONNA KICK FROM HOW I'M APPROACHING? SHE'S NO BEGINNER...
BUT EXECUTION IS SOME-THING ELSE ENTIRELY!
THE BALL HEADS TO THE OPPOSITE SIDE OF THE GOAL!!

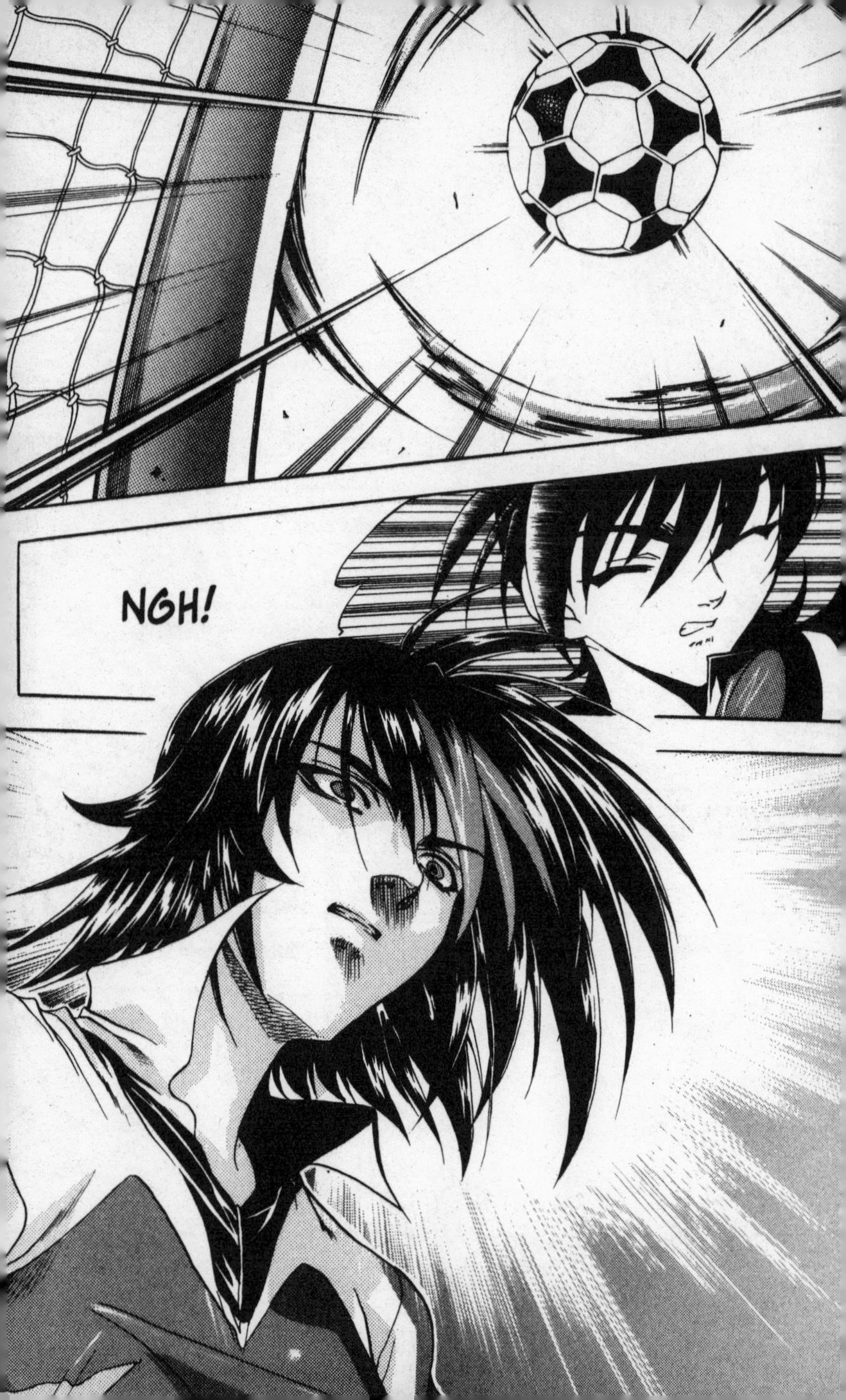
NGH!

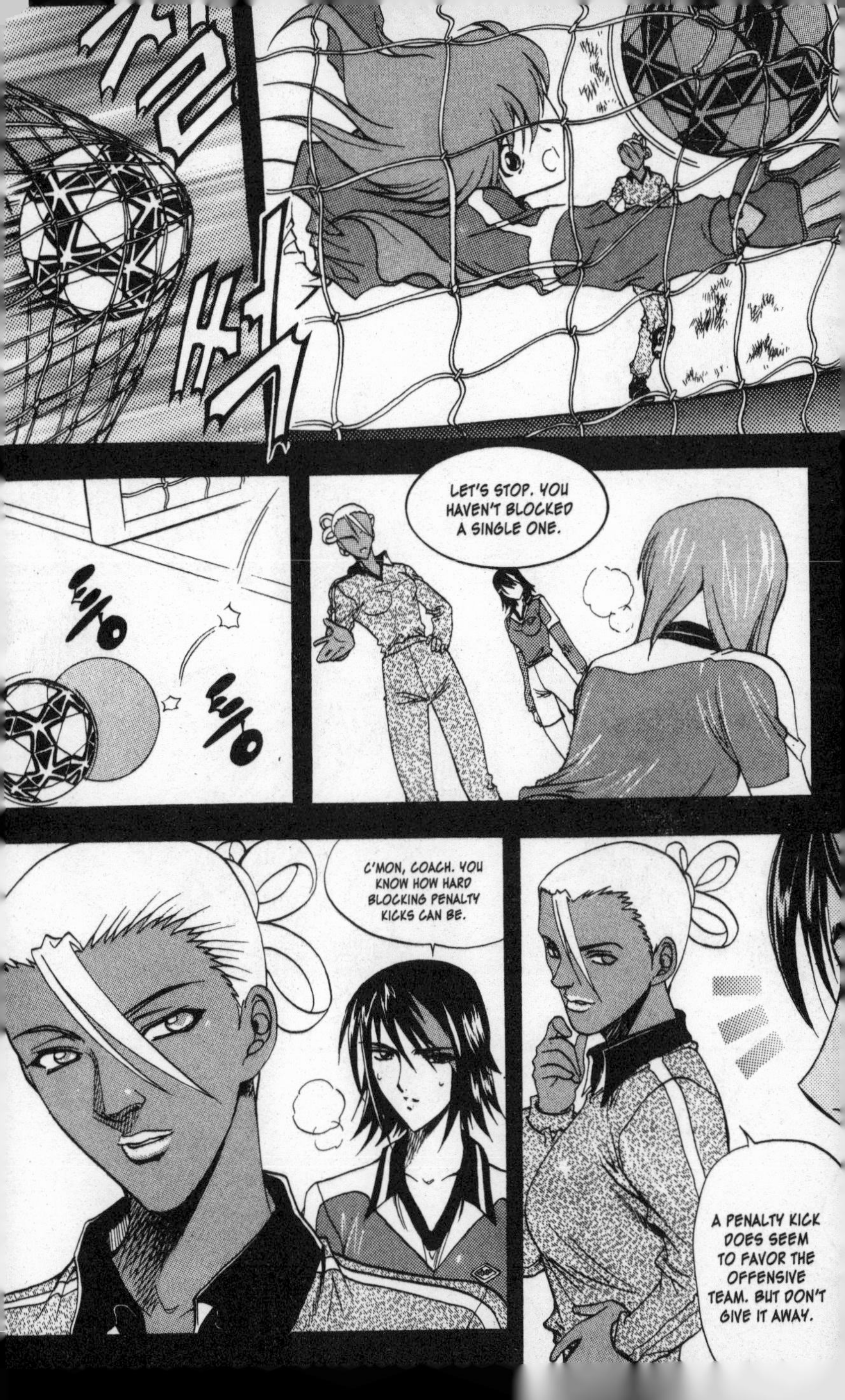
LET'S STOP. YOU HAVEN'T BLOCKED A SINGLE ONE.
C'MON, COACH. YOU KNOW HOW HARD BLOCKING PENALTY KICKS CAN BE.
A PENALTY KICK DOES SEEM TO FAVOR THE OFFENSIVE TEAM. BUT DON'T GIVE IT AWAY.

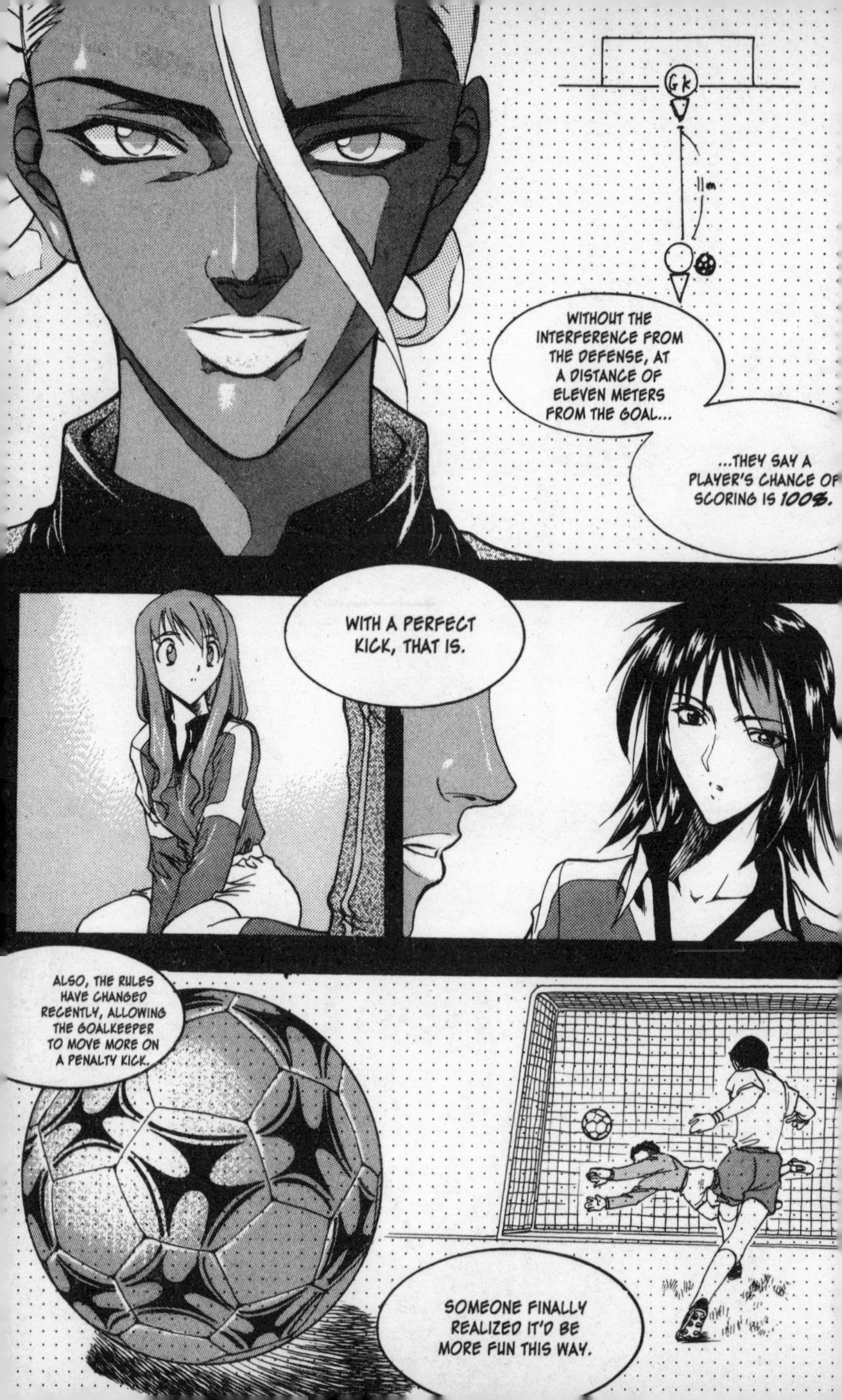
GK
WITHOUT THE INTERFERENCE FROM THE DEFENSE, AT A DISTANCE OF ELEVEN METERS FROM THE GOAL...
...THEY SAY A PLAYER'S CHANCE OF SCORING IS 100%.
WITH A PERFECT KICK, THAT IS.
ALSO, THE RULES HAVE CHANGED RECENTLY, ALLOWING THE GOALKEEPER TO MOVE MORE ON A PENALTY KICK.
SOMEONE FINALLY REALIZED IT'D BE MORE FUN THIS WAY.

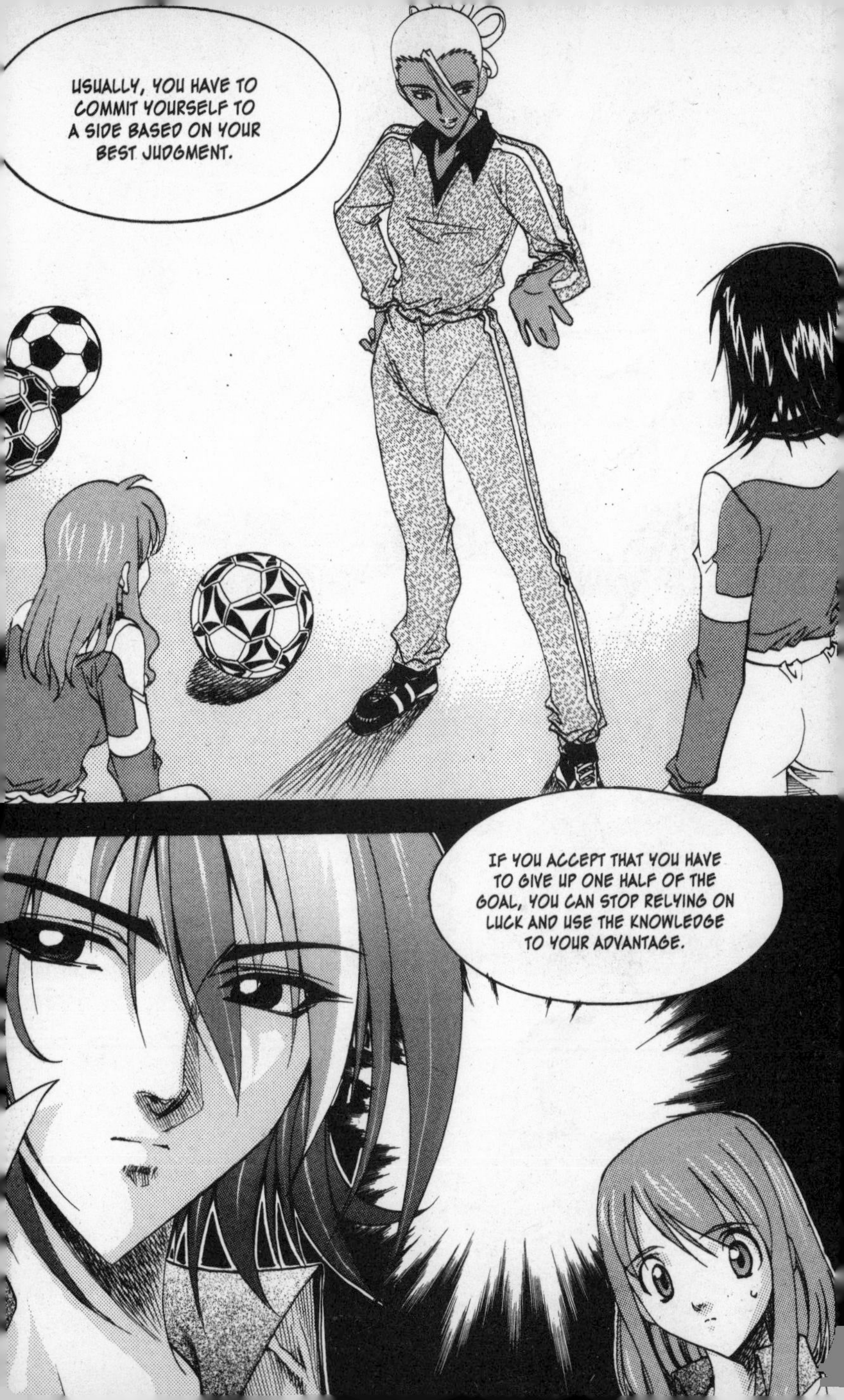
USUALLY, YOU HAVE TO COMMIT YOURSELF TO A SIDE BASED ON YOUR BEST JUDGMENT.
IF YOU ACCEPT THAT YOU HAVE TO GIVE UP ONE HALF OF THE GOAL, YOU CAN STOP RELYING ON LUCK AND USE THE KNOWLEDGE TO YOUR ADVANTAGE.

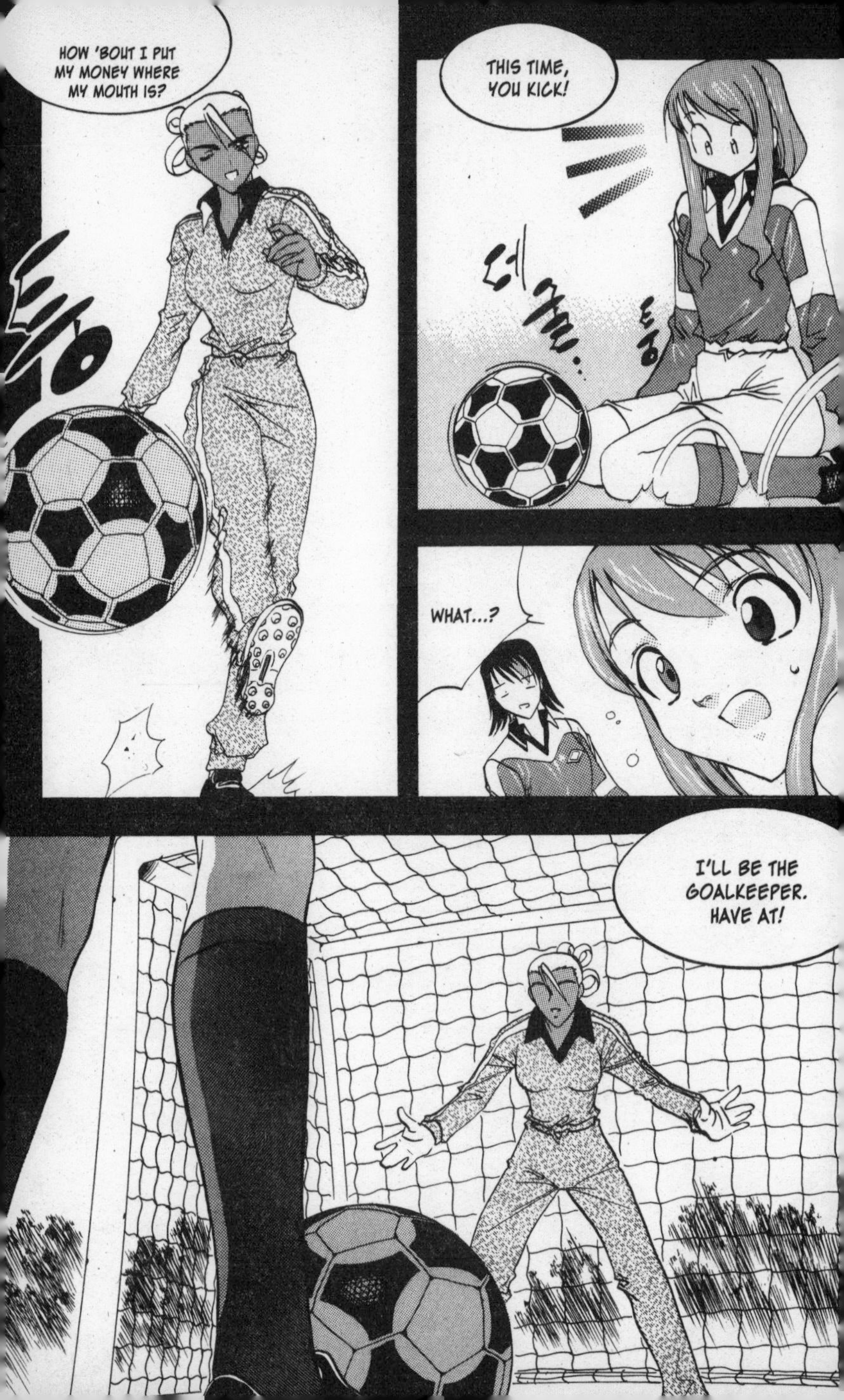
HOW 'BOUT I PUT MY MONEY WHERE MY MOUTH IS?
THIS TIME, YOU KICK!
WHAT...?
I'LL BE THE GOALKEEPER. HAVE AT!

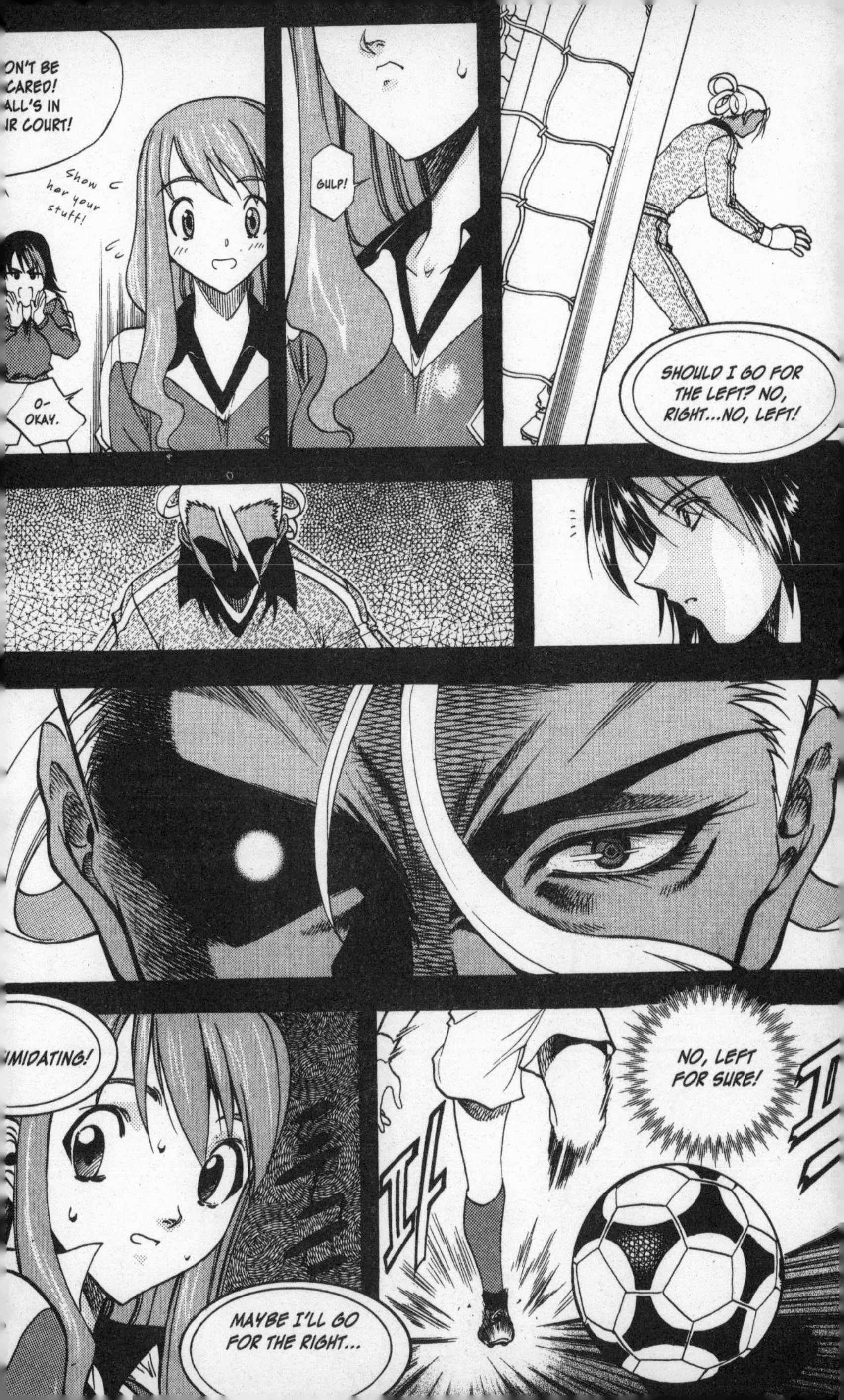
ON'T BE
CARED!
ALL'S IN
R COURT!
Show her your stuff!
O-OKAY.
GULP!
SHOULD I GO FOR THE LEFT? NO, RIGHT...NO, LEFT!
IMIDATING!
MAYBE I'LL GO FOR THE RIGHT...
NO, LEFT FOR SURE!

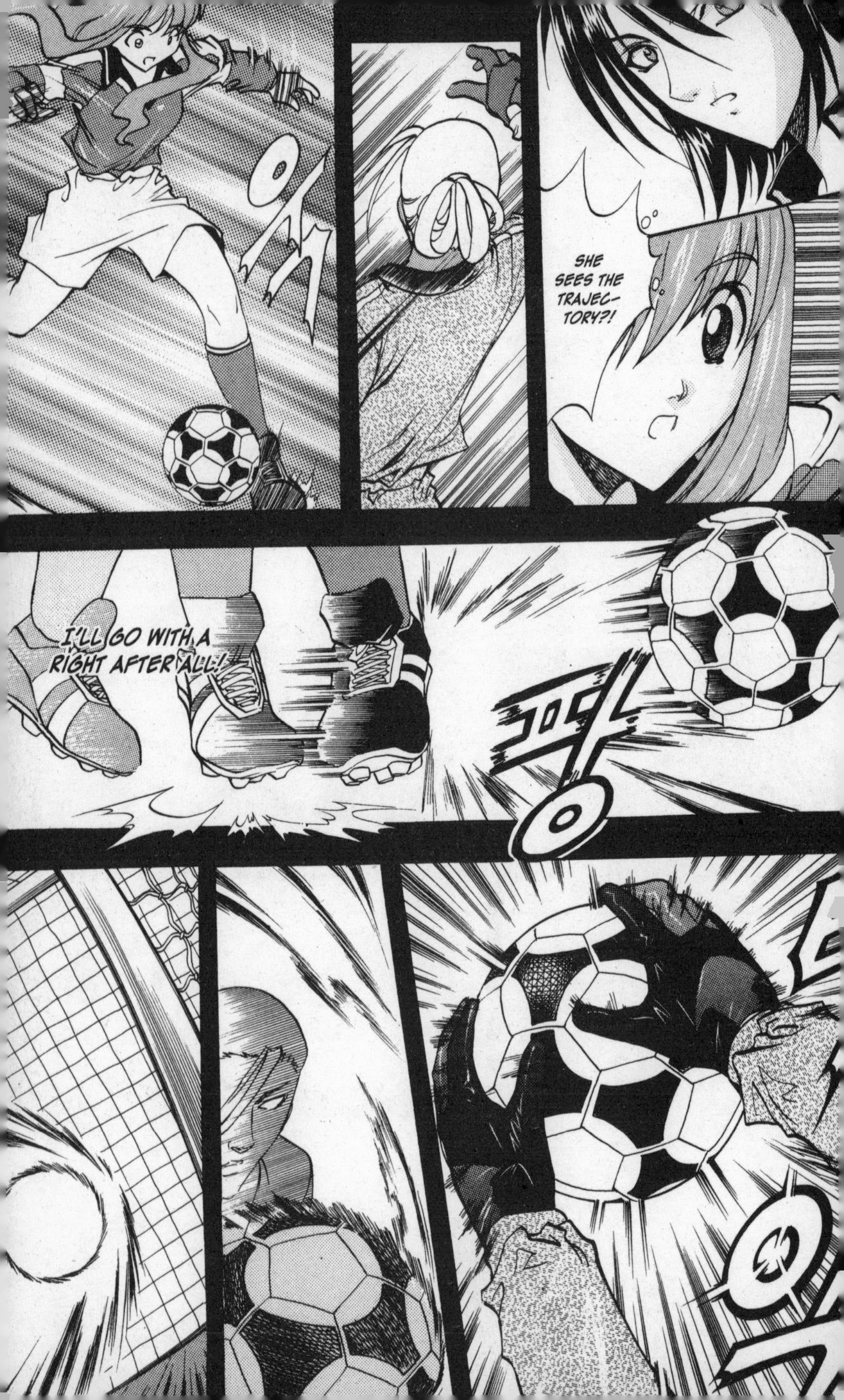
SHE SEES THE TRAJECTORY?!
I'LL GO WITH A RIGHT AFTER ALL!

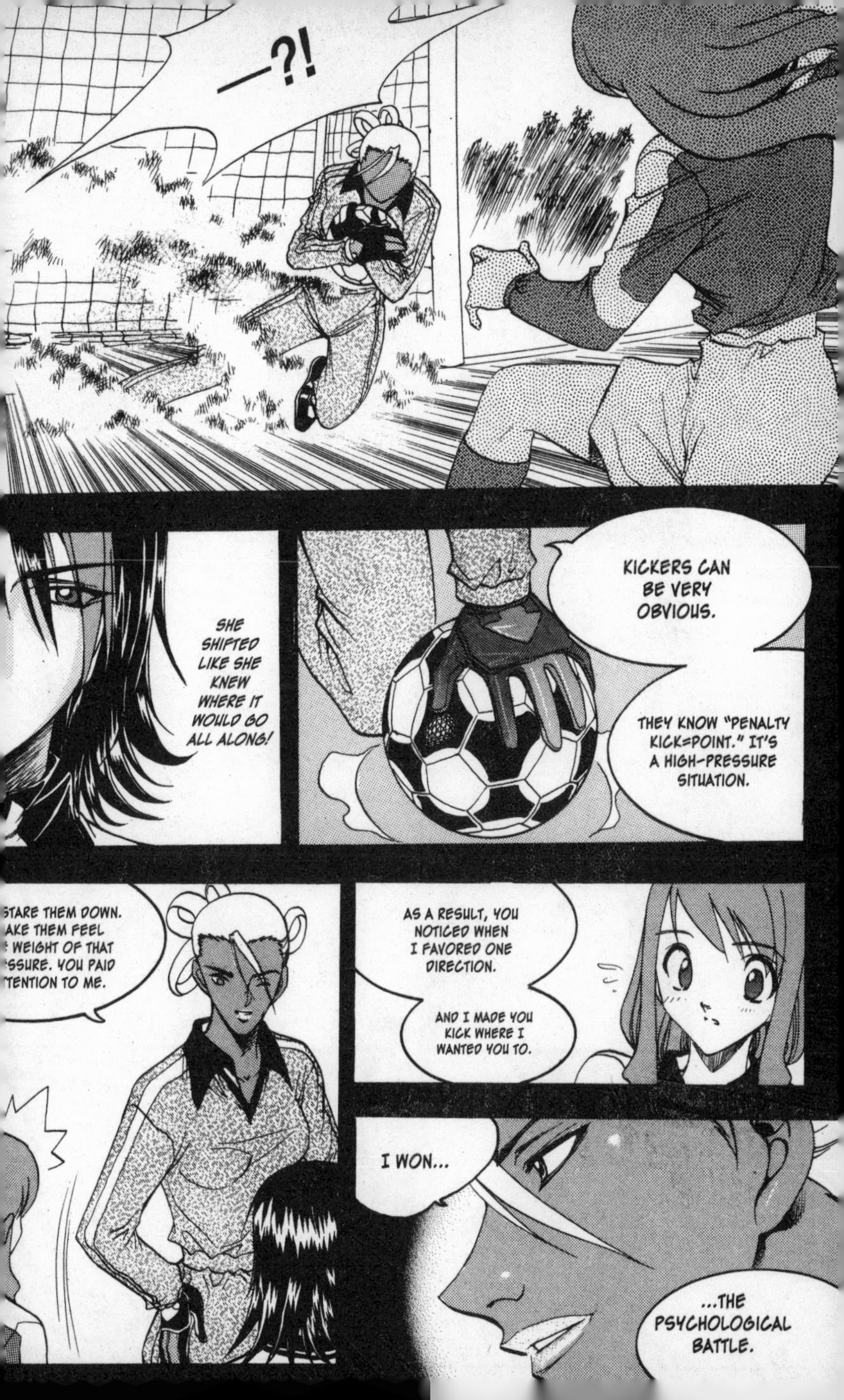
—?!
SHE SHIFTED LIKE SHE KNEW WHERE IT WOULD GO ALL ALONG!
KICKERS CAN BE VERY OBVIOUS.
THEY KNOW "PENALTY KICK=POINT." IT'S A HIGH-PRESSURE SITUATION.
STARE THEM DOWN. AKE THEM FEEL WEIGHT OF THAT SSURE. YOU PAID TENTION TO ME.
AS A RESULT, YOU NOTICED WHEN I FAVORED ONE DIRECTION.
AND I MADE YOU KICK WHERE I WANTED YOU TO.
I WON...
...THE PSYCHOLOGICAL BATTLE.

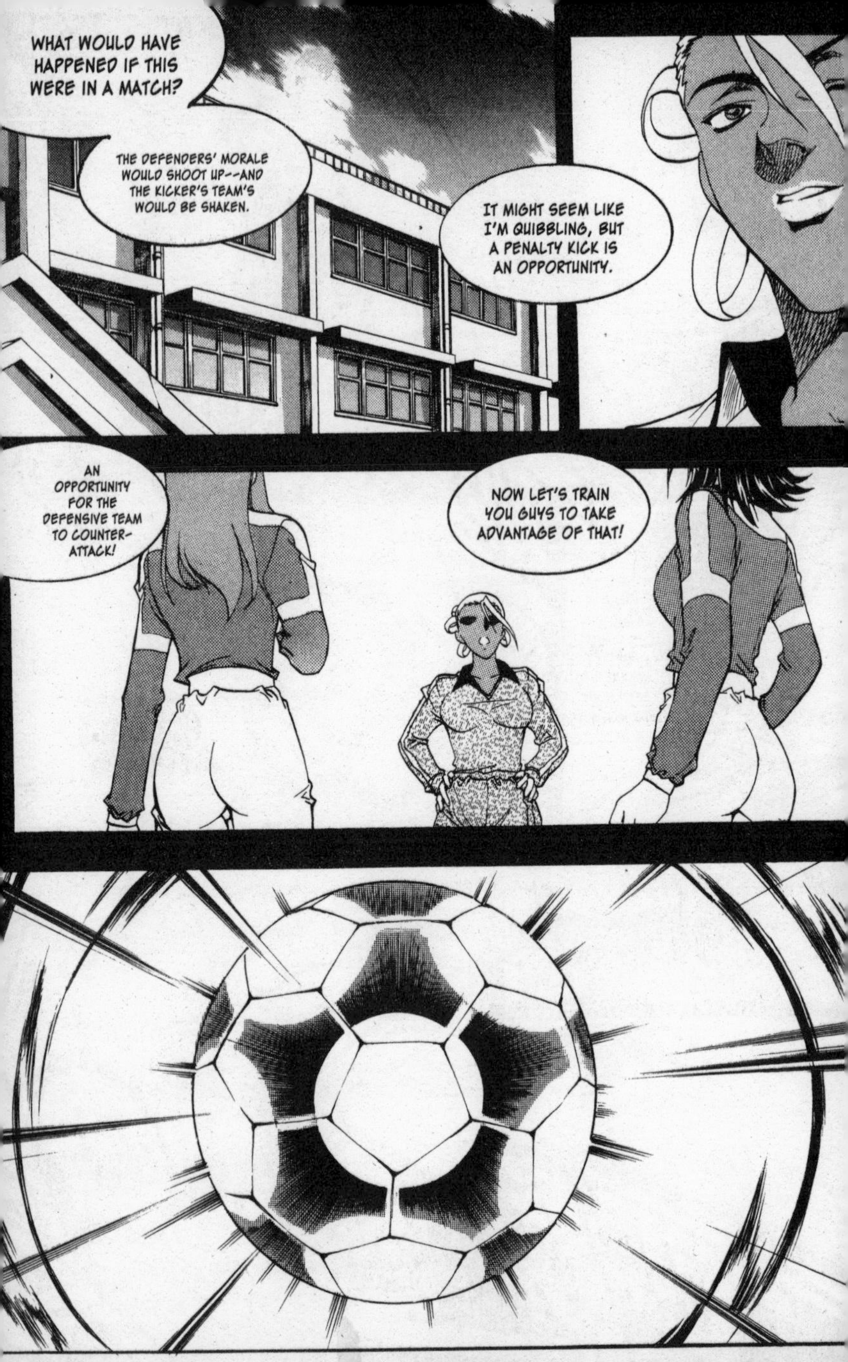
WHAT WOULD HAVE HAPPENED IF THIS WERE IN A MATCH?
THE DEFENDERS' MORALE WOULD SHOOT UP--AND THE KICKER'S TEAM'S WOULD BE SHAKEN.
IT MIGHT SEEM LIKE I'M QUIBBLING, BUT A PENALTY KICK IS AN OPPORTUNITY.
AN OPPORTUNITY FOR THE DEFENSIVE TEAM TO COUNTER-ATTACK!
NOW LET'S TRAIN YOU GUYS TO TAKE ADVANTAGE OF THAT!

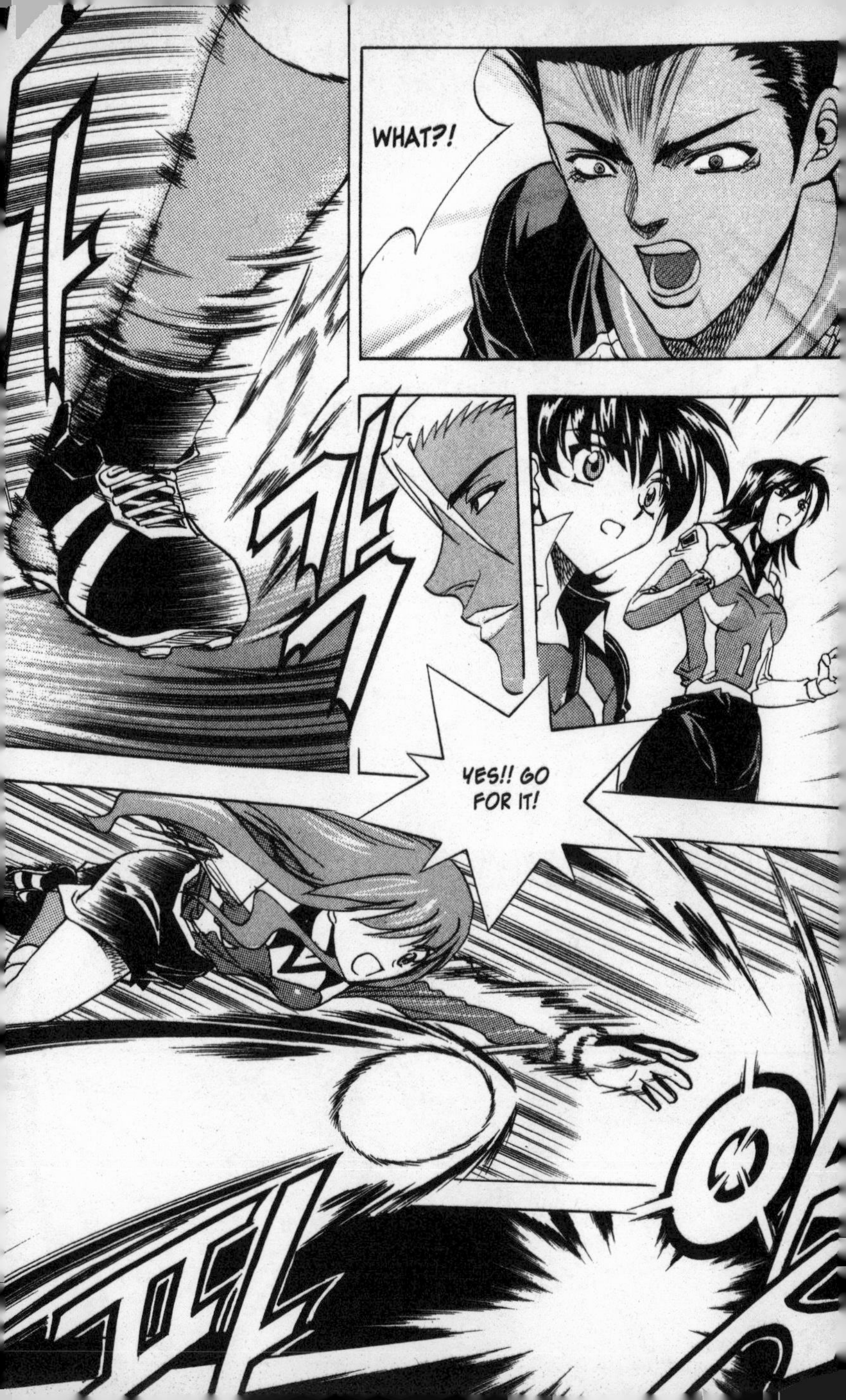
WHAT?!
YES!! GO FOR IT!

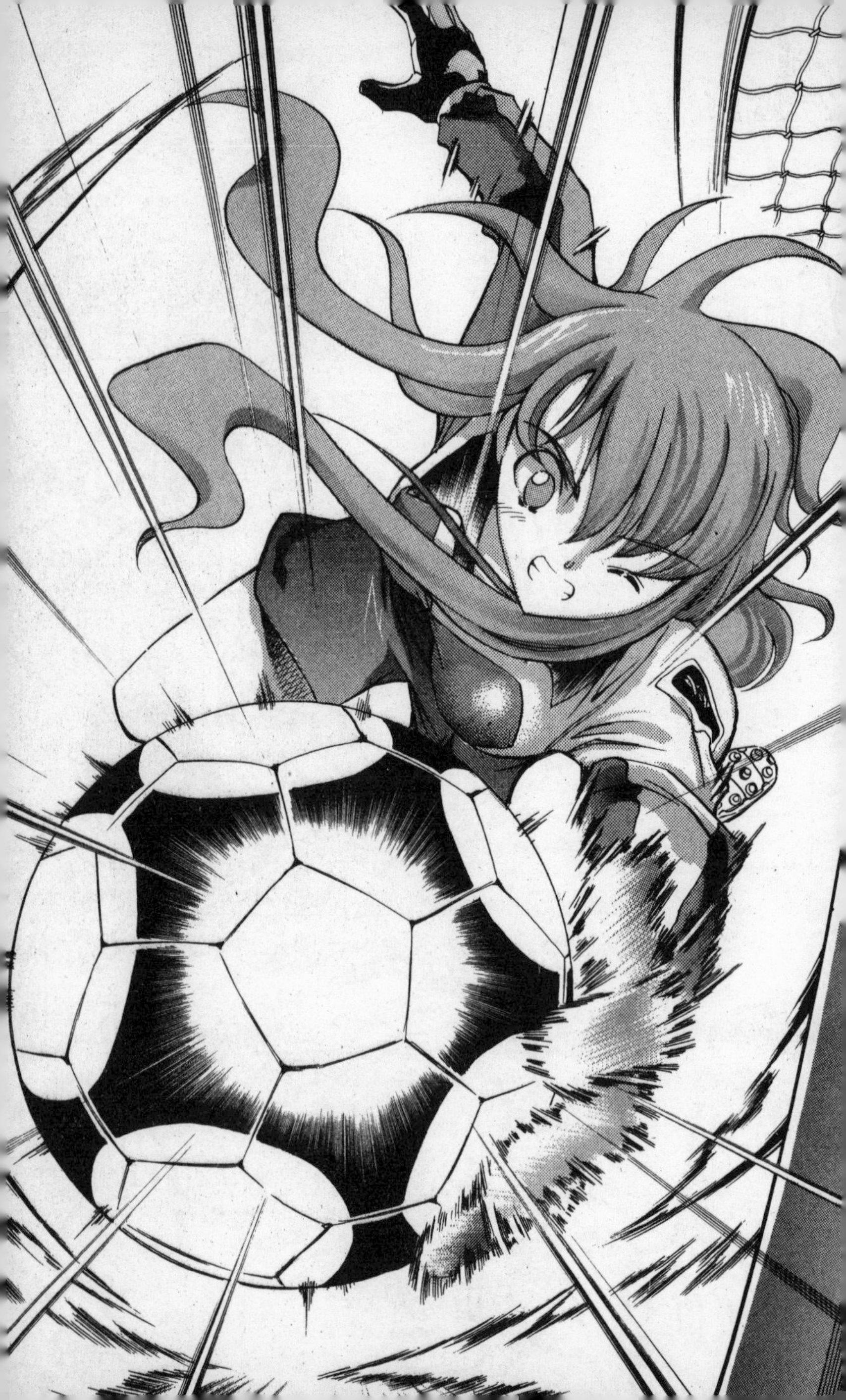

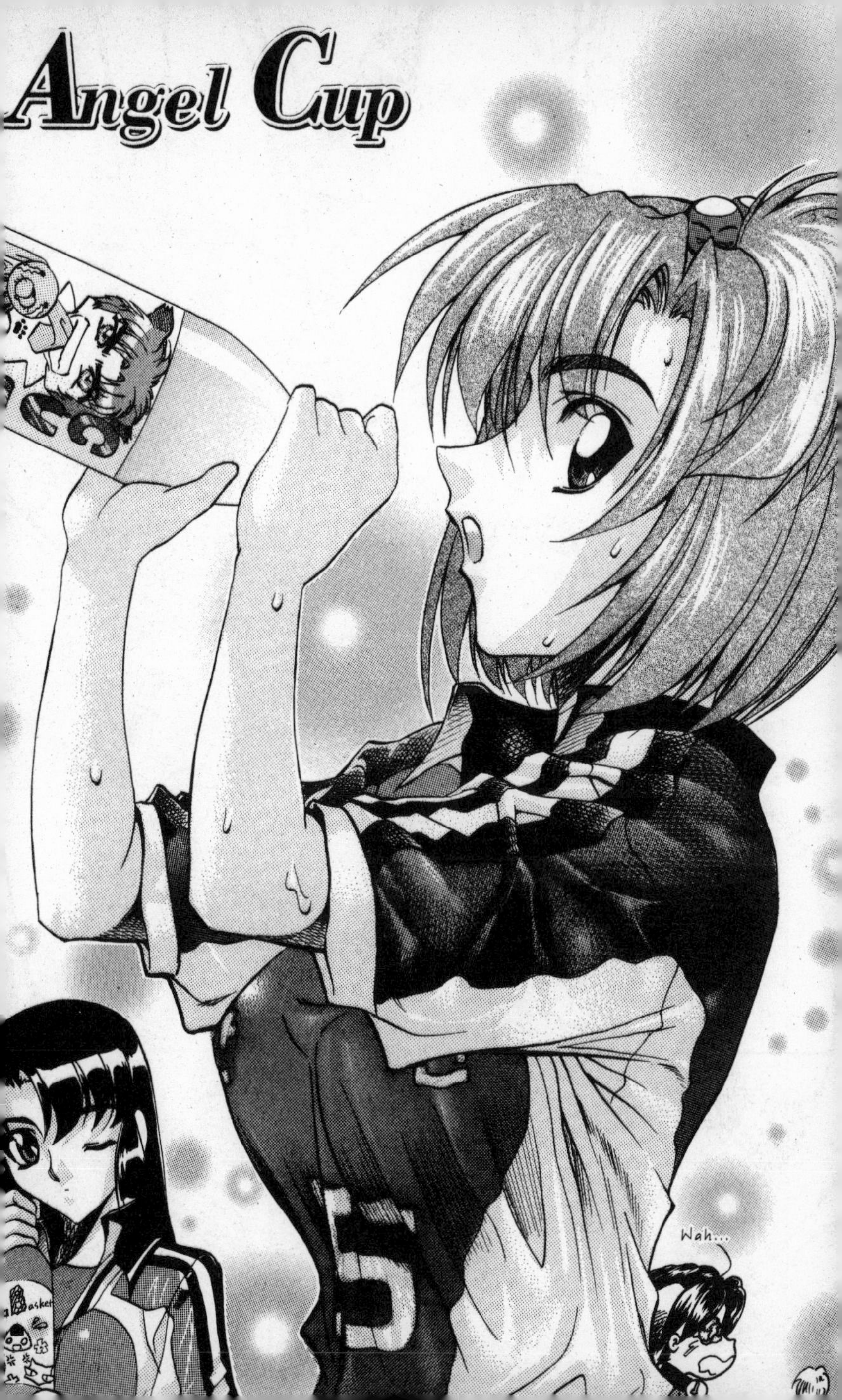
Angel Cup
Wah...

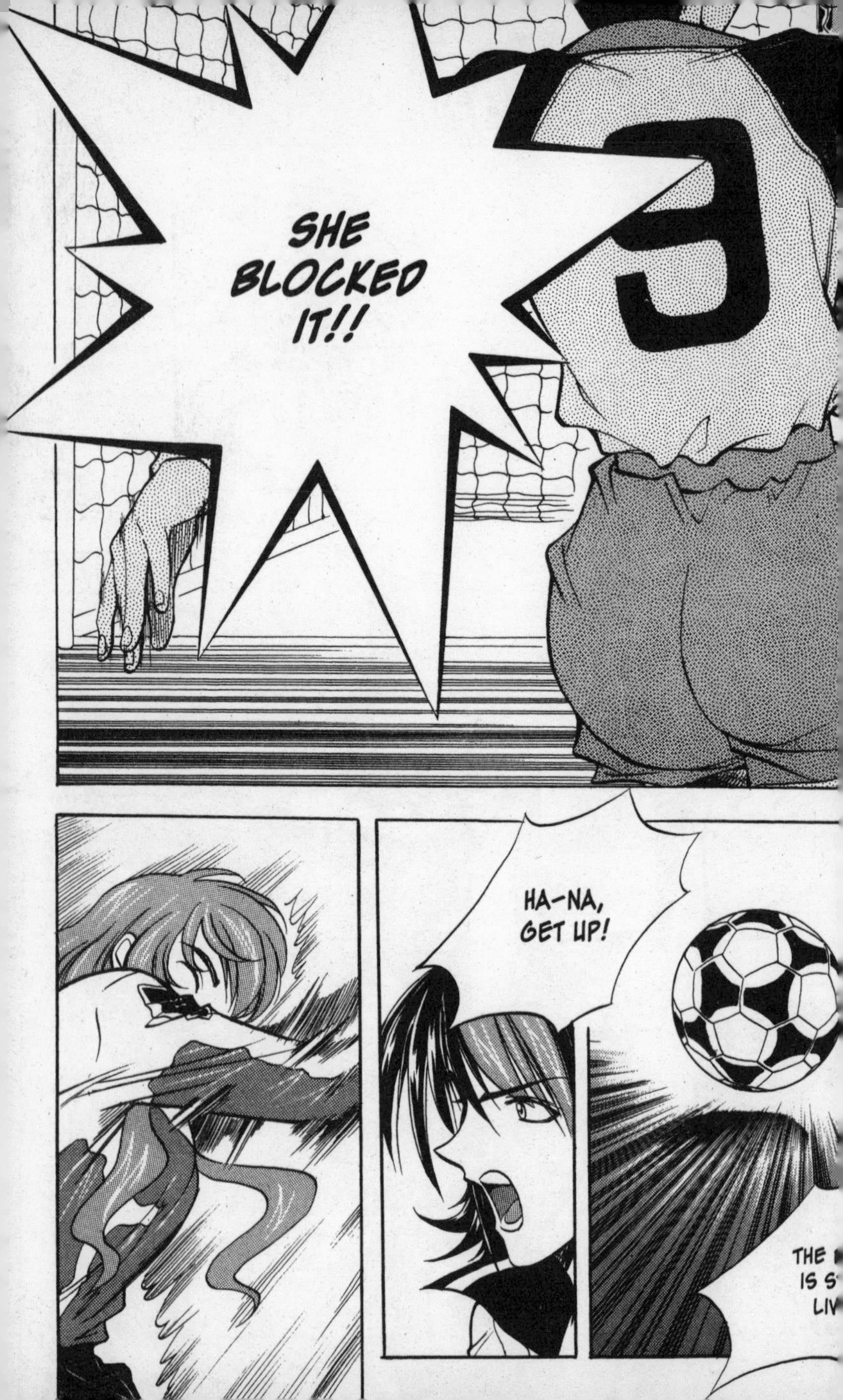
SHE BLOCKED IT!!
HA-NA, GET UP!

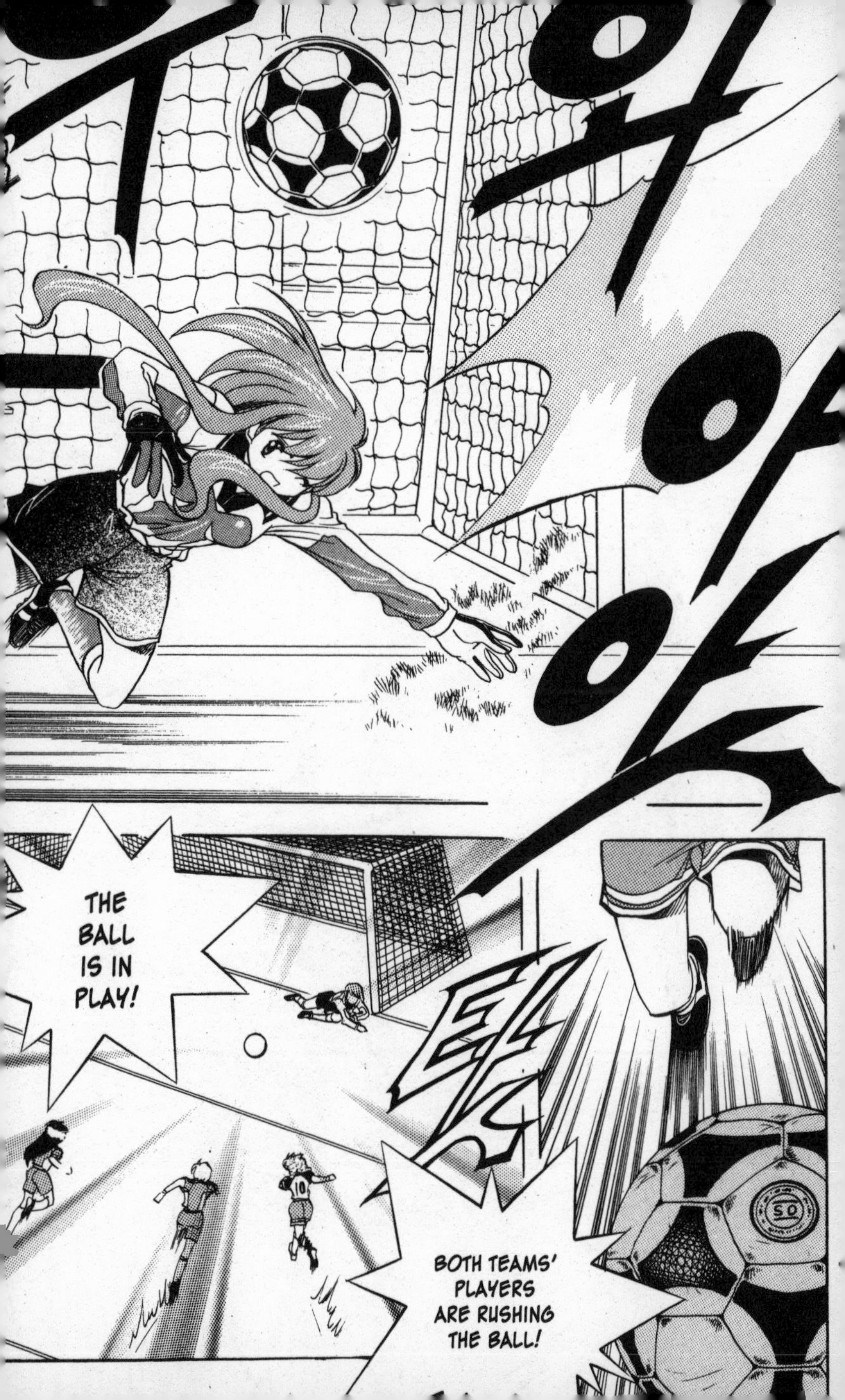
THE BALL IS IN PLAY!
BOTH TEAMS' PLAYERS ARE RUSHING THE BALL!

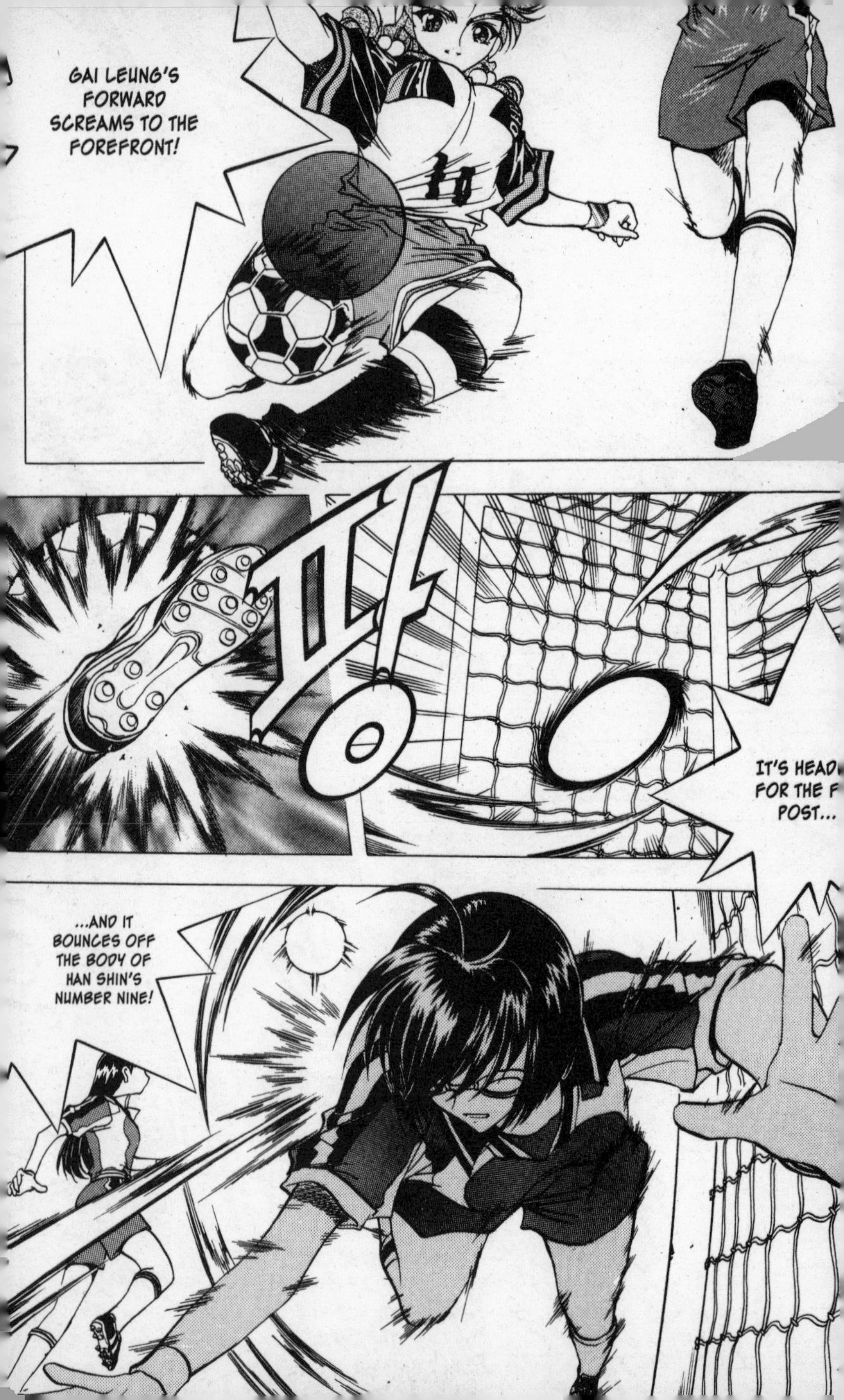
GAI LEUNG'S FORWARD SCREAMS TO THE FOREFRONT!
IT'S HEAD FOR THE F POST...
...AND IT BOUNCES OFF THE BODY OF HAN SHIN'S NUMBER NINE!

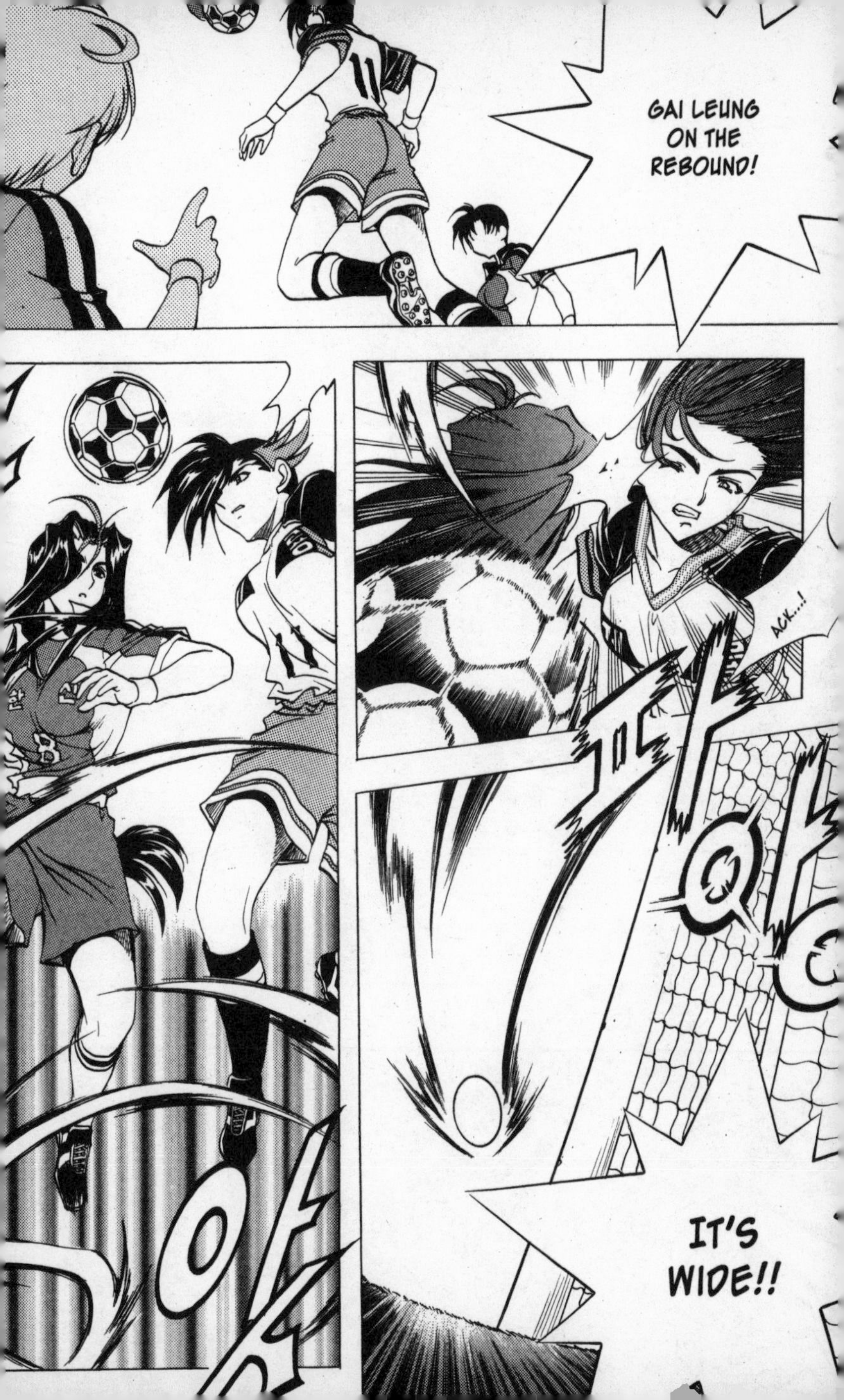

GAI LEUNG ON THE REBOUND!
ACK...!
IT'S WIDE!!

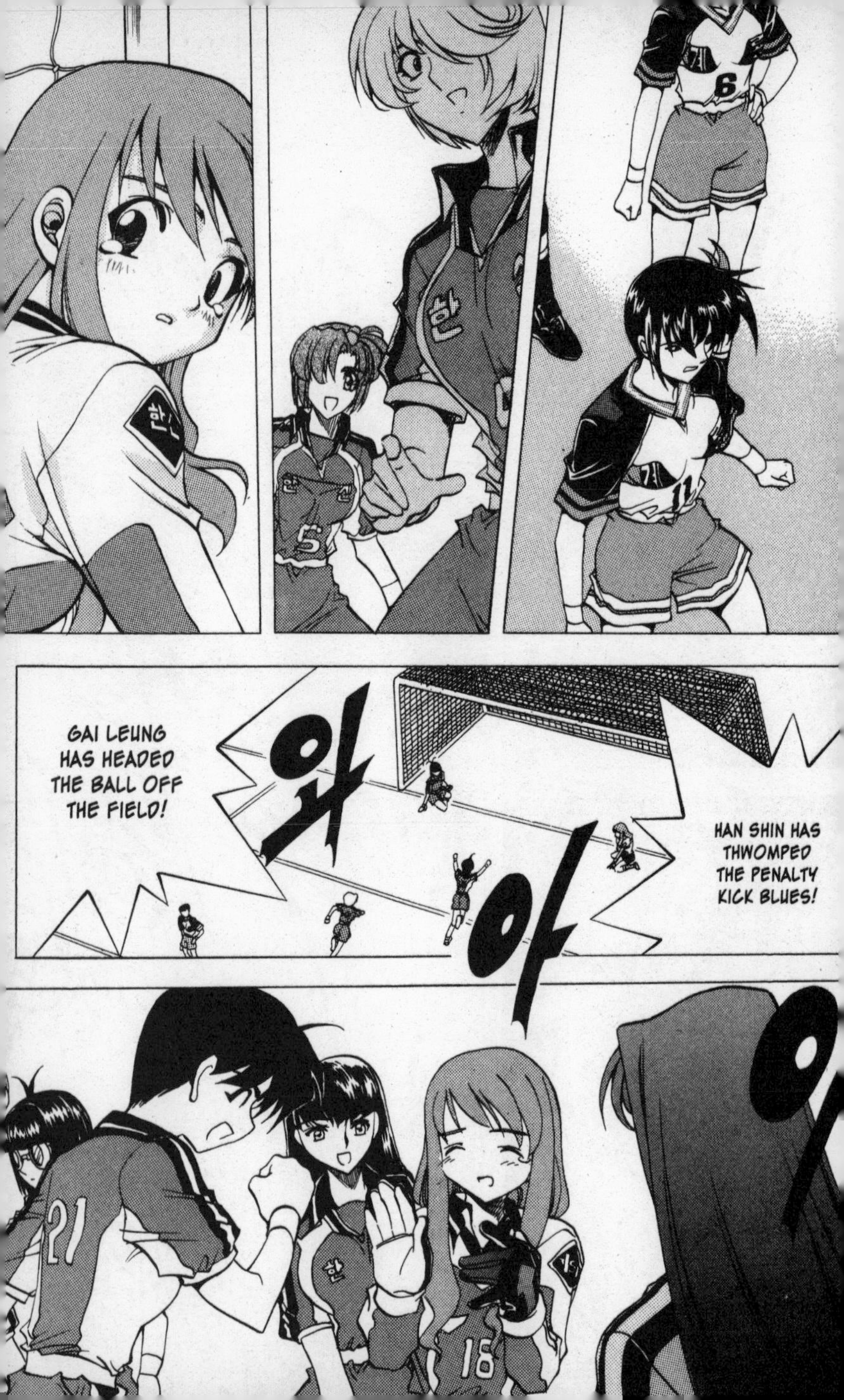
GAI LEUNG HAS HEADED THE BALL OFF THE FIELD!
와
HAN SHIN HAS THWOMPED THE PENALTY KICK BLUES!
아

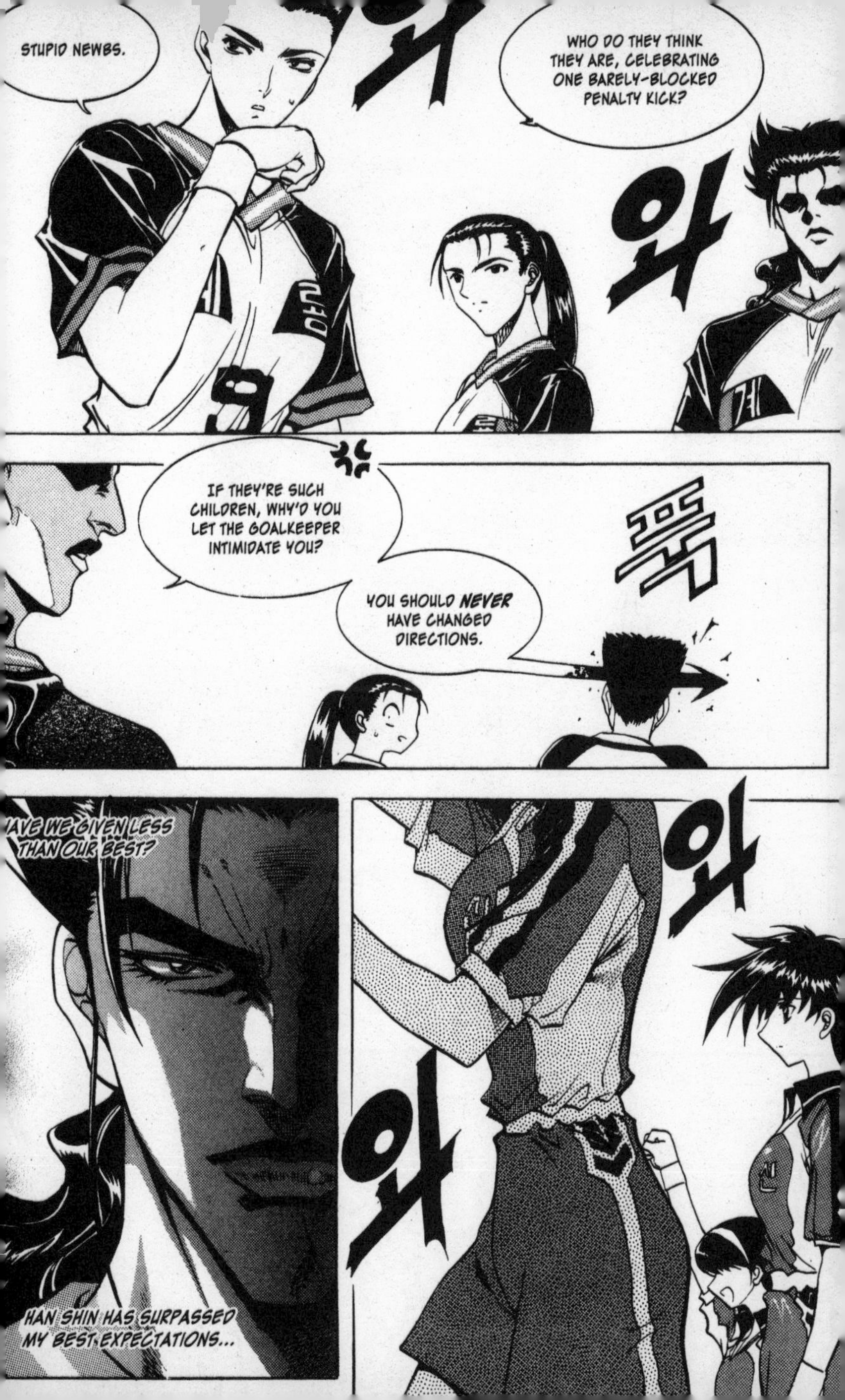
STUPID NEWBS.
WHO DO THEY THINK THEY ARE, CELEBRATING ONE BARELY-BLOCKED PENALTY KICK?
와
IF THEY'RE SUCH CHILDREN, WHY'D YOU LET THE GOALKEEPER INTIMIDATE YOU?
푹
YOU SHOULD **NEVER** HAVE CHANGED DIRECTIONS.
AVE WE GIVEN LESS THAN OUR BEST?
HAN SHIN HAS SURPASSED MY BEST EXPECTATIONS...
와
와

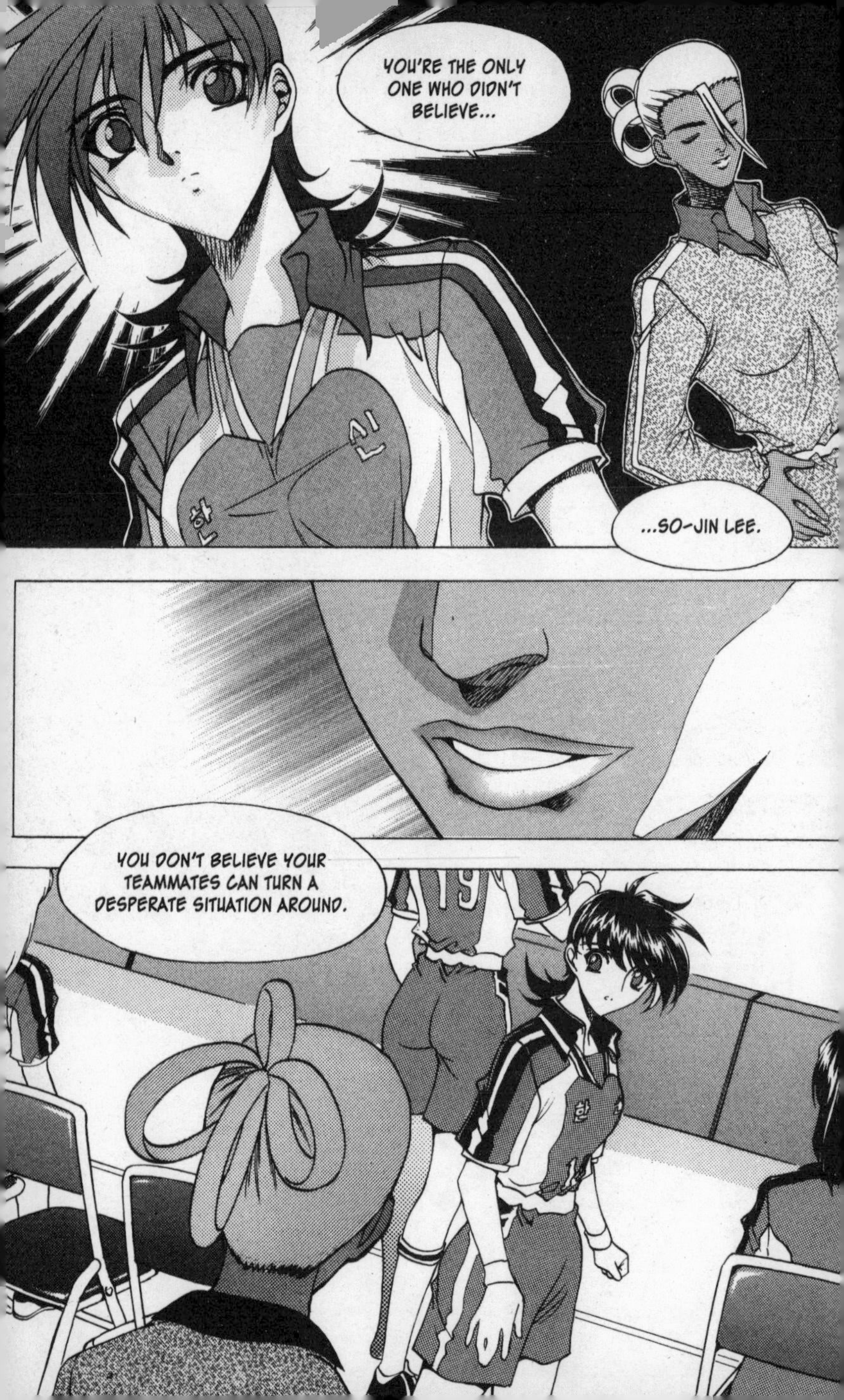
YOU'RE THE ONLY ONE WHO DIDN'T BELIEVE...
...SO-JIN LEE.
YOU DON'T BELIEVE YOUR TEAMMATES CAN TURN A DESPERATE SITUATION AROUND.

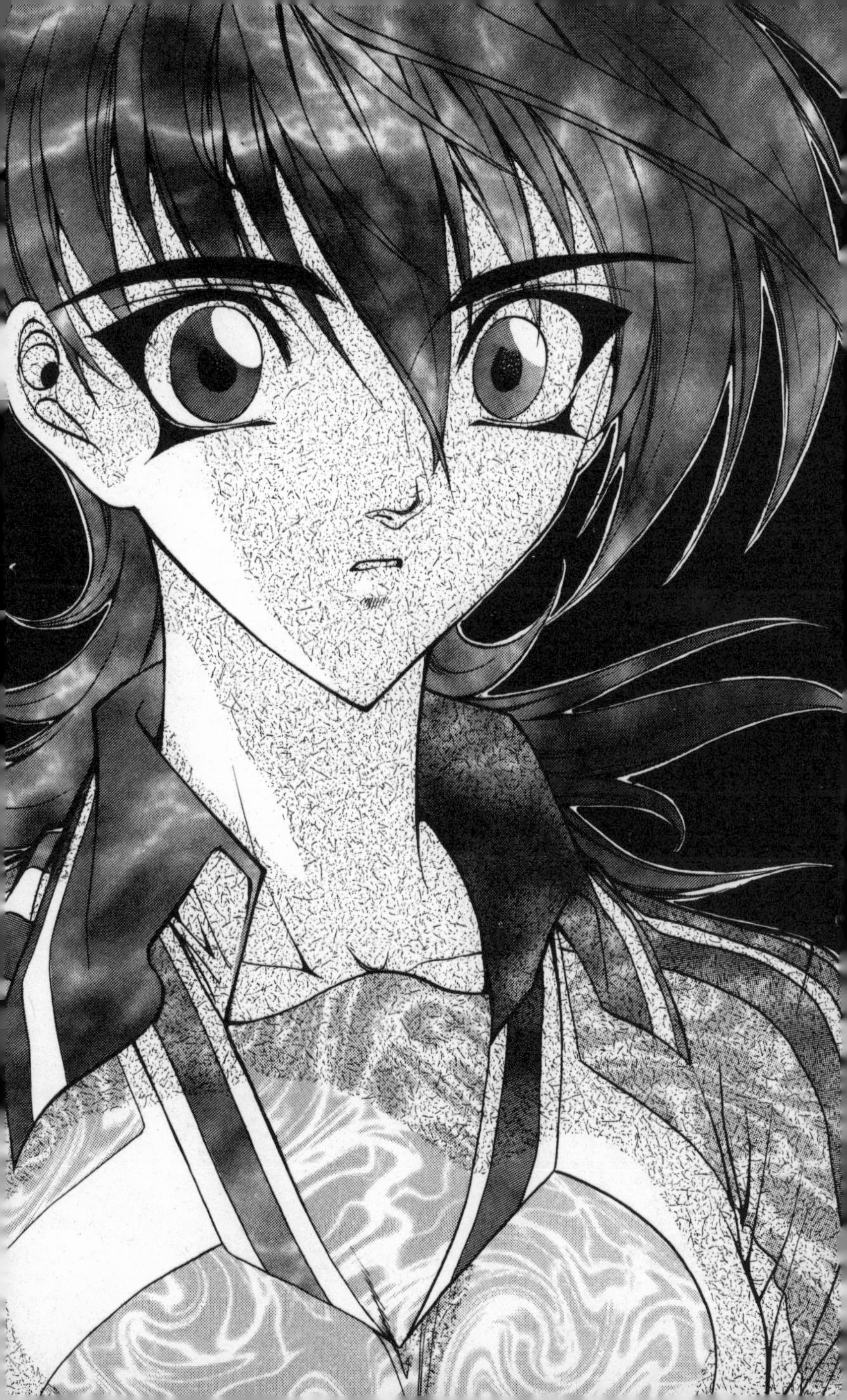

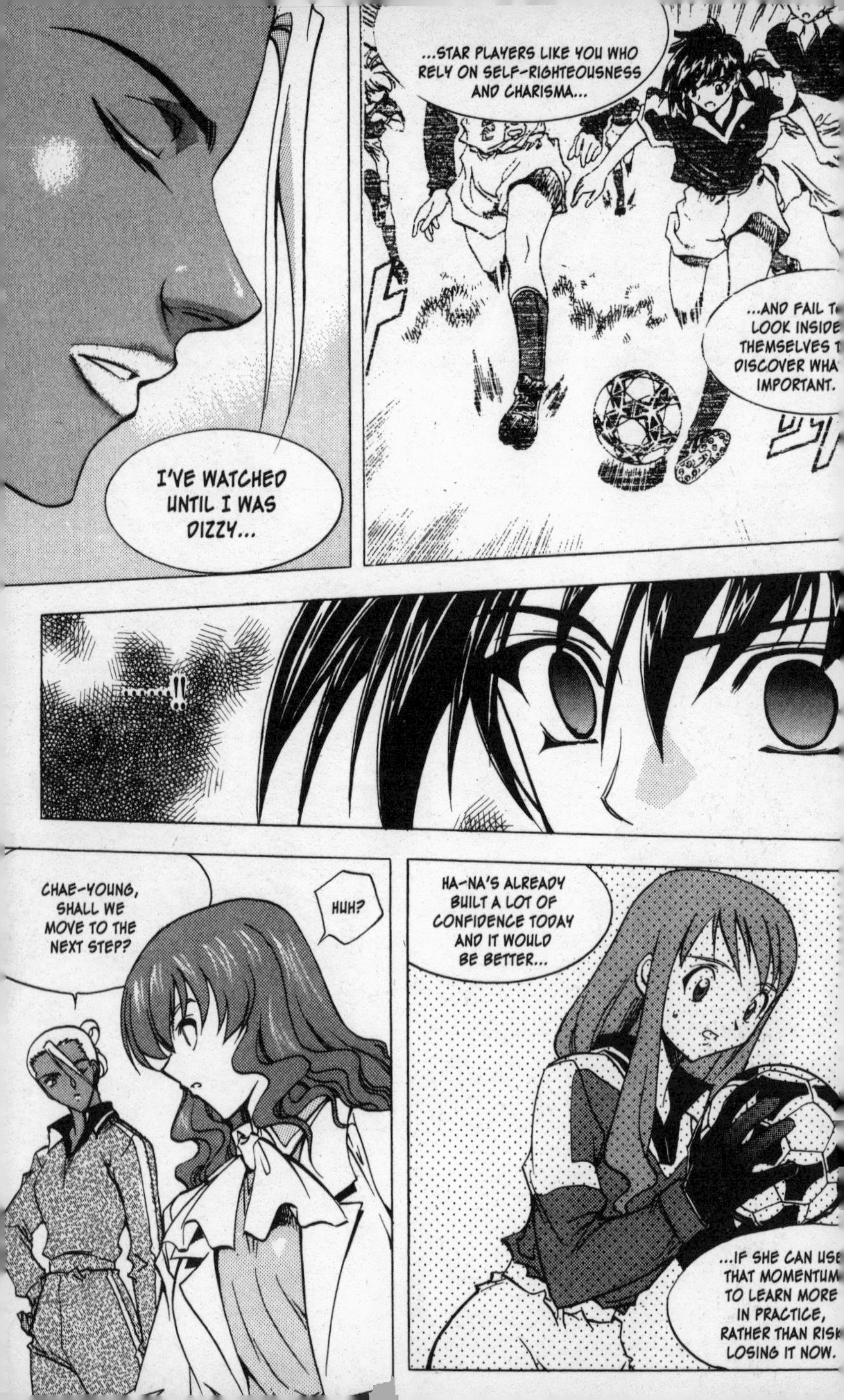
I'VE WATCHED UNTIL I WAS DIZZY...
...STAR PLAYERS LIKE YOU WHO RELY ON SELF-RIGHTEOUSNESS AND CHARISMA...
...AND FAIL T LOOK INSIDE THEMSELVES T DISCOVER WHA IMPORTANT.
CHAE-YOUNG, SHALL WE MOVE TO THE NEXT STEP?
HUH?
HA-NA'S ALREADY BUILT A LOT OF CONFIDENCE TODAY AND IT WOULD BE BETTER...
...IF SHE CAN USE THAT MOMENTUM TO LEARN MORE IN PRACTICE, RATHER THAN RISK LOSING IT NOW.

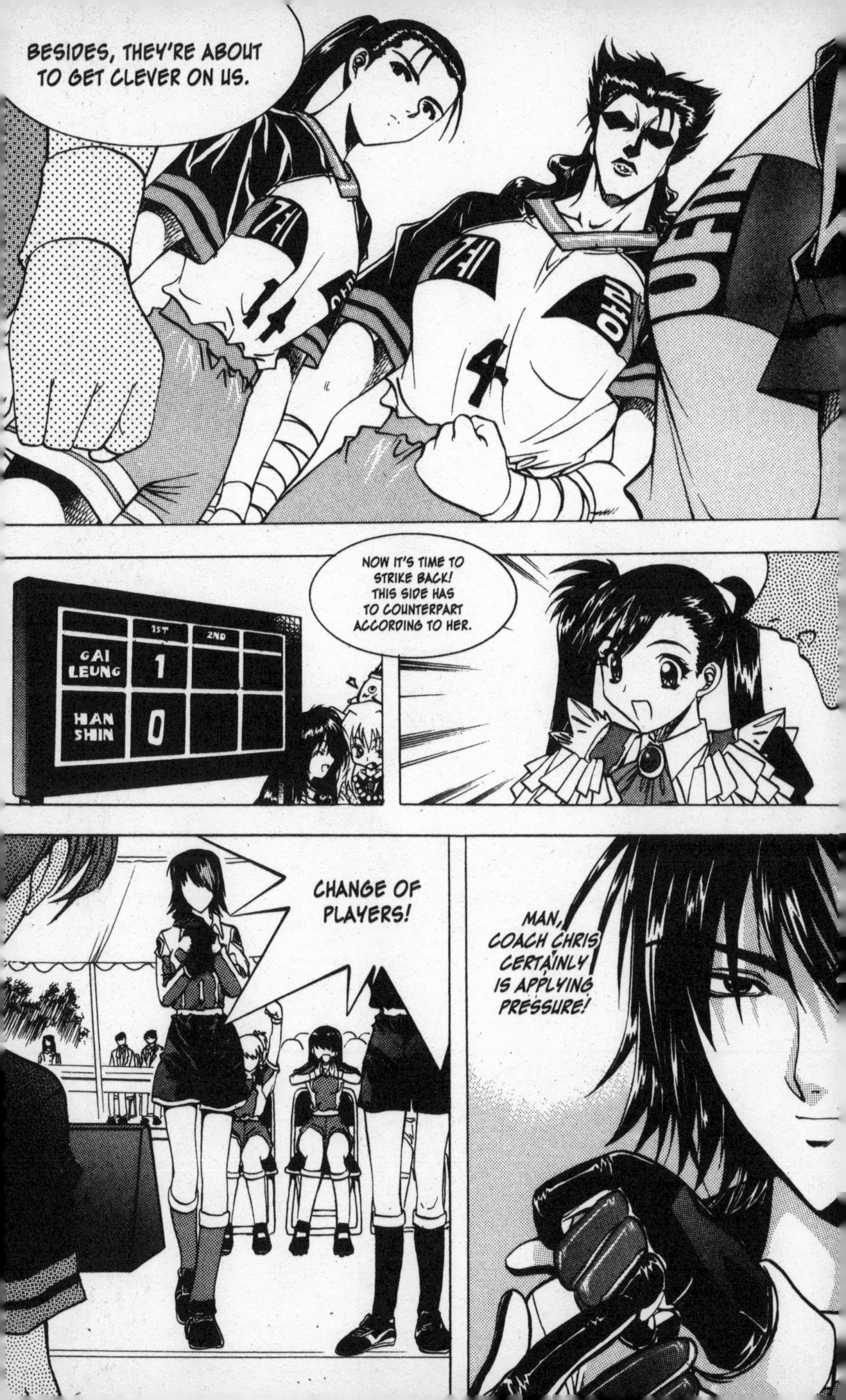
BESIDES, THEY'RE ABOUT TO GET CLEVER ON US.
4
14
1ST
2ND
GAI LEUNG
1
HAN SHIN
0
NOW IT'S TIME TO STRIKE BACK! THIS SIDE HAS TO COUNTERPART ACCORDING TO HER.
CHANGE OF PLAYERS!
MAN, COACH CHRIS CERTAINLY IS APPLYING PRESSURE!

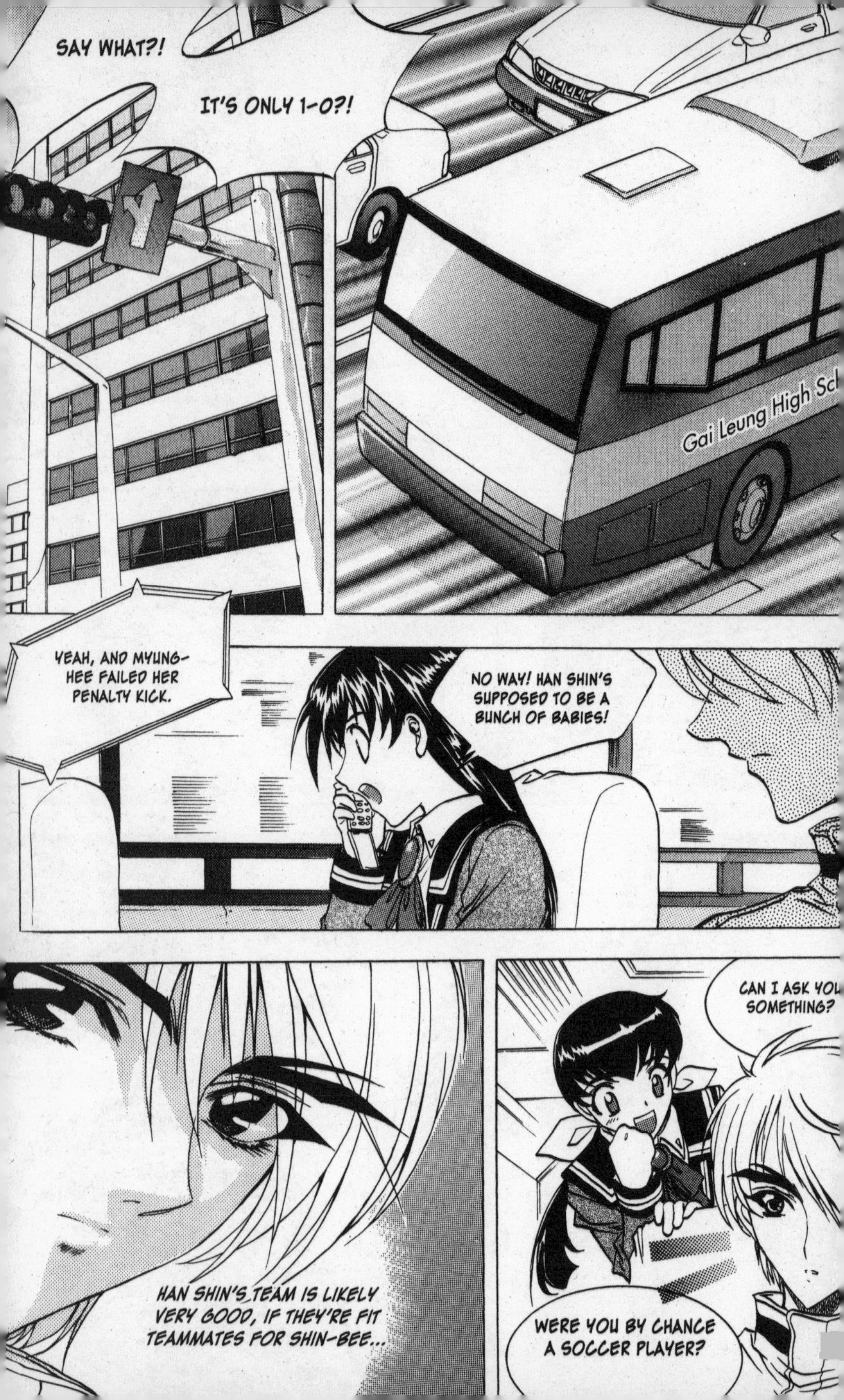
SAY WHAT?!
IT'S ONLY 1-0?!
Gai Leung High Sch
YEAH, AND MYUNG-HEE FAILED HER PENALTY KICK.
NO WAY! HAN SHIN'S SUPPOSED TO BE A BUNCH OF BABIES!
HAN SHIN'S TEAM IS LIKELY VERY GOOD, IF THEY'RE FIT TEAMMATES FOR SHIN-BEE...
CAN I ASK YOU SOMETHING?
WERE YOU BY CHANCE A SOCCER PLAYER?

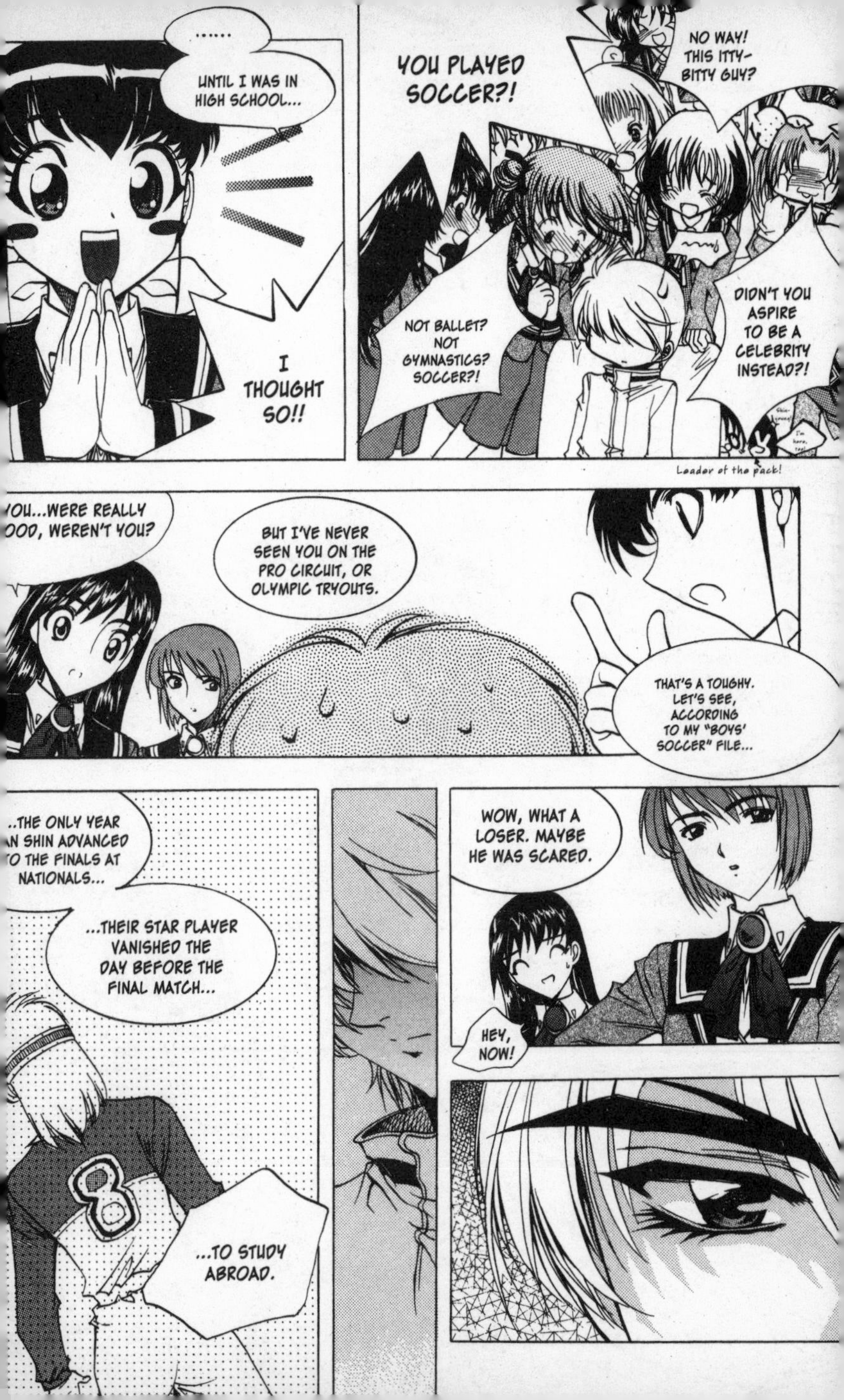
......
UNTIL I WAS IN HIGH SCHOOL...
I THOUGHT SO!!
YOU PLAYED SOCCER?!
NO WAY! THIS ITTY-BITTY GUY?
NOT BALLET? NOT GYMNASTICS? SOCCER?!
DIDN'T YOU ASPIRE TO BE A CELEBRITY INSTEAD?!
I'm here, too!
Leader of the pack!
YOU...WERE REALLY GOOD, WEREN'T YOU?
BUT I'VE NEVER SEEN YOU ON THE PRO CIRCUIT, OR OLYMPIC TRYOUTS.
THAT'S A TOUGHY. LET'S SEE, ACCORDING TO MY "BOYS' SOCCER" FILE...
...THE ONLY YEAR AN SHIN ADVANCED TO THE FINALS AT NATIONALS...
...THEIR STAR PLAYER VANISHED THE DAY BEFORE THE FINAL MATCH...
...TO STUDY ABROAD.
WOW, WHAT A LOSER. MAYBE HE WAS SCARED.
HEY, NOW!

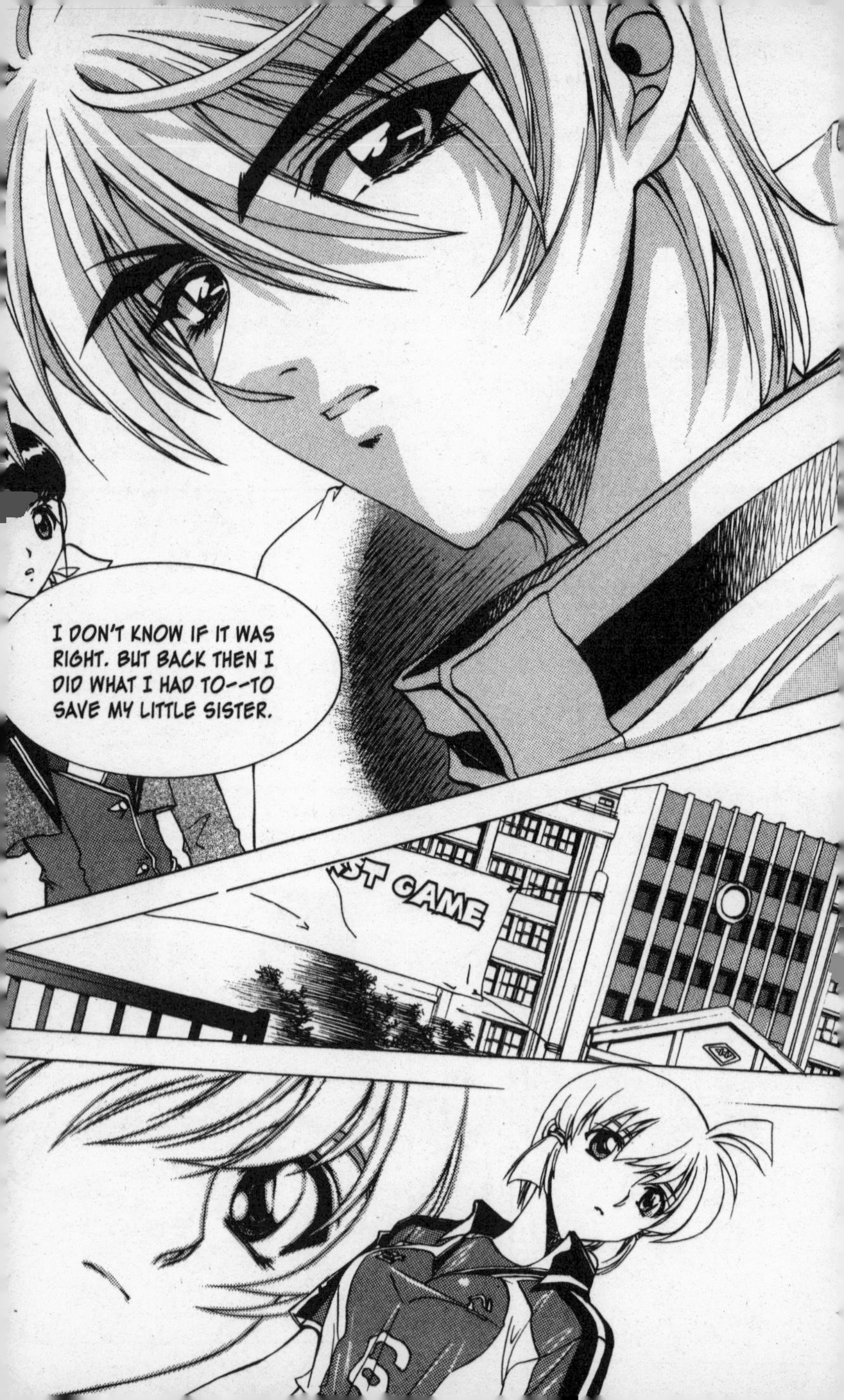
I DON'T KNOW IF IT WAS RIGHT. BUT BACK THEN I DID WHAT I HAD TO--TO SAVE MY LITTLE SISTER.
GAME

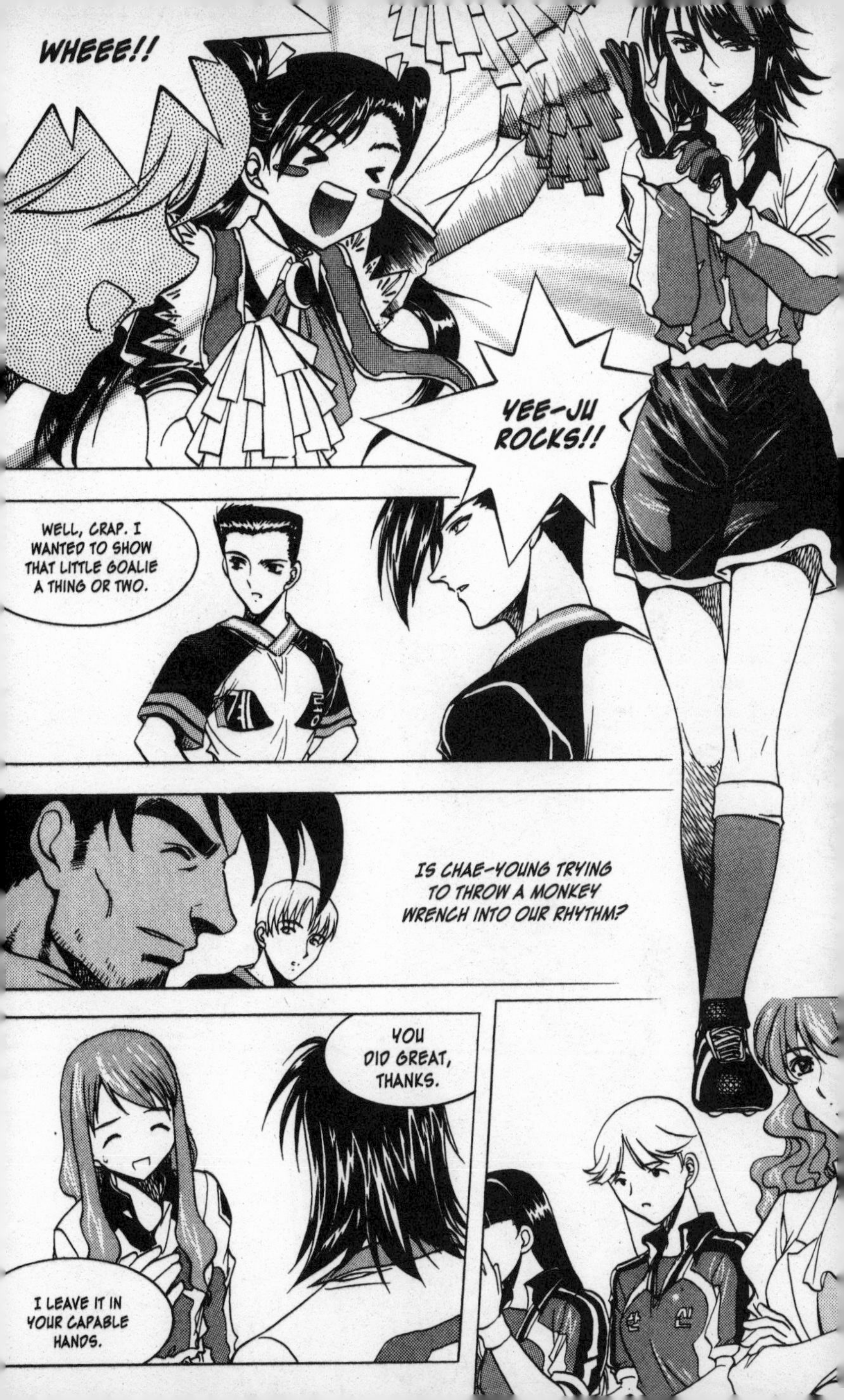
WHEEEE!!
YEE-JU ROCKS!!
WELL, CRAP. I WANTED TO SHOW THAT LITTLE GOALIE A THING OR TWO.
IS CHAE-YOUNG TRYING TO THROW A MONKEY WRENCH INTO OUR RHYTHM?
YOU DID GREAT, THANKS.
I LEAVE IT IN YOUR CAPABLE HANDS.

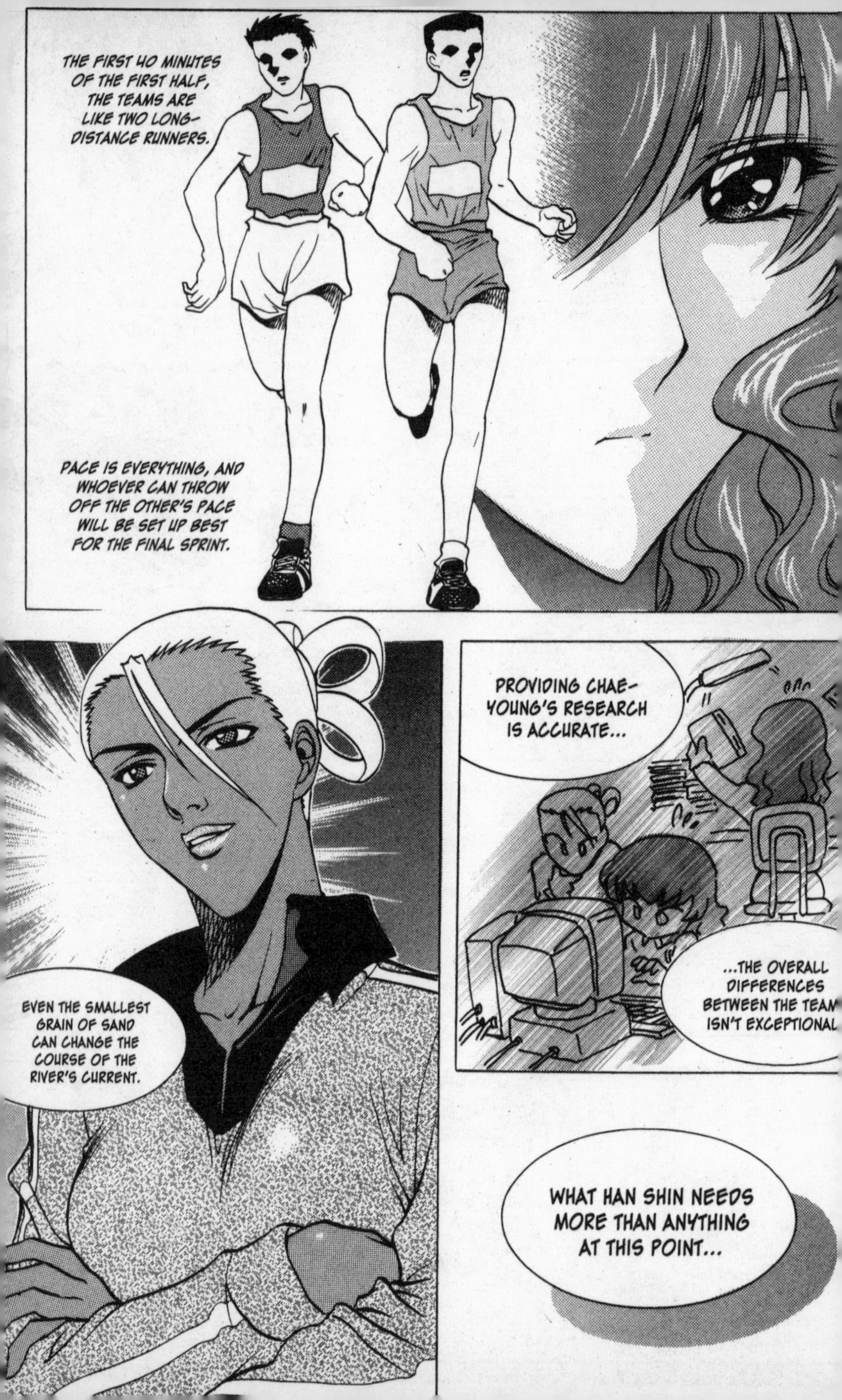

THE FIRST 40 MINUTES OF THE FIRST HALF, THE TEAMS ARE LIKE TWO LONG-DISTANCE RUNNERS.
PACE IS EVERYTHING, AND WHOEVER CAN THROW OFF THE OTHER'S PACE WILL BE SET UP BEST FOR THE FINAL SPRINT.
EVEN THE SMALLEST GRAIN OF SAND CAN CHANGE THE COURSE OF THE RIVER'S CURRENT.
PROVIDING CHAE-YOUNG'S RESEARCH IS ACCURATE...
...THE OVERALL DIFFERENCES BETWEEN THE TEAM ISN'T EXCEPTIONAL
WHAT HAN SHIN NEEDS MORE THAN ANYTHING AT THIS POINT...

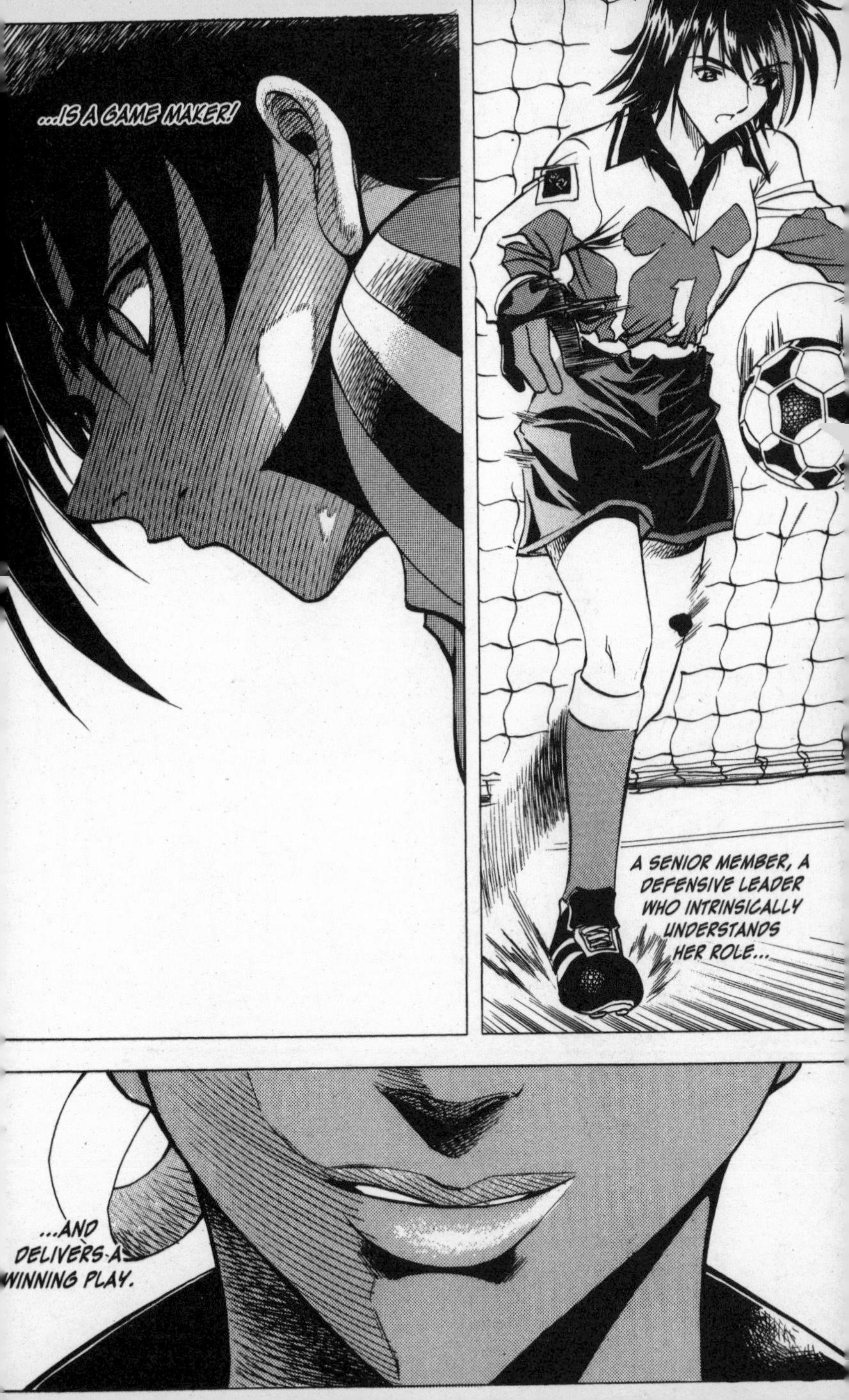
...IS A GAME MAKER!
A SENIOR MEMBER, A DEFENSIVE LEADER WHO INTRINSICALLY UNDERSTANDS HER ROLE...
...AND DELIVERS A WINNING PLAY.

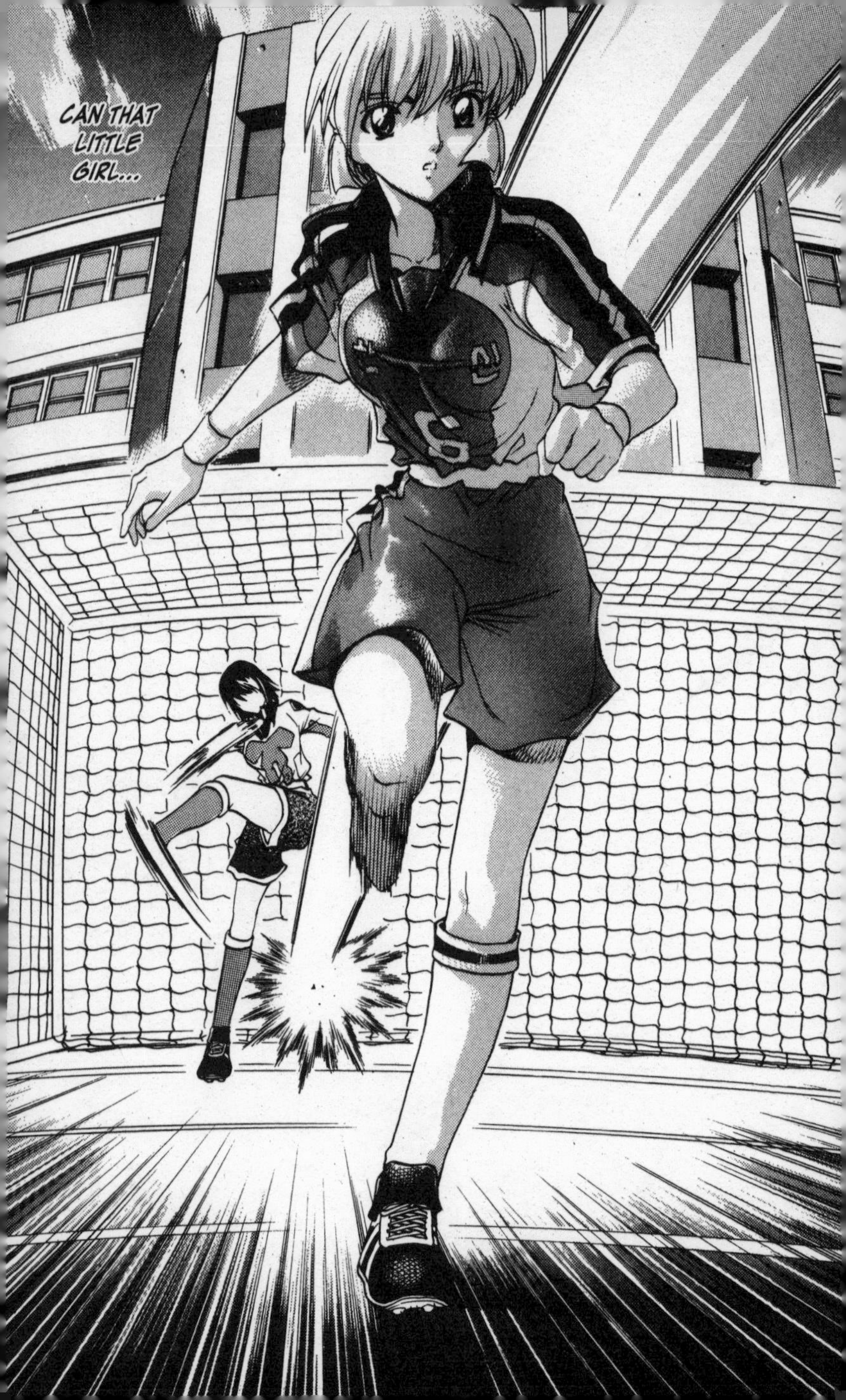
CAN THAT LITTLE GIRL...

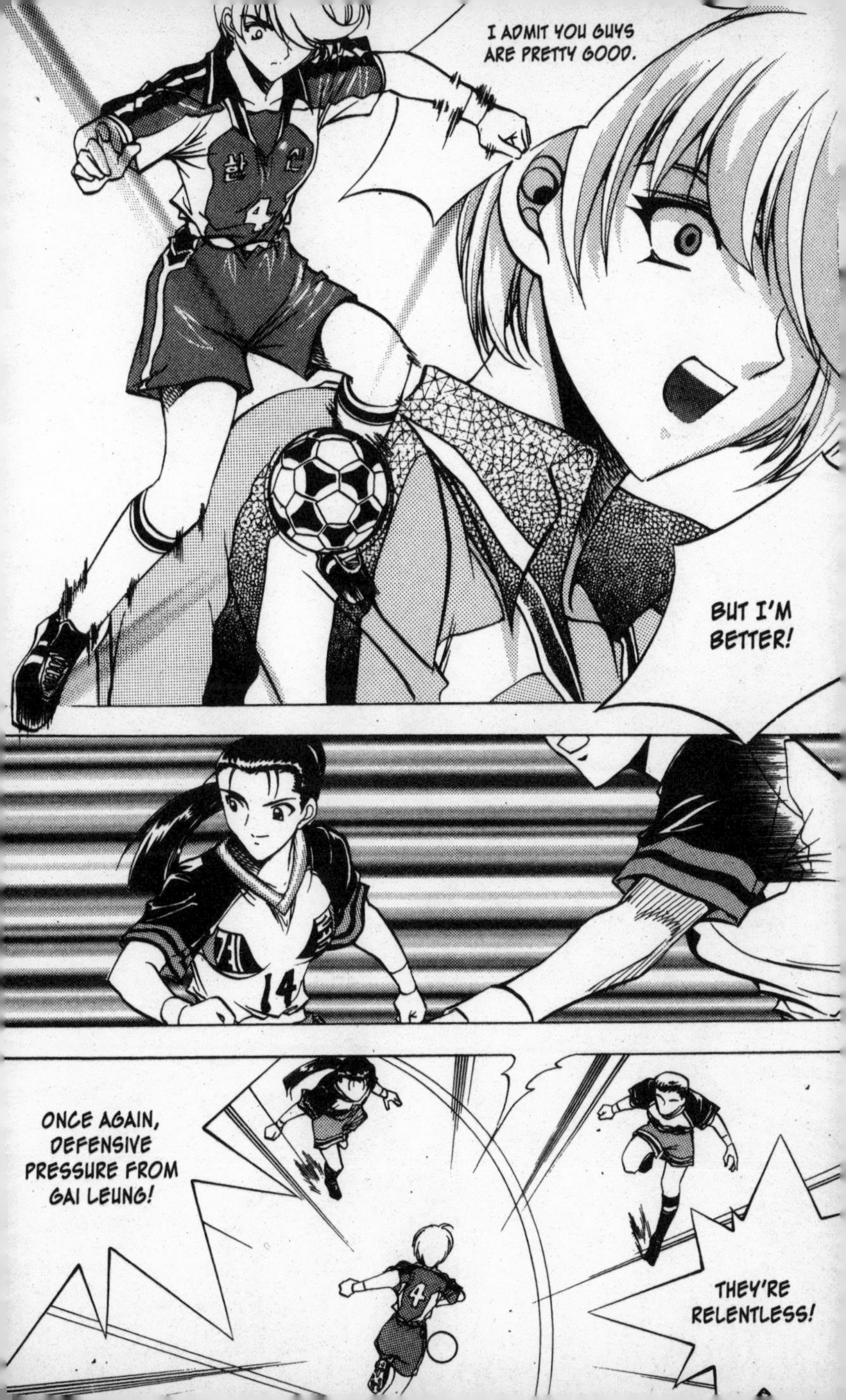
I ADMIT YOU GUYS ARE PRETTY GOOD.
BUT I'M BETTER!
ONCE AGAIN, DEFENSIVE PRESSURE FROM GAI LEUNG!
THEY'RE RELENTLESS!

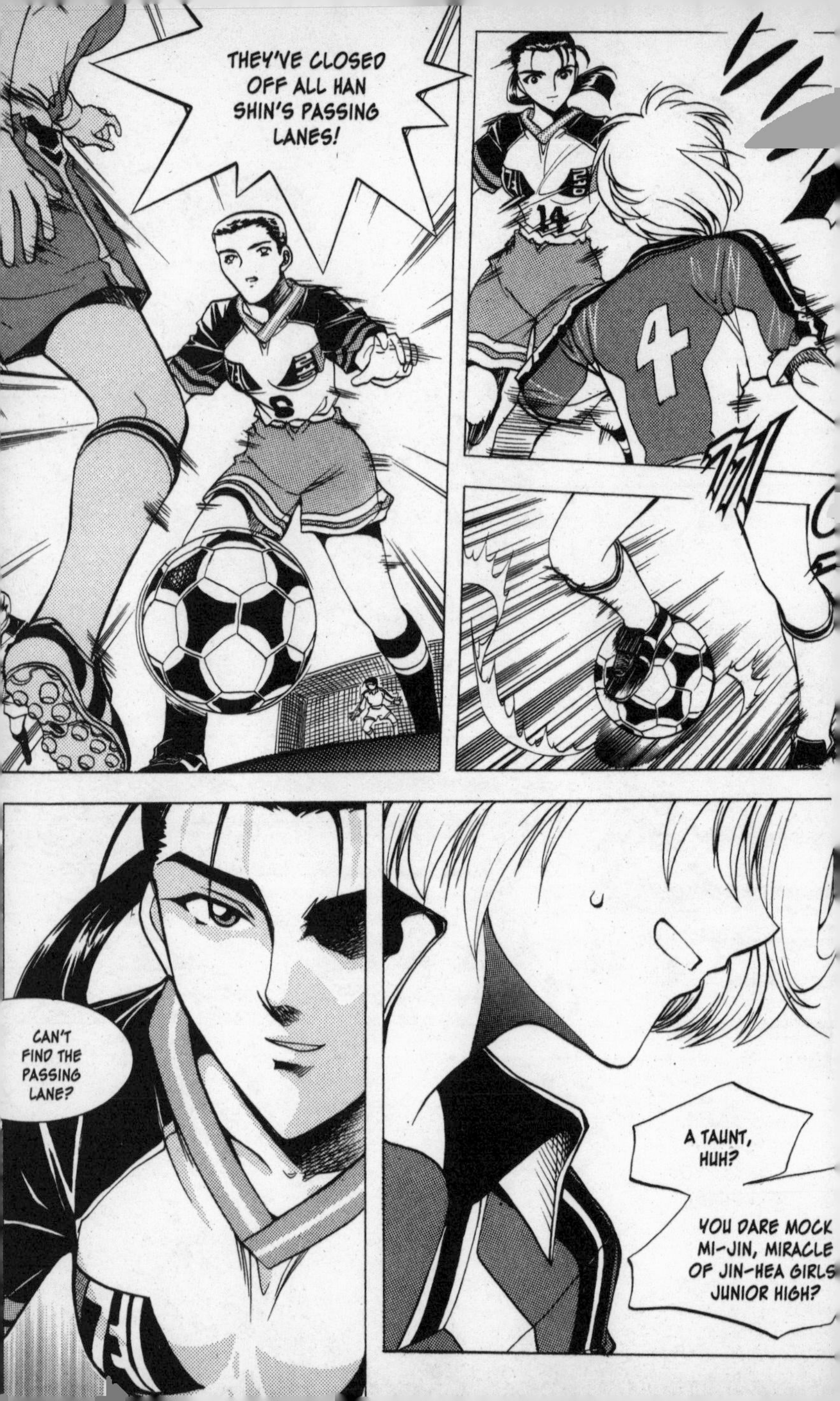
THEY'VE CLOSED OFF ALL HAN SHIN'S PASSING LANES!
CAN'T FIND THE PASSING LANE?
A TAUNT, HUH?
YOU DARE MOCK MI-JIN, MIRACLE OF JIN-HEA GIRLS JUNIOR HIGH?

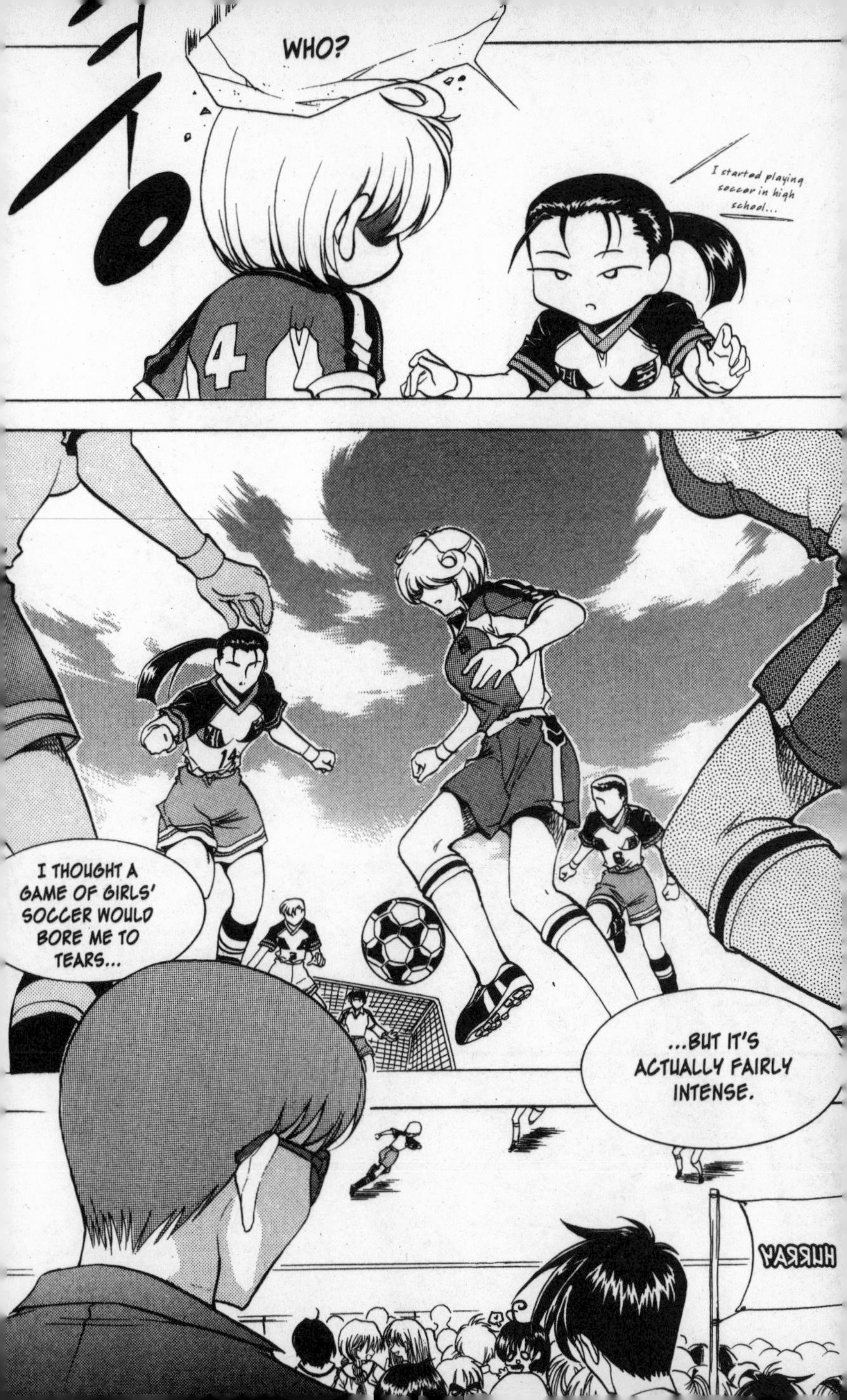
WHO?
I started playing soccer in high school...
I THOUGHT A GAME OF GIRLS' SOCCER WOULD BORE ME TO TEARS...
...BUT IT'S ACTUALLY FAIRLY INTENSE.
HURRAY

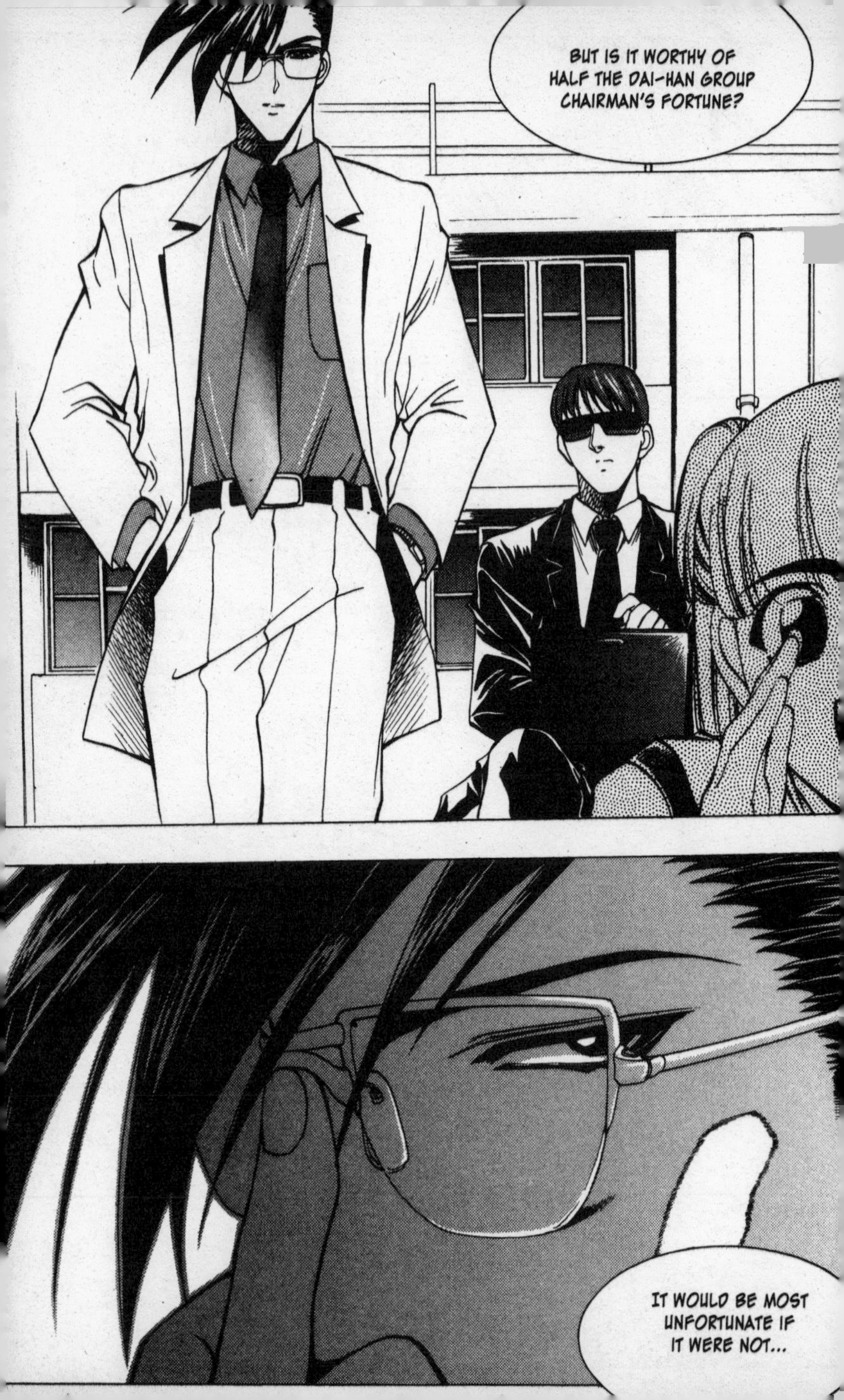
BUT IS IT WORTHY OF HALF THE DAI-HAN GROUP CHAIRMAN'S FORTUNE?
IT WOULD BE MOST UNFORTUNATE IF IT WERE NOT...

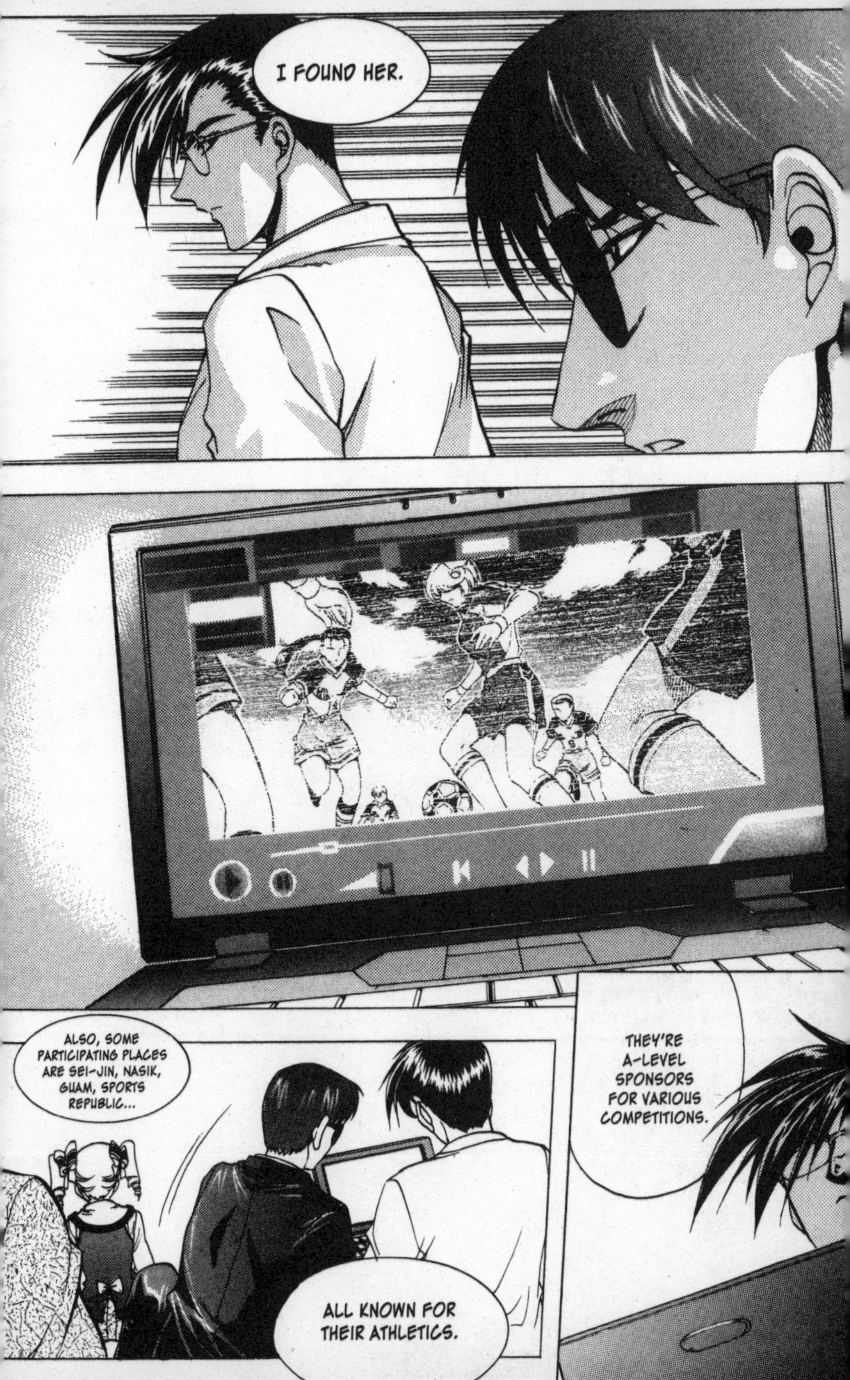
I FOUND HER.
ALSO, SOME PARTICIPATING PLACES ARE SEI-JIN, NASIK, GUAM, SPORTS REPUBLIC...
ALL KNOWN FOR THEIR ATHLETICS.
THEY'RE A-LEVEL SPONSORS FOR VARIOUS COMPETITIONS.

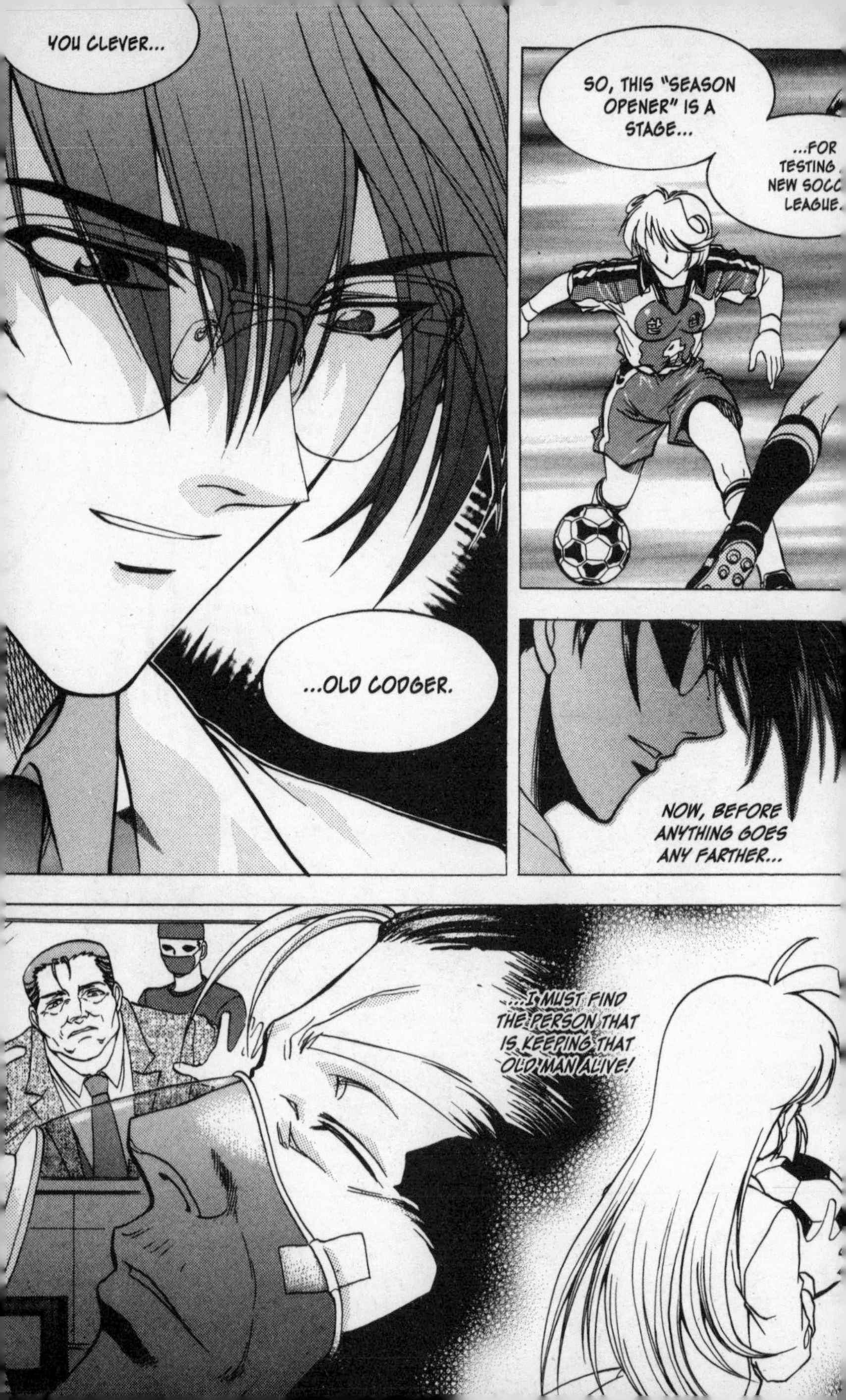
YOU CLEVER...
...OLD CODGER.
SO, THIS "SEASON OPENER" IS A STAGE...
...FOR TESTING NEW SOCC LEAGUE.
NOW, BEFORE ANYTHING GOES ANY FARTHER...
...I MUST FIND THE PERSON THAT IS KEEPING THAT OLD MAN ALIVE!

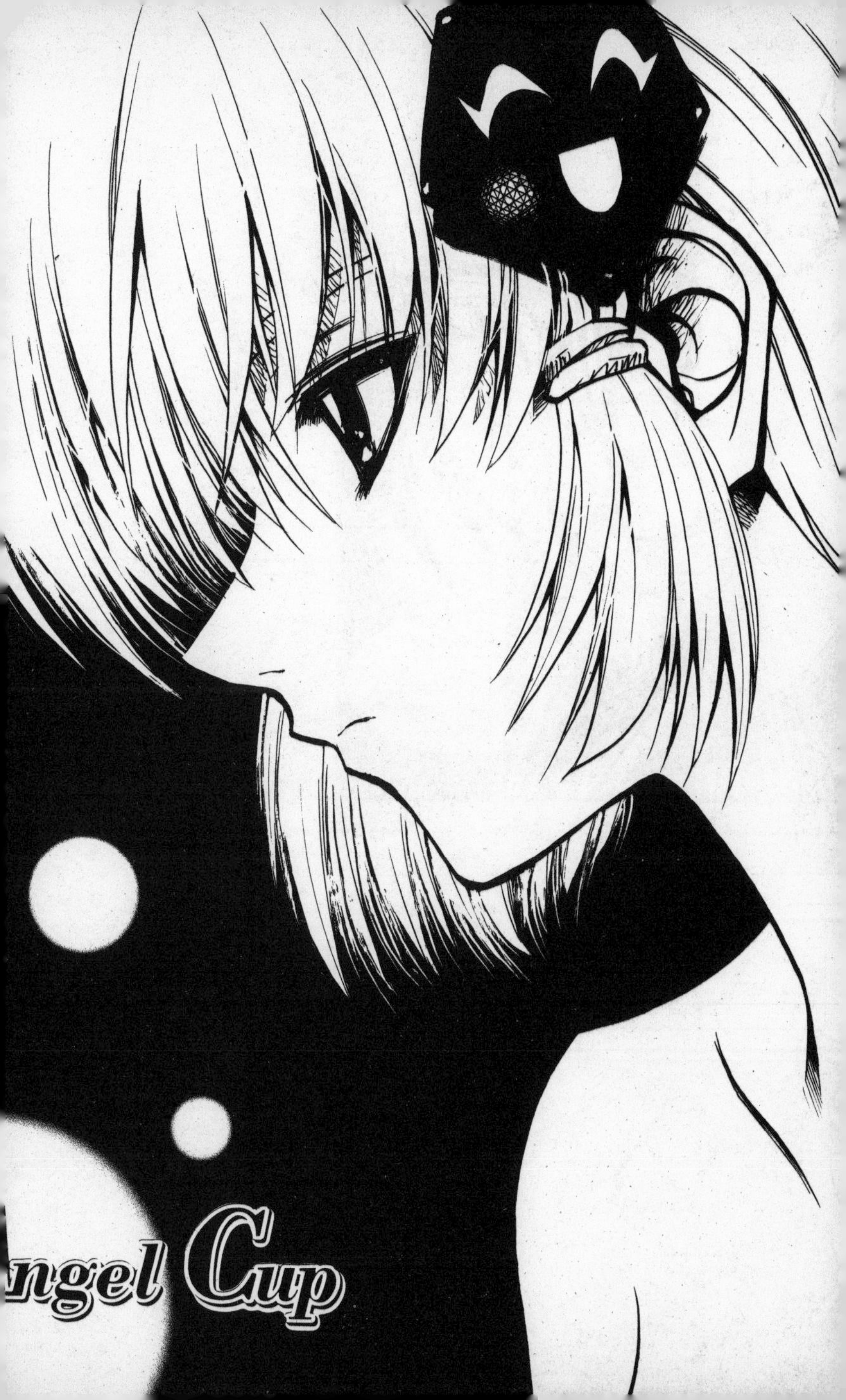
ngel Cup

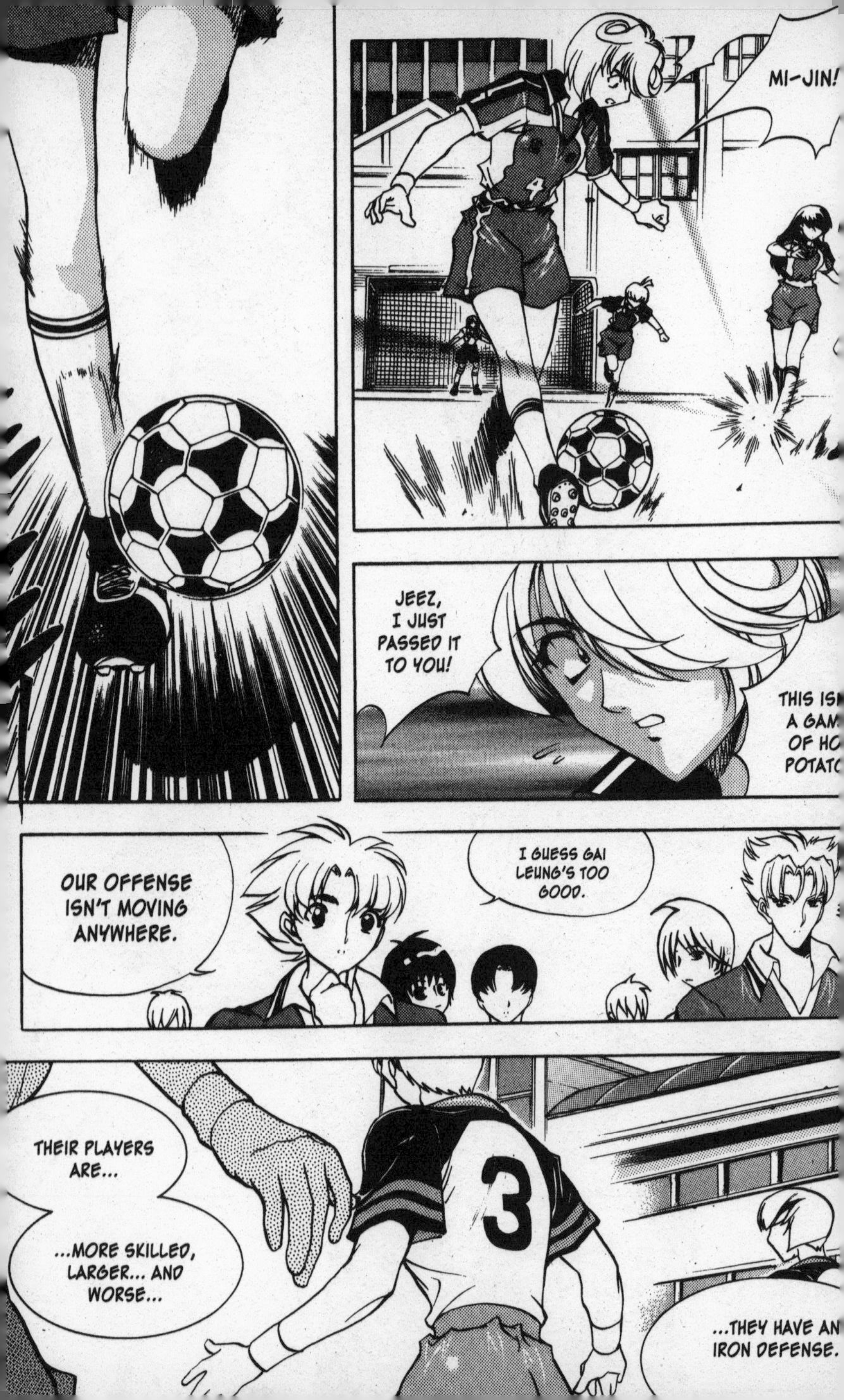
MI-JIN!
JEEZ, I JUST PASSED IT TO YOU!
THIS ISN A GAM OF HO POTATO
OUR OFFENSE ISN'T MOVING ANYWHERE.
I GUESS GAI LEUNG'S TOO GOOD.
THEIR PLAYERS ARE...
...MORE SKILLED, LARGER... AND WORSE...
...THEY HAVE AN IRON DEFENSE.

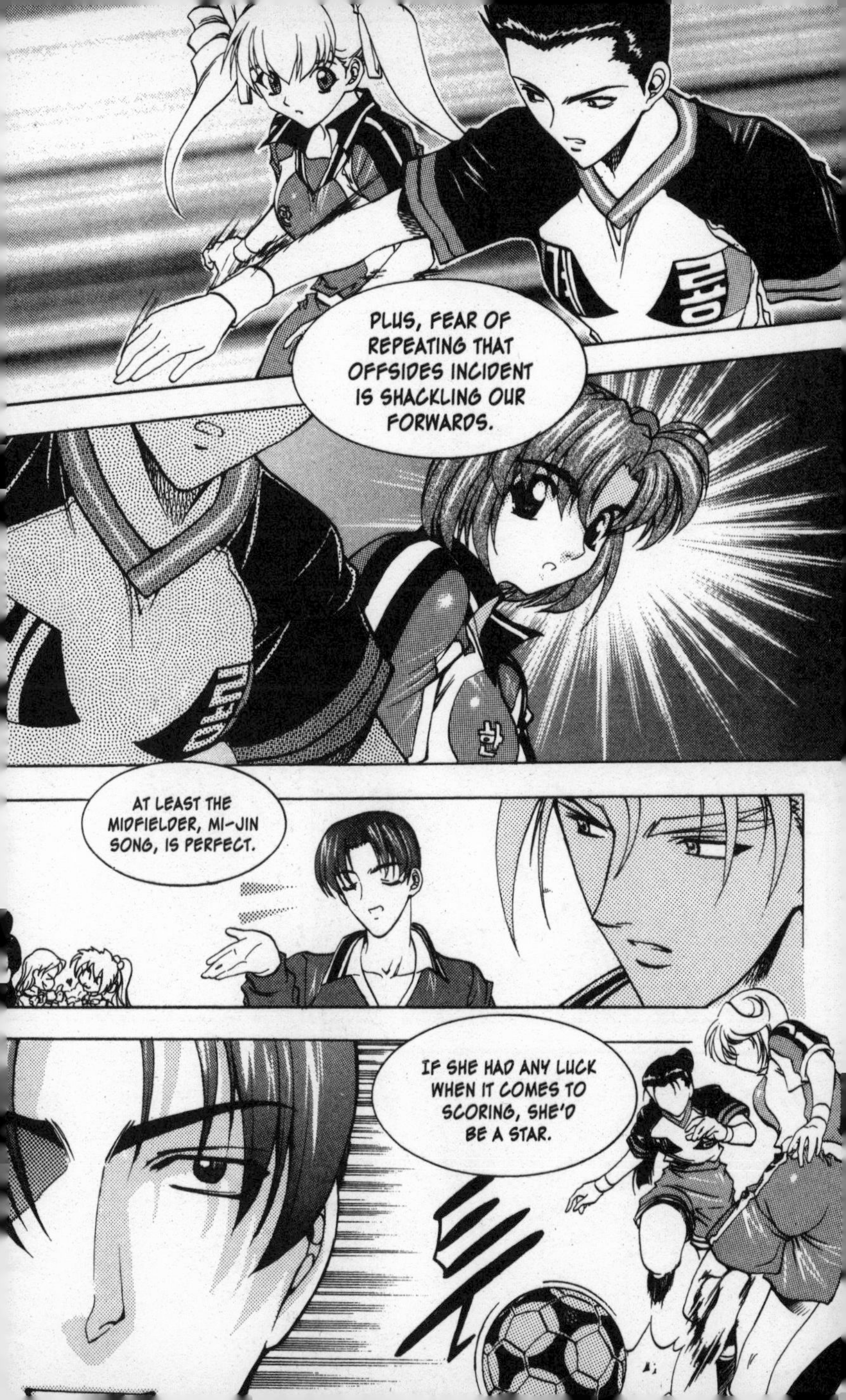
PLUS, FEAR OF REPEATING THAT OFFSIDES INCIDENT IS SHACKLING OUR FORWARDS.
AT LEAST THE MIDFIELDER, MI-JIN SONG, IS PERFECT.
IF SHE HAD ANY LUCK WHEN IT COMES TO SCORING, SHE'D BE A STAR.

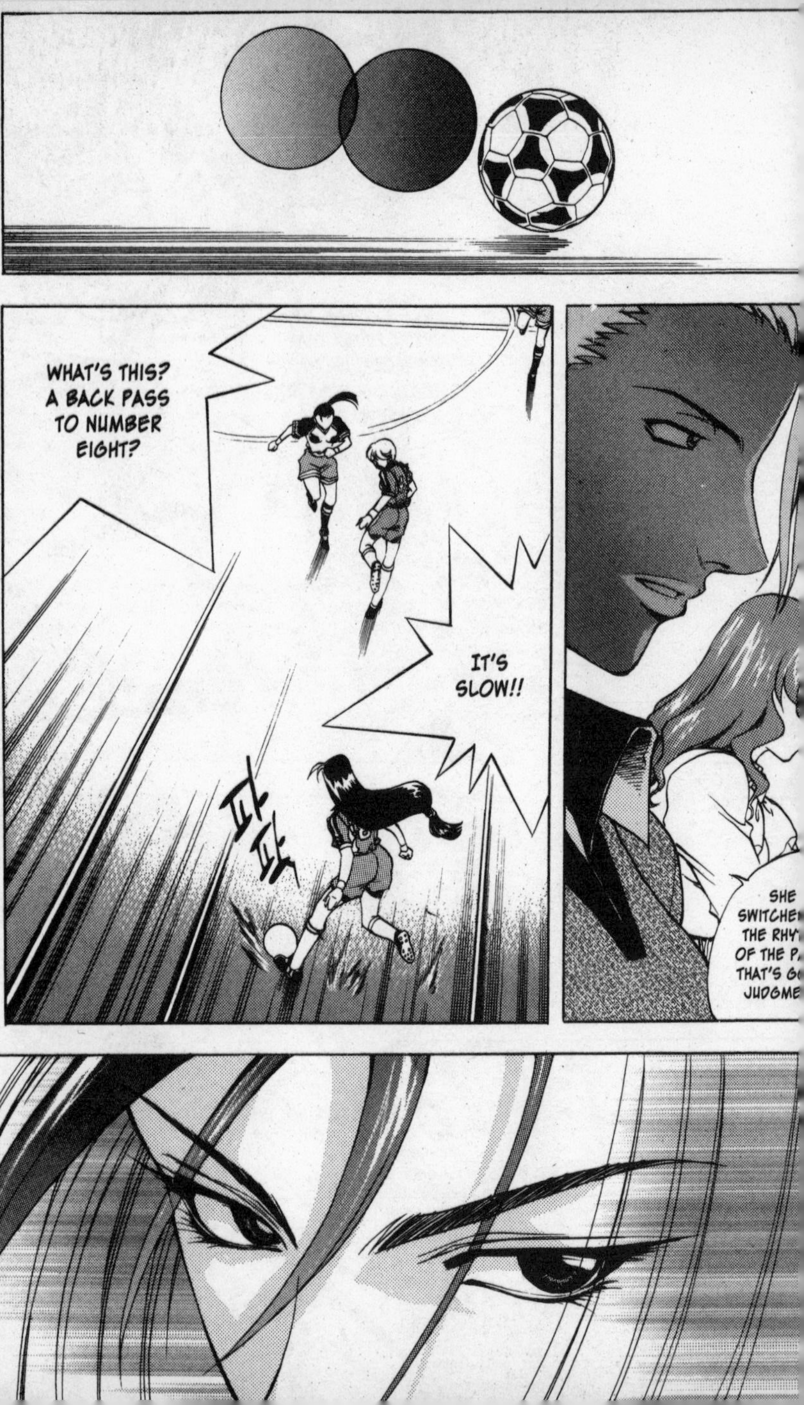
WHAT'S THIS? A BACK PASS TO NUMBER EIGHT?
IT'S SLOW!!
SHE SWITCHE THE RHY OF THE PA THAT'S G JUDGME

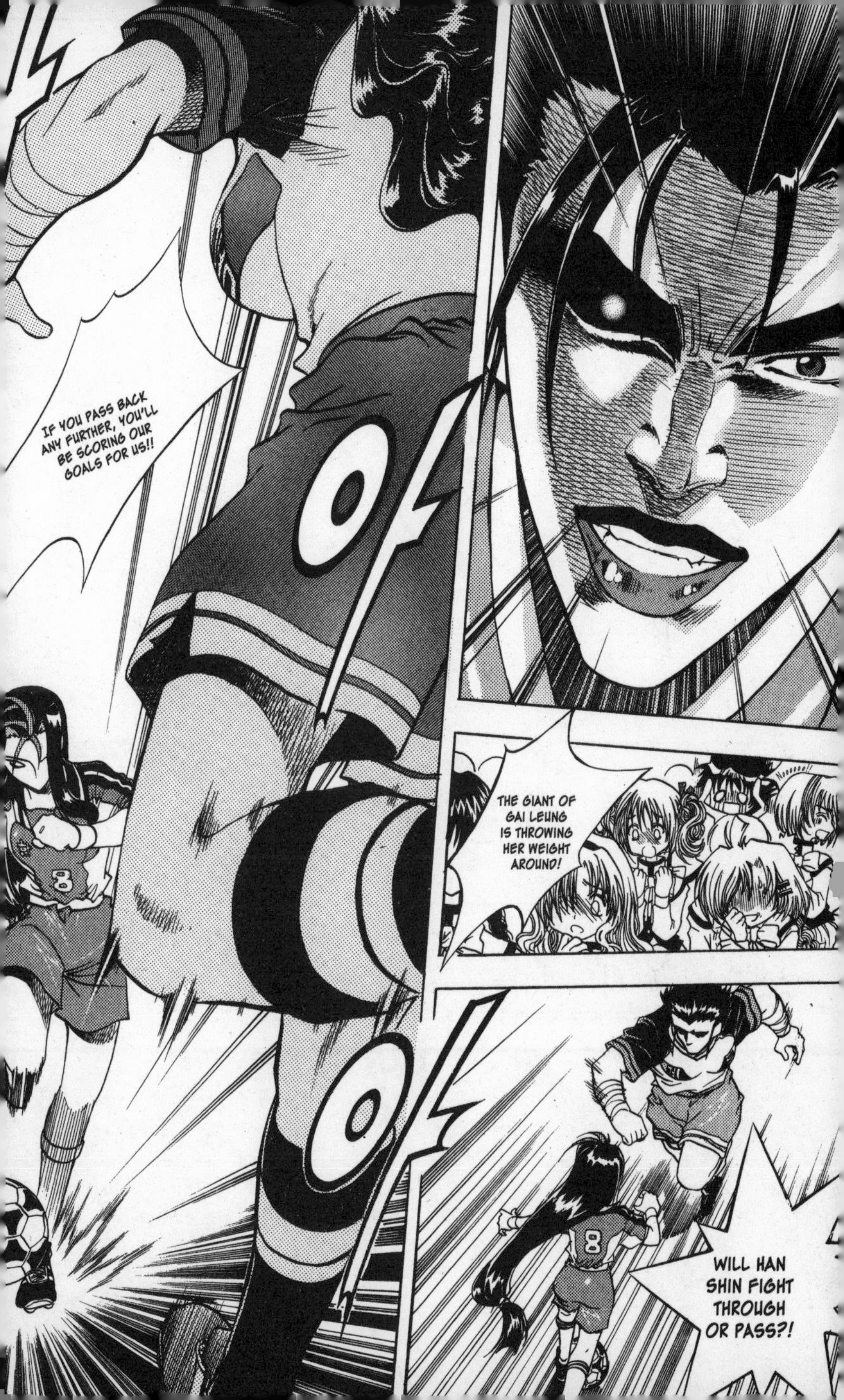
IF YOU PASS BACK ANY FURTHER, YOU'LL BE SCORING OUR GOALS FOR US!!
THE GIANT OF GAI LEUNG IS THROWING HER WEIGHT AROUND!
Noooooo!!
WILL HAN SHIN FIGHT THROUGH OR PASS?!

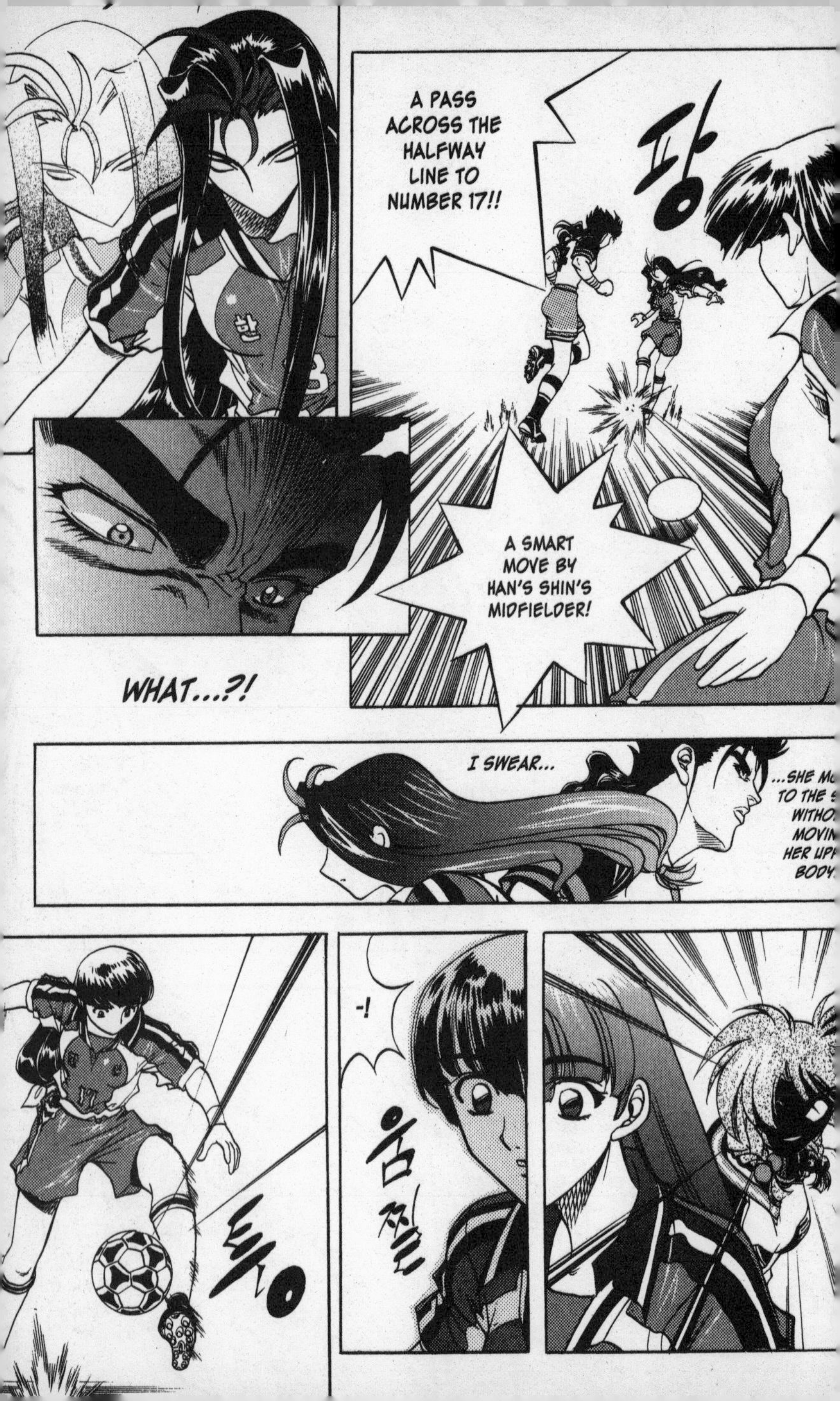
WHAT...?!
A PASS ACROSS THE HALFWAY LINE TO NUMBER 17!!
팡
A SMART MOVE BY HAN'S SHIN'S MIDFIELDER!
I SWEAR...
...SHE MO TO THE S WITHO MOVIN HER UPP BODY.
-!
움찔

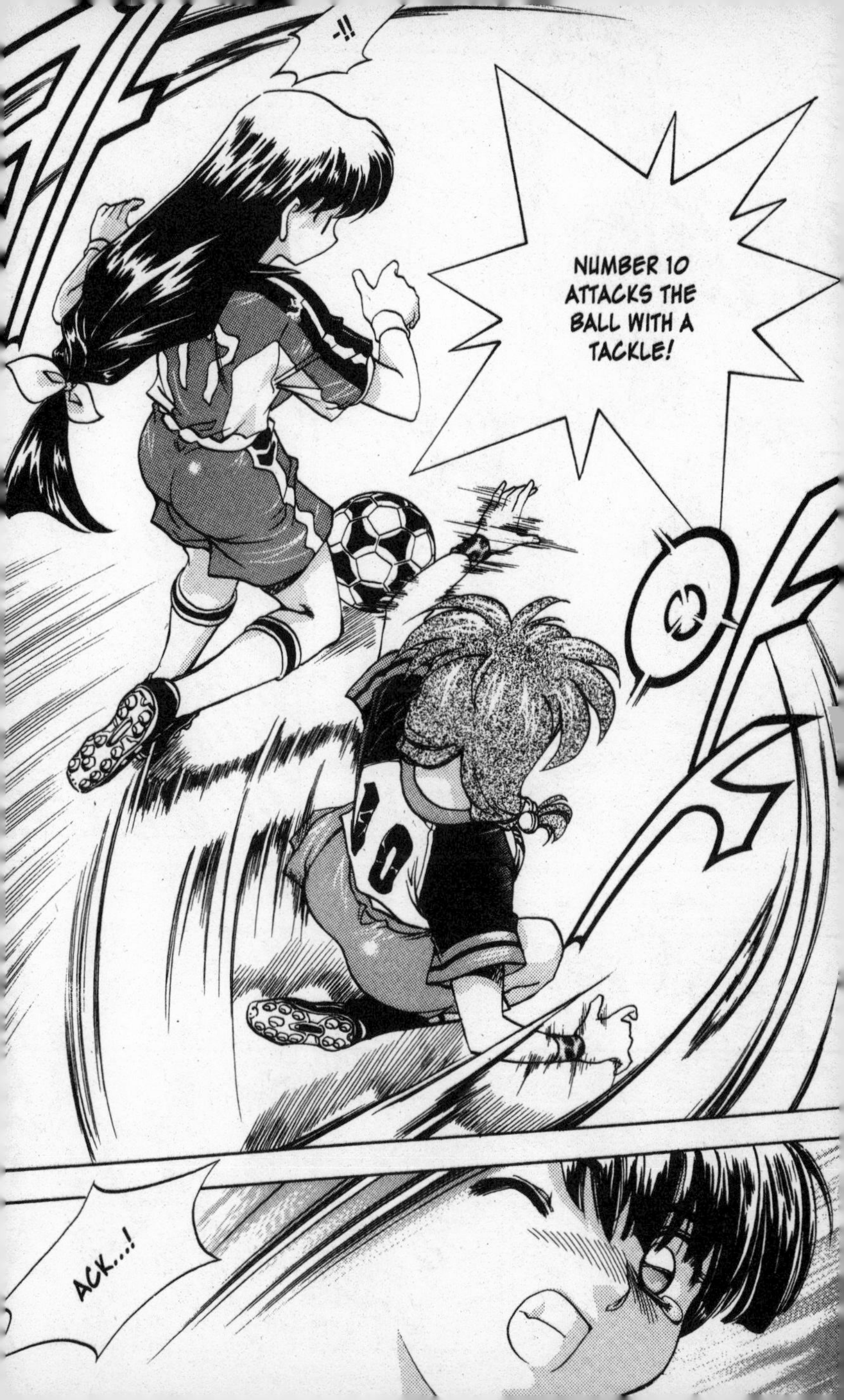
-!!
NUMBER 10 ATTACKS THE BALL WITH A TACKLE!
ACK...!

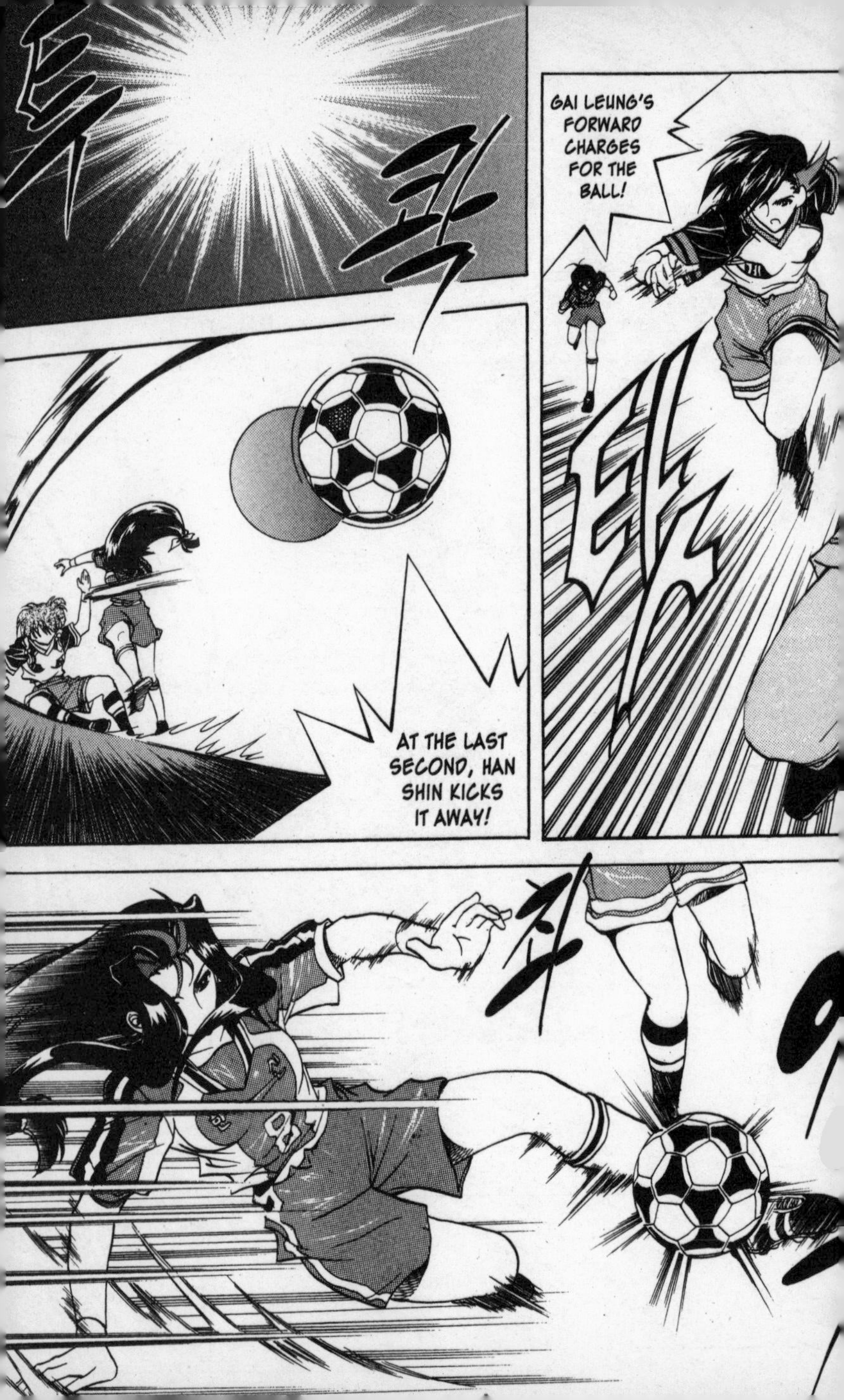

AT THE LAST SECOND, HAN SHIN KICKS IT AWAY!
GAI LEUNG'S FORWARD CHARGES FOR THE BALL!

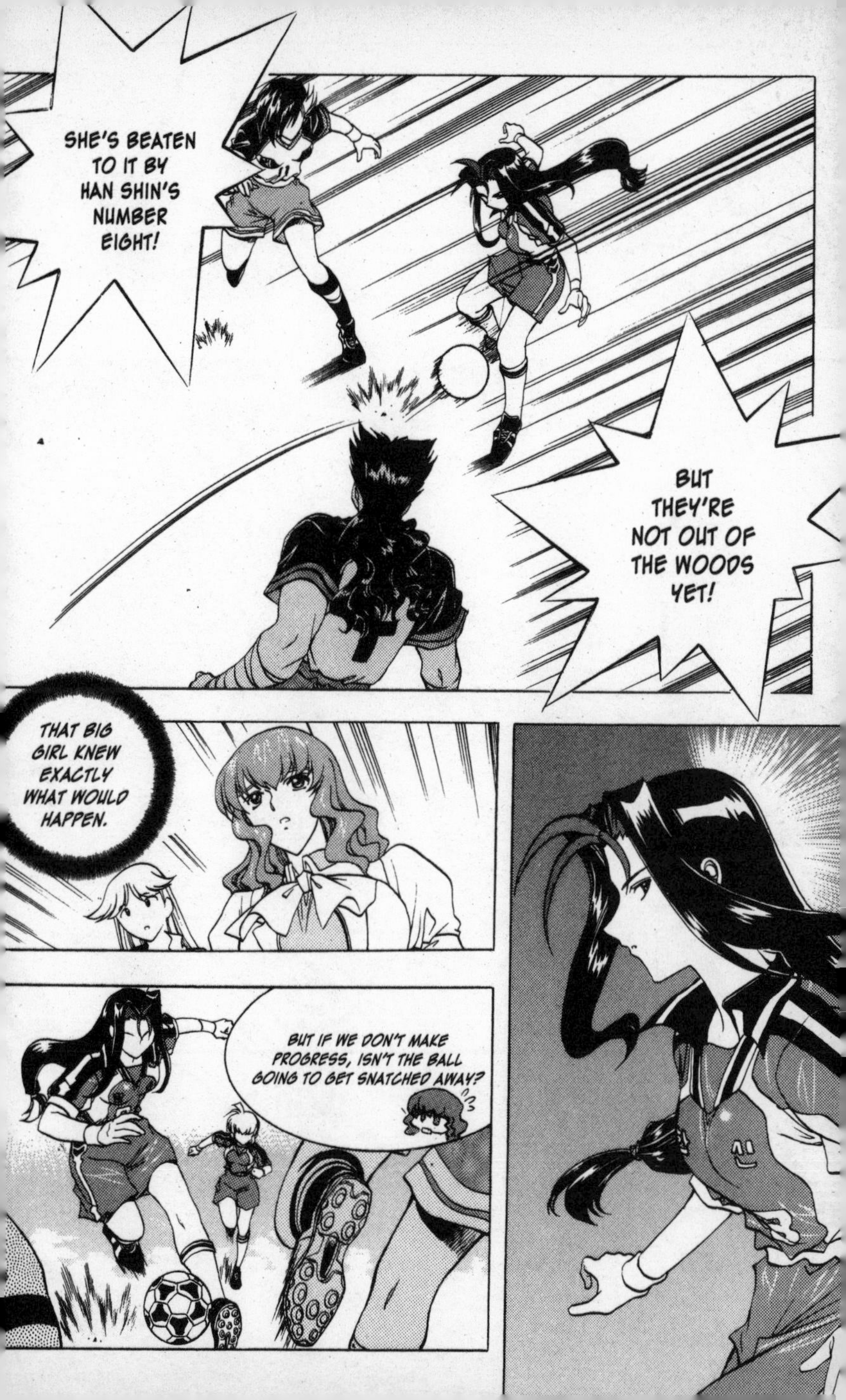
SHE'S BEATEN TO IT BY HAN SHIN'S NUMBER EIGHT!
BUT THEY'RE NOT OUT OF THE WOODS YET!
THAT BIG GIRL KNEW EXACTLY WHAT WOULD HAPPEN.
BUT IF WE DON'T MAKE PROGRESS, ISN'T THE BALL GOING TO GET SNATCHED AWAY?

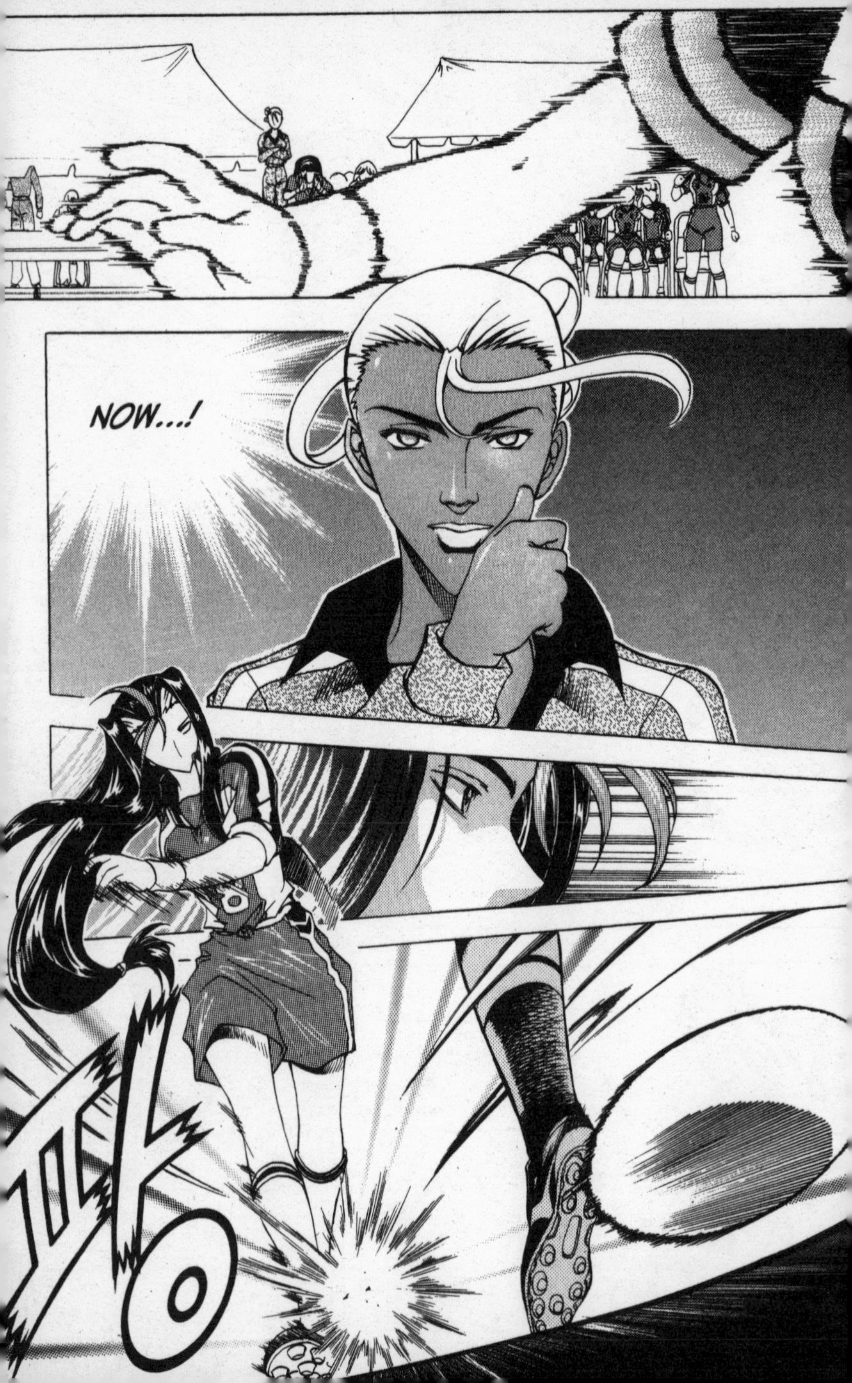
NOW...!

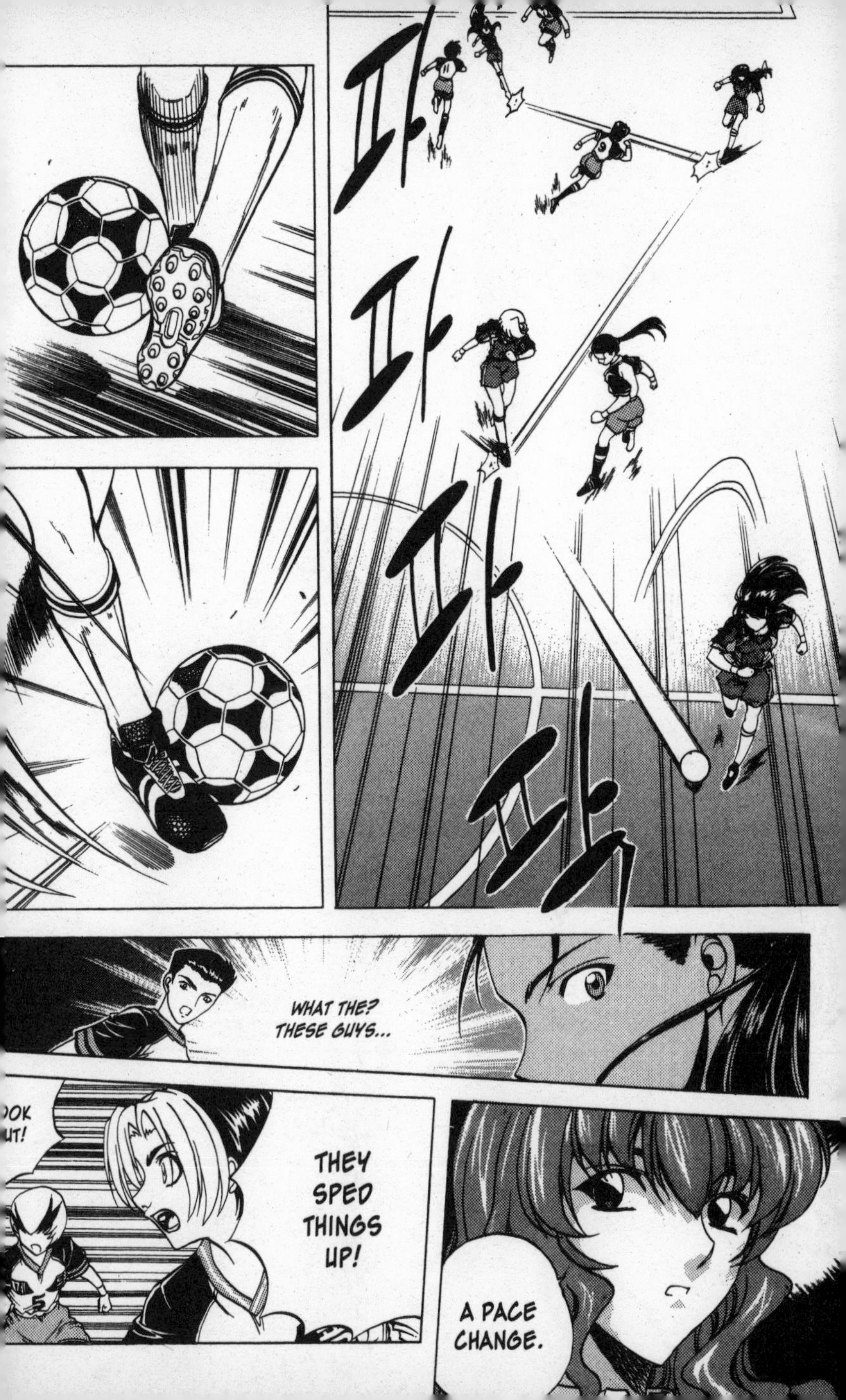
파파파팟
WHAT THE? THESE GUYS...
THEY SPED THINGS UP!
A PACE CHANGE.

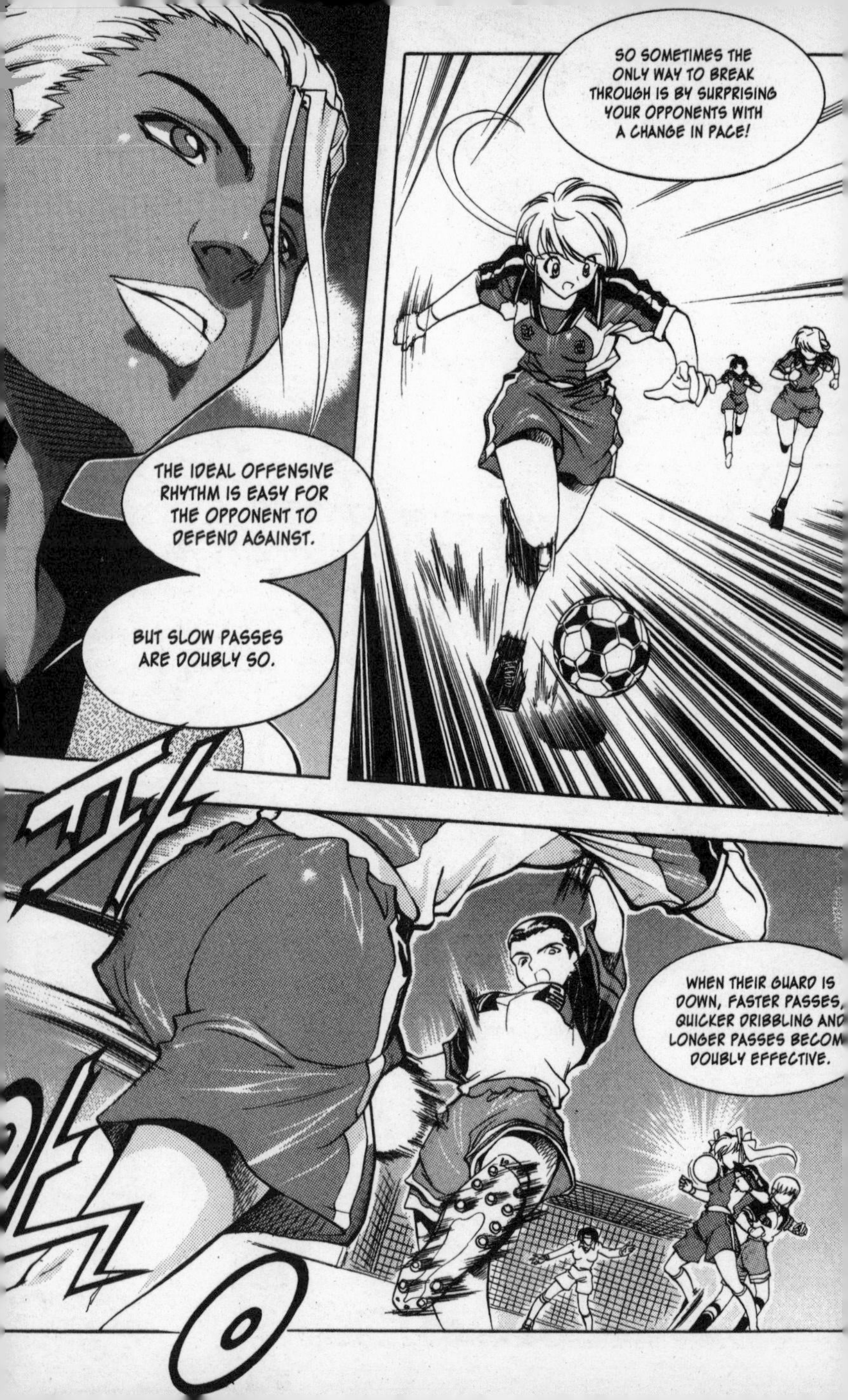
THE IDEAL OFFENSIVE RHYTHM IS EASY FOR THE OPPONENT TO DEFEND AGAINST.
BUT SLOW PASSES ARE DOUBLY SO.
SO SOMETIMES THE ONLY WAY TO BREAK THROUGH IS BY SURPRISING YOUR OPPONENTS WITH A CHANGE IN PACE!
WHEN THEIR GUARD IS DOWN, FASTER PASSES, QUICKER DRIBBLING AND LONGER PASSES BECOM DOUBLY EFFECTIVE.

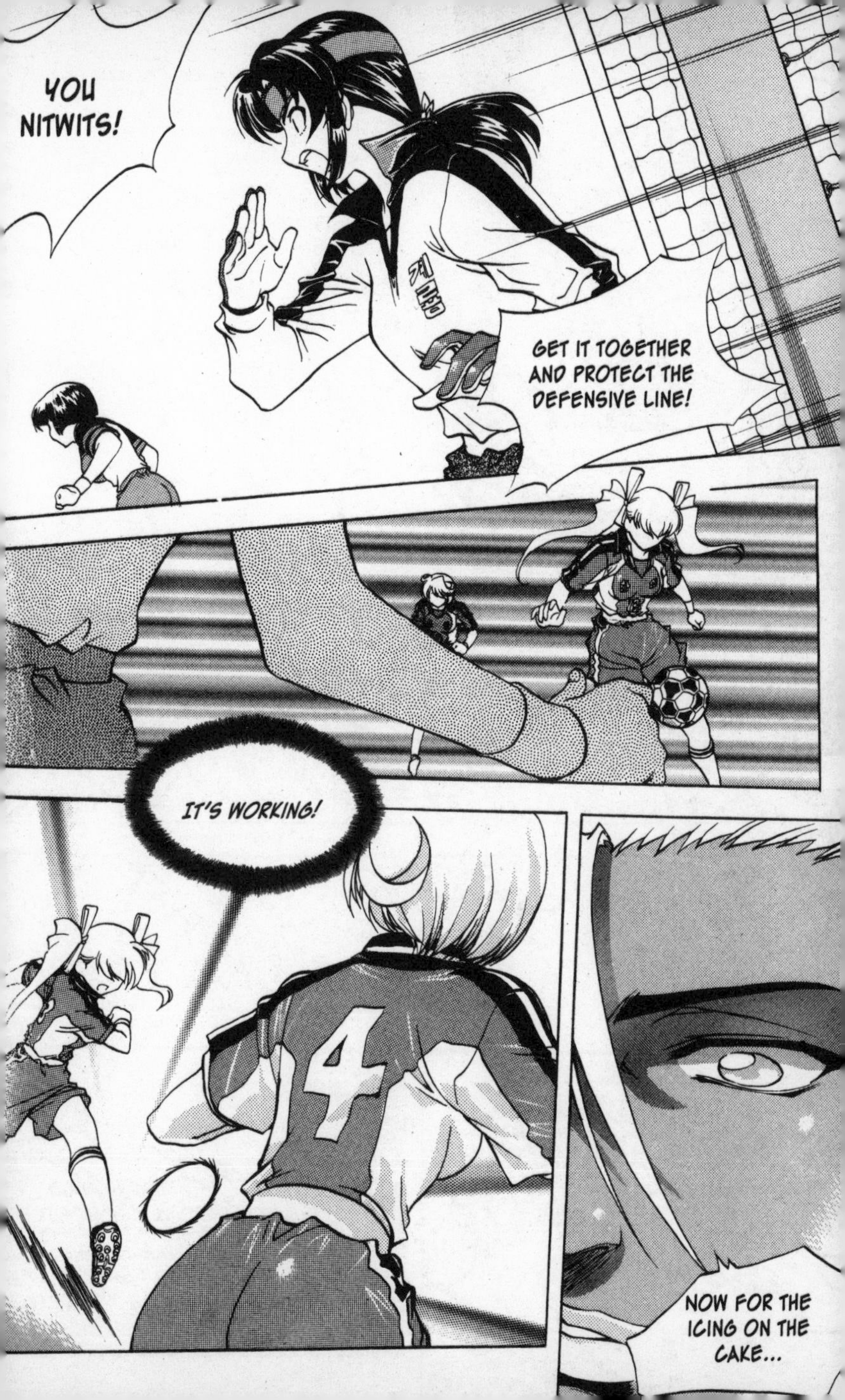
YOU NITWITS!
GET IT TOGETHER AND PROTECT THE DEFENSIVE LINE!
IT'S WORKING!
NOW FOR THE ICING ON THE CAKE...

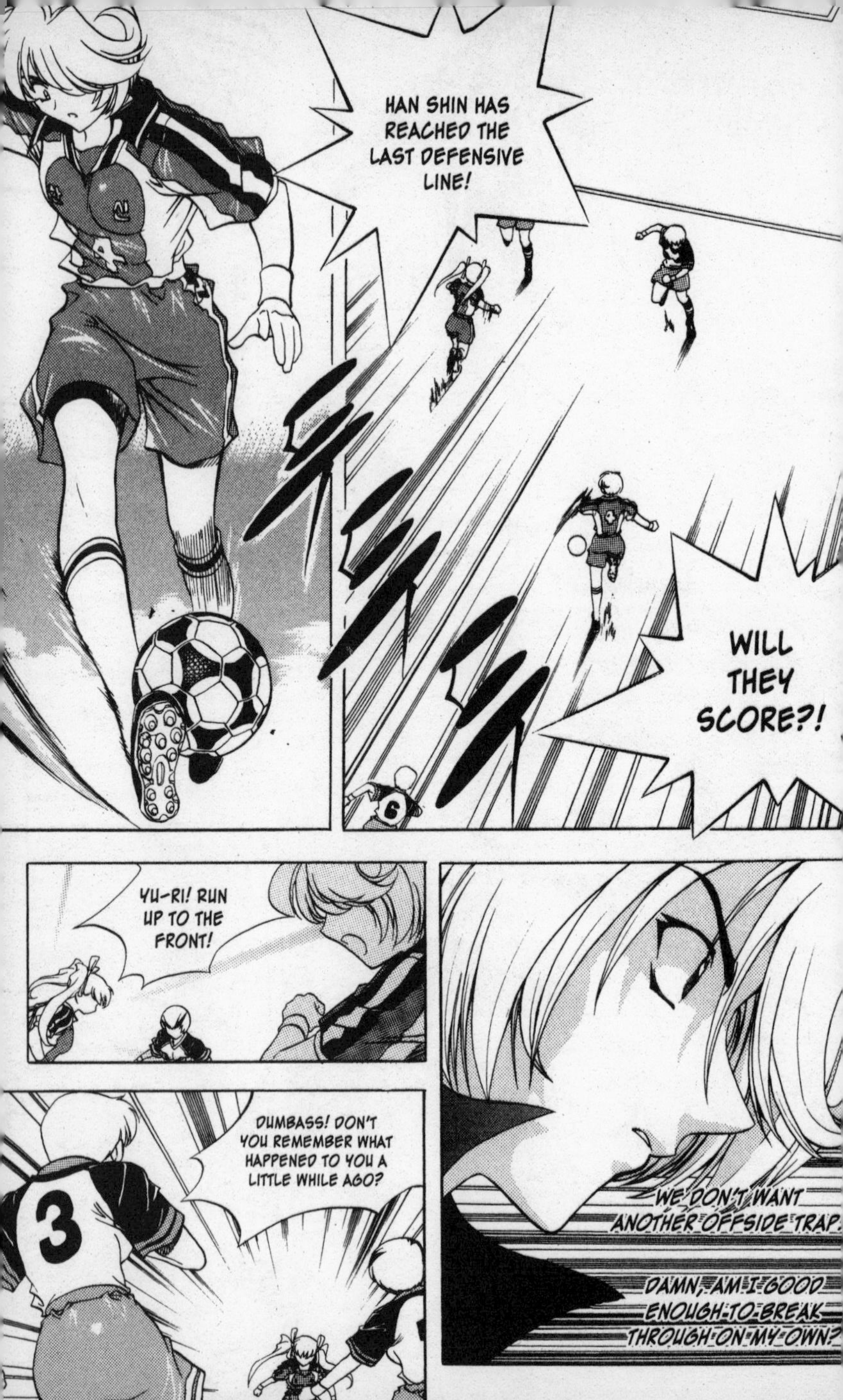
HAN SHIN HAS REACHED THE LAST DEFENSIVE LINE!
WILL THEY SCORE?!
YU-RI! RUN UP TO THE FRONT!
WE DON'T WANT ANOTHER OFFSIDE TRAP.
DAMN, AM I GOOD ENOUGH TO BREAK THROUGH ON MY OWN?
DUMBASS! DON'T YOU REMEMBER WHAT HAPPENED TO YOU A LITTLE WHILE AGO?

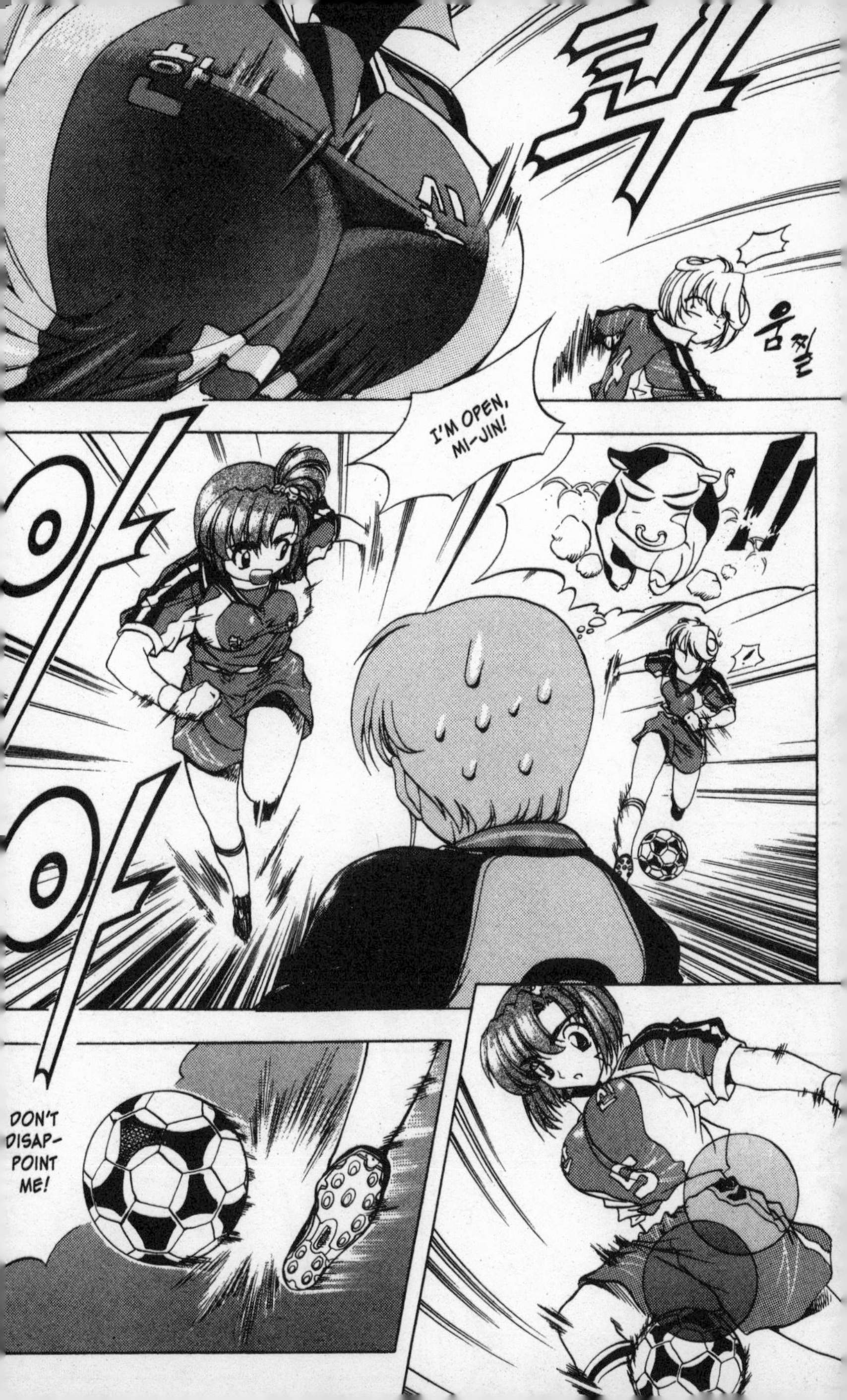
움찔
I'M OPEN, MI-JIN!
DON'T DISAP-POINT ME!

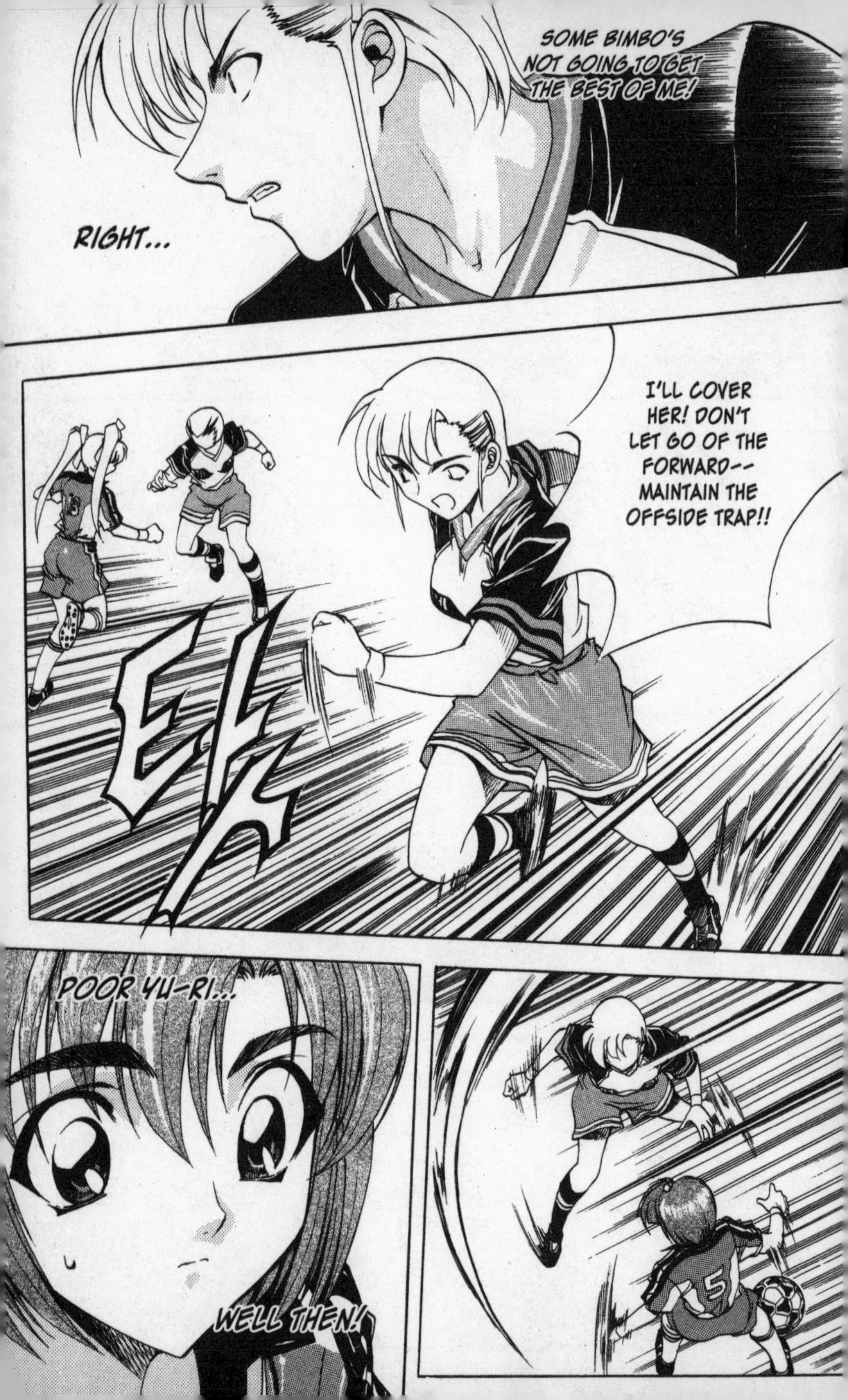
SOME BIMBO'S NOT GOING TO GET THE BEST OF ME!
RIGHT...
I'LL COVER HER! DON'T LET GO OF THE FORWARD--MAINTAIN THE OFFSIDE TRAP!!
POOR YU-RI...
WELL THEN!

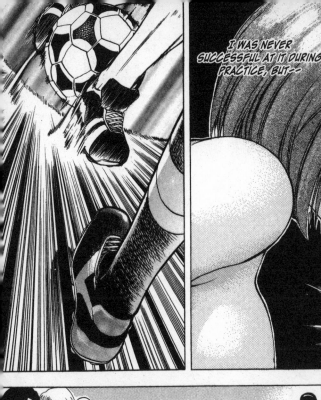

I WAS NEVER SUCCESSFUL AT IT DURING PRACTICE, BUT--

-!!

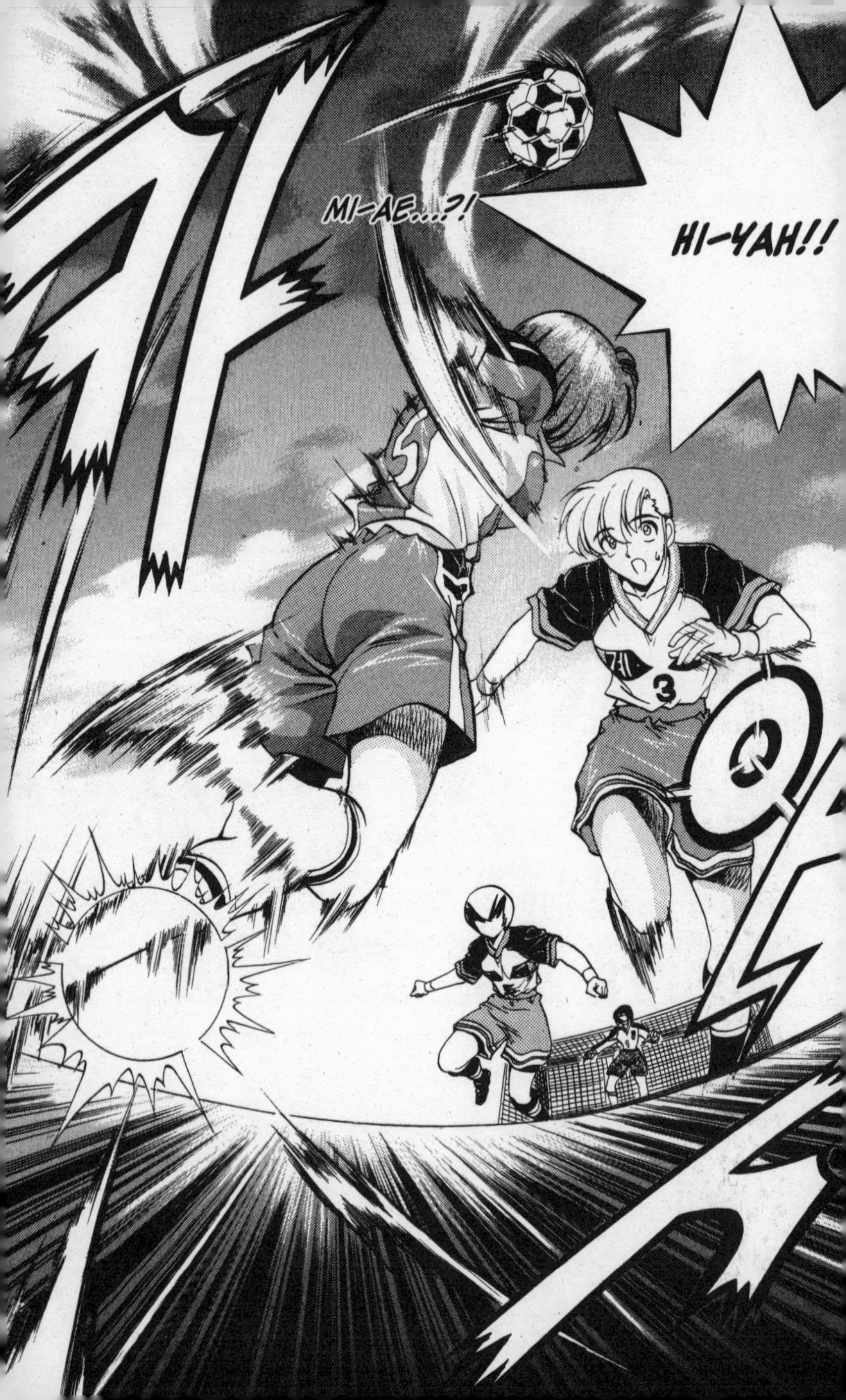
MI-AE...?!
HI-YAH!!

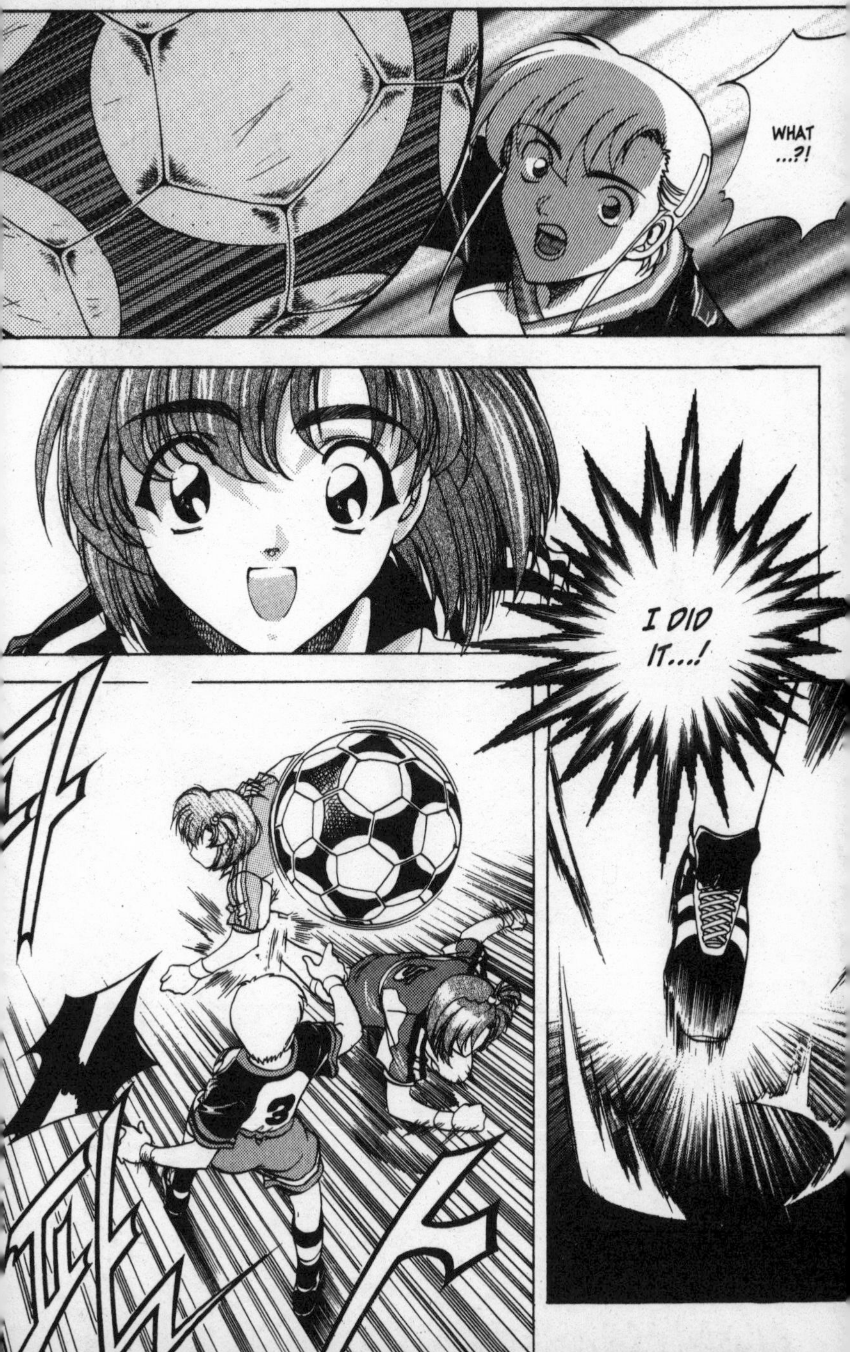
WHAT ...?!
I DID IT...!

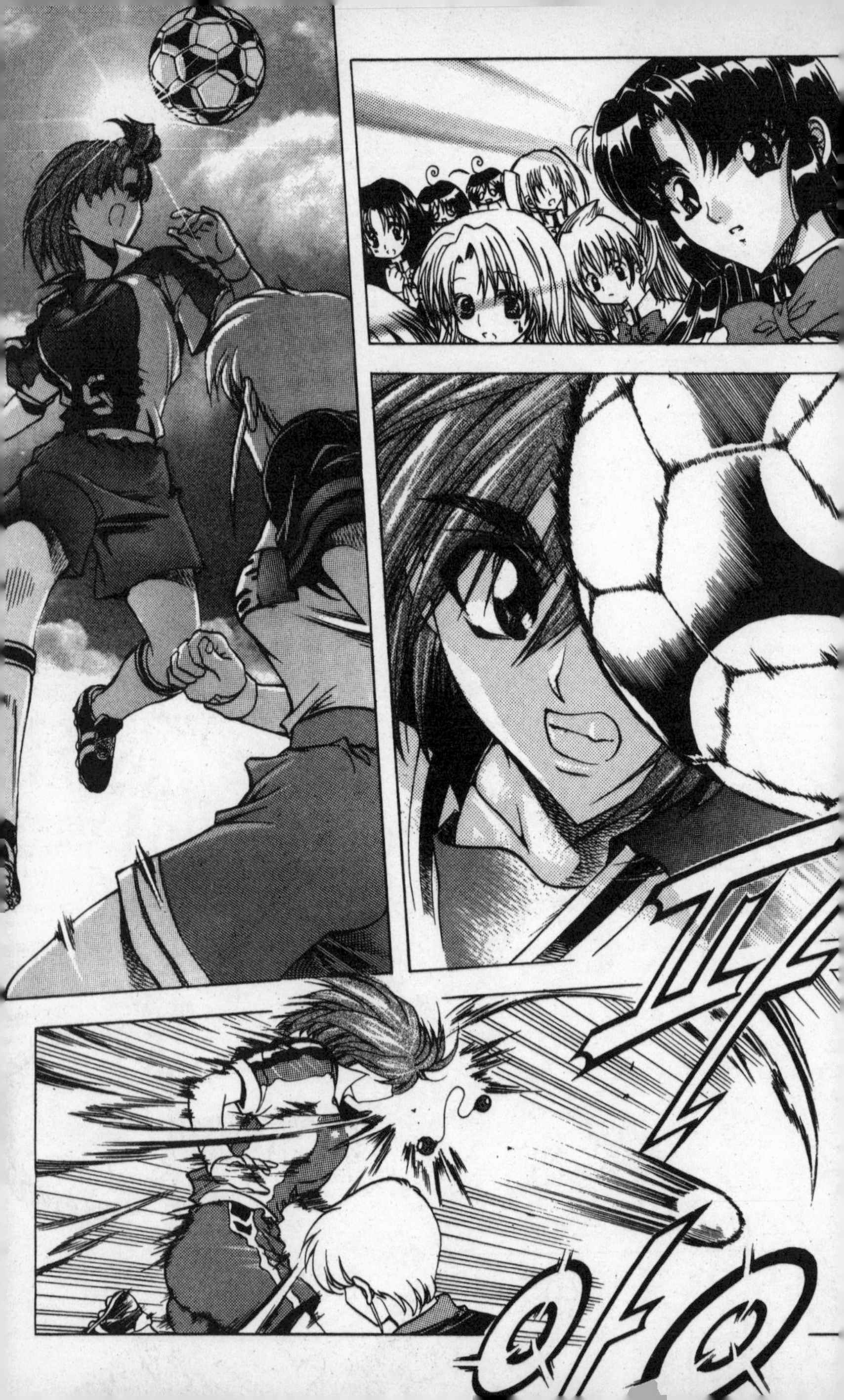

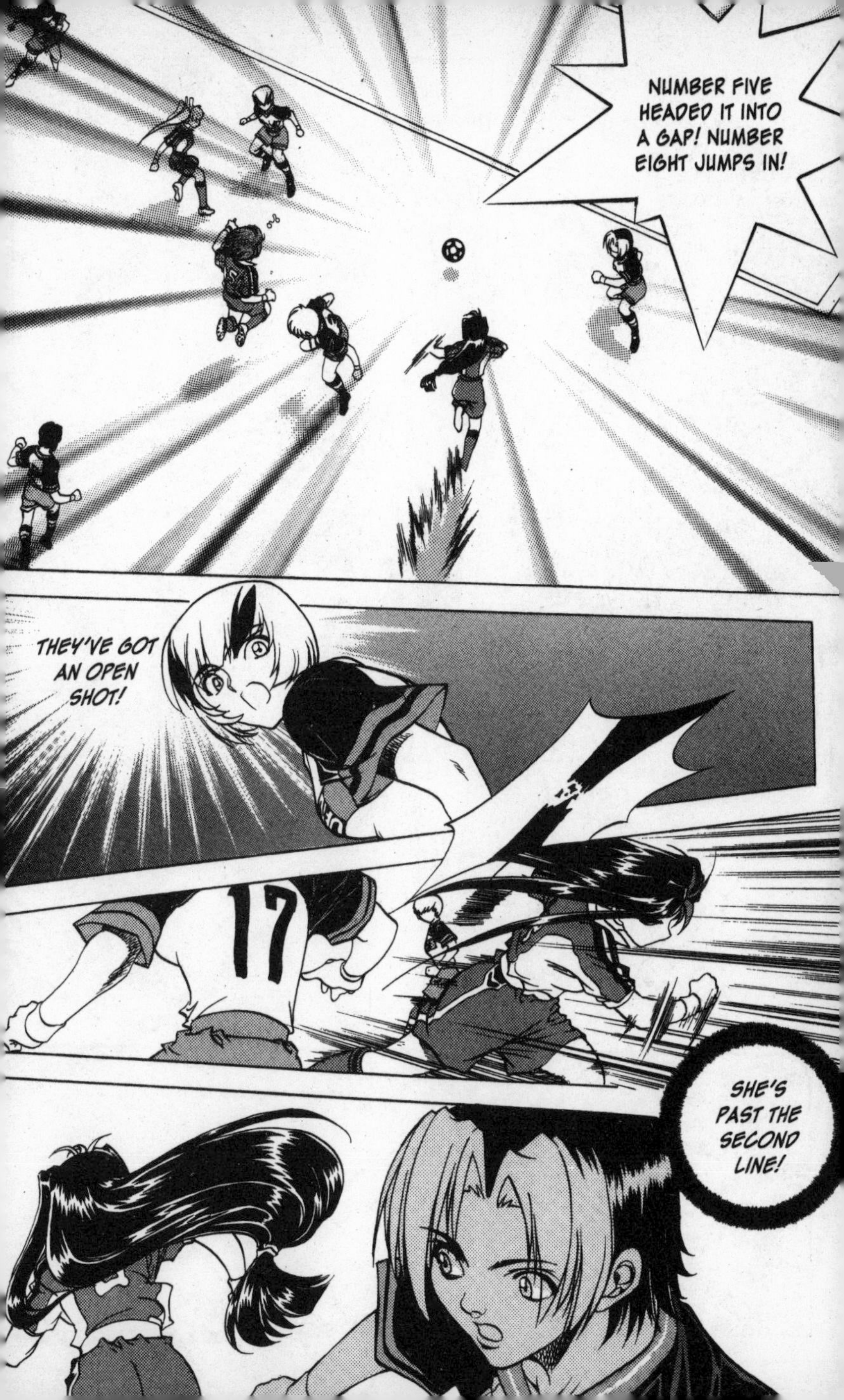
NUMBER FIVE HEADED IT INTO A GAP! NUMBER EIGHT JUMPS IN!
THEY'VE GOT AN OPEN SHOT!
17
SHE'S PAST THE SECOND LINE!

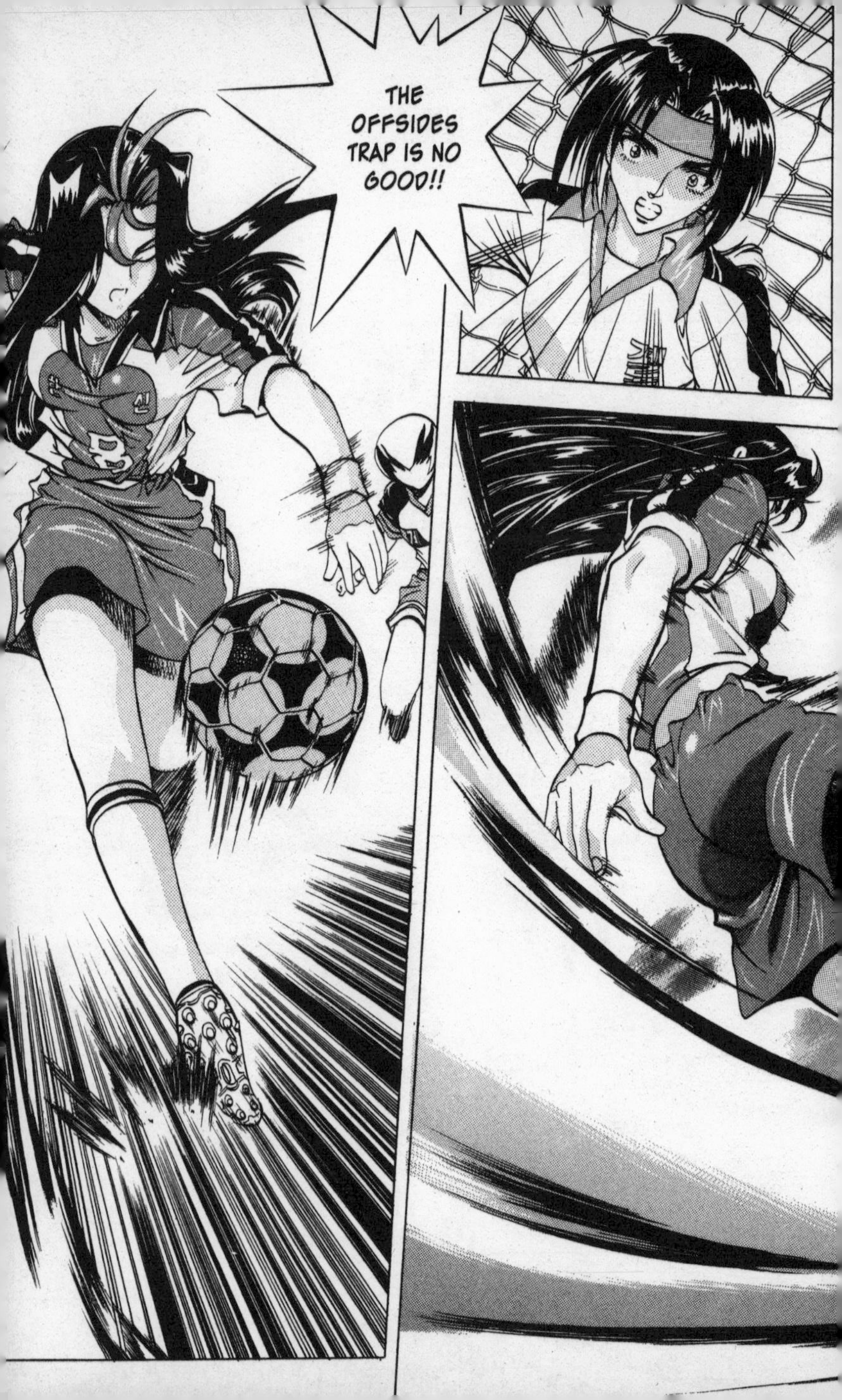
THE OFFSIDES TRAP IS NO GOOD!!

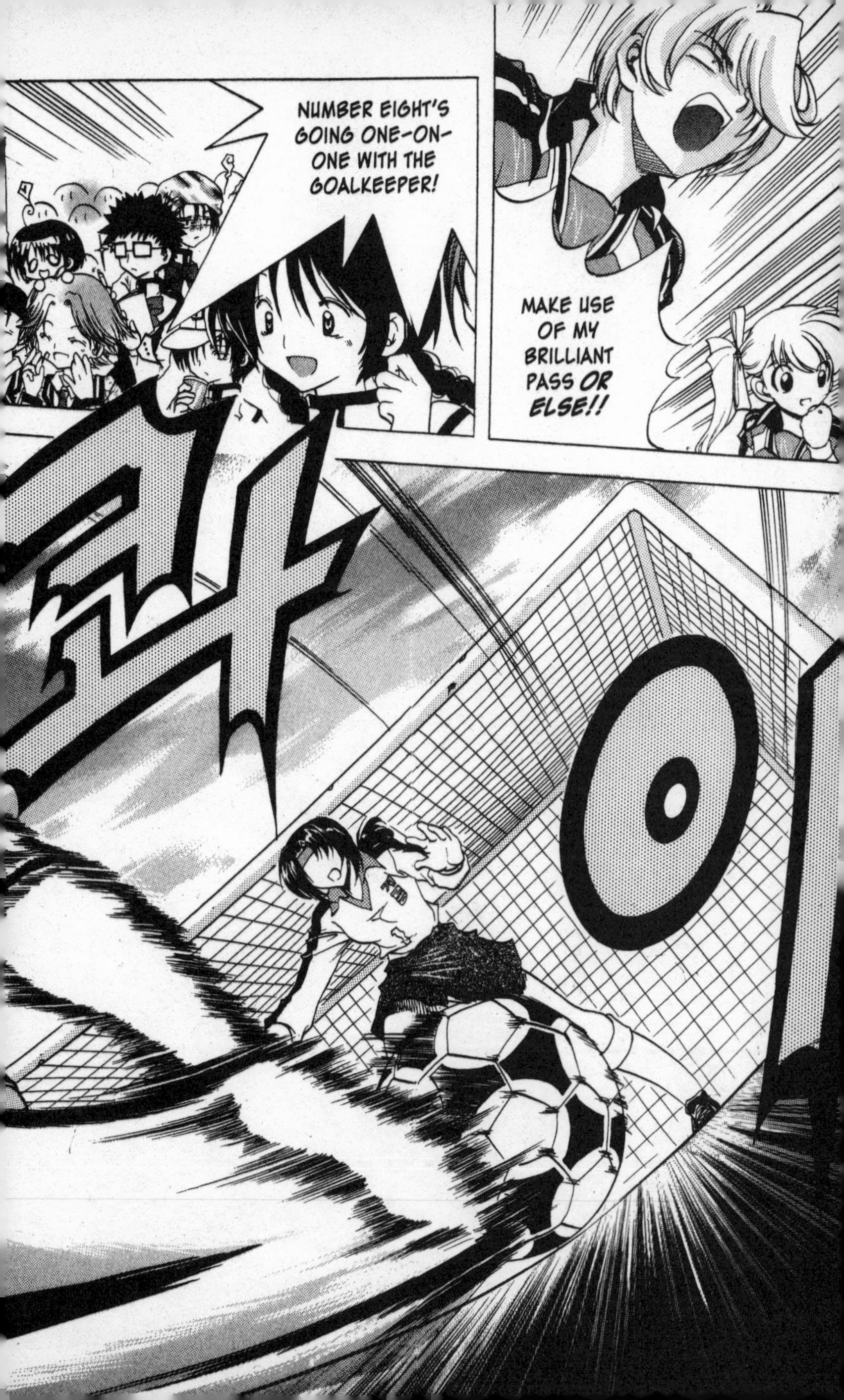
NUMBER EIGHT'S GOING ONE-ON-ONE WITH THE GOALKEEPER!
MAKE USE OF MY BRILLIANT PASS *OR ELSE!!*

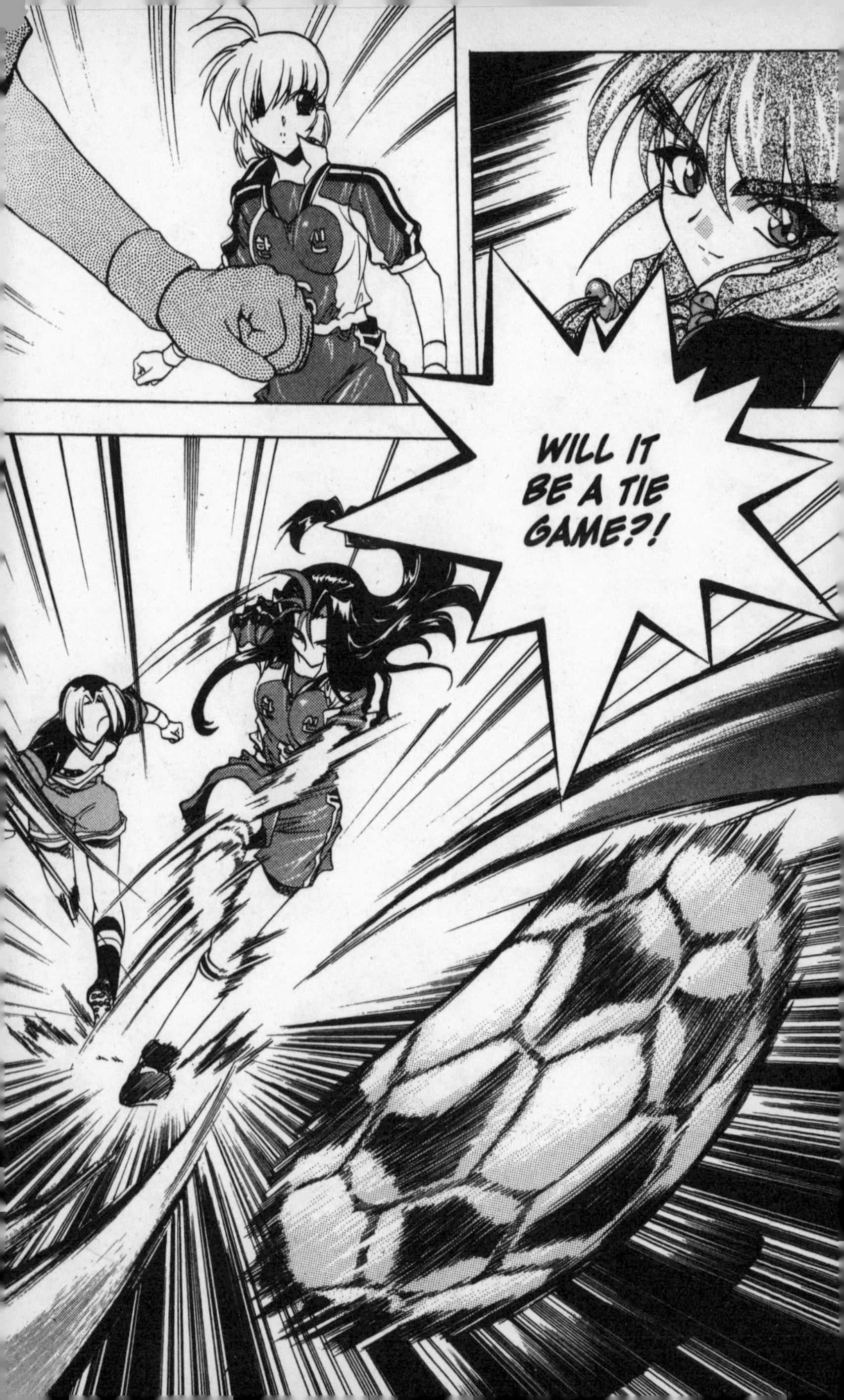
WILL IT BE A TIE GAME?!

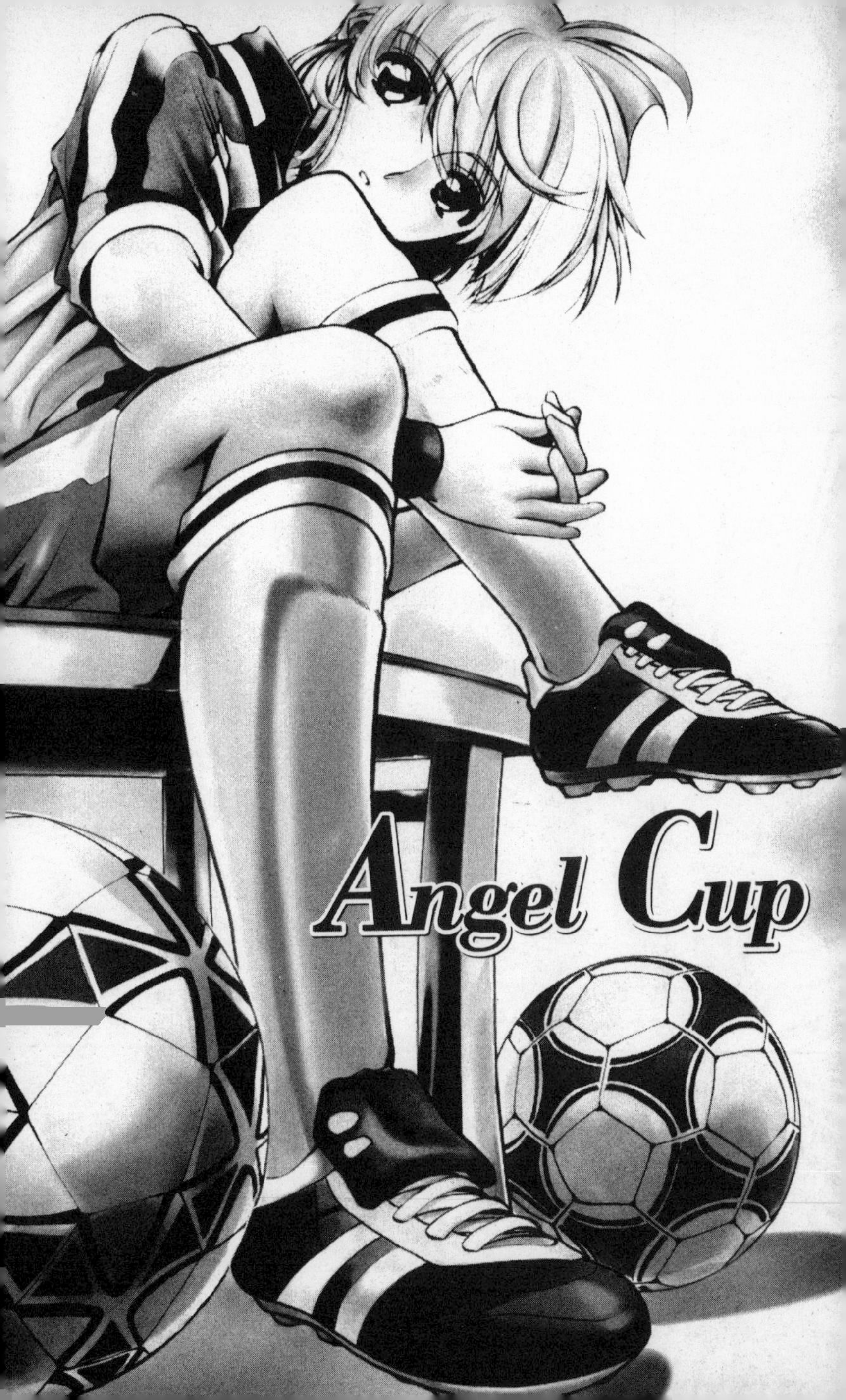
Angel Cup

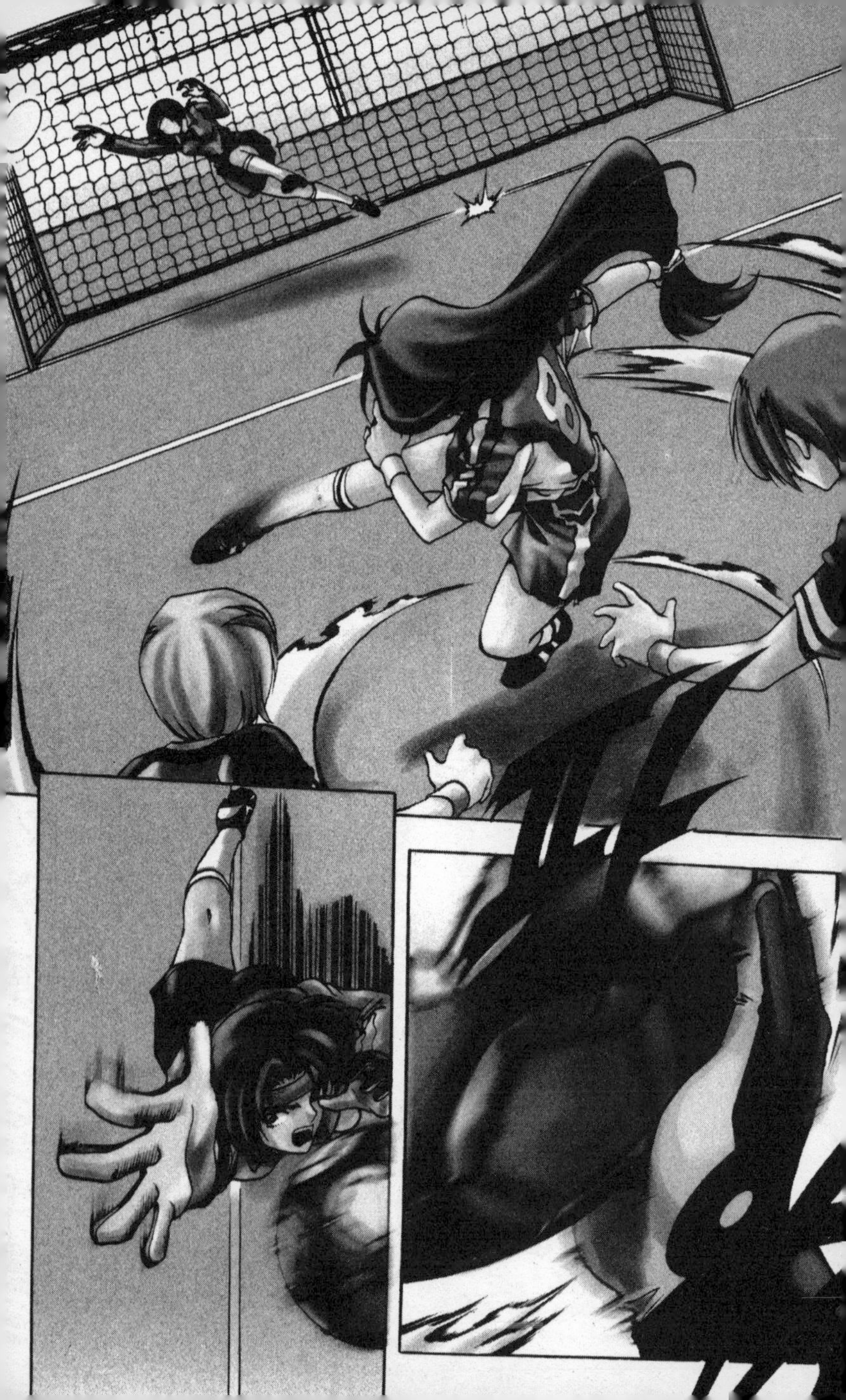

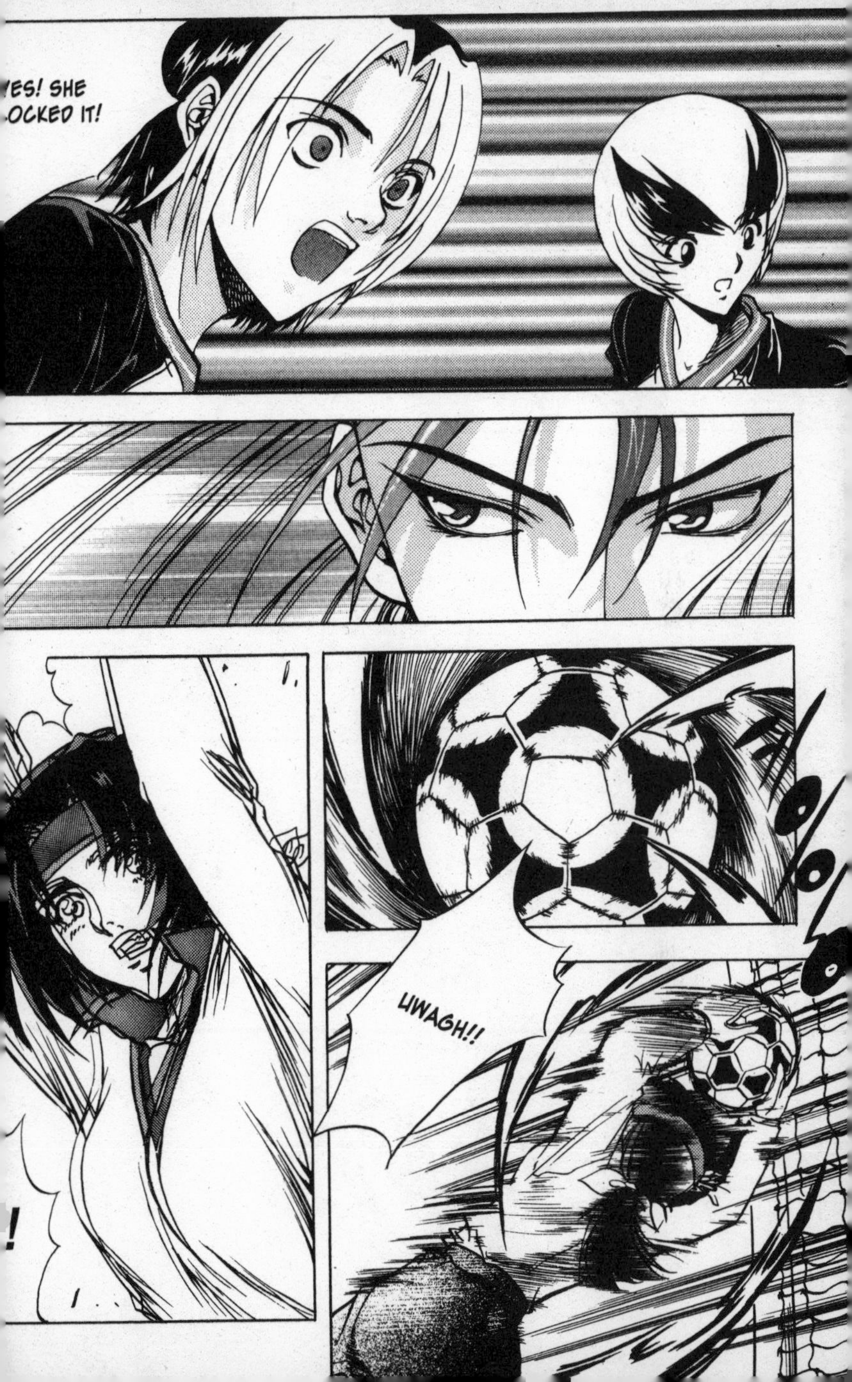

YES! SHE
BLOCKED IT!
UWAGH!!

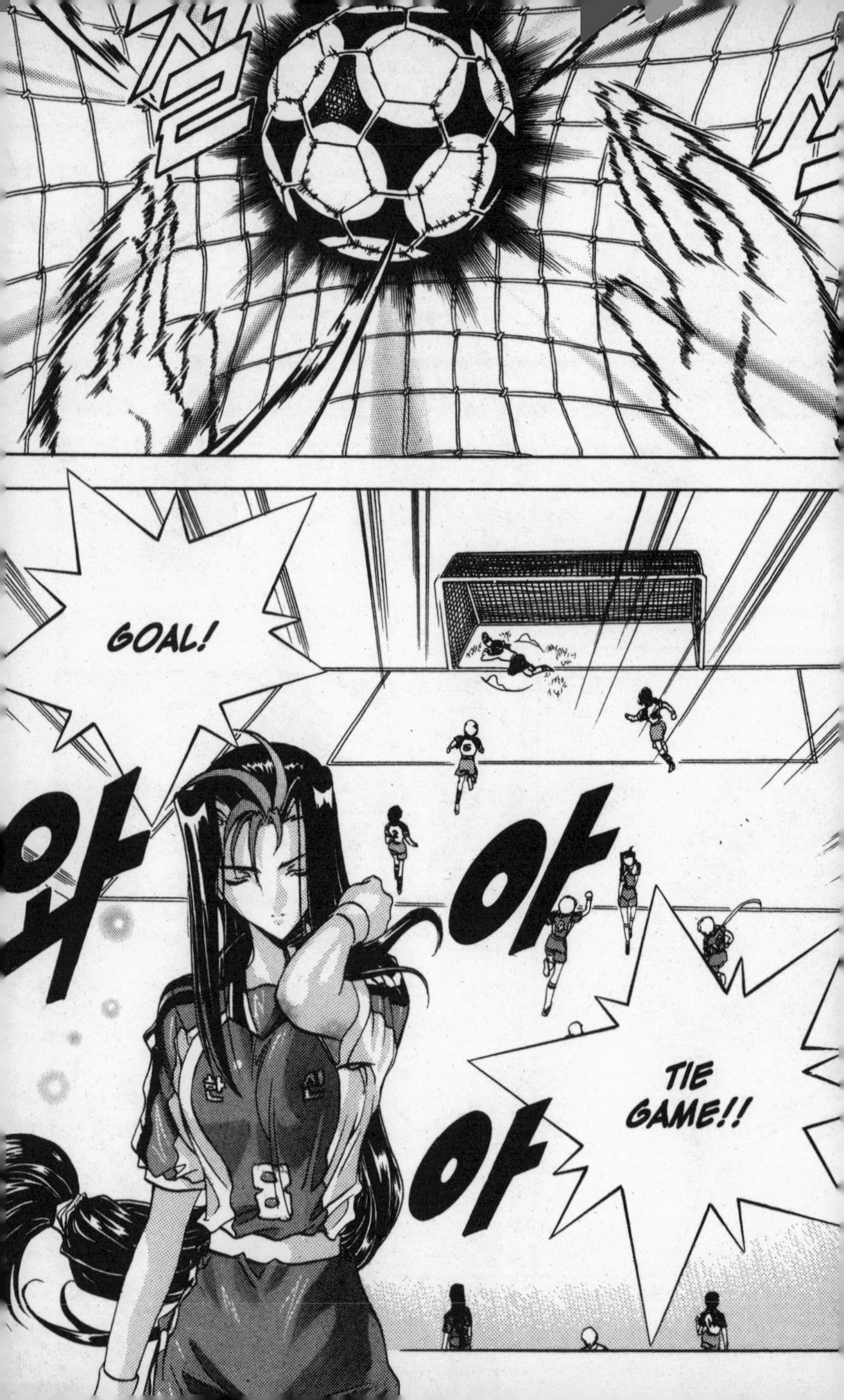
GOAL!
와아아
TIE GAME!!

SHIN-AE!

WHAT HAPPENED? HEY.

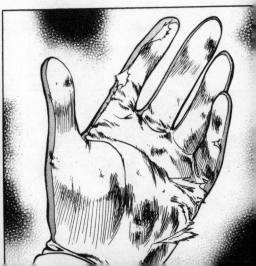

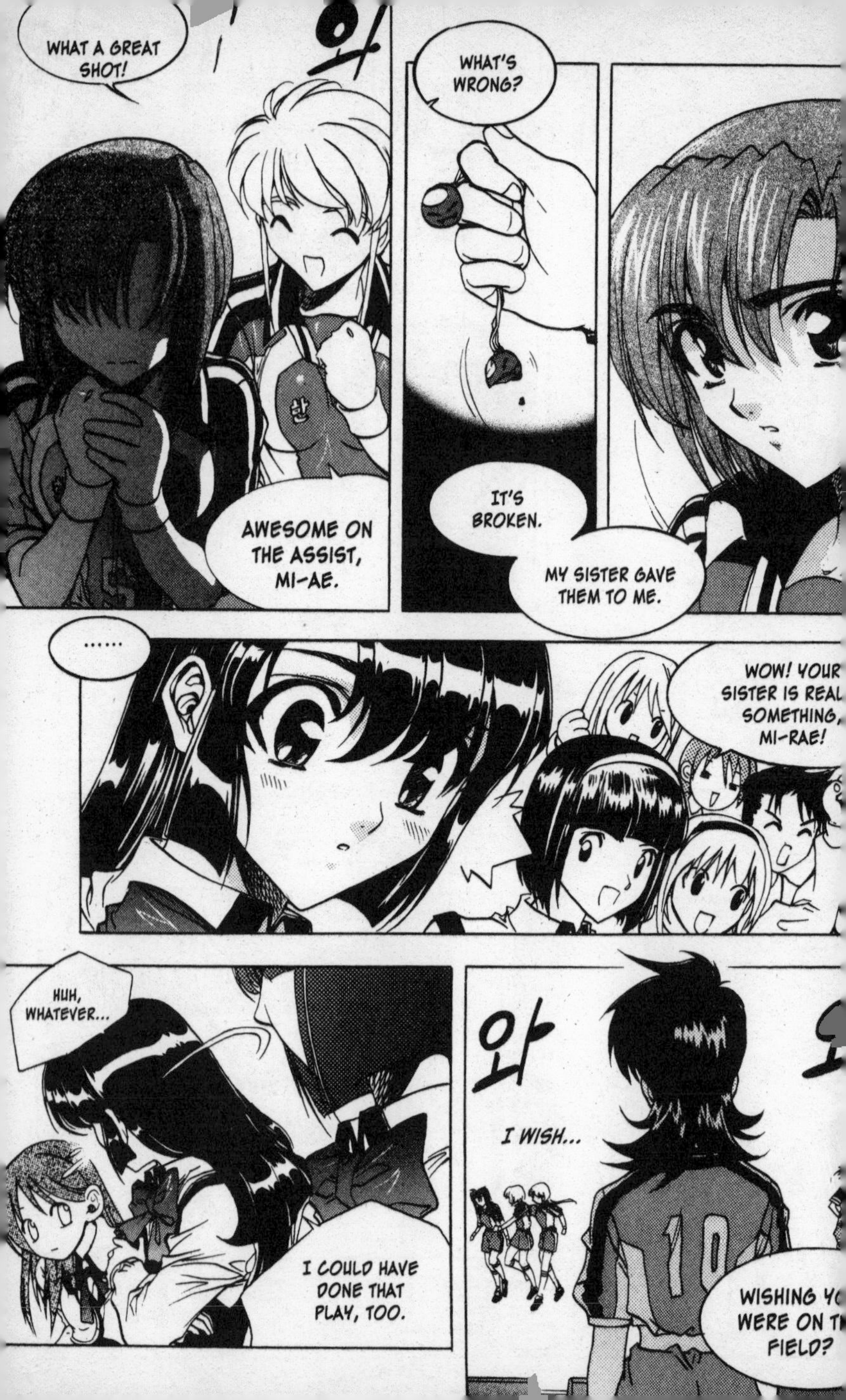

WHAT A GREAT SHOT!
와
AWESOME ON THE ASSIST, MI-AE.
WHAT'S WRONG?
IT'S BROKEN.
MY SISTER GAVE THEM TO ME.
......
WOW! YOUR SISTER IS REAL SOMETHING, MI-RAE!
HUH, WHATEVER...
I COULD HAVE DONE THAT PLAY, TOO.
와
I WISH...
WISHING YO WERE ON T FIELD?

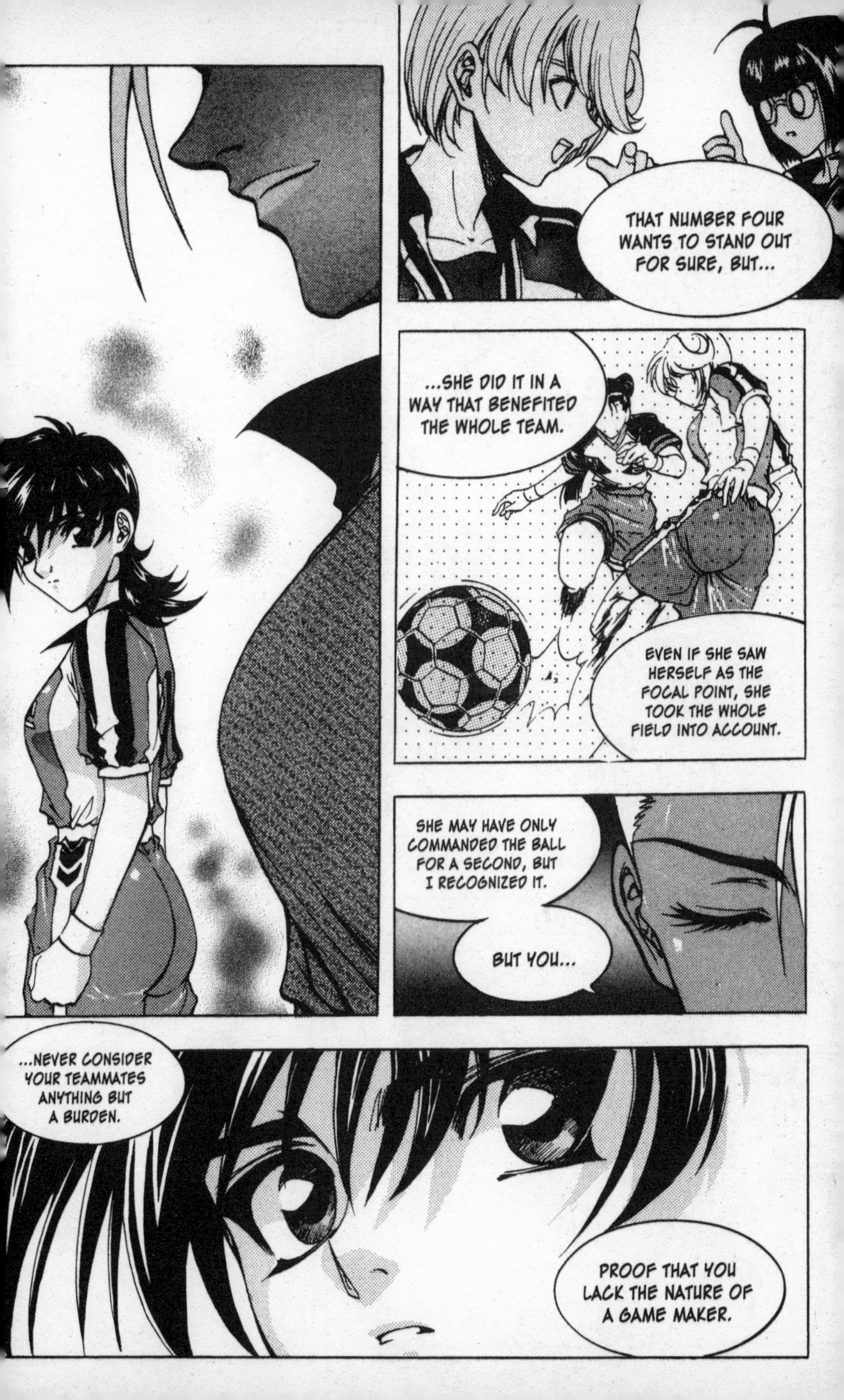
THAT NUMBER FOUR WANTS TO STAND OUT FOR SURE, BUT...
...SHE DID IT IN A WAY THAT BENEFITED THE WHOLE TEAM.
EVEN IF SHE SAW HERSELF AS THE FOCAL POINT, SHE TOOK THE WHOLE FIELD INTO ACCOUNT.
SHE MAY HAVE ONLY COMMANDED THE BALL FOR A SECOND, BUT I RECOGNIZED IT.
BUT YOU...
...NEVER CONSIDER YOUR TEAMMATES ANYTHING BUT A BURDEN.
PROOF THAT YOU LACK THE NATURE OF A GAME MAKER.

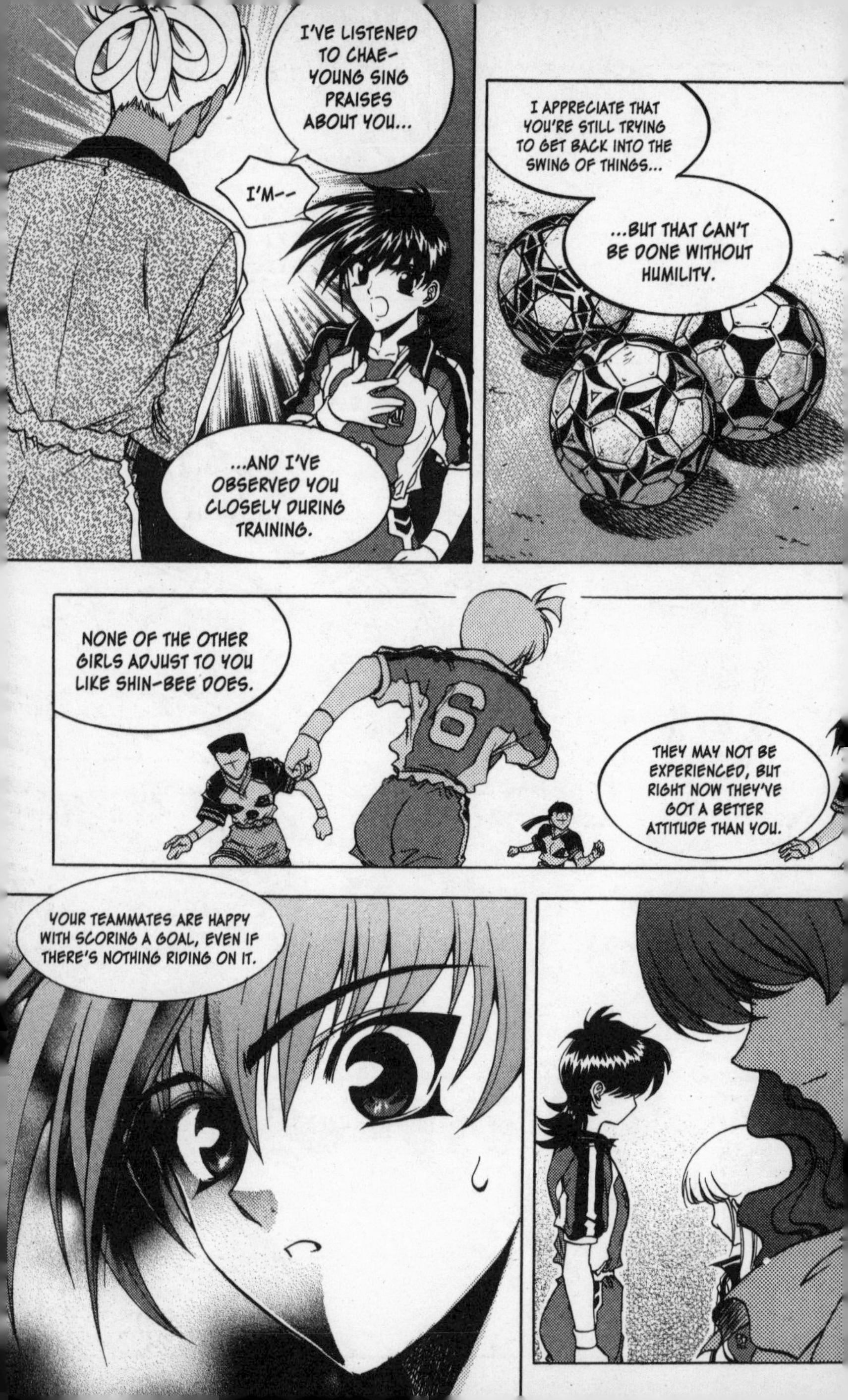
I'VE LISTENED TO CHAE-YOUNG SING PRAISES ABOUT YOU...
I'M--
...AND I'VE OBSERVED YOU CLOSELY DURING TRAINING.
I APPRECIATE THAT YOU'RE STILL TRYING TO GET BACK INTO THE SWING OF THINGS...
...BUT THAT CAN'T BE DONE WITHOUT HUMILITY.
NONE OF THE OTHER GIRLS ADJUST TO YOU LIKE SHIN-BEE DOES.
THEY MAY NOT BE EXPERIENCED, BUT RIGHT NOW THEY'VE GOT A BETTER ATTITUDE THAN YOU.
YOUR TEAMMATES ARE HAPPY WITH SCORING A GOAL, EVEN IF THERE'S NOTHING RIDING ON IT.

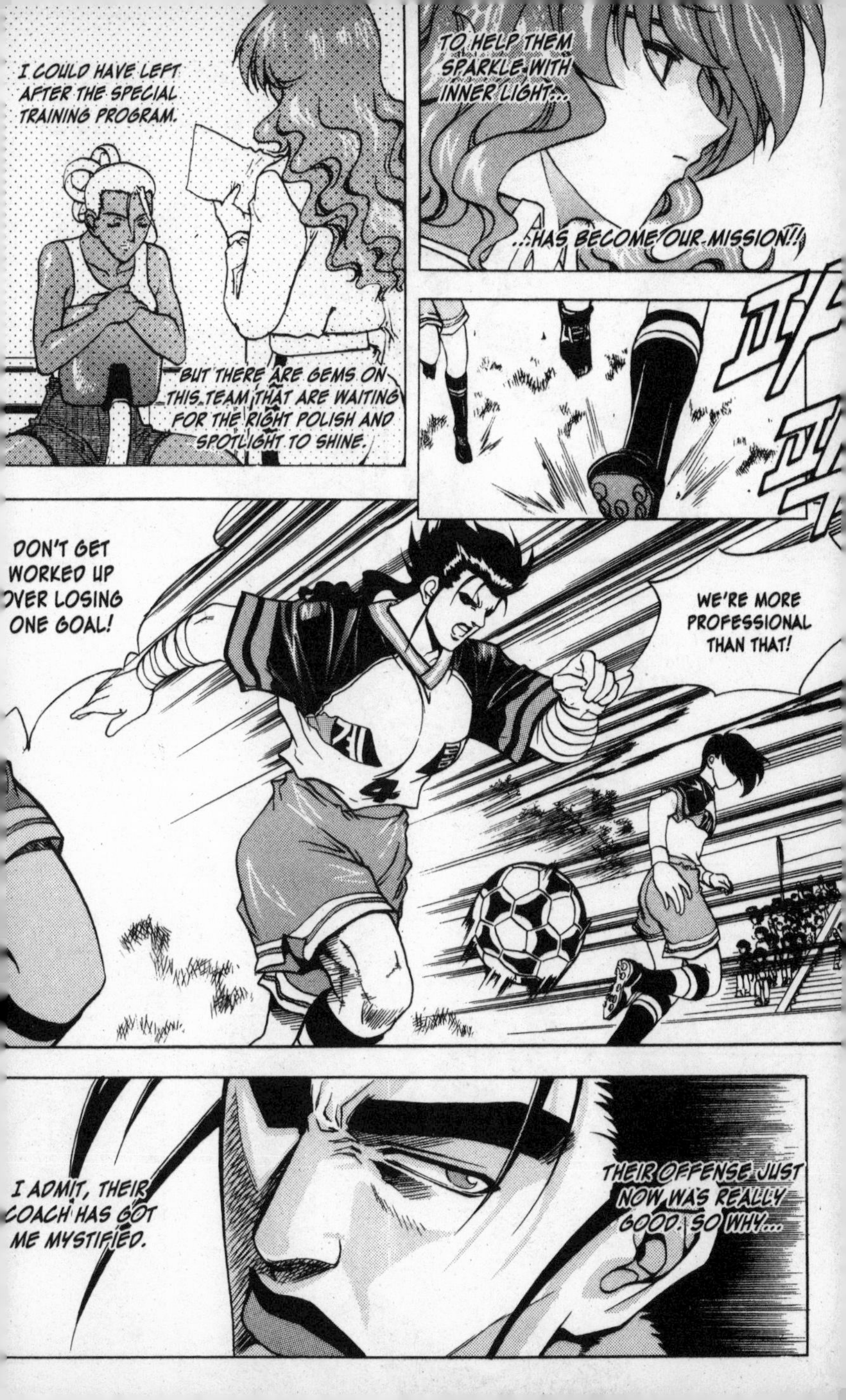
I COULD HAVE LEFT AFTER THE SPECIAL TRAINING PROGRAM.
BUT THERE ARE GEMS ON THIS TEAM THAT ARE WAITING FOR THE RIGHT POLISH AND SPOTLIGHT TO SHINE.
TO HELP THEM SPARKLE WITH INNER LIGHT...
...HAS BECOME OUR MISSION!!
DON'T GET WORKED UP OVER LOSING ONE GOAL!
WE'RE MORE PROFESSIONAL THAN THAT!
I ADMIT, THEIR COACH HAS GOT ME MYSTIFIED.
THEIR OFFENSE JUST NOW WAS REALLY GOOD. SO WHY...

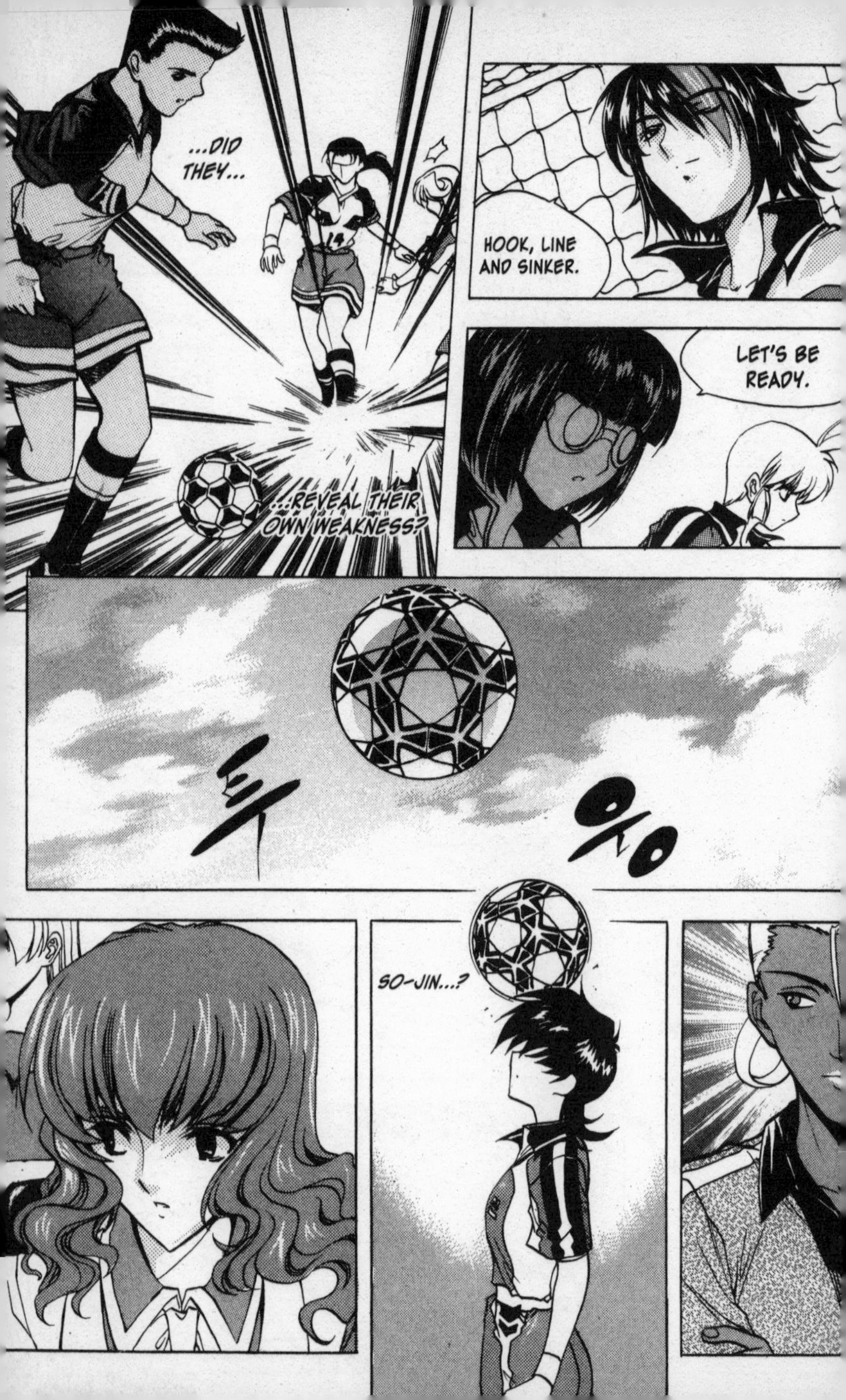
...DID THEY...
...REVEAL THEIR OWN WEAKNESS?
HOOK, LINE AND SINKER.
LET'S BE READY.
SO-JIN...?

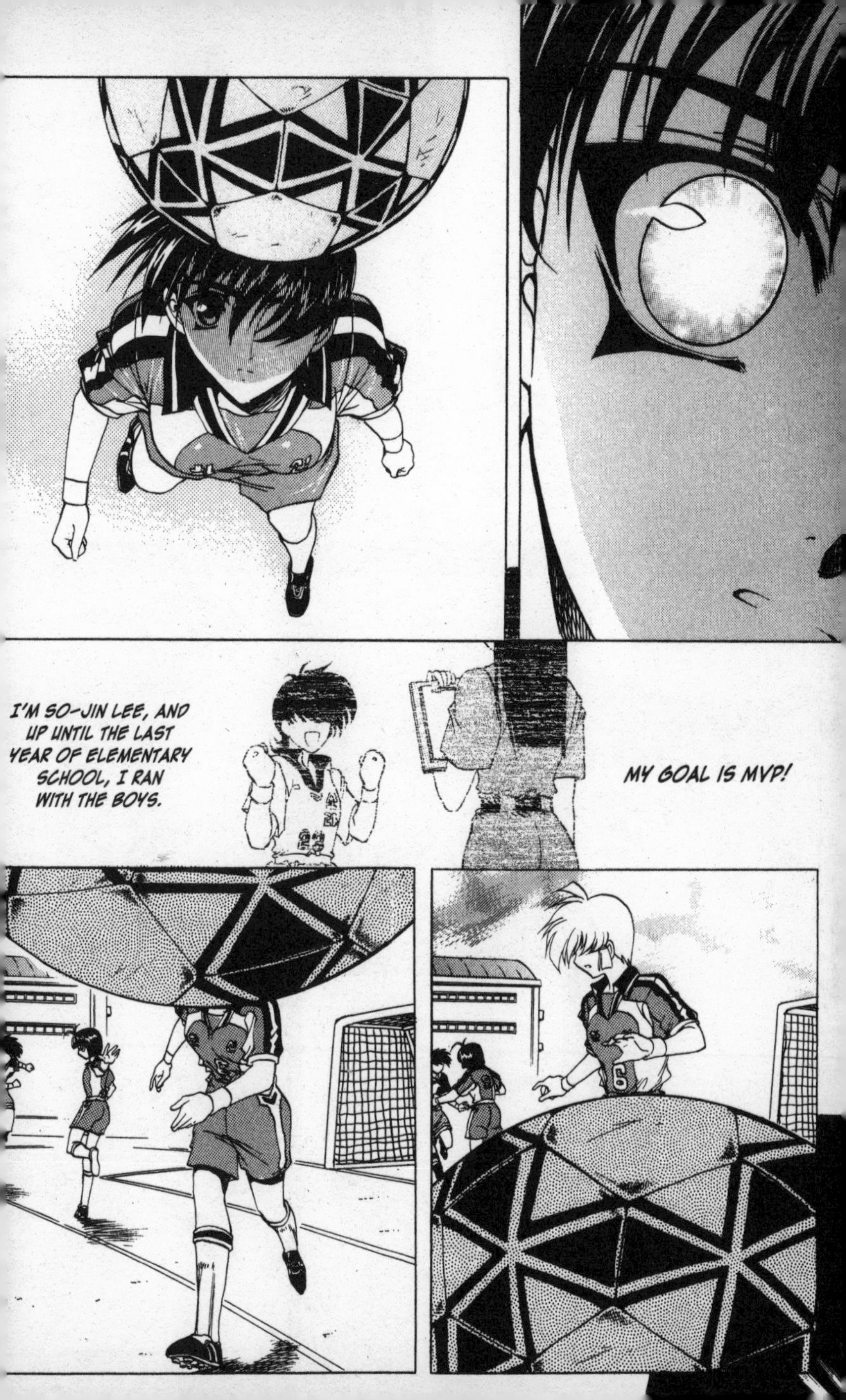
I'M SO-JIN LEE, AND UP UNTIL THE LAST YEAR OF ELEMENTARY SCHOOL, I RAN WITH THE BOYS.
MY GOAL IS MVP!

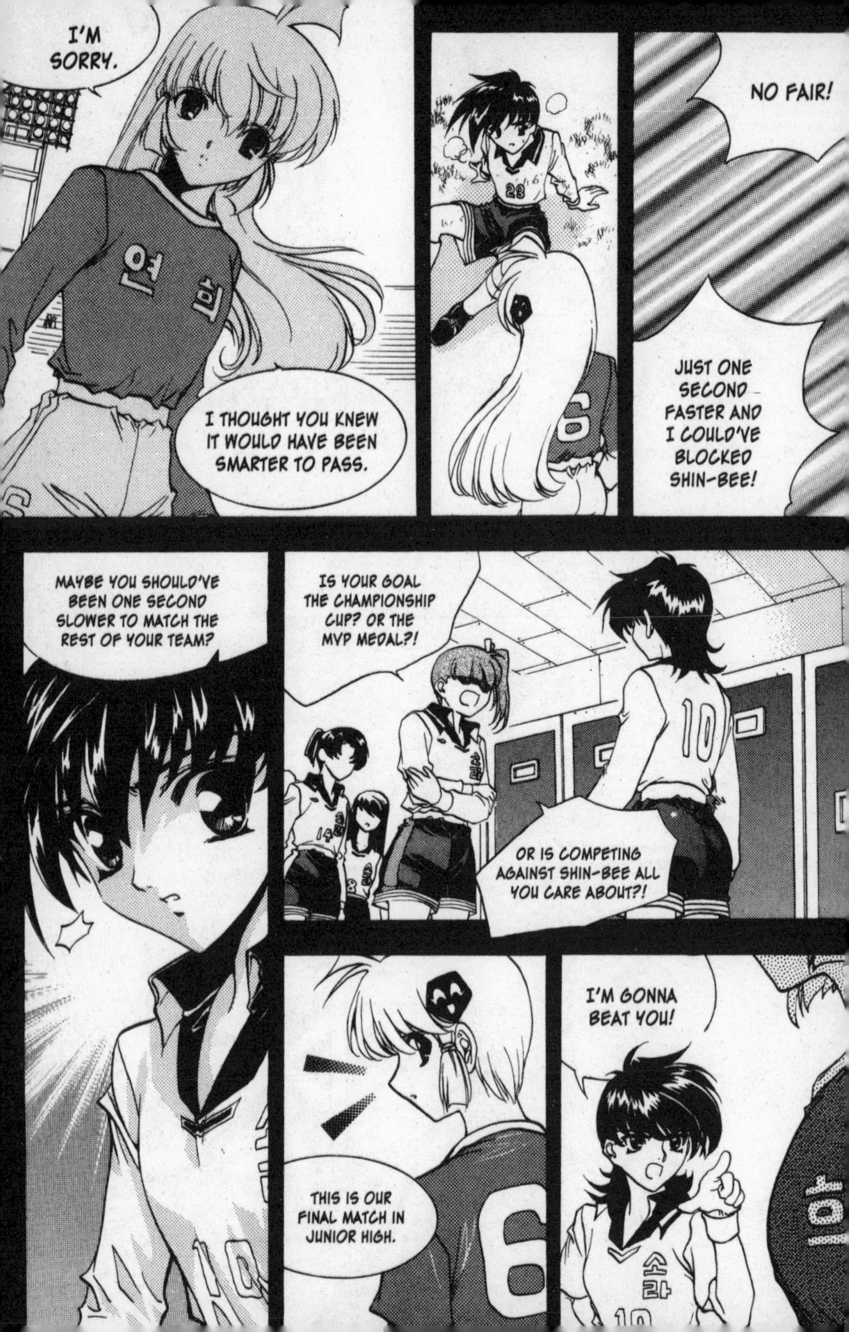
I'M SORRY.
I THOUGHT YOU KNEW IT WOULD HAVE BEEN SMARTER TO PASS.
NO FAIR!
JUST ONE SECOND FASTER AND I COULD'VE BLOCKED SHIN-BEE!
MAYBE YOU SHOULD'VE BEEN ONE SECOND SLOWER TO MATCH THE REST OF YOUR TEAM?
IS YOUR GOAL THE CHAMPIONSHIP CUP? OR THE MVP MEDAL?!
OR IS COMPETING AGAINST SHIN-BEE ALL YOU CARE ABOUT?!
THIS IS OUR FINAL MATCH IN JUNIOR HIGH.
I'M GONNA BEAT YOU!

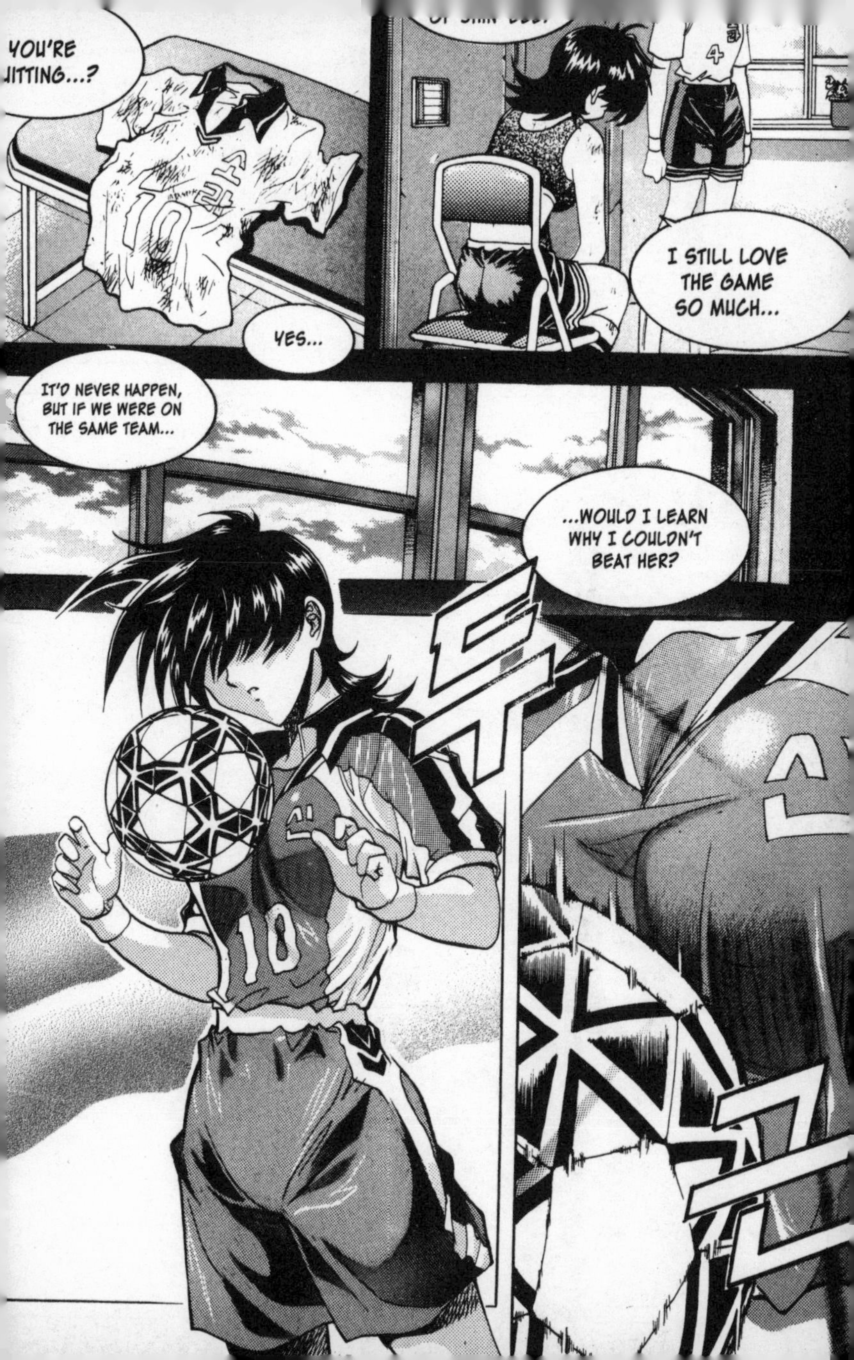
YOU'RE ITTING...?
YES...
I STILL LOVE THE GAME SO MUCH...
IT'D NEVER HAPPEN, BUT IF WE WERE ON THE SAME TEAM...
...WOULD I LEARN WHY I COULDN'T BEAT HER?

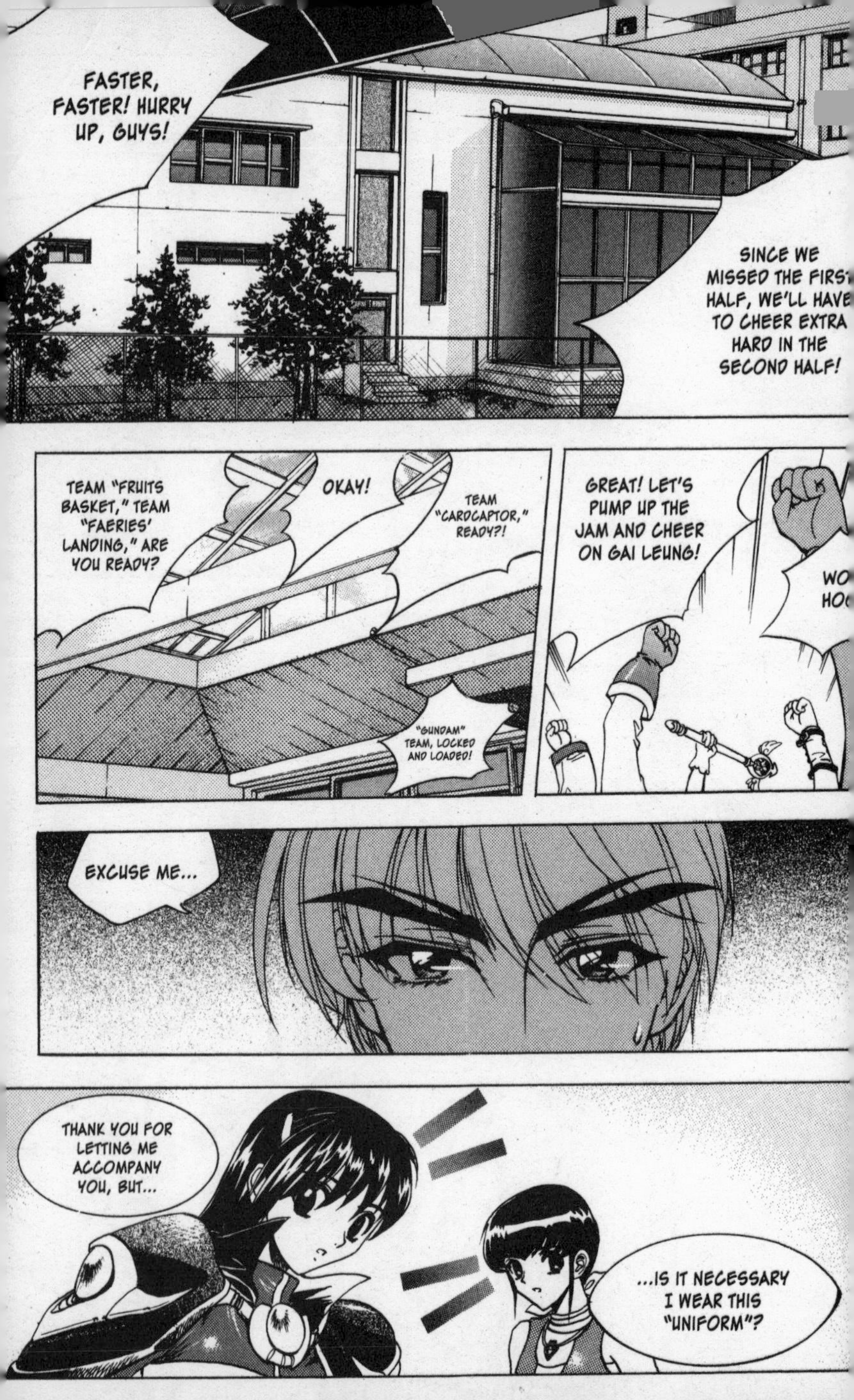
FASTER, FASTER! HURRY UP, GUYS!
SINCE WE MISSED THE FIRST HALF, WE'LL HAVE TO CHEER EXTRA HARD IN THE SECOND HALF!
TEAM "FRUITS BASKET," TEAM "FAERIES' LANDING," ARE YOU READY?
OKAY!
TEAM "CARDCAPTOR," READY?!
"GUNDAM" TEAM, LOCKED AND LOADED!
GREAT! LET'S PUMP UP THE JAM AND CHEER ON GAI LEUNG!
EXCUSE ME...
THANK YOU FOR LETTING ME ACCOMPANY YOU, BUT...
...IS IT NECESSARY I WEAR THIS "UNIFORM"?

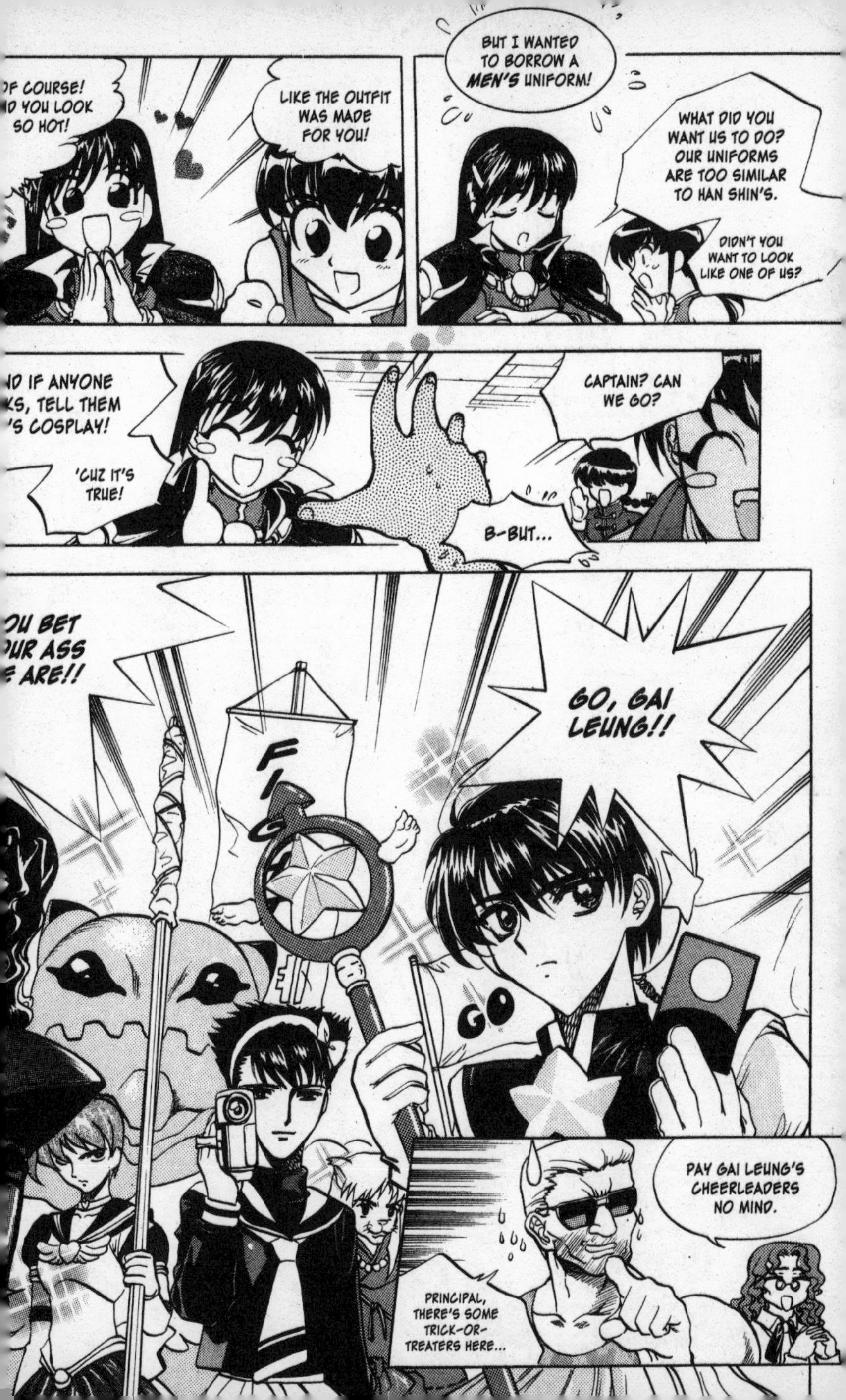
F COURSE! D YOU LOOK SO HOT!
LIKE THE OUTFIT WAS MADE FOR YOU!
BUT I WANTED TO BORROW A *MEN'S* UNIFORM!
WHAT DID YOU WANT US TO DO? OUR UNIFORMS ARE TOO SIMILAR TO HAN SHIN'S.
DIDN'T YOU WANT TO LOOK LIKE ONE OF US?
D IF ANYONE KS, TELL THEM 'S COSPLAY!
'CUZ IT'S TRUE!
CAPTAIN? CAN WE GO?
B-BUT...
OU BET OUR ASS E ARE!!
GO, GAI LEUNG!!
GO
PRINCIPAL, THERE'S SOME TRICK-OR-TREATERS HERE...
PAY GAI LEUNG'S CHEERLEADERS NO MIND.

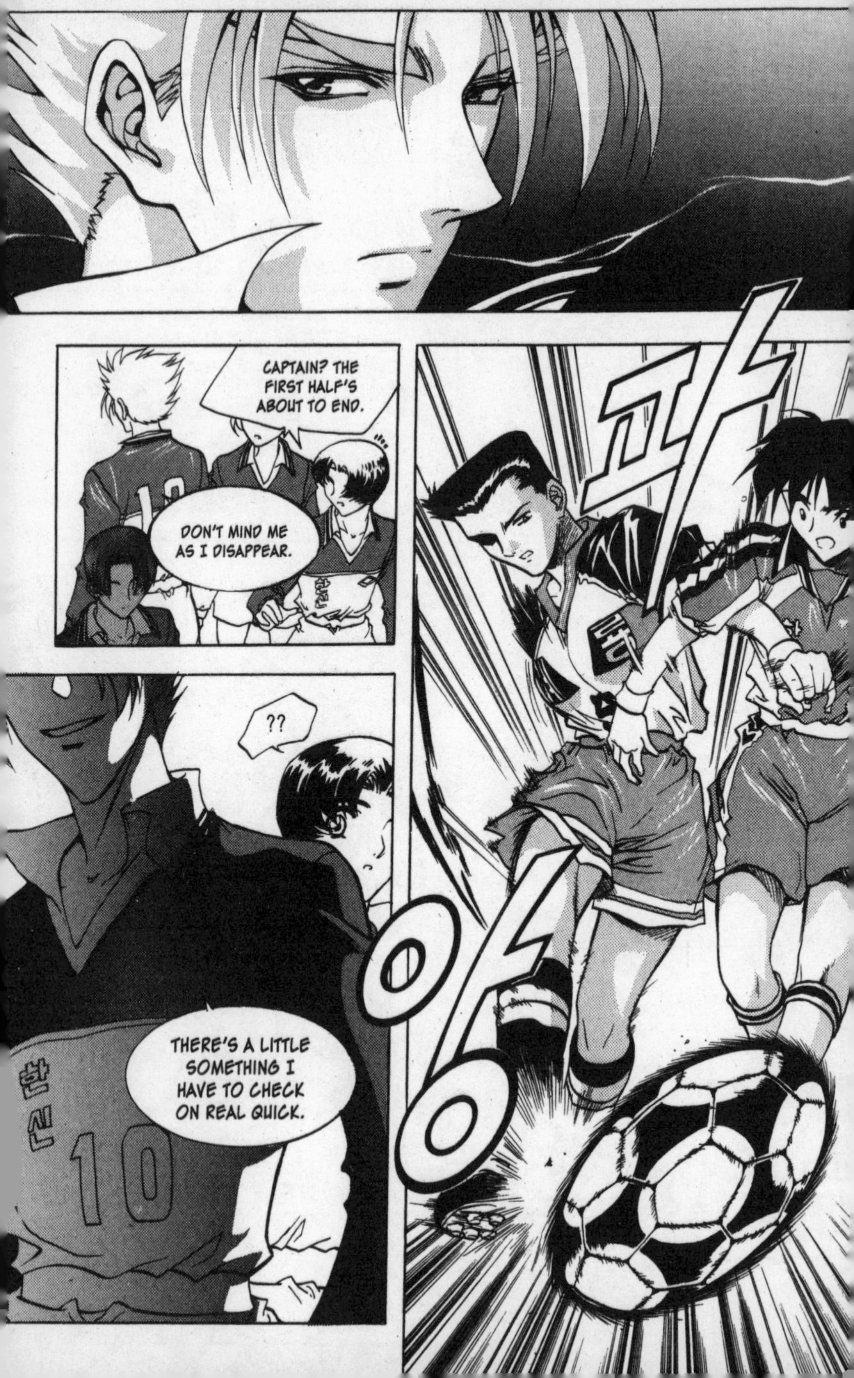
CAPTAIN? THE FIRST HALF'S ABOUT TO END.
DON'T MIND ME AS I DISAPPEAR.
??
THERE'S A LITTLE SOMETHING I HAVE TO CHECK ON REAL QUICK.

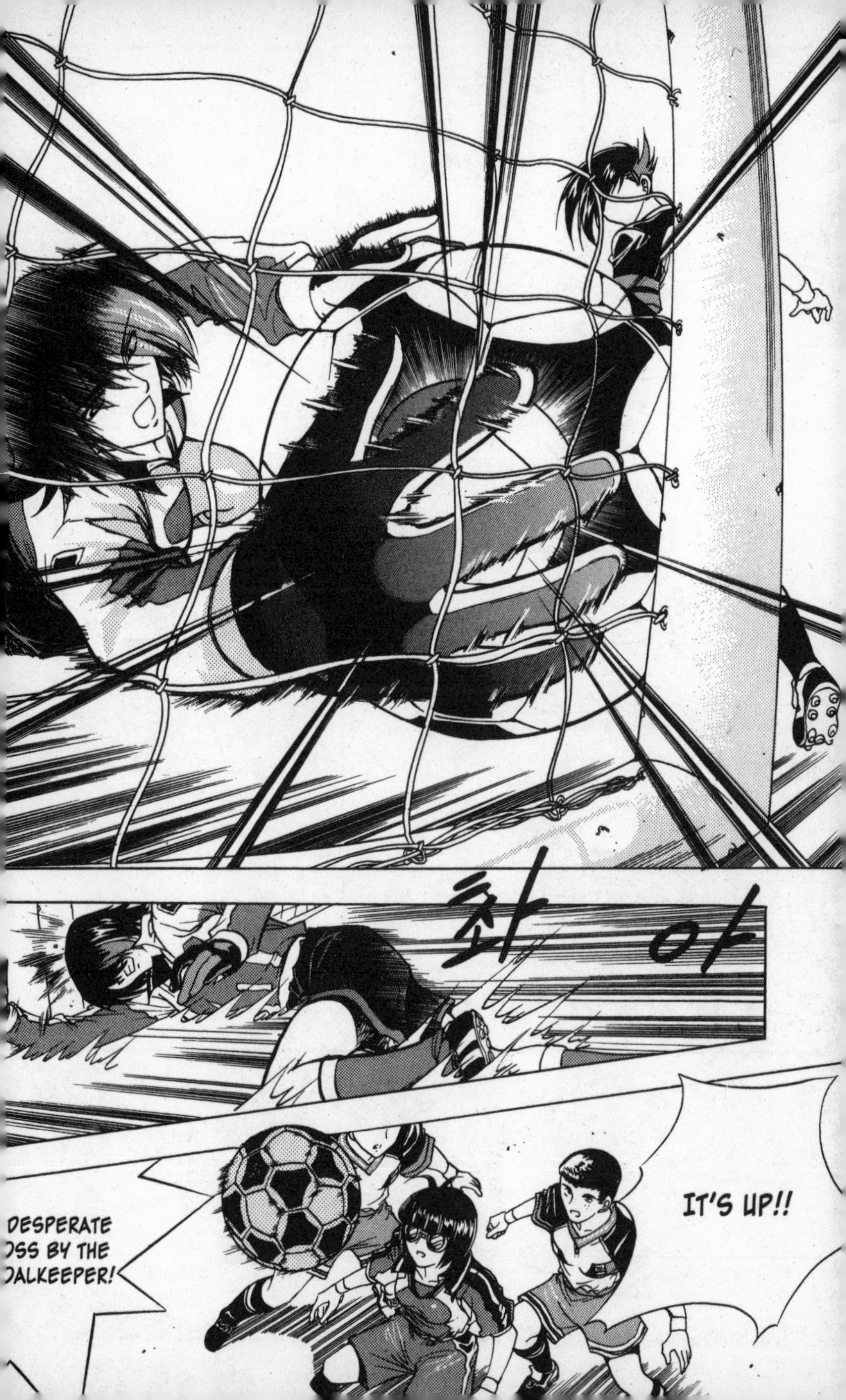

좌 아
DESPERATE
OSS BY THE
OALKEEPER!
IT'S UP!!

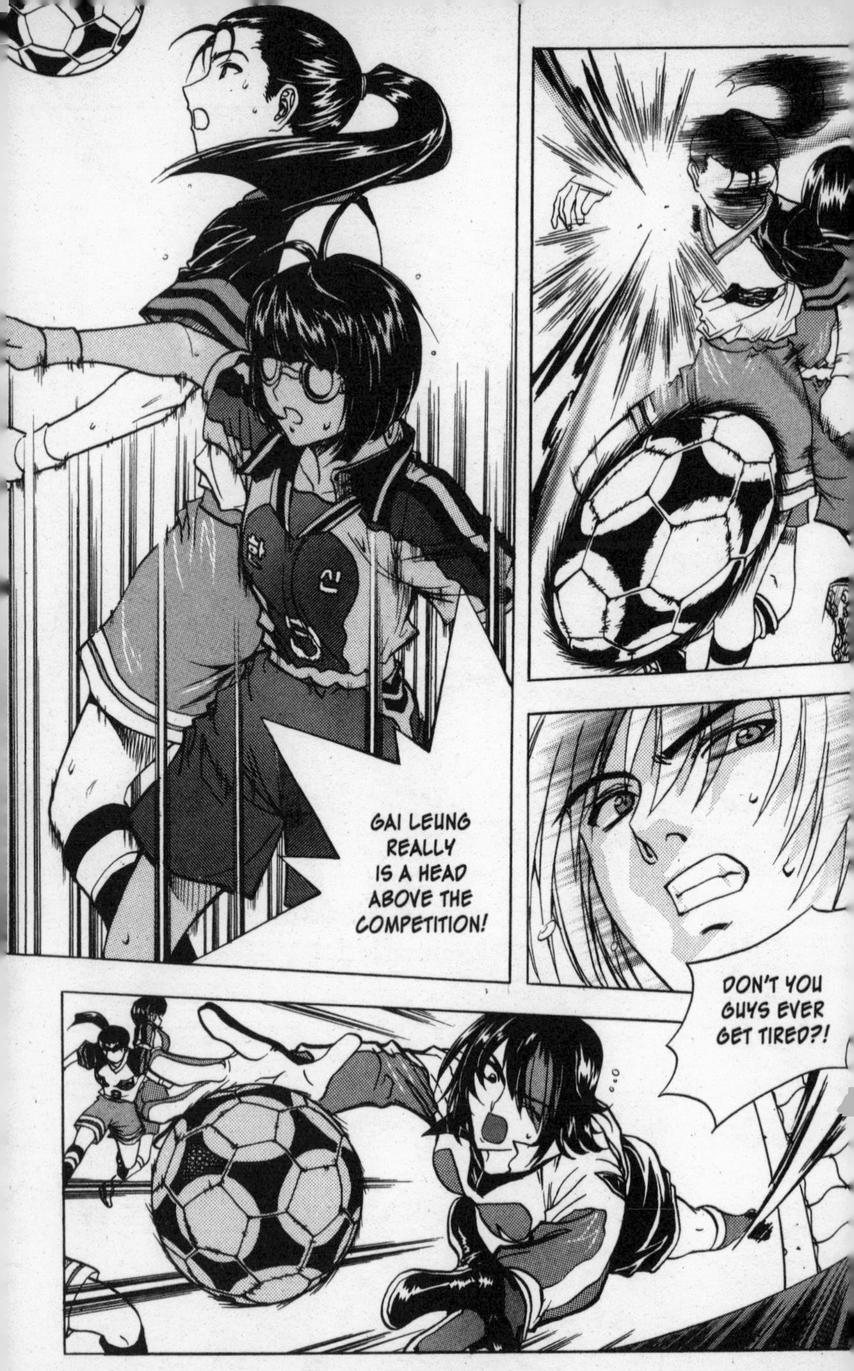
GAI LEUNG
REALLY
IS A HEAD
ABOVE THE
COMPETITION!
DON'T YOU
GUYS EVER
GET TIRED?!

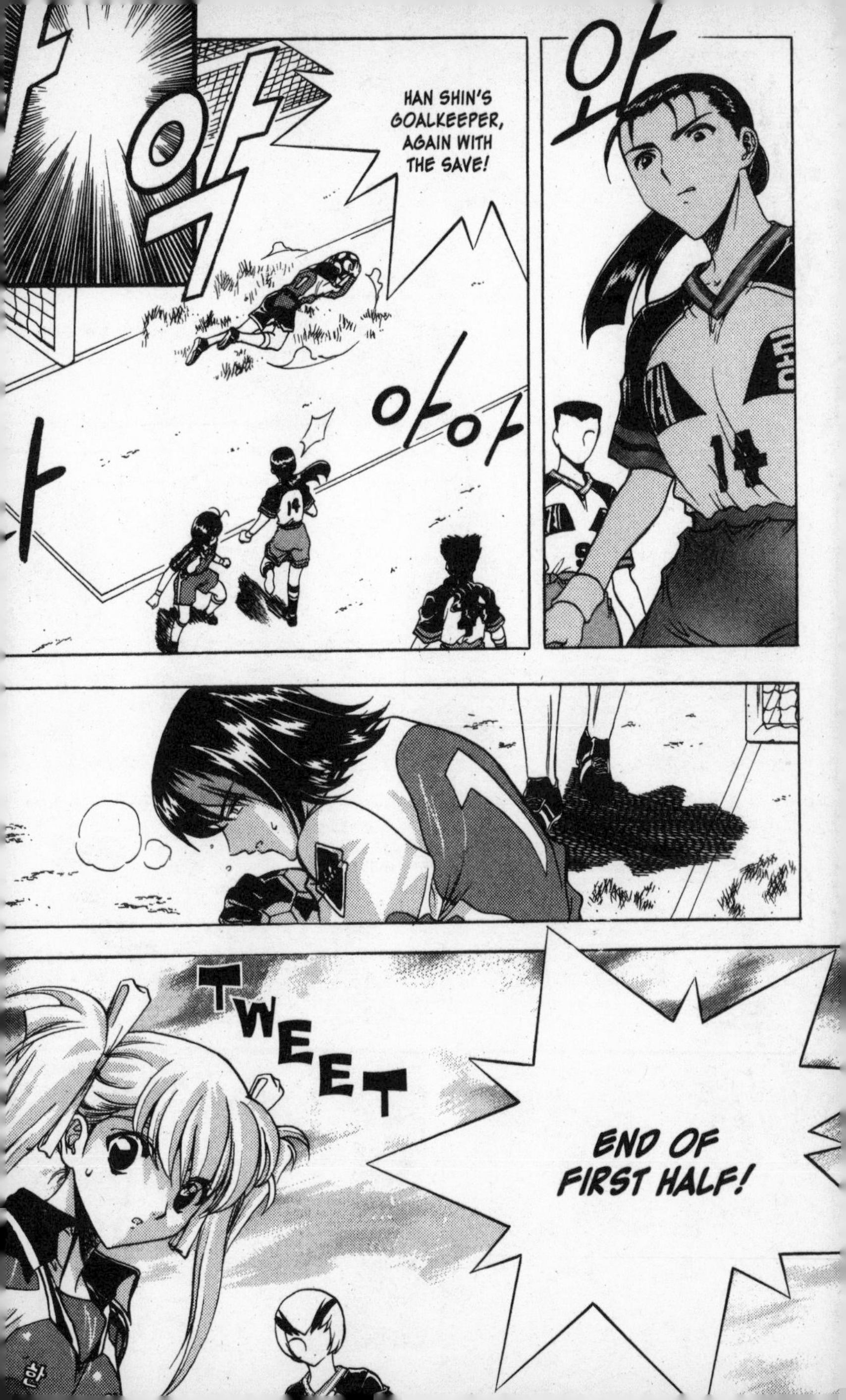
HAN SHIN'S GOALKEEPER, AGAIN WITH THE SAVE!
TWEET
END OF FIRST HALF!

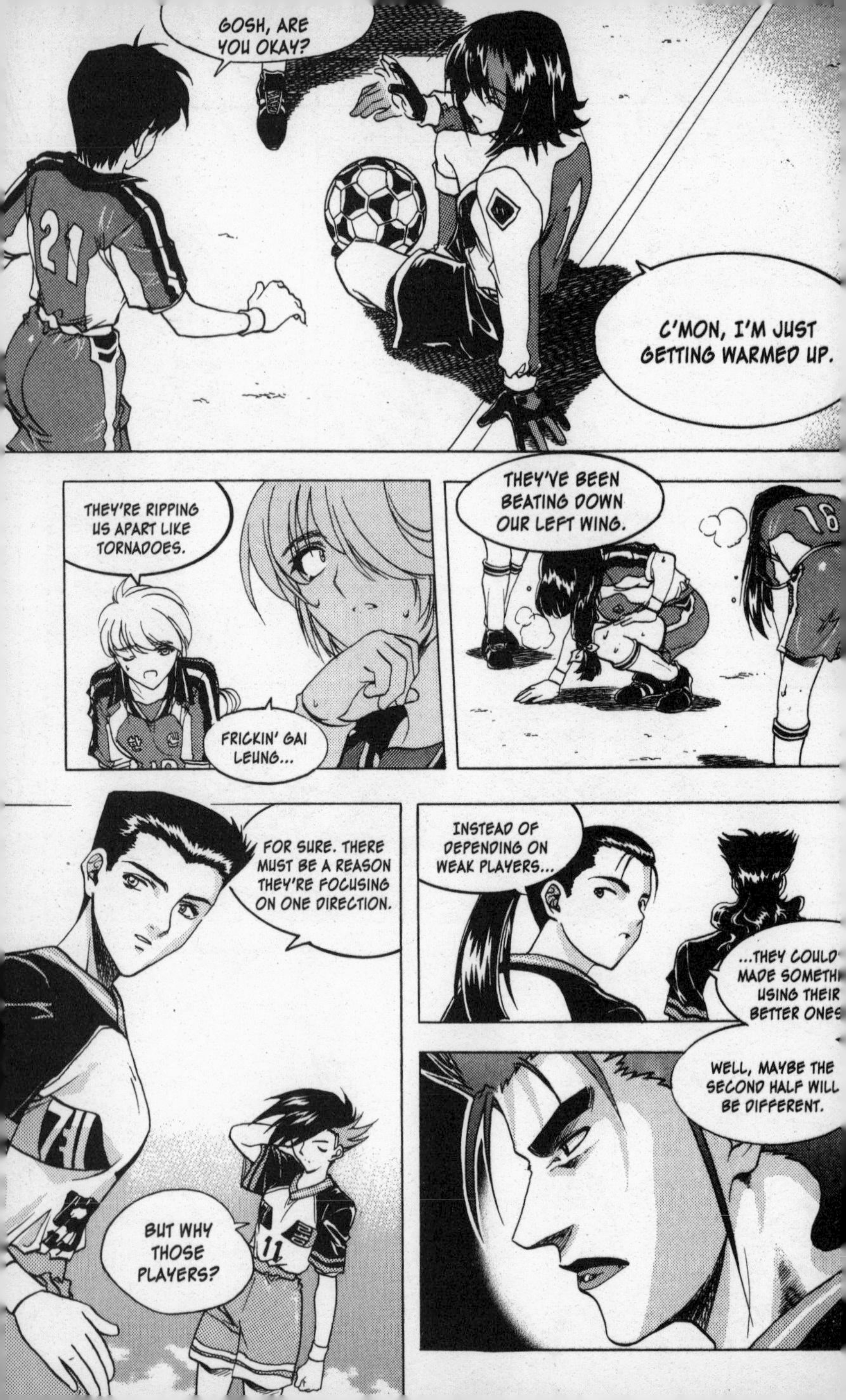
GOSH, ARE YOU OKAY?
C'MON, I'M JUST GETTING WARMED UP.
THEY'RE RIPPING US APART LIKE TORNADOES.
FRICKIN' GAI LEUNG...
THEY'VE BEEN BEATING DOWN OUR LEFT WING.
FOR SURE. THERE MUST BE A REASON THEY'RE FOCUSING ON ONE DIRECTION.
BUT WHY THOSE PLAYERS?
INSTEAD OF DEPENDING ON WEAK PLAYERS...
...THEY COULD MADE SOMETHI USING THEIR BETTER ONES
WELL, MAYBE THE SECOND HALF WILL BE DIFFERENT.

PLAY WILL RESUME AFTER HALFTIME!

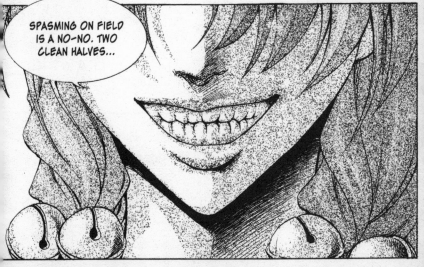

SPASMING ON FIELD IS A NO-NO. TWO CLEAN HALVES...

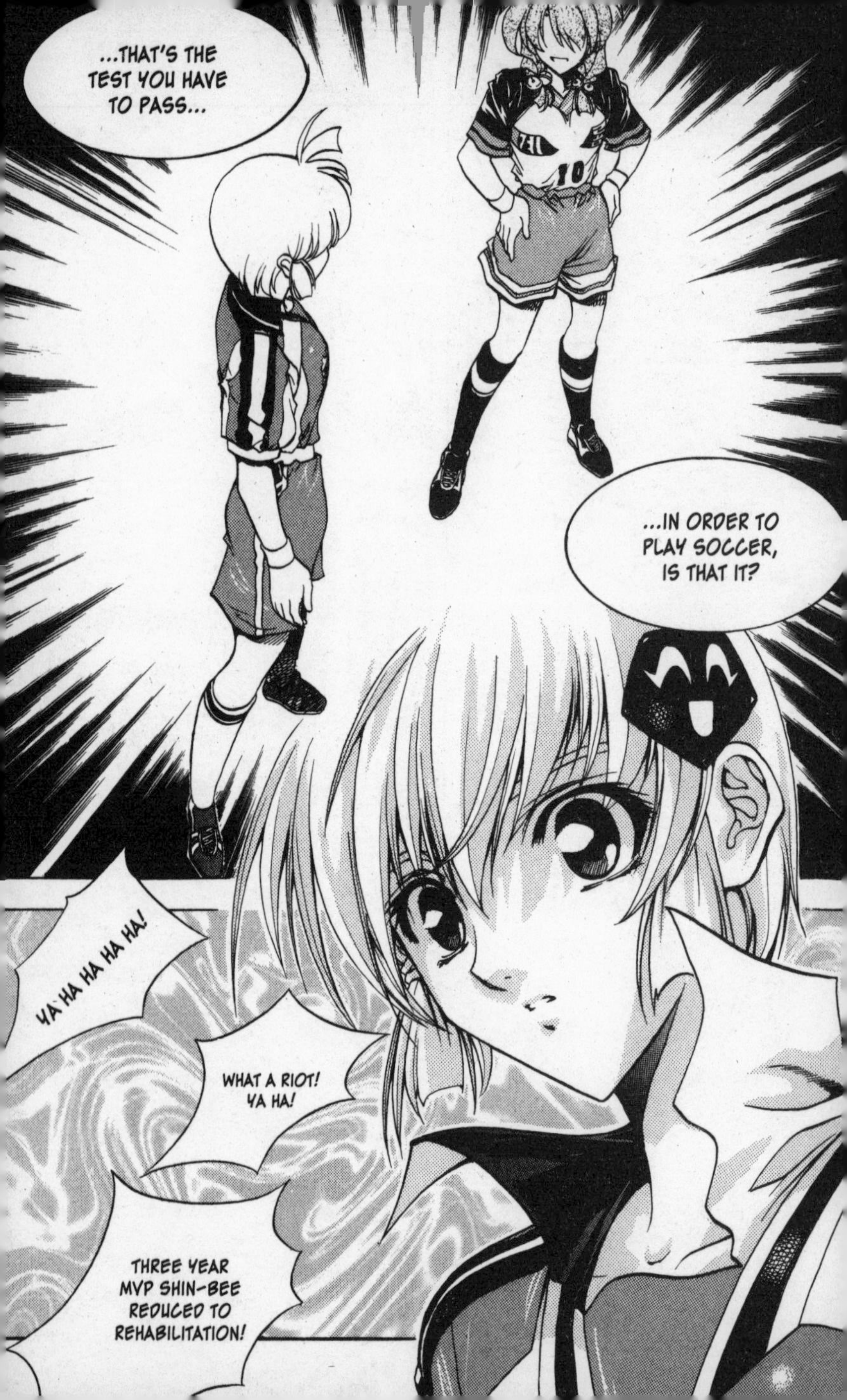
...THAT'S THE TEST YOU HAVE TO PASS...
...IN ORDER TO PLAY SOCCER, IS THAT IT?
YA HA HA HA HA!
WHAT A RIOT! YA HA!
THREE YEAR MVP SHIN-BEE REDUCED TO REHABILITATION!

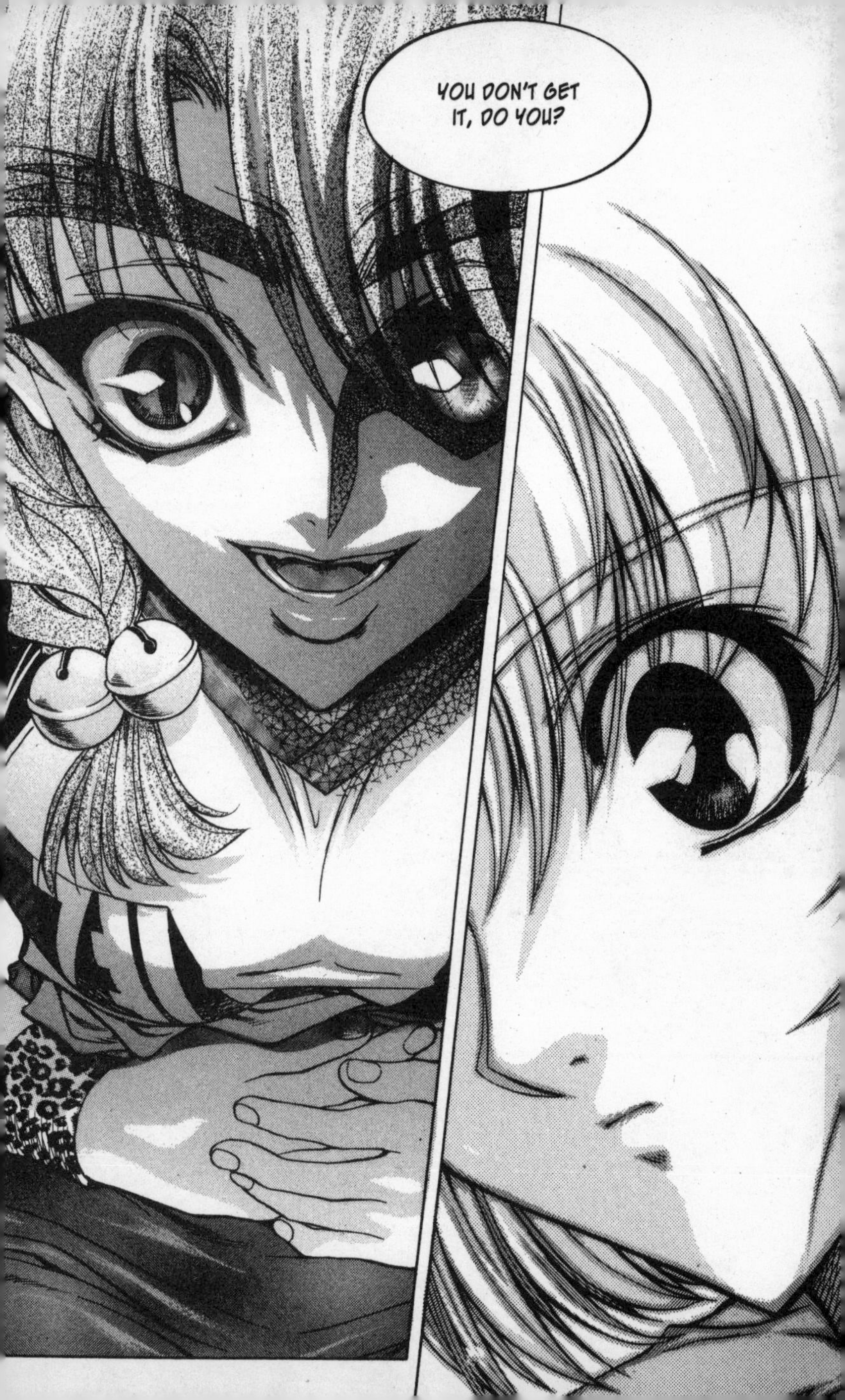
YOU DON'T GET IT, DO YOU?

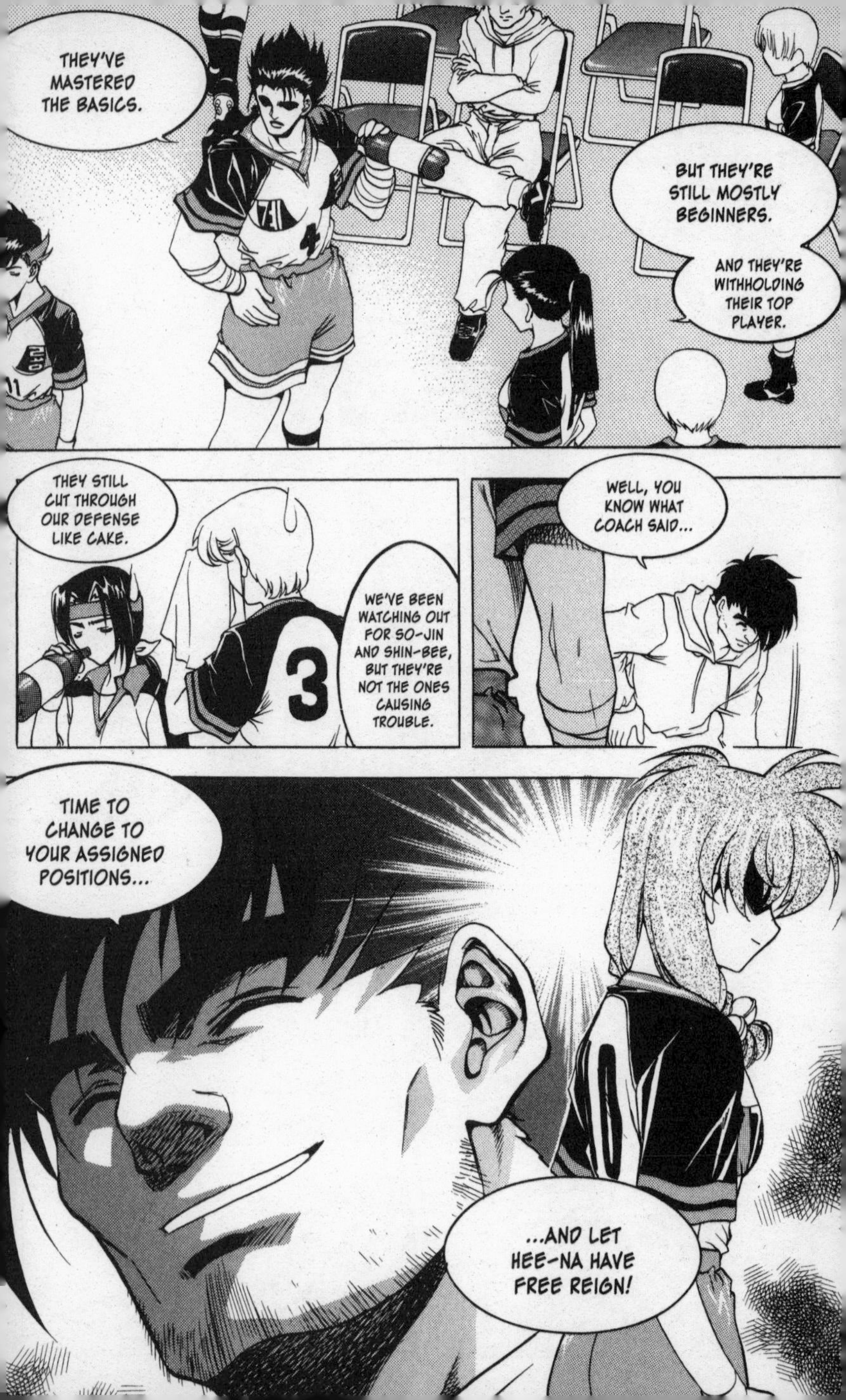
THEY'VE MASTERED THE BASICS.
BUT THEY'RE STILL MOSTLY BEGINNERS.
AND THEY'RE WITHHOLDING THEIR TOP PLAYER.
THEY STILL CUT THROUGH OUR DEFENSE LIKE CAKE.
WE'VE BEEN WATCHING OUT FOR SO-JIN AND SHIN-BEE, BUT THEY'RE NOT THE ONES CAUSING TROUBLE.
WELL, YOU KNOW WHAT COACH SAID...
TIME TO CHANGE TO YOUR ASSIGNED POSITIONS...
...AND LET HEE-NA HAVE FREE REIGN!

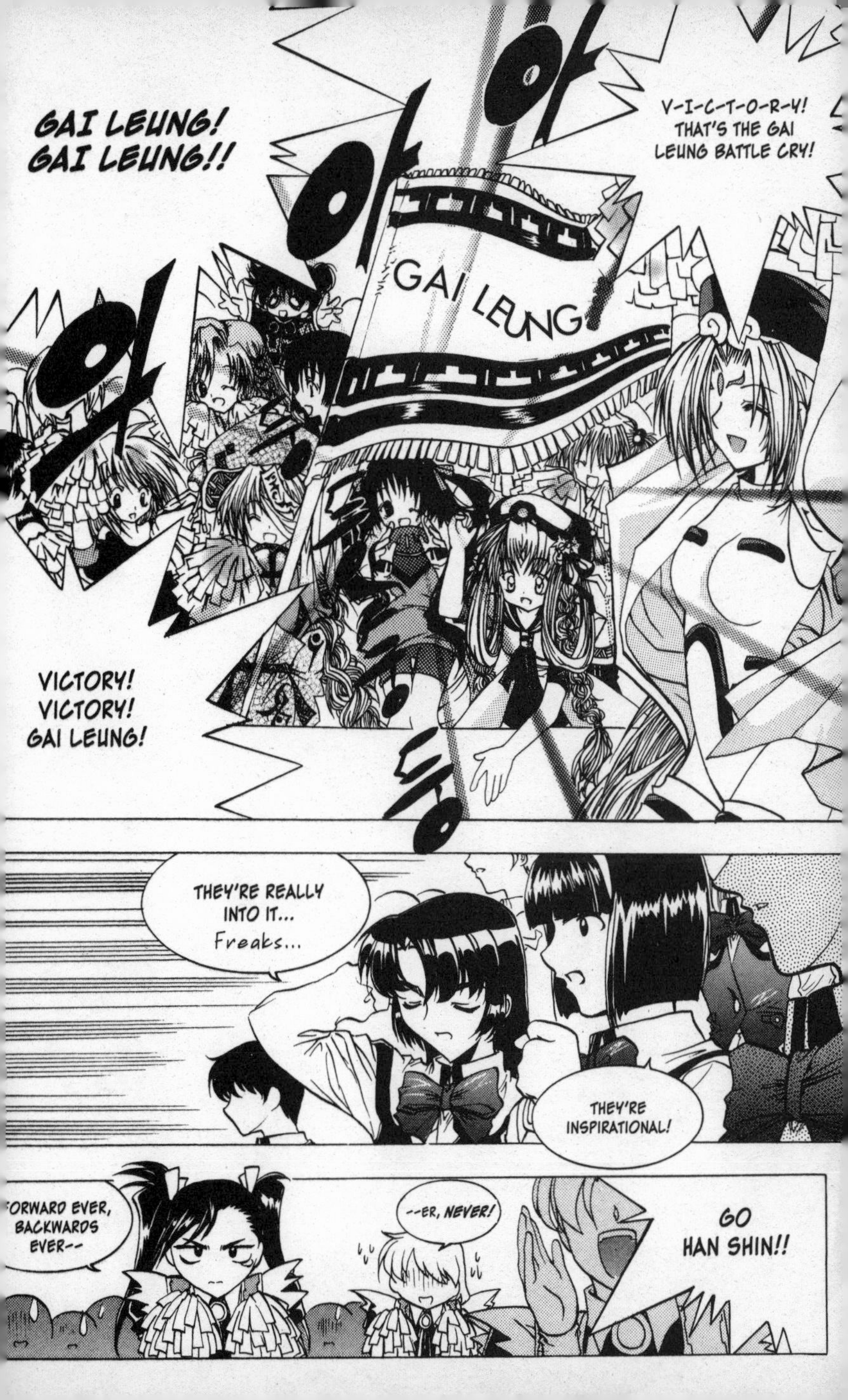
GAI LEUNG! GAI LEUNG!!
GAI LEUNG
V-I-C-T-O-R-Y! THAT'S THE GAI LEUNG BATTLE CRY!
VICTORY! VICTORY! GAI LEUNG!
THEY'RE REALLY INTO IT... Freaks...
THEY'RE INSPIRATIONAL!
FORWARD EVER, BACKWARDS EVER--
--ER, NEVER!
GO HAN SHIN!!

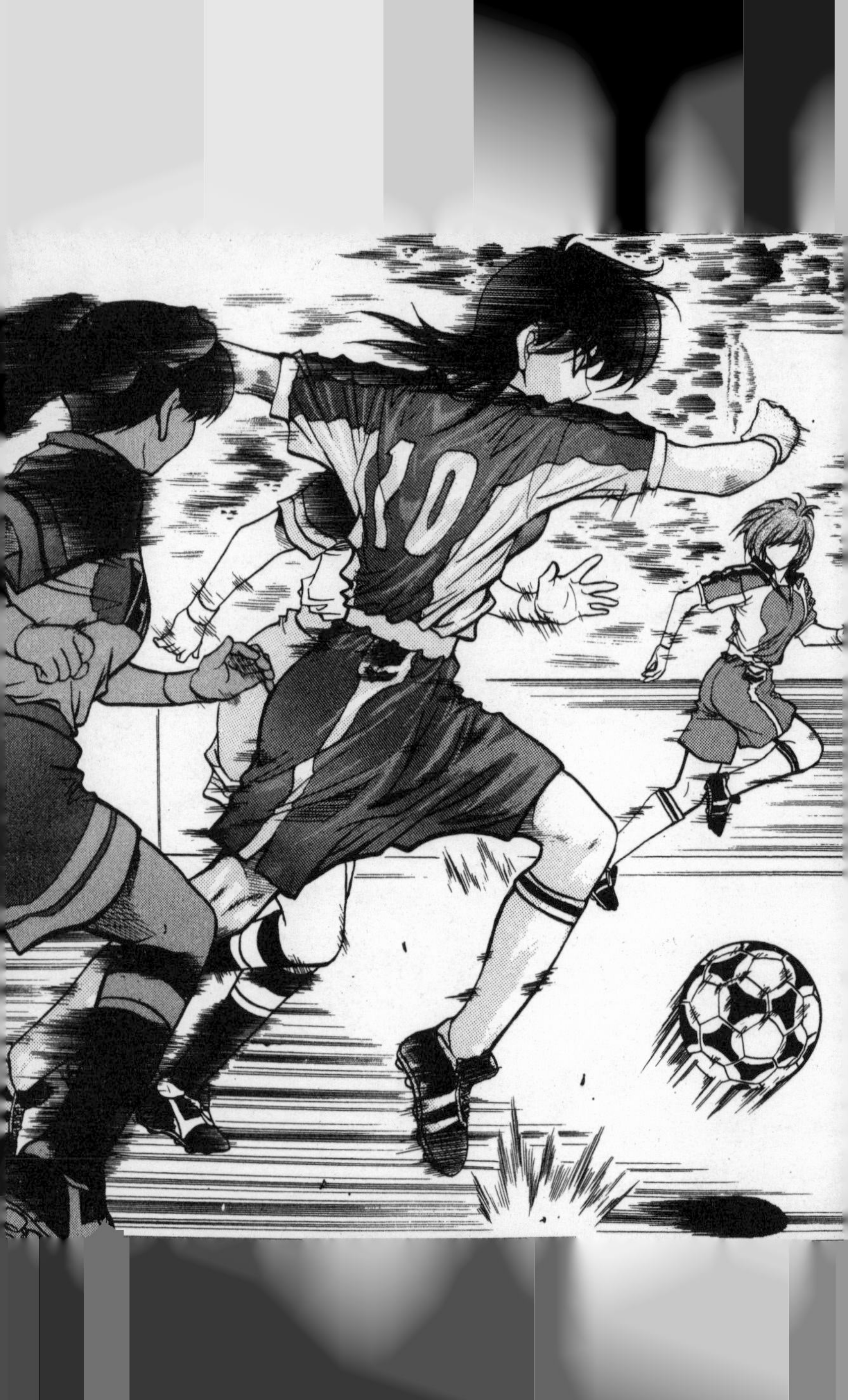

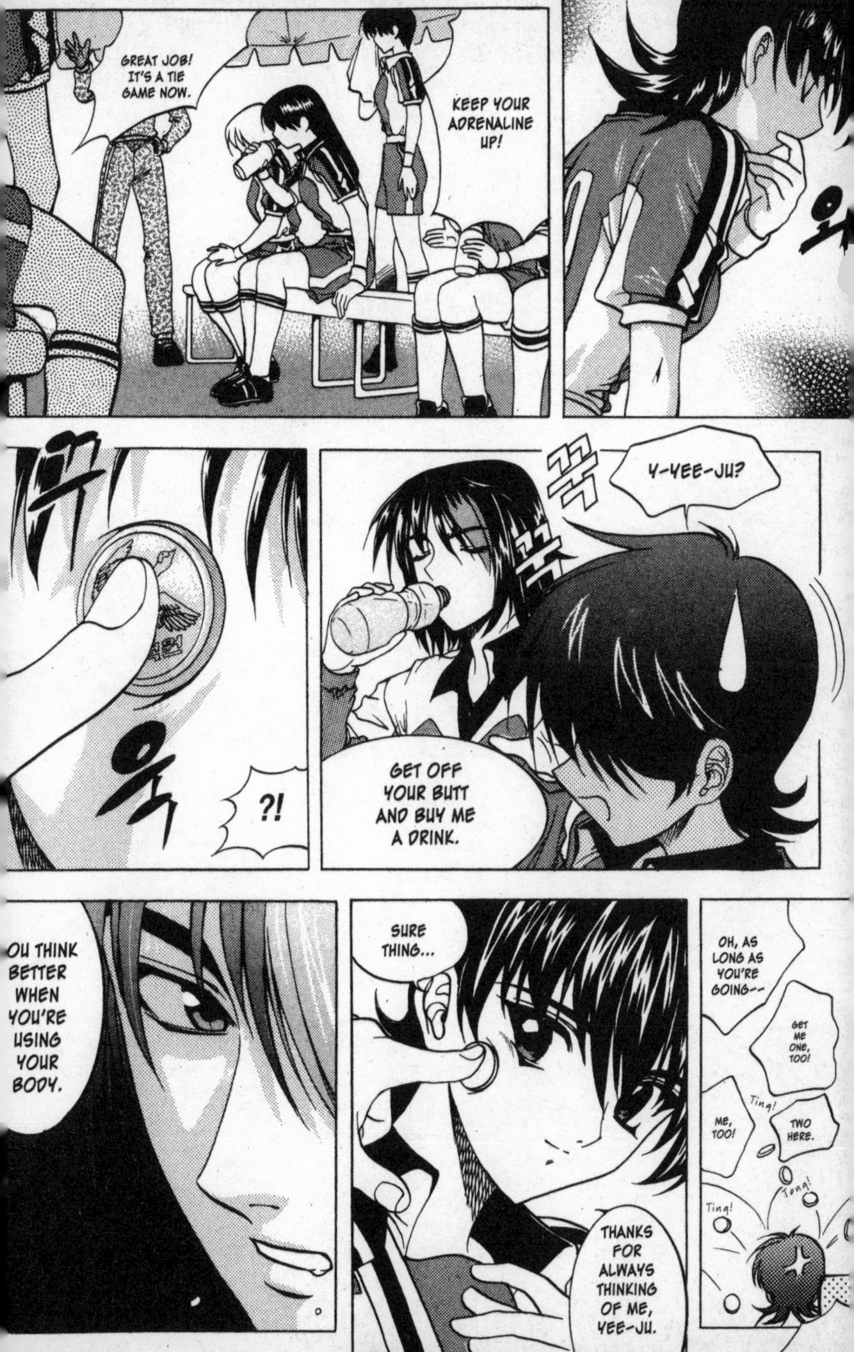
GREAT JOB! IT'S A TIE GAME NOW.
KEEP YOUR ADRENALINE UP!
?!
Y-YEE-JU?
GET OFF YOUR BUTT AND BUY ME A DRINK.
OU THINK BETTER WHEN YOU'RE USING YOUR BODY.
SURE THING...
THANKS FOR ALWAYS THINKING OF ME, YEE-JU.
OH, AS LONG AS YOU'RE GOING--
GET ME ONE, TOO!
Ting!
ME, TOO!
TWO HERE.
Ting!
Tong!

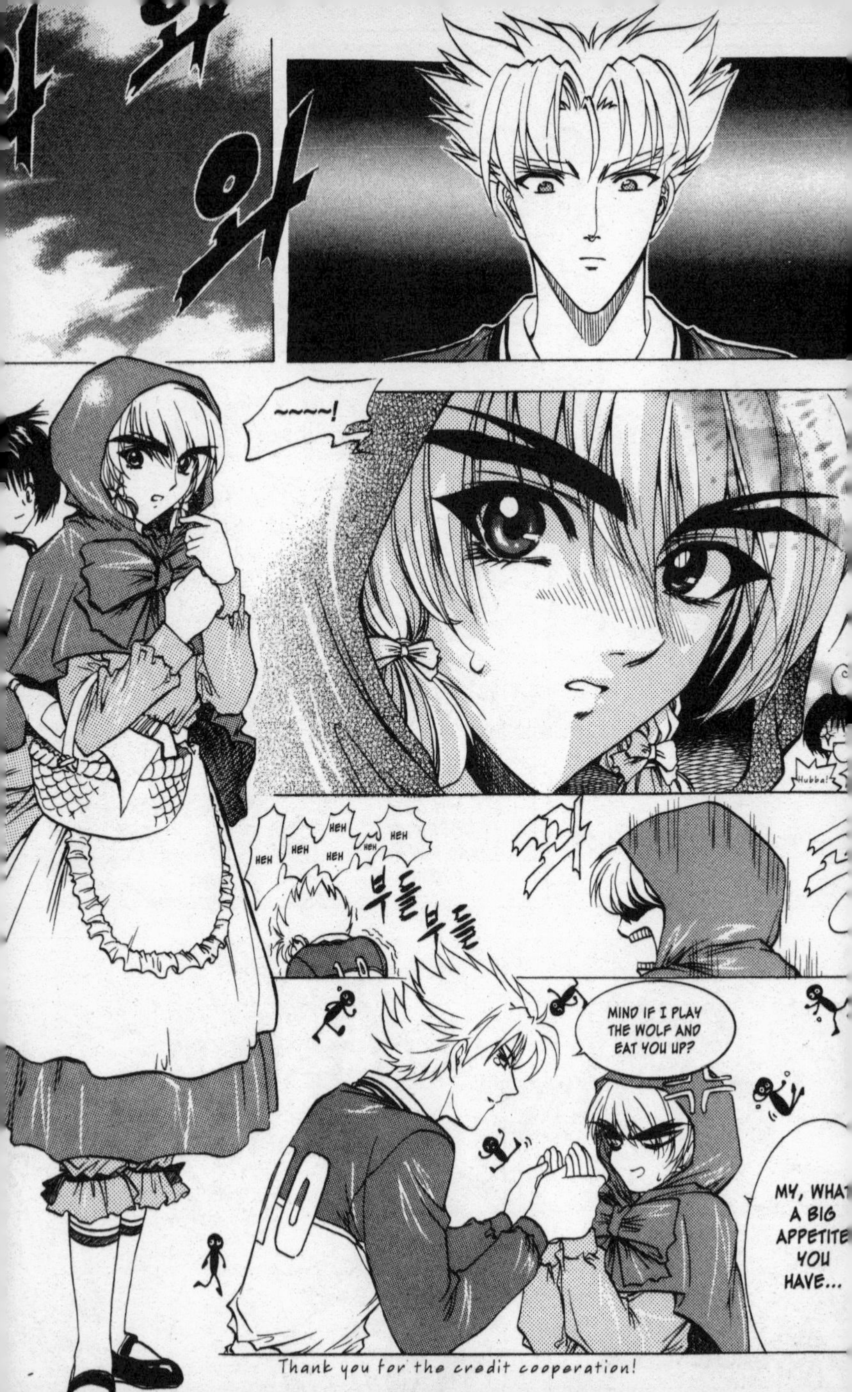

~~~~!
Hubba!
HEH
HEH
HEH
HEH
HEH
HEH
MIND IF I PLAY THE WOLF AND EAT YOU UP?
MY, WHAT A BIG APPETITE YOU HAVE...

Thank you for the credit cooperation!
~~~~

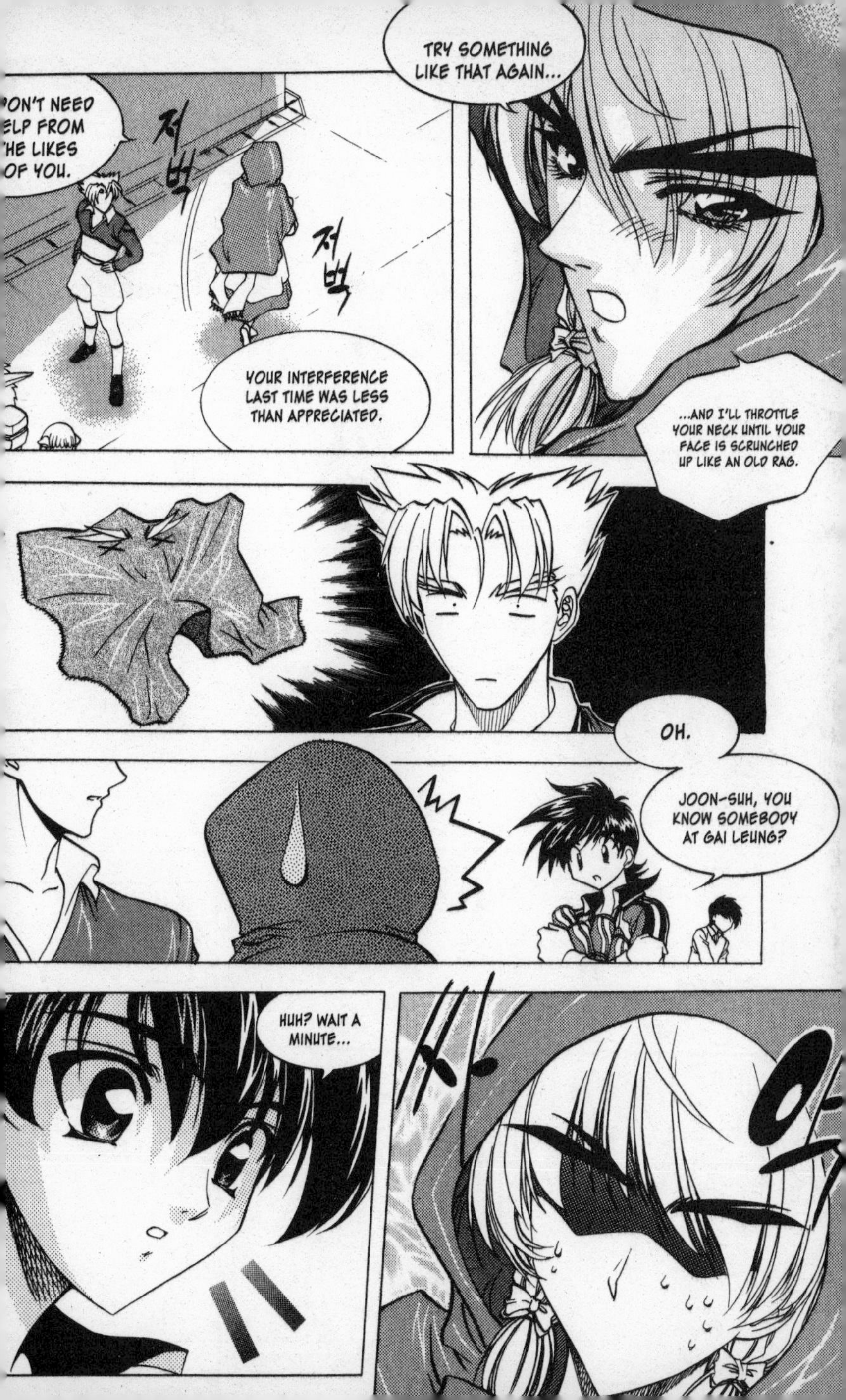

'ON'T NEED
ELP FROM
THE LIKES
OF YOU.
저벅
저벅
YOUR INTERFERENCE LAST TIME WAS LESS THAN APPRECIATED.
TRY SOMETHING LIKE THAT AGAIN...
...AND I'LL THROTTLE YOUR NECK UNTIL YOUR FACE IS SCRUNCHED UP LIKE AN OLD RAG.
OH.
JOON-SUH, YOU KNOW SOMEBODY AT GAI LEUNG?
HUH? WAIT A MINUTE...

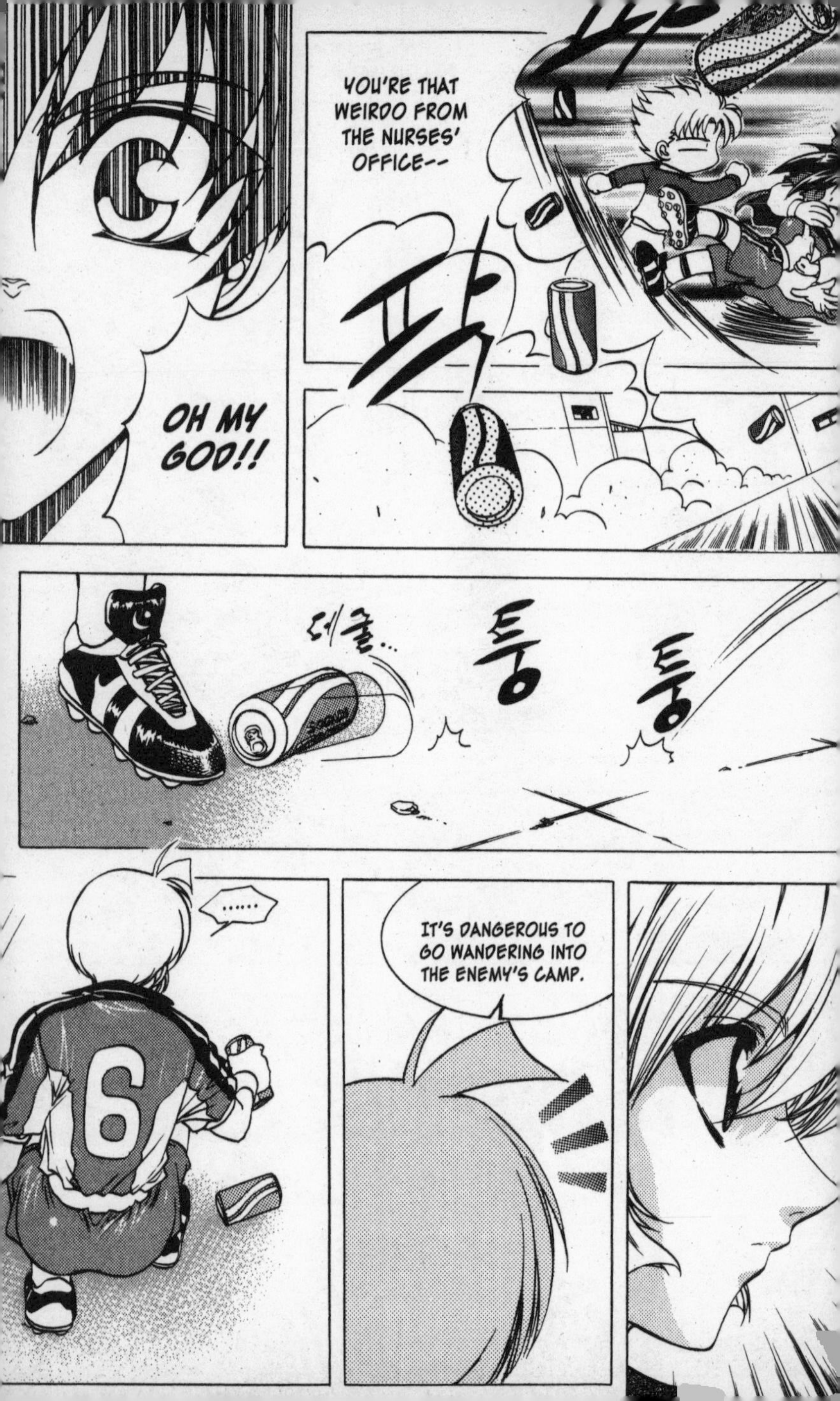
OH MY GOD!!
YOU'RE THAT WEIRDO FROM THE NURSES' OFFICE--
팍
데굴...
퉁
퉁
......
IT'S DANGEROUS TO GO WANDERING INTO THE ENEMY'S CAMP.

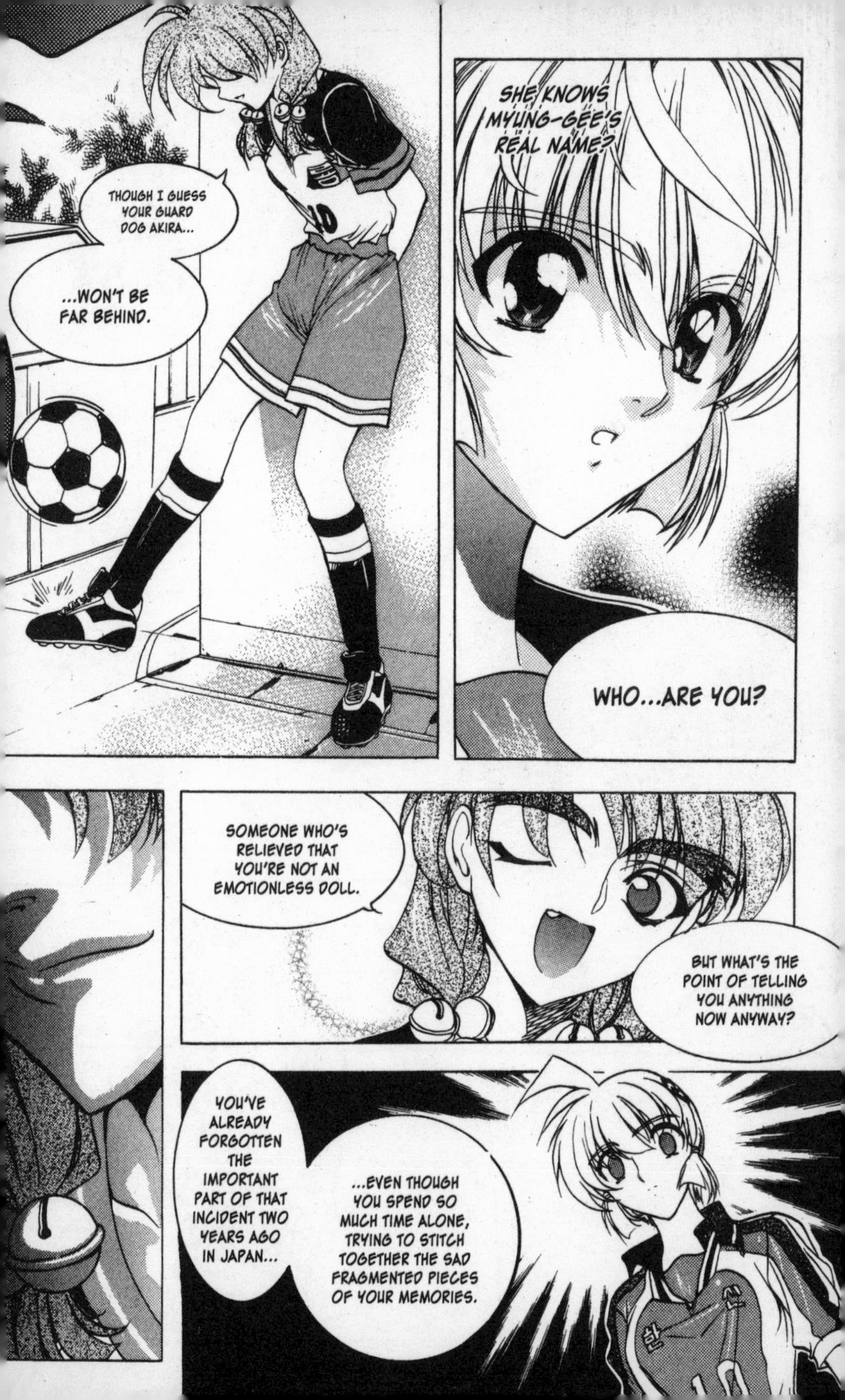

THOUGH I GUESS YOUR GUARD DOG AKIRA...
...WON'T BE FAR BEHIND.
SHE KNOWS MYUNG-GEE'S REAL NAME?
WHO...ARE YOU?
SOMEONE WHO'S RELIEVED THAT YOU'RE NOT AN EMOTIONLESS DOLL.
BUT WHAT'S THE POINT OF TELLING YOU ANYTHING NOW ANYWAY?
YOU'VE ALREADY FORGOTTEN THE IMPORTANT PART OF THAT INCIDENT TWO YEARS AGO IN JAPAN...
...EVEN THOUGH YOU SPEND SO MUCH TIME ALONE, TRYING TO STITCH TOGETHER THE SAD FRAGMENTED PIECES OF YOUR MEMORIES.

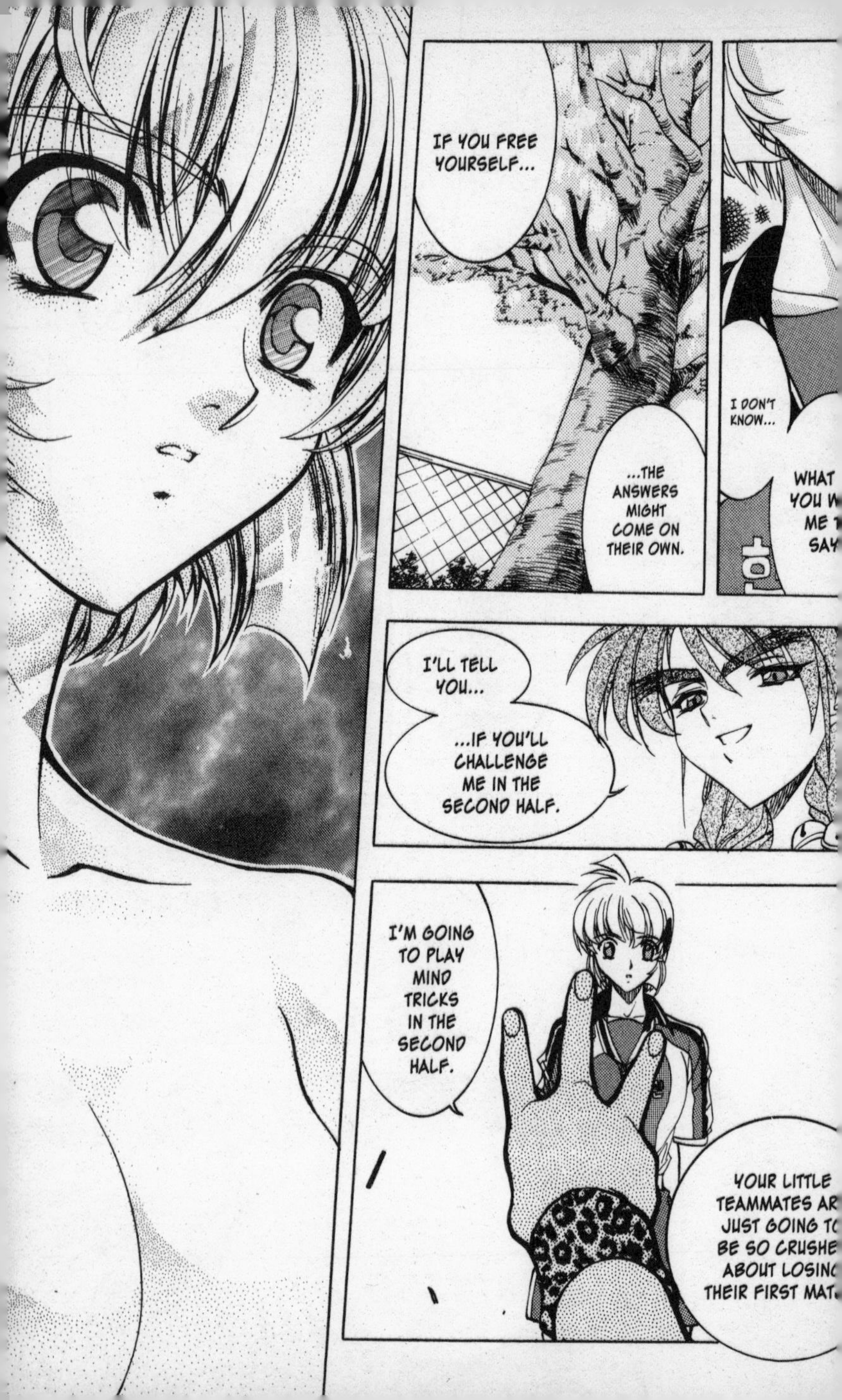
IF YOU FREE YOURSELF...
...THE ANSWERS MIGHT COME ON THEIR OWN.
I DON'T KNOW...
WHAT YOU W ME SAY
I'LL TELL YOU...
...IF YOU'LL CHALLENGE ME IN THE SECOND HALF.
I'M GOING TO PLAY MIND TRICKS IN THE SECOND HALF.
YOUR LITTLE TEAMMATES AR JUST GOING T BE SO CRUSHE ABOUT LOSIN THEIR FIRST MAT

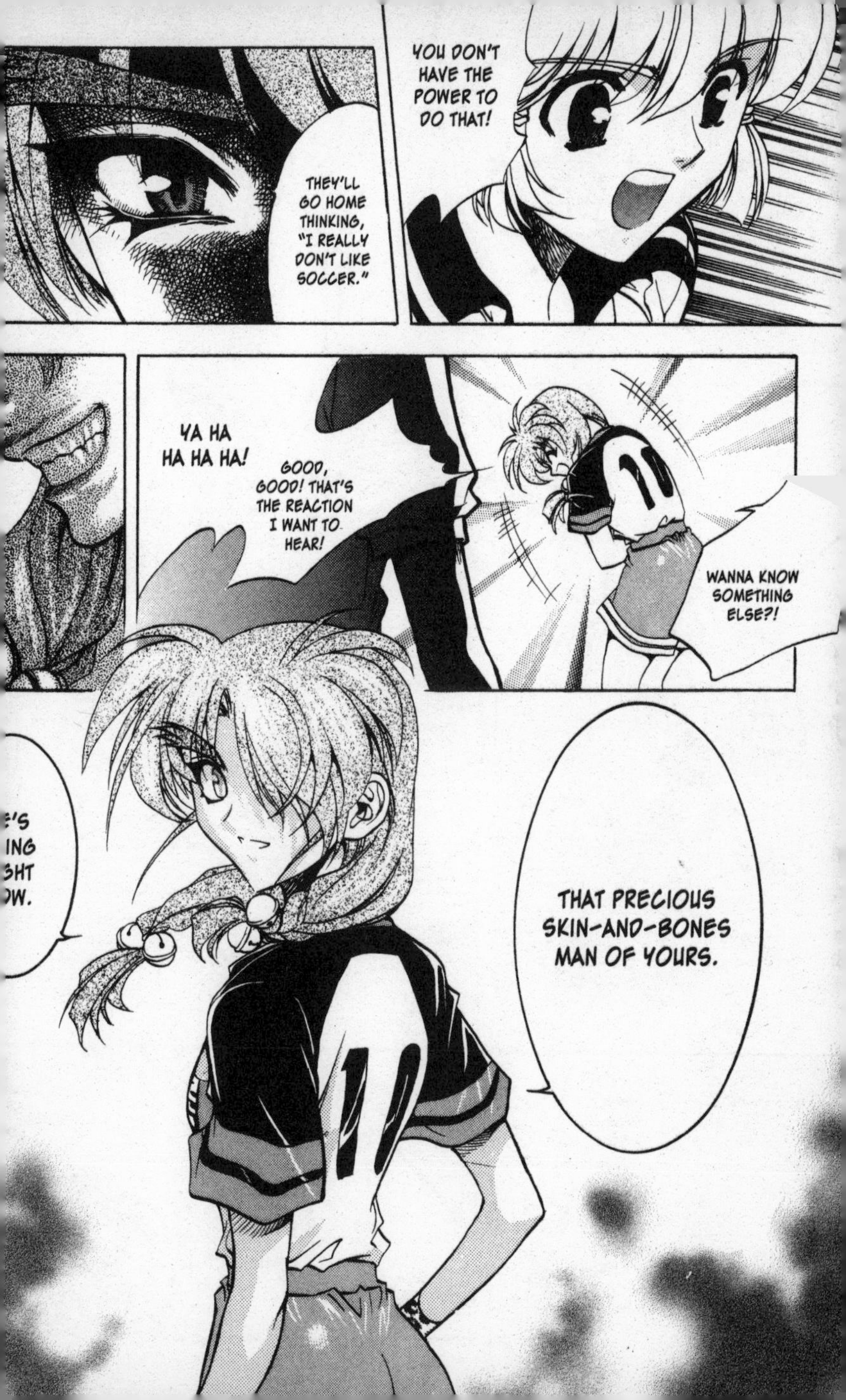
THEY'LL GO HOME THINKING, "I REALLY DON'T LIKE SOCCER."
YOU DON'T HAVE THE POWER TO DO THAT!
YA HA HA HA HA!
GOOD, GOOD! THAT'S THE REACTION I WANT TO HEAR!
WANNA KNOW SOMETHING ELSE?!
THAT PRECIOUS SKIN-AND-BONES MAN OF YOURS.

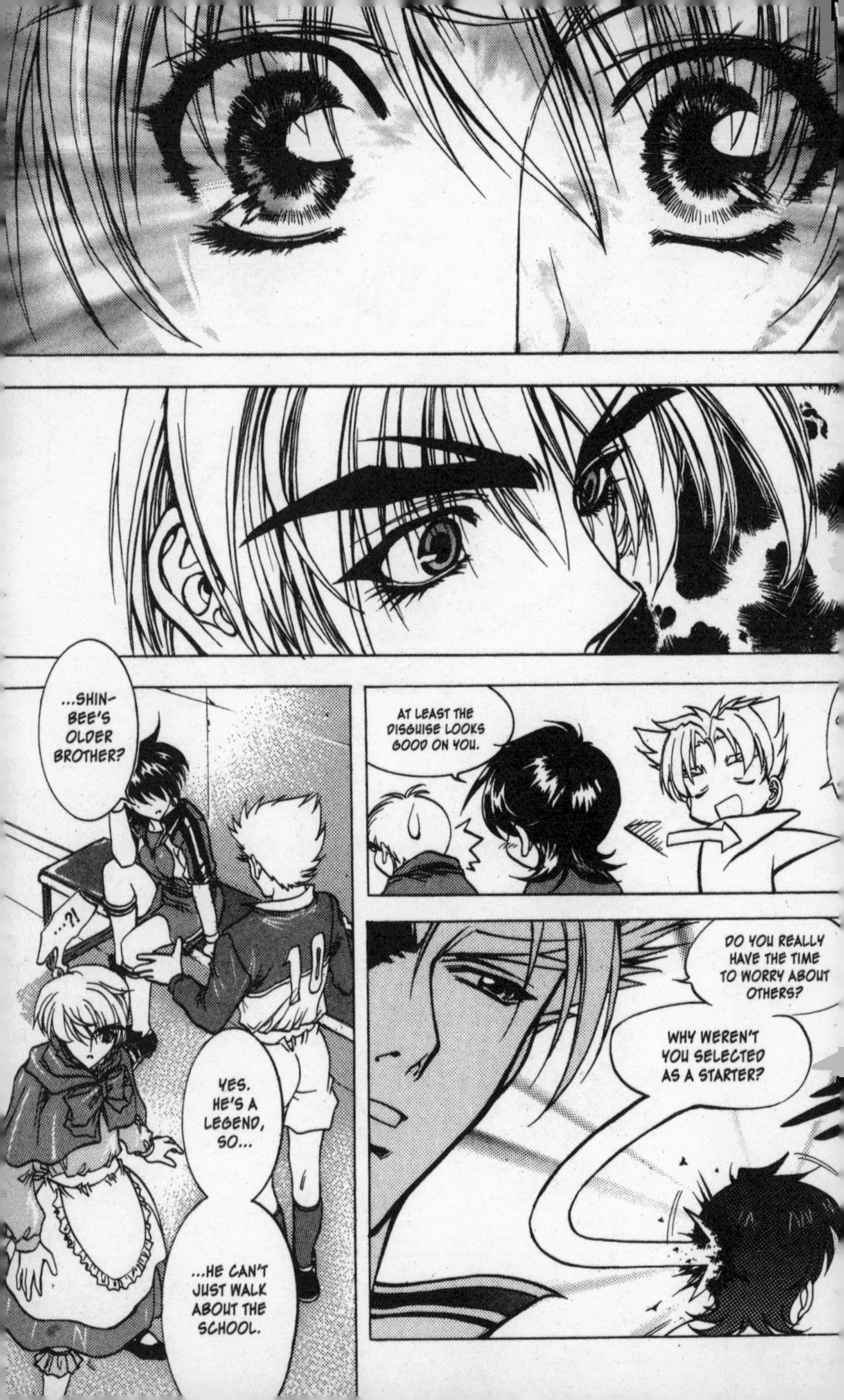
...SHIN-BEE'S OLDER BROTHER?
...?!
YES. HE'S A LEGEND, SO...
...HE CAN'T JUST WALK ABOUT THE SCHOOL.
AT LEAST THE DISGUISE LOOKS GOOD ON YOU.
DO YOU REALLY HAVE THE TIME TO WORRY ABOUT OTHERS?
WHY WEREN'T YOU SELECTED AS A STARTER?

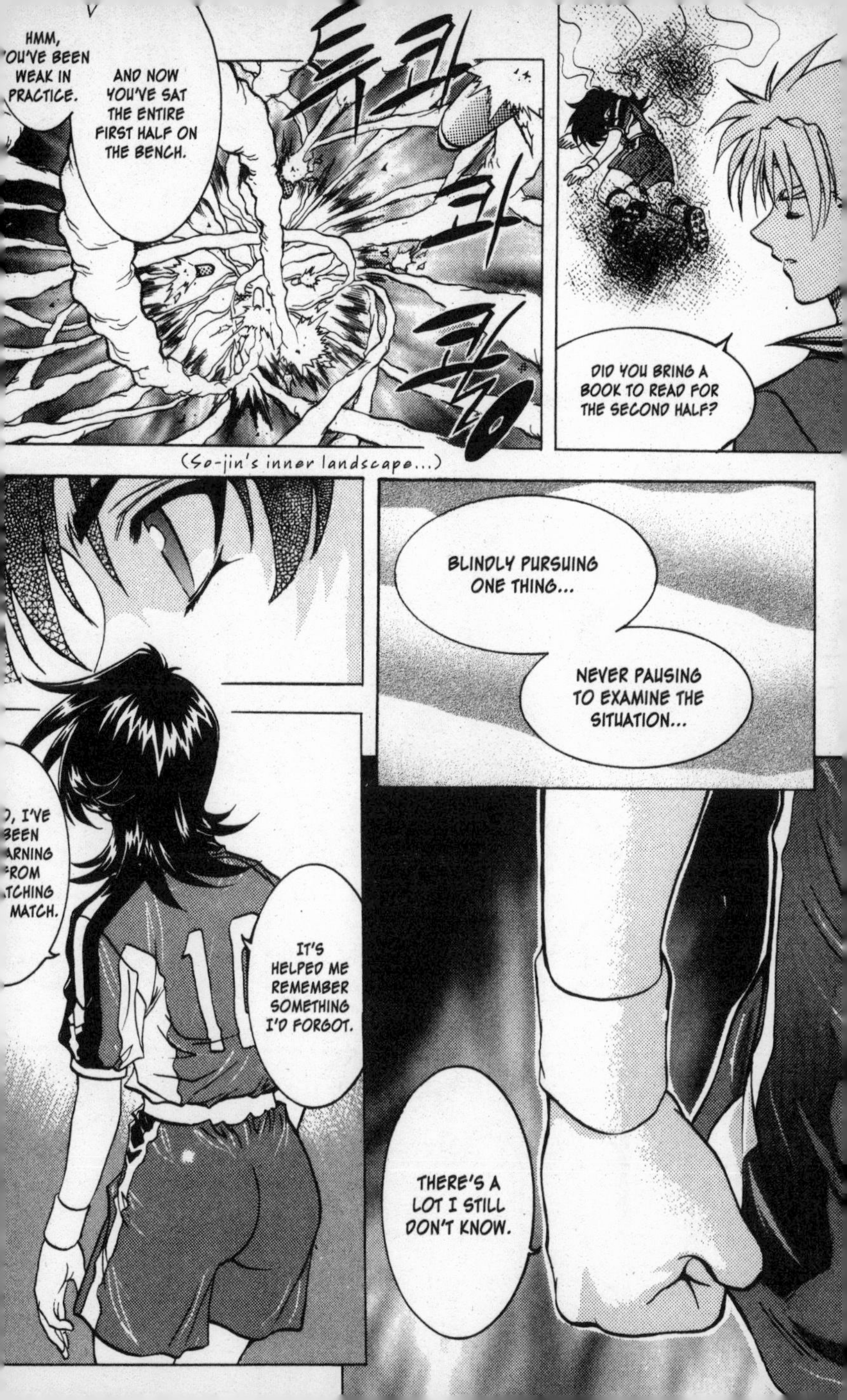
HMM, 'OU'VE BEEN WEAK IN PRACTICE.
AND NOW YOU'VE SAT THE ENTIRE FIRST HALF ON THE BENCH.
DID YOU BRING A BOOK TO READ FOR THE SECOND HALF?
(So-jin's inner landscape...)
BLINDLY PURSUING ONE THING...
NEVER PAUSING TO EXAMINE THE SITUATION...
O, I'VE BEEN ARNING FROM TCHING MATCH.
IT'S HELPED ME REMEMBER SOMETHING I'D FORGOT.
THERE'S A LOT I STILL DON'T KNOW.

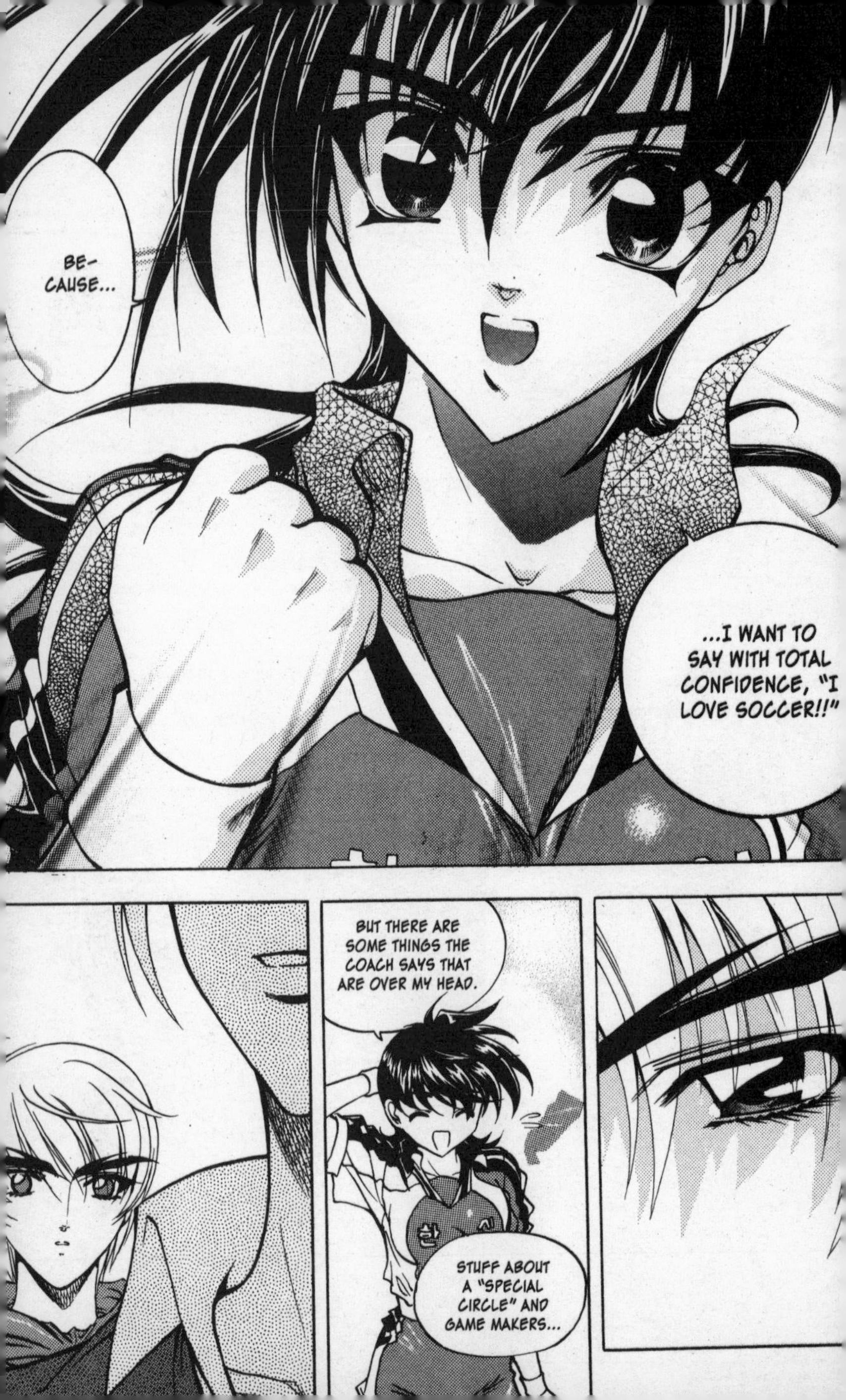
BE-CAUSE...
...I WANT TO SAY WITH TOTAL CONFIDENCE, "I LOVE SOCCER!!"
BUT THERE ARE SOME THINGS THE COACH SAYS THAT ARE OVER MY HEAD.
STUFF ABOUT A "SPECIAL CIRCLE" AND GAME MAKERS...

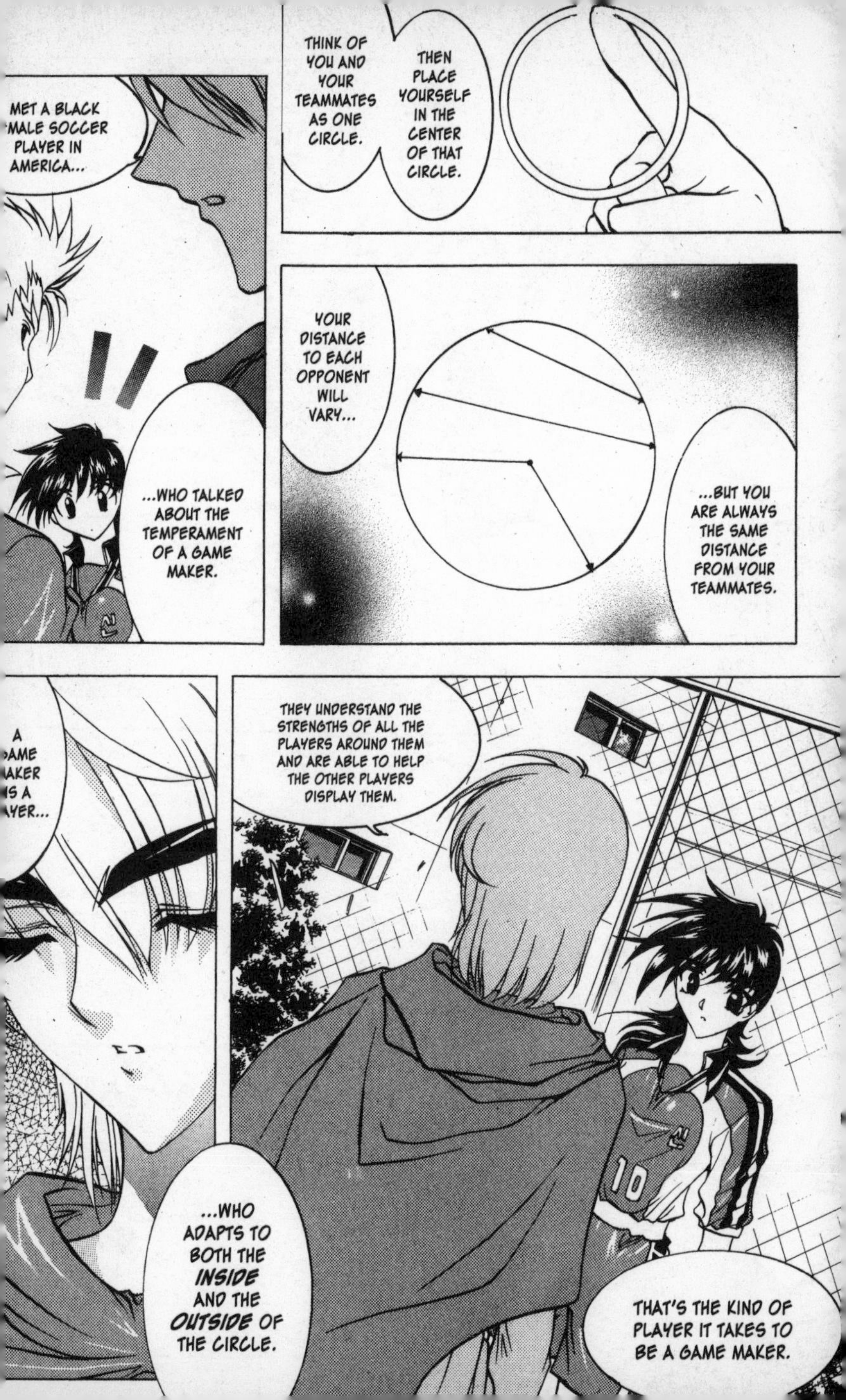

MET A BLACK MALE SOCCER PLAYER IN AMERICA...
...WHO TALKED ABOUT THE TEMPERAMENT OF A GAME MAKER.
THINK OF YOU AND YOUR TEAMMATES AS ONE CIRCLE.
THEN PLACE YOURSELF IN THE CENTER OF THAT CIRCLE.
YOUR DISTANCE TO EACH OPPONENT WILL VARY...
...BUT YOU ARE ALWAYS THE SAME DISTANCE FROM YOUR TEAMMATES.
A AME AKER S A AYER...
...WHO ADAPTS TO BOTH THE *INSIDE* AND THE *OUTSIDE* OF THE CIRCLE.
THEY UNDERSTAND THE STRENGTHS OF ALL THE PLAYERS AROUND THEM AND ARE ABLE TO HELP THE OTHER PLAYERS DISPLAY THEM.
THAT'S THE KIND OF PLAYER IT TAKES TO BE A GAME MAKER.

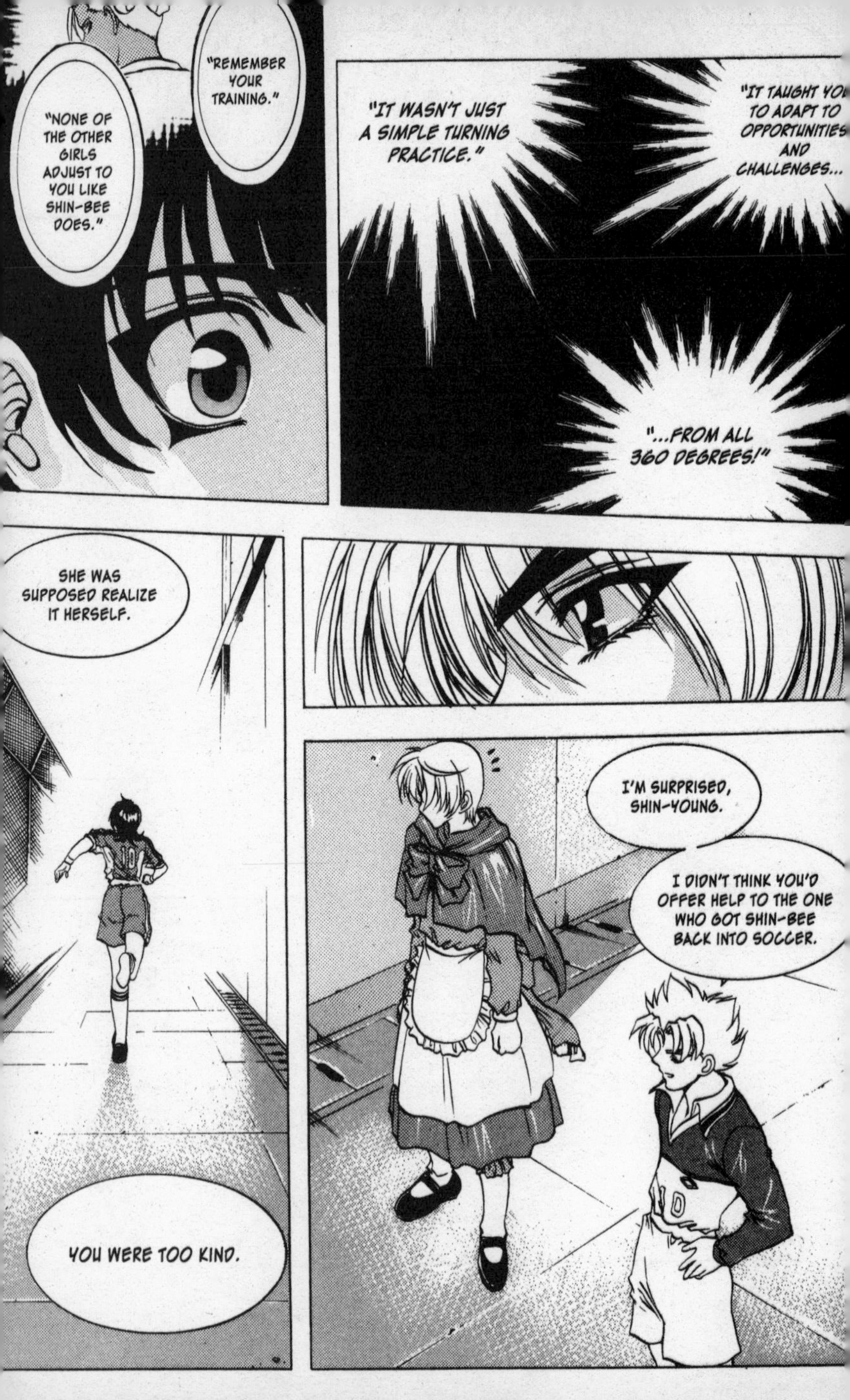
"NONE OF THE OTHER GIRLS ADJUST TO YOU LIKE SHIN-BEE DOES."
"REMEMBER YOUR TRAINING."
"IT WASN'T JUST A SIMPLE TURNING PRACTICE."
"IT TAUGHT YOU TO ADAPT TO OPPORTUNITIES AND CHALLENGES...
"...FROM ALL 360 DEGREES!"
SHE WAS SUPPOSED REALIZE IT HERSELF.
YOU WERE TOO KIND.
I'M SURPRISED, SHIN-YOUNG.
I DIDN'T THINK YOU'D OFFER HELP TO THE ONE WHO GOT SHIN-BEE BACK INTO SOCCER.

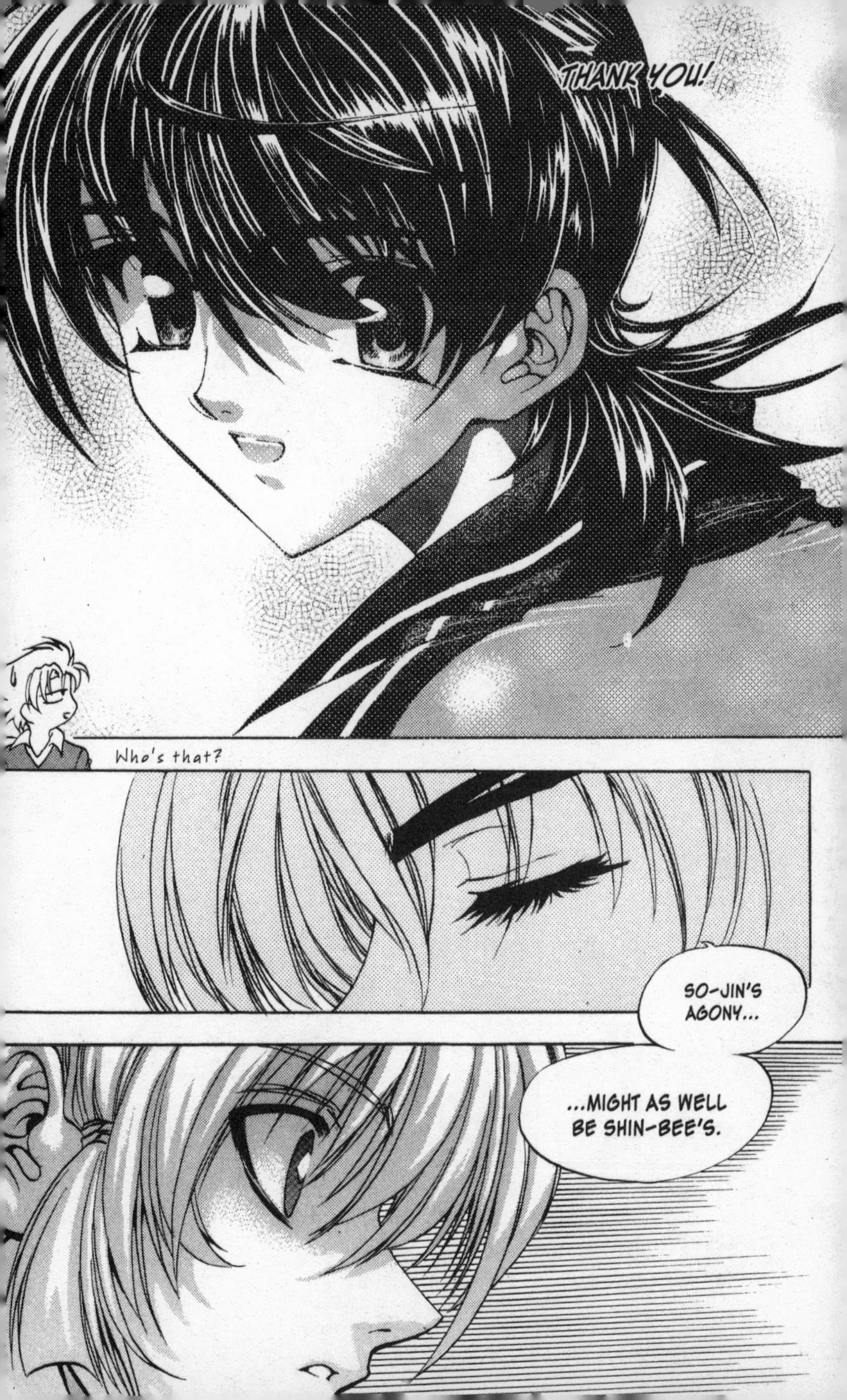
THANK YOU!
Who's that?
SO-JIN'S AGONY...
...MIGHT AS WELL BE SHIN-BEE'S.

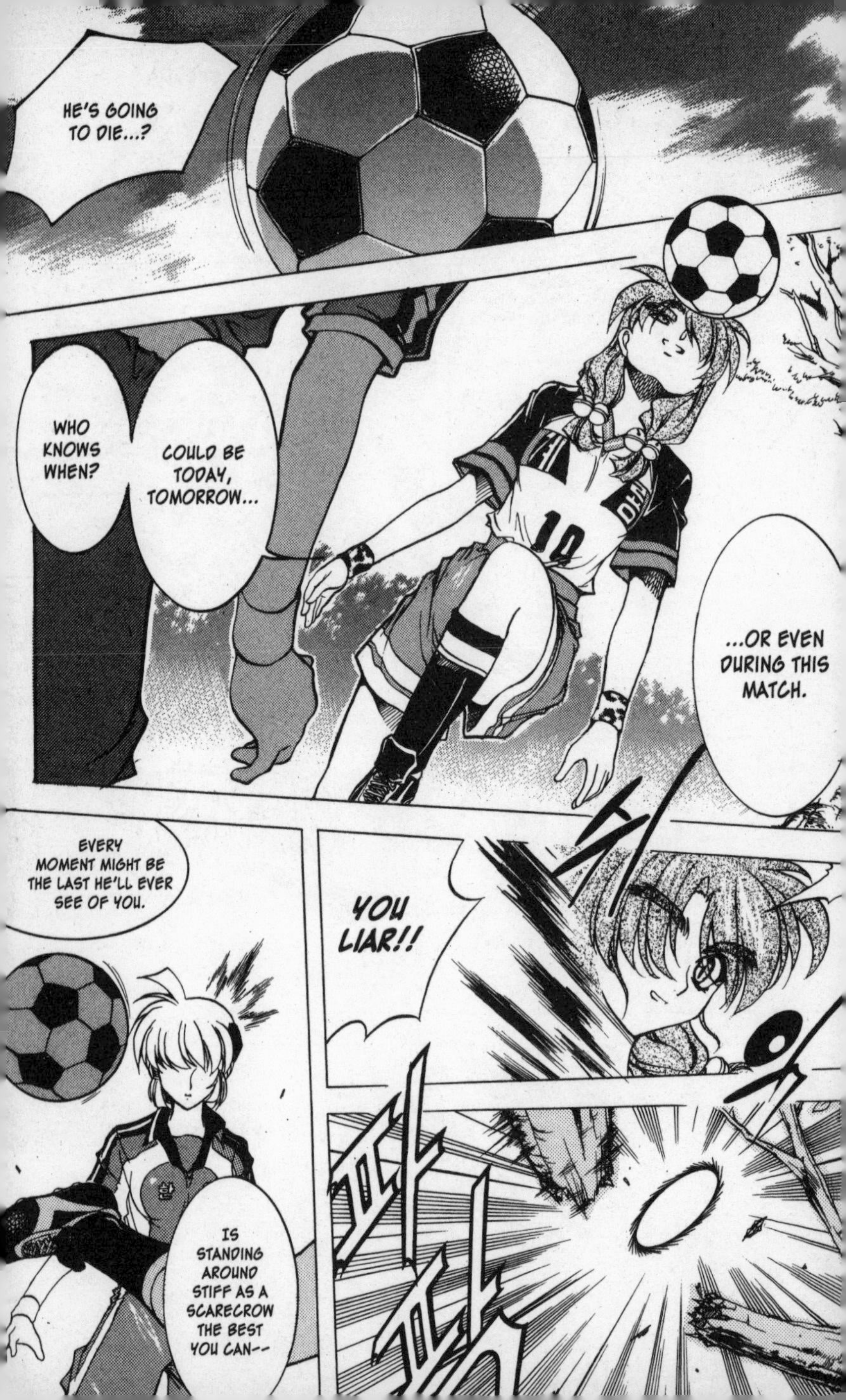
HE'S GOING TO DIE...?
WHO KNOWS WHEN?
COULD BE TODAY, TOMORROW...
...OR EVEN DURING THIS MATCH.
EVERY MOMENT MIGHT BE THE LAST HE'LL EVER SEE OF YOU.
IS STANDING AROUND STIFF AS A SCARECROW THE BEST YOU CAN--
YOU LIAR!!

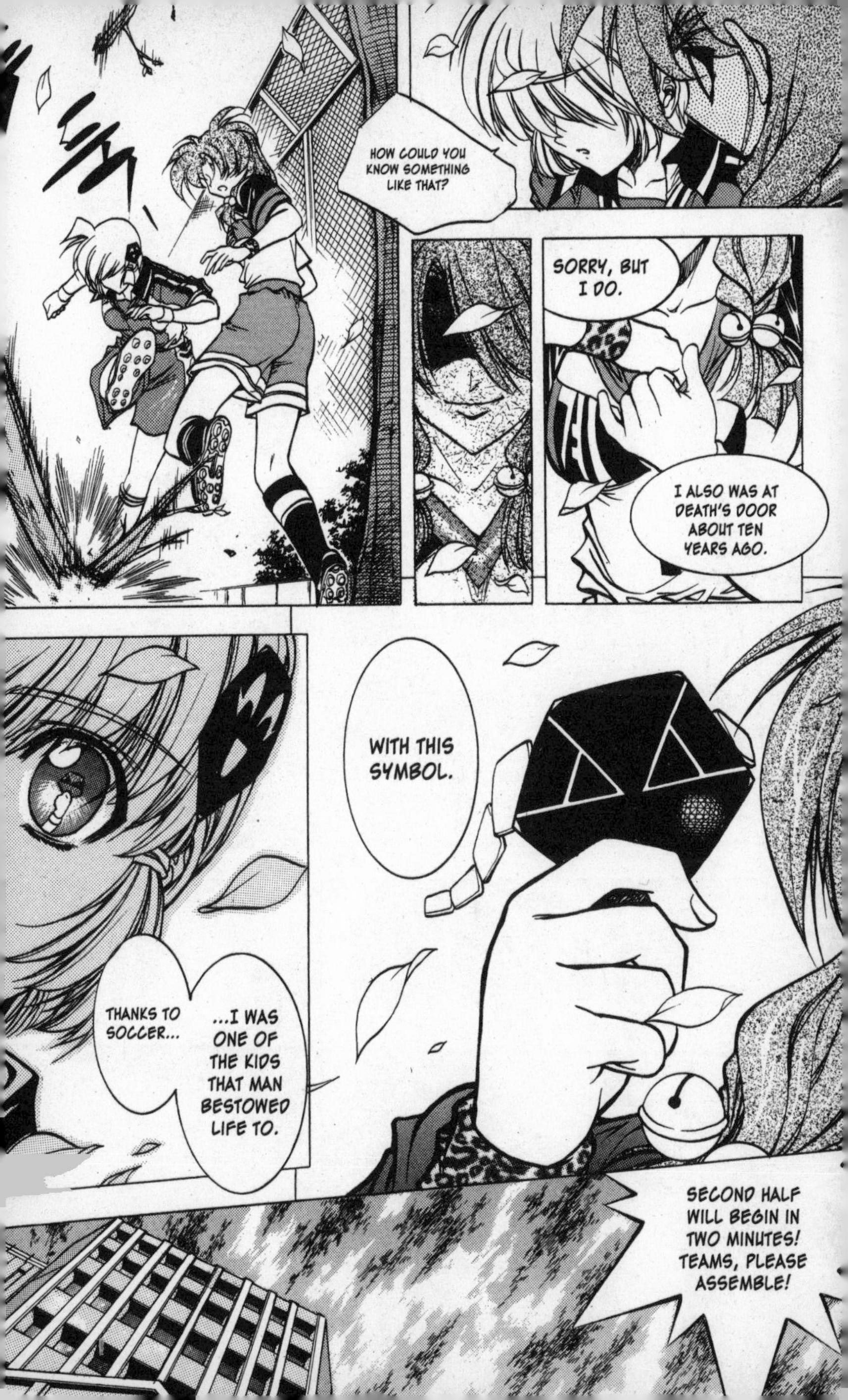
HOW COULD YOU KNOW SOMETHING LIKE THAT?
SORRY, BUT I DO.
I ALSO WAS AT DEATH'S DOOR ABOUT TEN YEARS AGO.
WITH THIS SYMBOL.
THANKS TO SOCCER...
...I WAS ONE OF THE KIDS THAT MAN BESTOWED LIFE TO.
SECOND HALF WILL BEGIN IN TWO MINUTES! TEAMS, PLEASE ASSEMBLE!

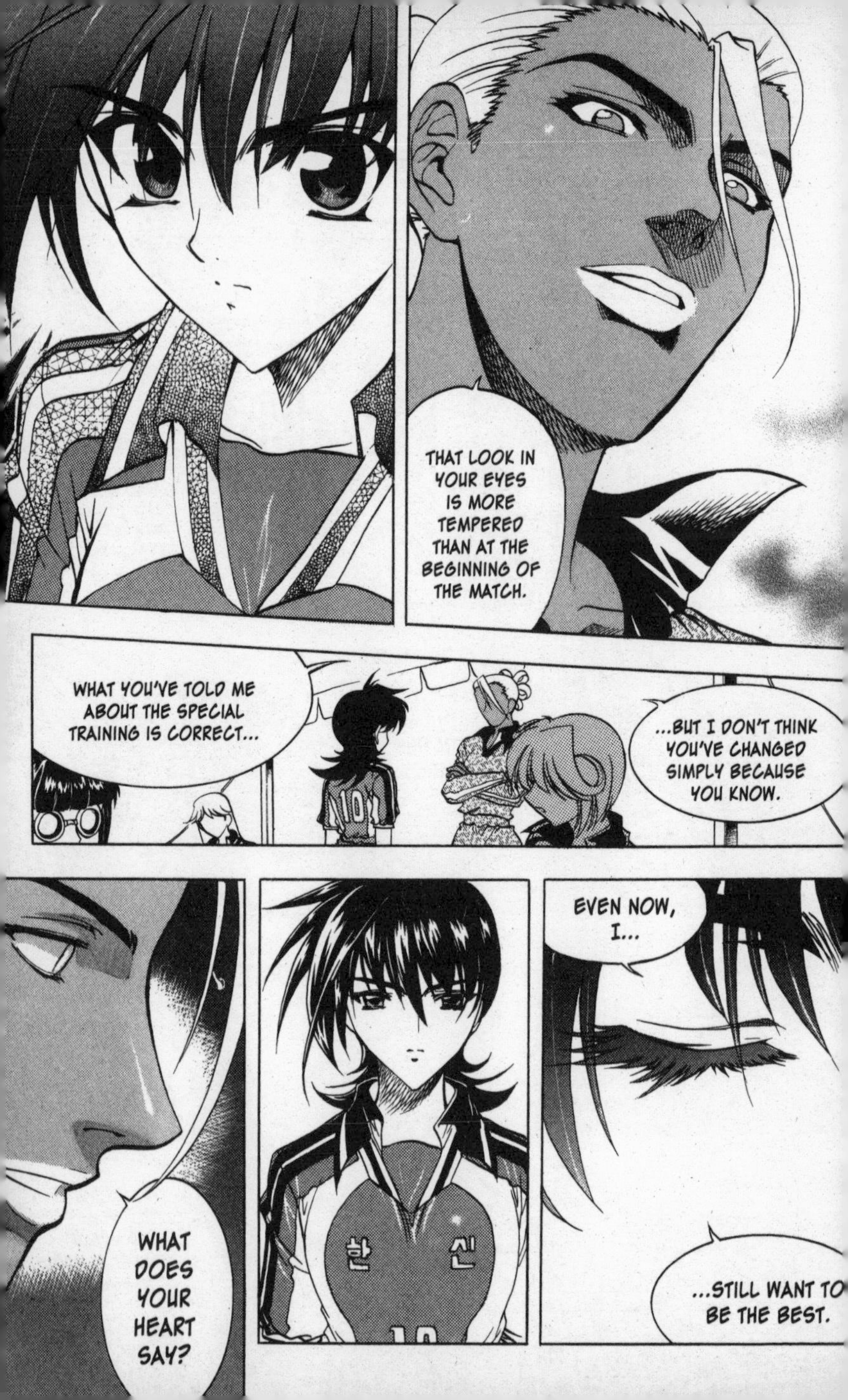
THAT LOOK IN YOUR EYES IS MORE TEMPERED THAN AT THE BEGINNING OF THE MATCH.
WHAT YOU'VE TOLD ME ABOUT THE SPECIAL TRAINING IS CORRECT...
...BUT I DON'T THINK YOU'VE CHANGED SIMPLY BECAUSE YOU KNOW.
WHAT DOES YOUR HEART SAY?
한 신
EVEN NOW, I...
...STILL WANT TO BE THE BEST.

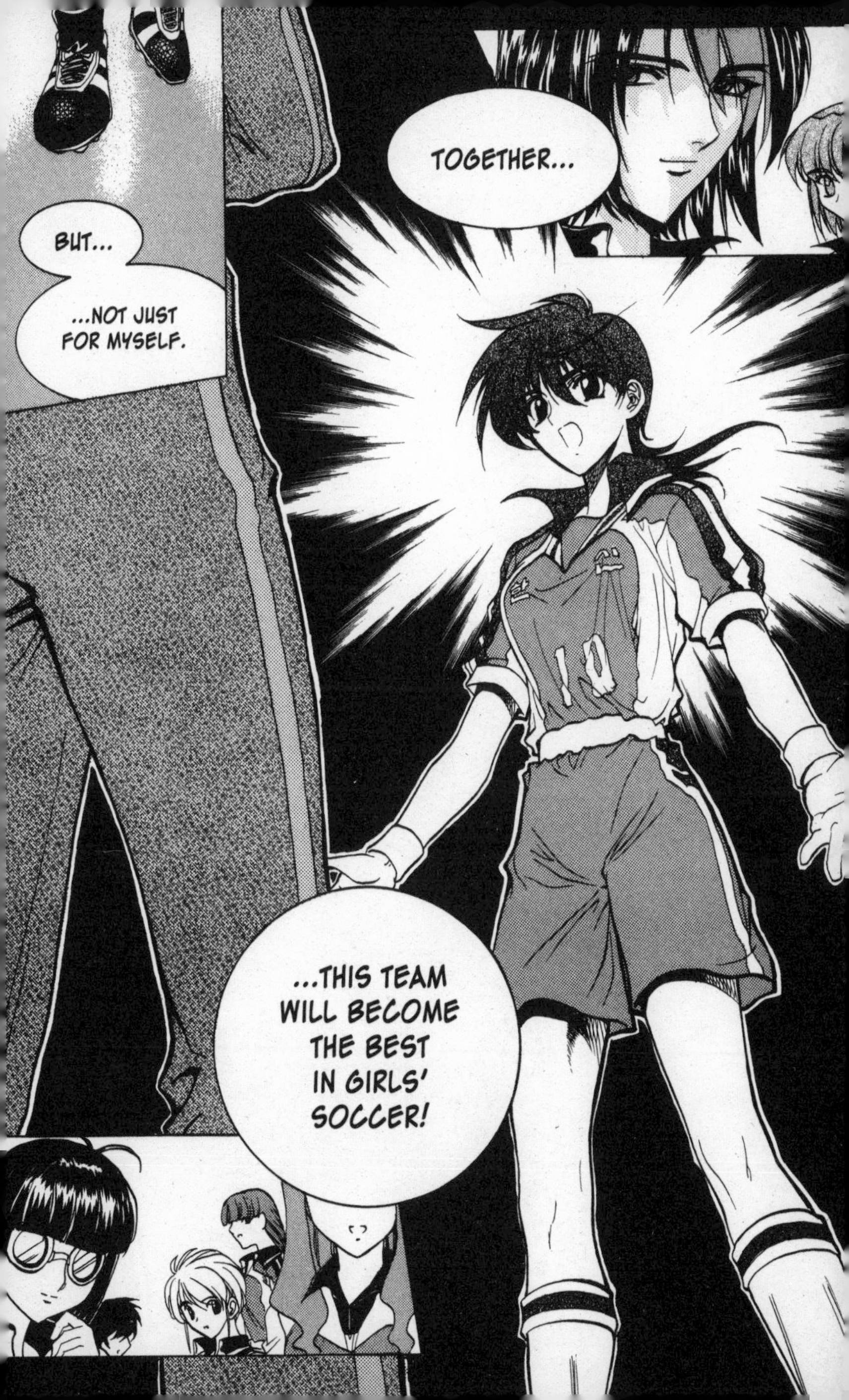
BUT...
...NOT JUST FOR MYSELF.
TOGETHER...
...THIS TEAM WILL BECOME THE BEST IN GIRLS' SOCCER!

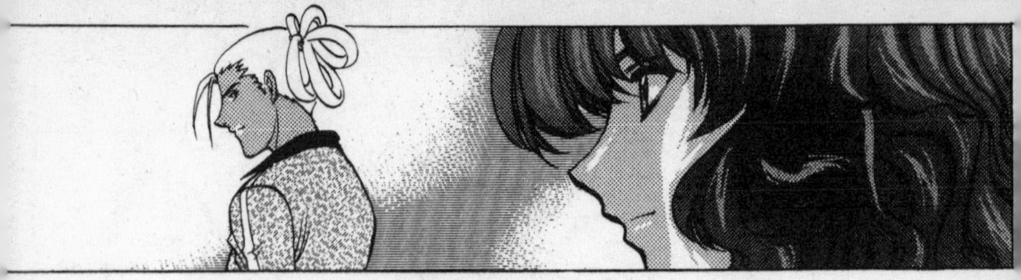

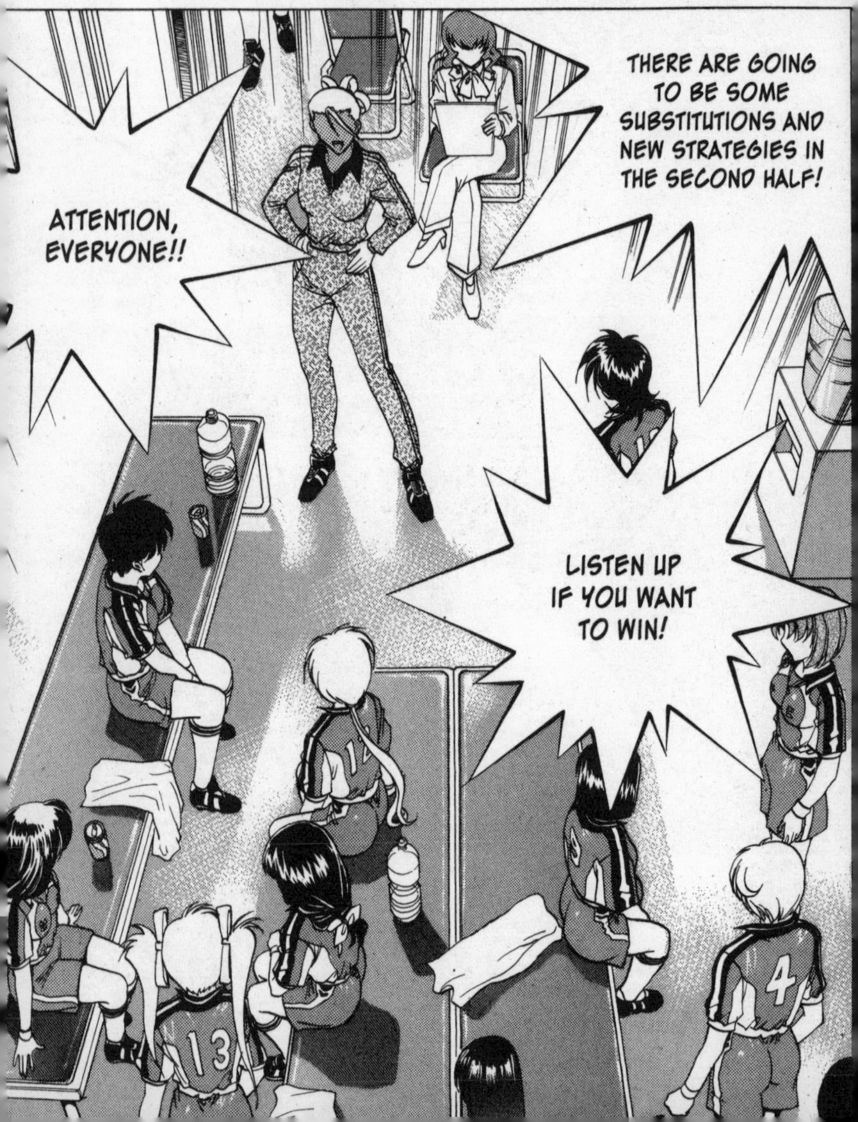
ATTENTION, EVERYONE!!
THERE ARE GOING TO BE SOME SUBSTITUTIONS AND NEW STRATEGIES IN THE SECOND HALF!
LISTEN UP IF YOU WANT TO WIN!

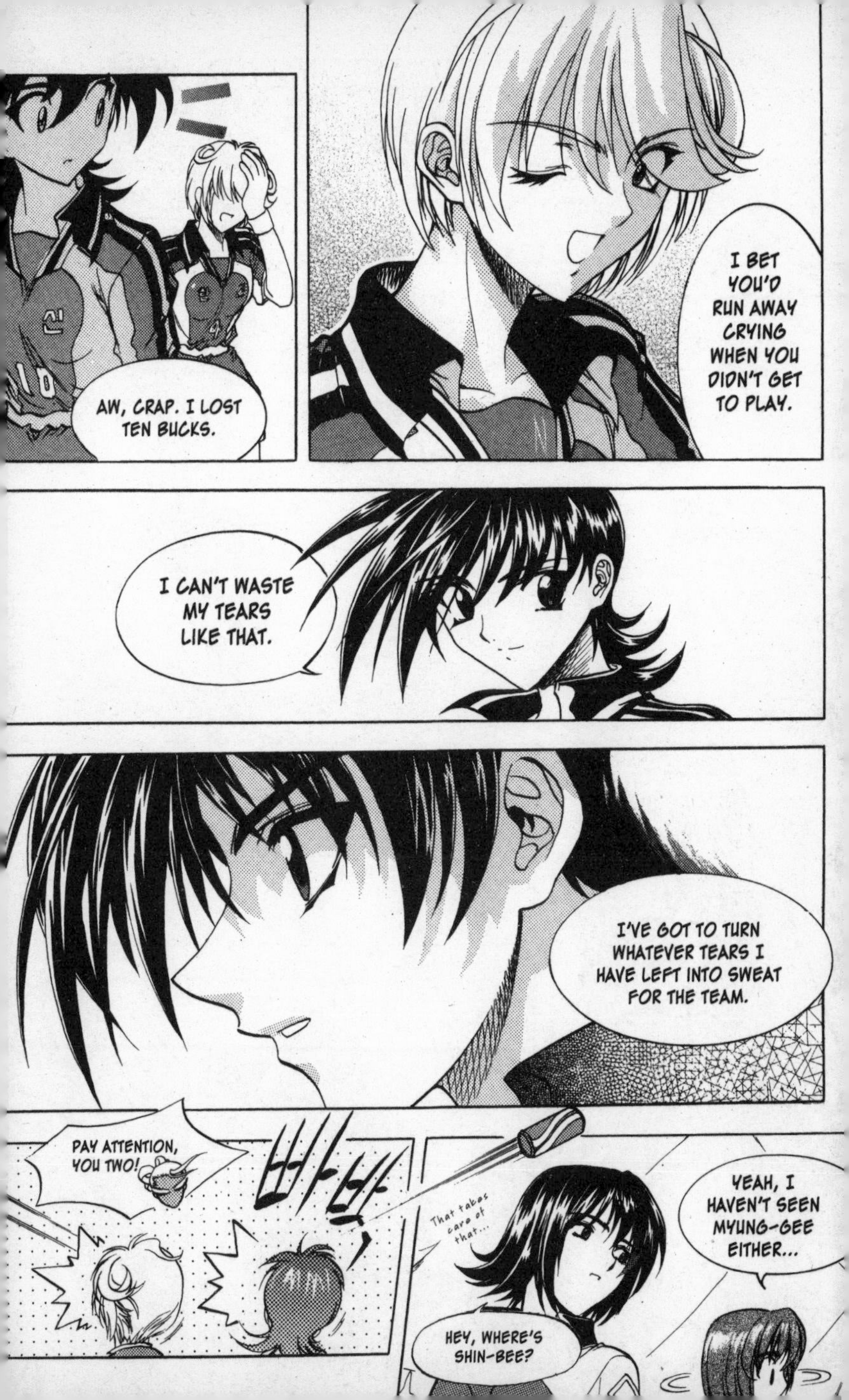

AW, CRAP. I LOST TEN BUCKS.
I BET YOU'D RUN AWAY CRYING WHEN YOU DIDN'T GET TO PLAY.
I CAN'T WASTE MY TEARS LIKE THAT.
I'VE GOT TO TURN WHATEVER TEARS I HAVE LEFT INTO SWEAT FOR THE TEAM.
PAY ATTENTION, YOU TWO!
That takes care of that...
HEY, WHERE'S SHIN-BEE?
YEAH, I HAVEN'T SEEN MYUNG-GEE EITHER...

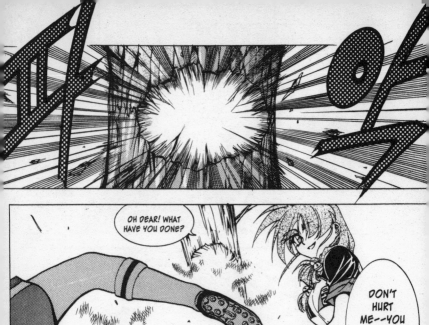

OH DEAR! WHAT HAVE YOU DONE?

DON'T HURT ME--YOU COULD GET IN TROUBLE.

LET'S...

...TAKE THIS TO THE FIELD.

YA HA HA HA!

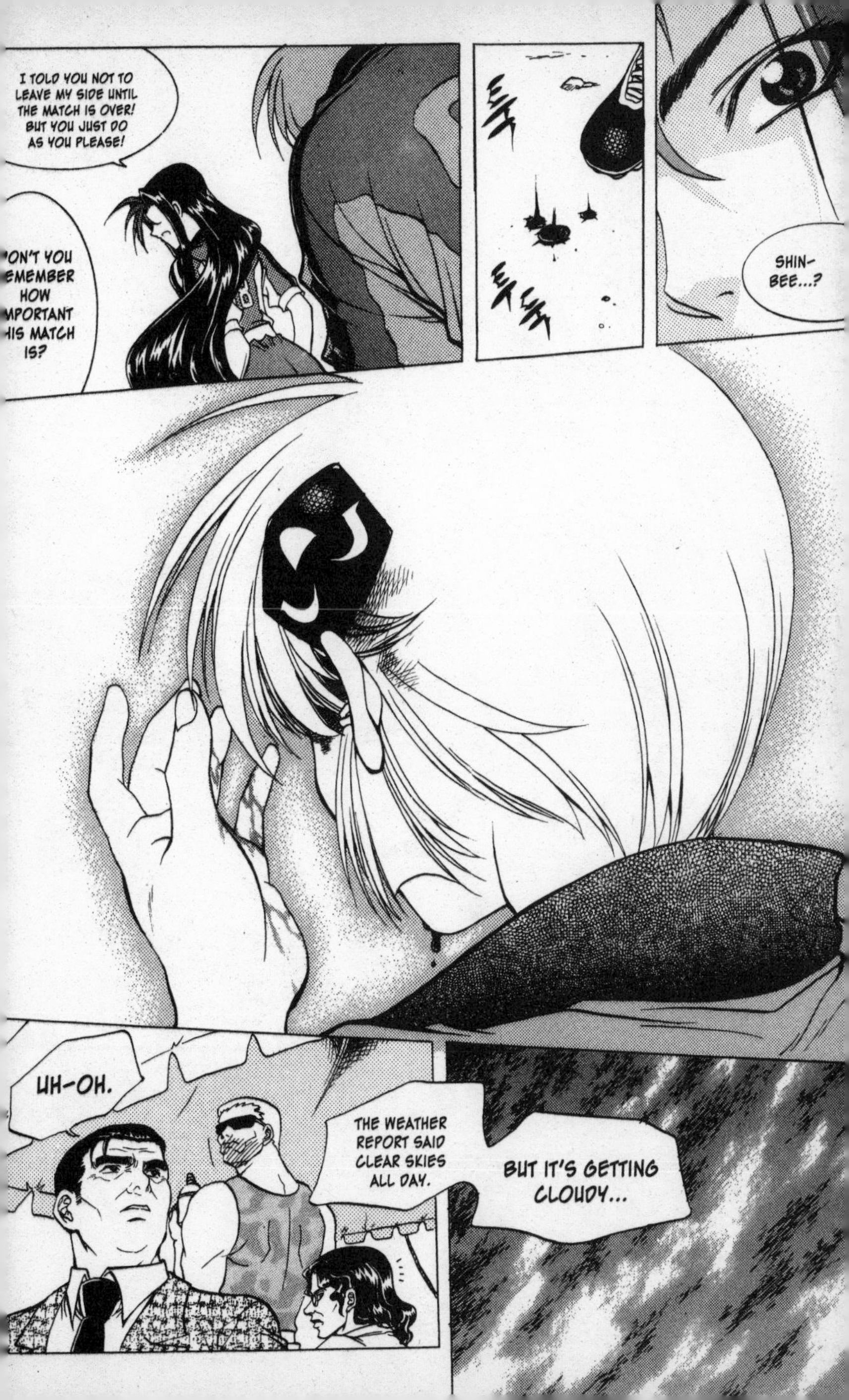
I TOLD YOU NOT TO LEAVE MY SIDE UNTIL THE MATCH IS OVER! BUT YOU JUST DO AS YOU PLEASE!
'ON'T YOU EMEMBER HOW MPORTANT HIS MATCH IS?
SHIN-BEE...?
UH-OH.
THE WEATHER REPORT SAID CLEAR SKIES ALL DAY.
BUT IT'S GETTING CLOUDY...

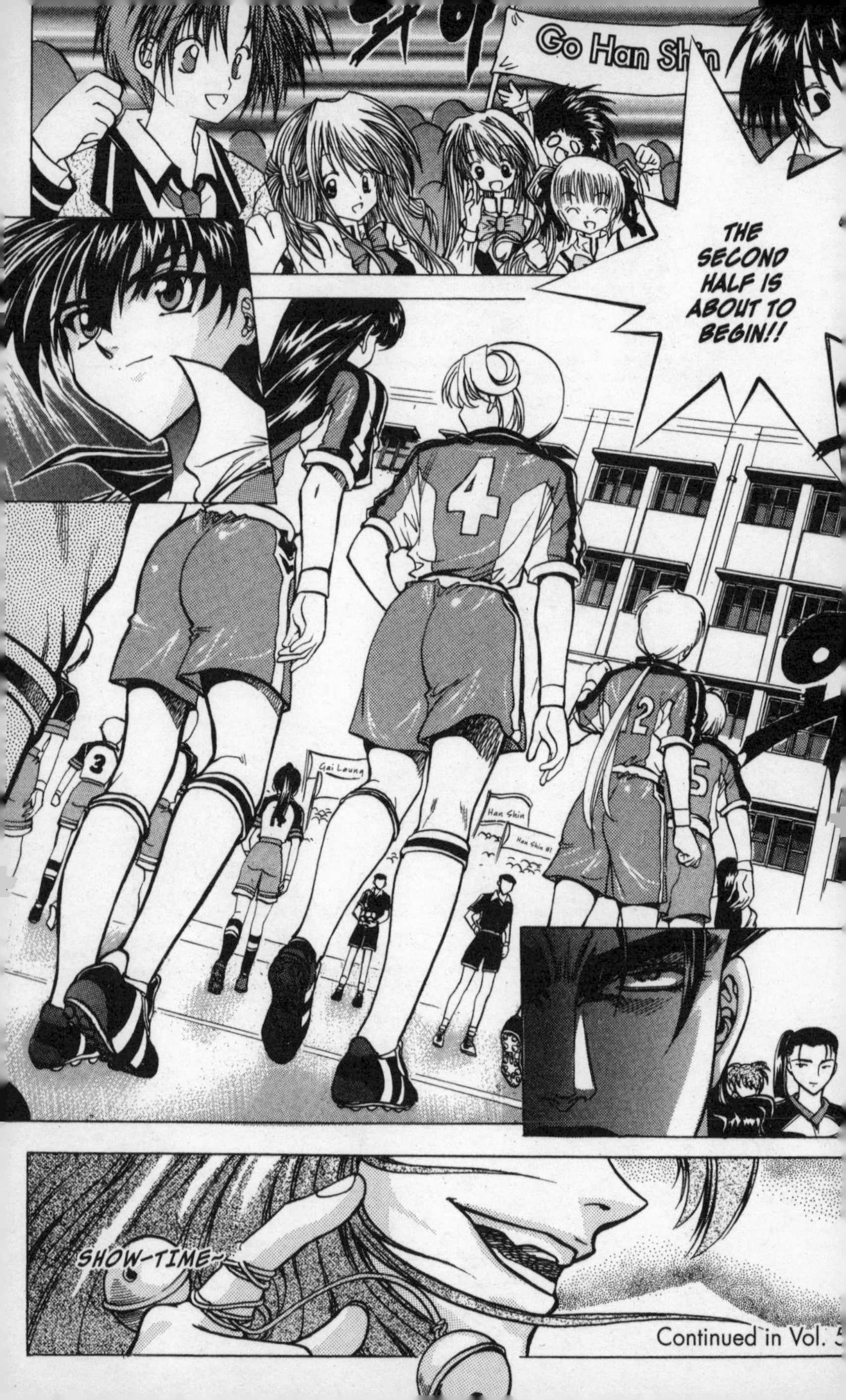

Go Han Shin
THE SECOND HALF IS ABOUT TO BEGIN!!
SHOW-TIME~
Continued in Vol. 5

Angelcup vol. 5

coming soon!!

ELDO's Crisis-Ridden Drawing Room

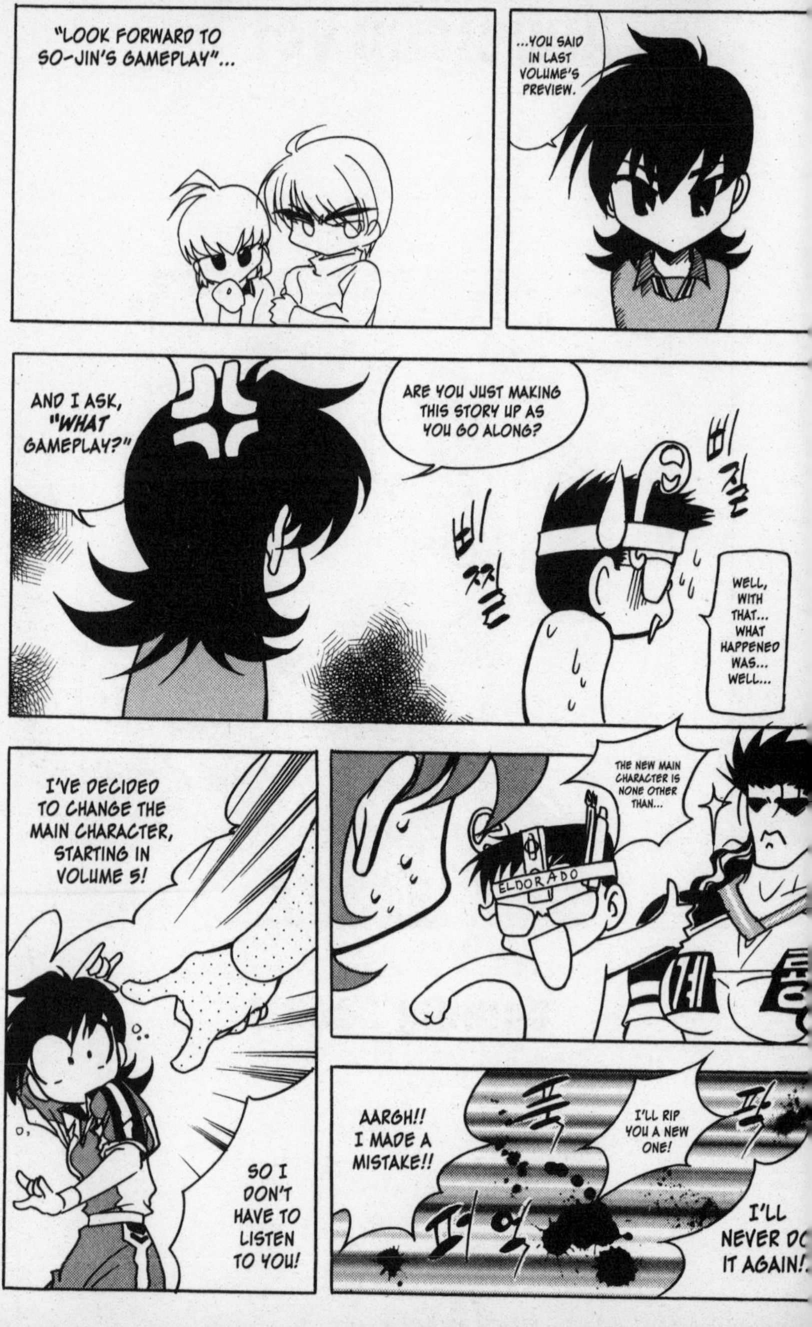

"LOOK FORWARD TO SO-JIN'S GAMEPLAY"...
...YOU SAID IN LAST VOLUME'S PREVIEW.
AND I ASK, "WHAT GAMEPLAY?"
ARE YOU JUST MAKING THIS STORY UP AS YOU GO ALONG?
삐질
삐질
WELL, WITH THAT... WHAT HAPPENED WAS... WELL...
I'VE DECIDED TO CHANGE THE MAIN CHARACTER, STARTING IN VOLUME 5!
SO I DON'T HAVE TO LISTEN TO YOU!
THE NEW MAIN CHARACTER IS NONE OTHER THAN...
ELDORADO
AARGH!! I MADE A MISTAKE!!
푹
I'LL RIP YOU A NEW ONE!
팍
퍼억
I'LL NEVER DO IT AGAIN!.

ASSISTANT #2

Mr. Hai-Tai's Birth

by Rudy

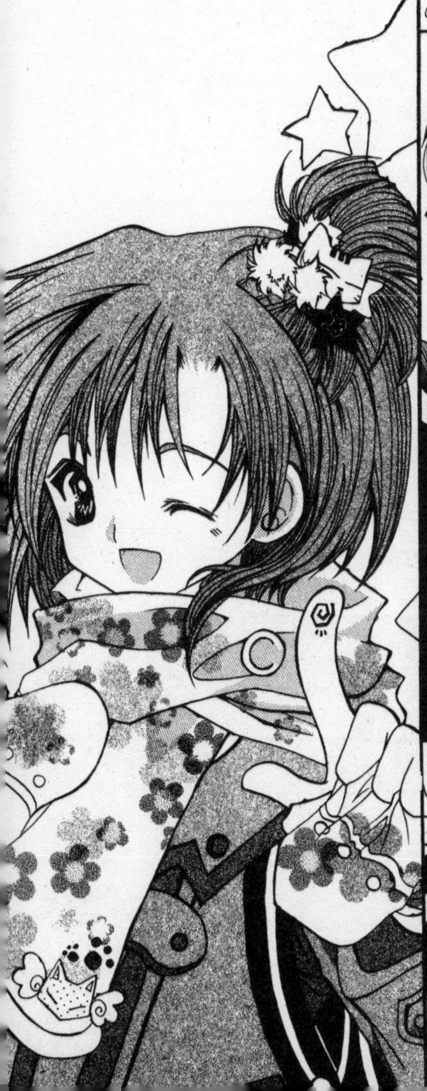

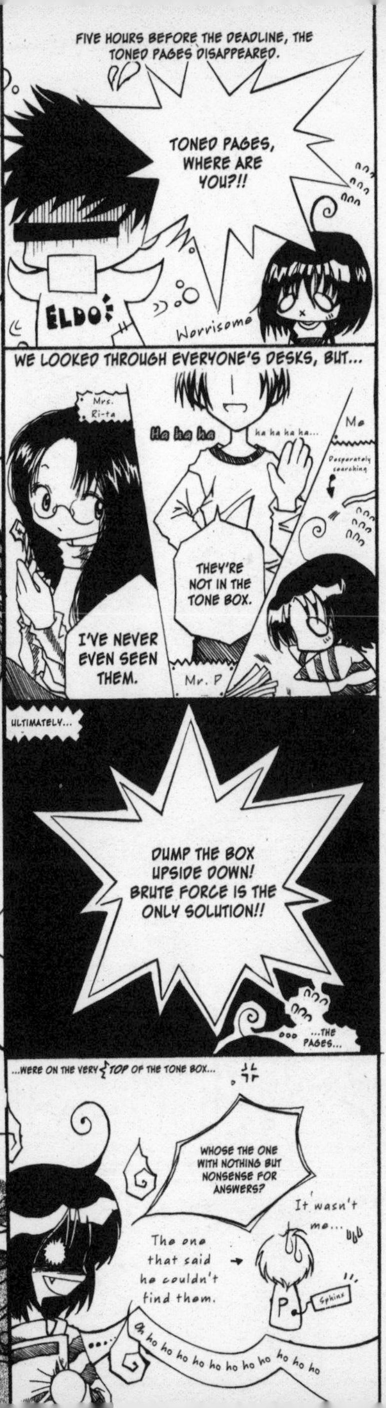
FIVE HOURS BEFORE THE DEADLINE, THE TONED PAGES DISAPPEARED.
TONED PAGES, WHERE ARE YOU?!!
ELDO
Worrisome
WE LOOKED THROUGH EVERYONE'S DESKS, BUT...
Mrs. Ri-ta
Ha ha ha
ha ha ha ha...
Me
Desperately searching
THEY'RE NOT IN THE TONE BOX.
I'VE NEVER EVEN SEEN THEM.
Mr. P
ULTIMATELY...
DUMP THE BOX UPSIDE DOWN! BRUTE FORCE IS THE ONLY SOLUTION!!
...THE PAGES...
...WERE ON THE VERY TOP OF THE TONE BOX...
WHOSE THE ONE WITH NOTHING BUT NONSENSE FOR ANSWERS?
It wasn't me...
The one that said he couldn't find them.
P
Sphinx
Oh ho ho ho ho ho ho ho ho ho ho ho

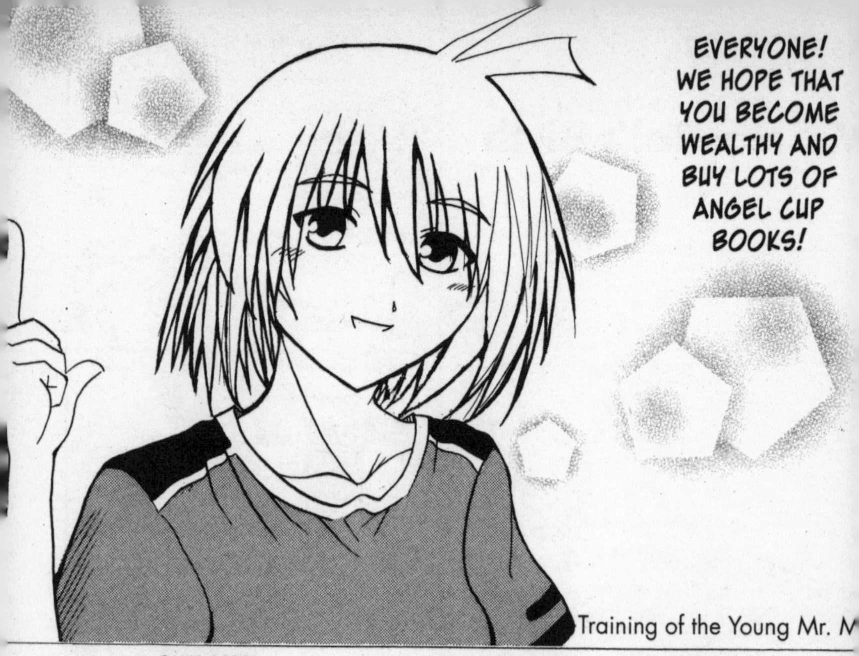
EVERYONE! WE HOPE THAT YOU BECOME WEALTHY AND BUY LOTS OF ANGEL CUP BOOKS!

Training of the Young Mr. M

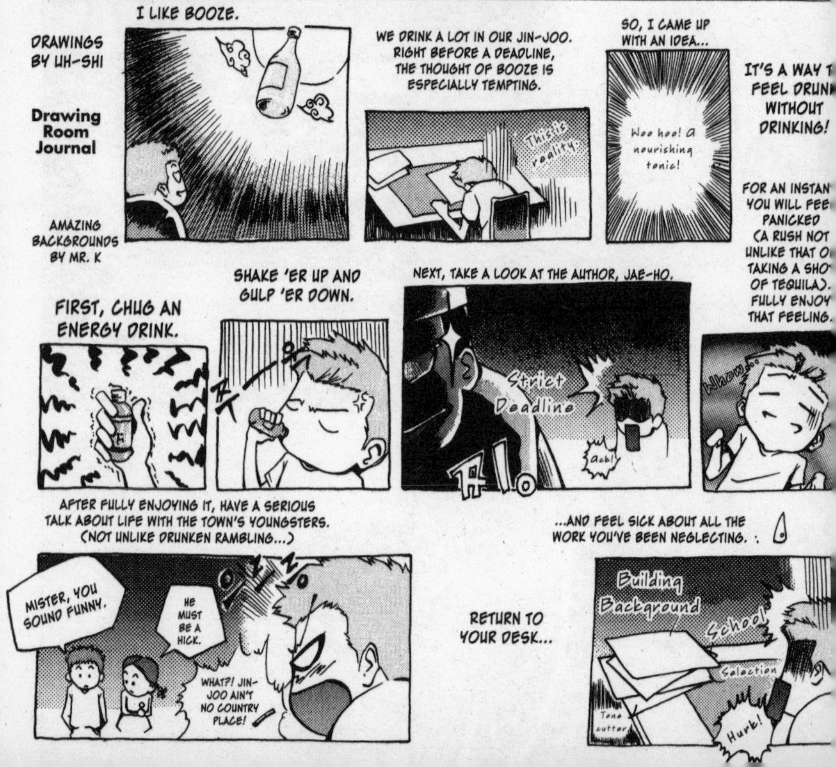
DRAWINGS BY UH-SHI
Drawing Room Journal
AMAZING BACKGROUNDS BY MR. K
I LIKE BOOZE.
WE DRINK A LOT IN OUR JIN-JOO. RIGHT BEFORE A DEADLINE, THE THOUGHT OF BOOZE IS ESPECIALLY TEMPTING.
This is reality.
SO, I CAME UP WITH AN IDEA...
Woo hoo! A nourishing tonic!
IT'S A WAY T FEEL DRUN WITHOUT DRINKING!
FIRST, CHUG AN ENERGY DRINK.
SHAKE 'ER UP AND GULP 'ER DOWN.
NEXT, TAKE A LOOK AT THE AUTHOR, JAE-HO.
Strict Deadline
Ack!
FOR AN INSTAN YOU WILL FEE PANICKED (A RUSH NOT UNLIKE THAT O TAKING A SHO OF TEQUILA). FULLY ENJOY THAT FEELING.
Whew...
AFTER FULLY ENJOYING IT, HAVE A SERIOUS TALK ABOUT LIFE WITH THE TOWN'S YOUNGSTERS. (NOT UNLIKE DRUNKEN RAMBLING...)
MISTER, YOU SOUND FUNNY.
HE MUST BE A HICK.
WHAT?! JIN-JOO AIN'T NO COUNTRY PLACE!
...AND FEEL SICK ABOUT ALL THE WORK YOU'VE BEEN NEGLECTING.
RETURN TO YOUR DESK...
Building Background
School
Selection
Tone cutter
Hurk!

In the next volume of:

The fateful game has already reached the 2nd half. Han Shin and Gai Leung are tied...for now, but will the introduction of Han Shin's best tip the scales in their favor? So-jin and Shin-bee make their long-awaited return to the field, and there will be more than the game on the line...

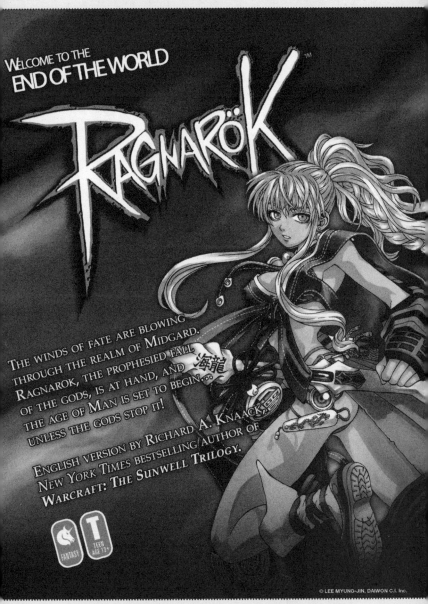

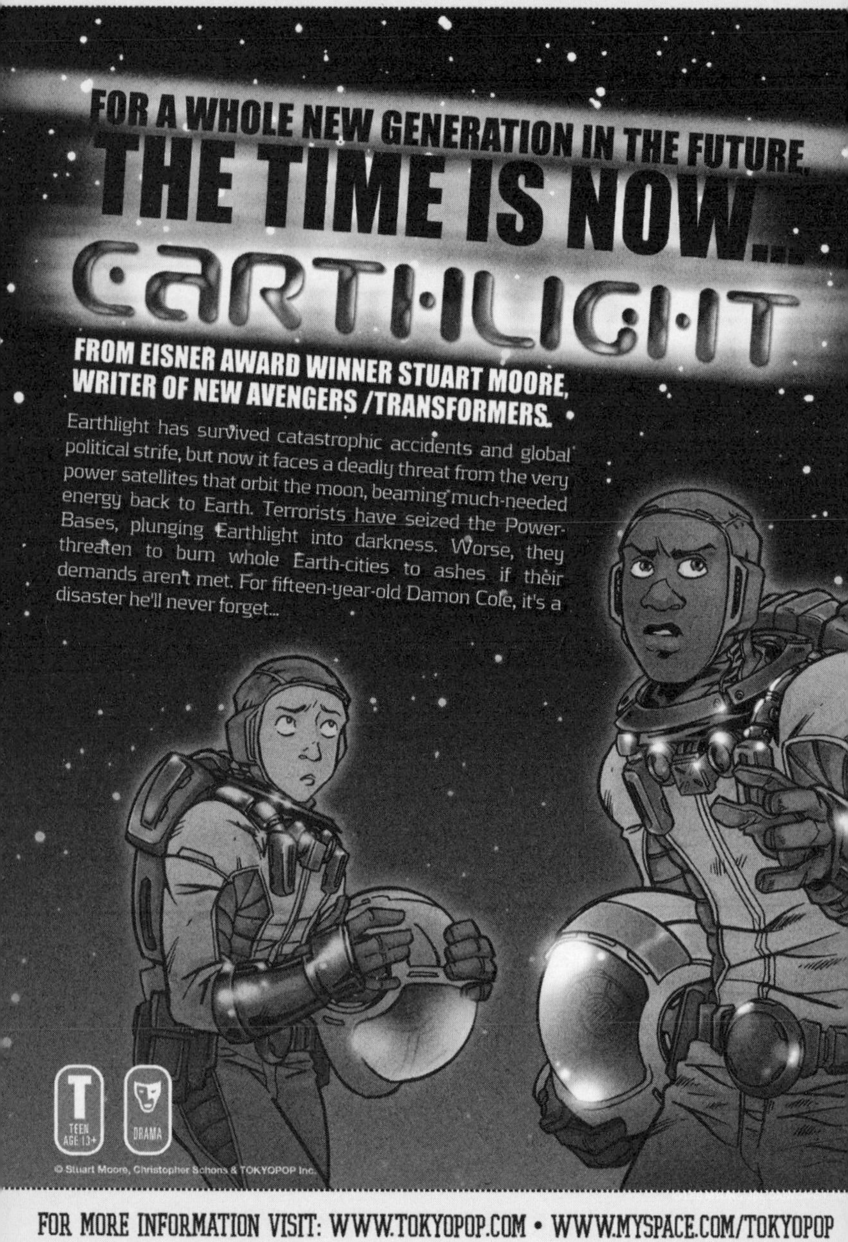
FOR A WHOLE NEW GENERATION IN THE FUTURE.
THE TIME IS NOW...
EARTHLIGHT
FROM EISNER AWARD WINNER STUART MOORE, WRITER OF NEW AVENGERS /TRANSFORMERS.
Earthlight has survived catastrophic accidents and global political strife, but now it faces a deadly threat from the very power satellites that orbit the moon, beaming much-needed energy back to Earth. Terrorists have seized the Power-Bases, plunging Earthlight into darkness. Worse, they threaten to burn whole Earth-cities to ashes if their demands aren't met. For fifteen-year-old Damon Cole, it's a disaster he'll never forget...
T TEEN AGE 13+
DRAMA
© Stuart Moore, Christopher Schons & TOKYOPOP Inc.

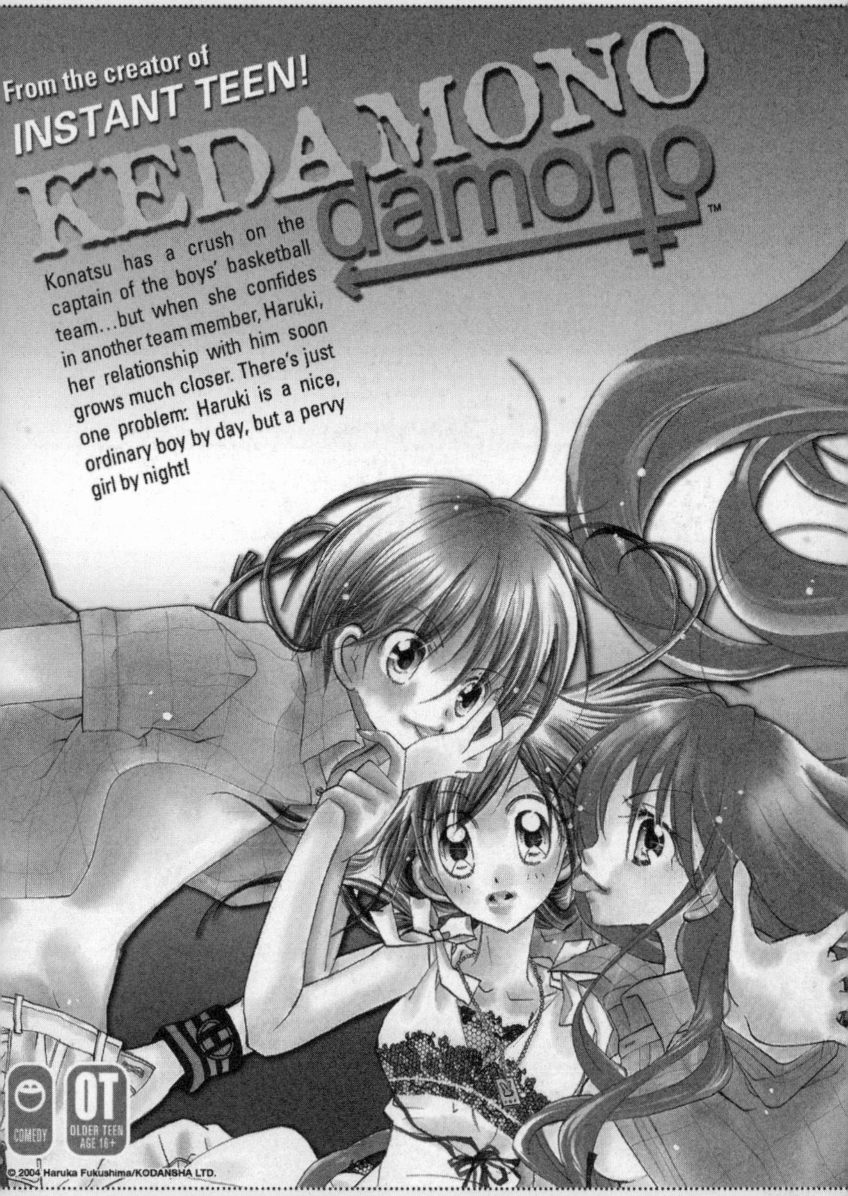
From the creator of
INSTANT TEEN!
KEDAMONO damono™
Konatsu has a crush on the captain of the boys' basketball team...but when she confides in another team member, Haruki, her relationship with him soon grows much closer. There's just one problem: Haruki is a nice, ordinary boy by day, but a pervy girl by night!
COMEDY
OT
OLDER TEEN AGE 16+
© 2004 Haruka Fukushima/KODANSHA LTD.

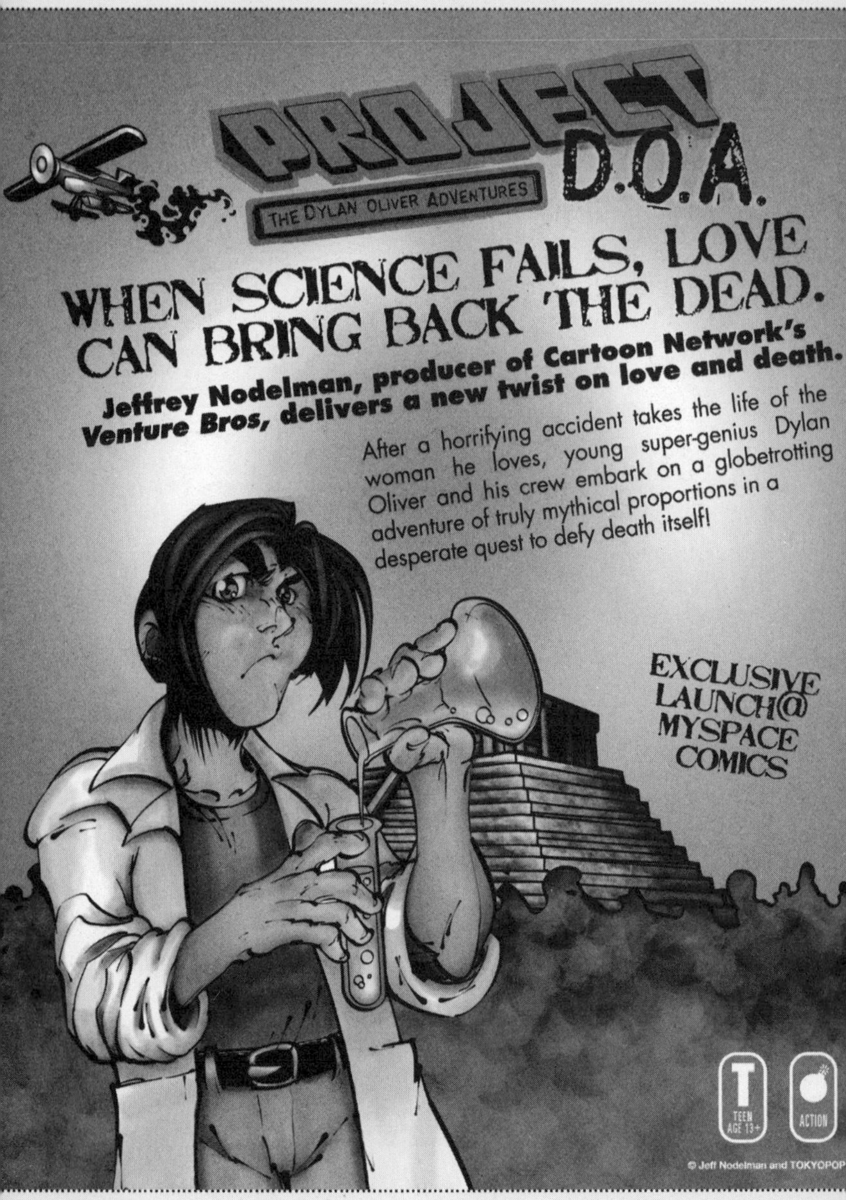
PROJECT D.O.A.
THE DYLAN OLIVER ADVENTURES
WHEN SCIENCE FAILS, LOVE CAN BRING BACK THE DEAD.
Jeffrey Nodelman, producer of Cartoon Network's Venture Bros, delivers a new twist on love and death.
After a horrifying accident takes the life of the woman he loves, young super-genius Dylan Oliver and his crew embark on a globetrotting adventure of truly mythical proportions in a desperate quest to defy death itself!
EXCLUSIVE LAUNCH@ MYSPACE COMICS
T TEEN AGE 13+
ACTION
© Jeff Nodelman and TOKYOPOP

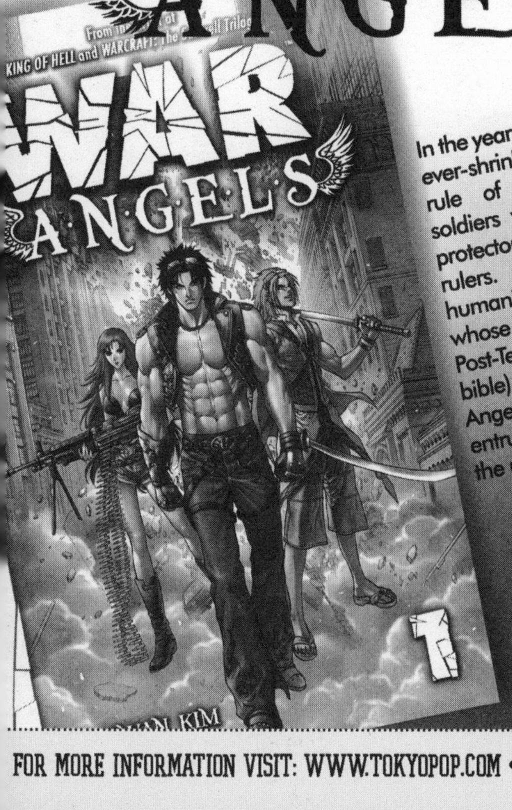
WAR
ANGELS
1

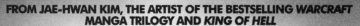

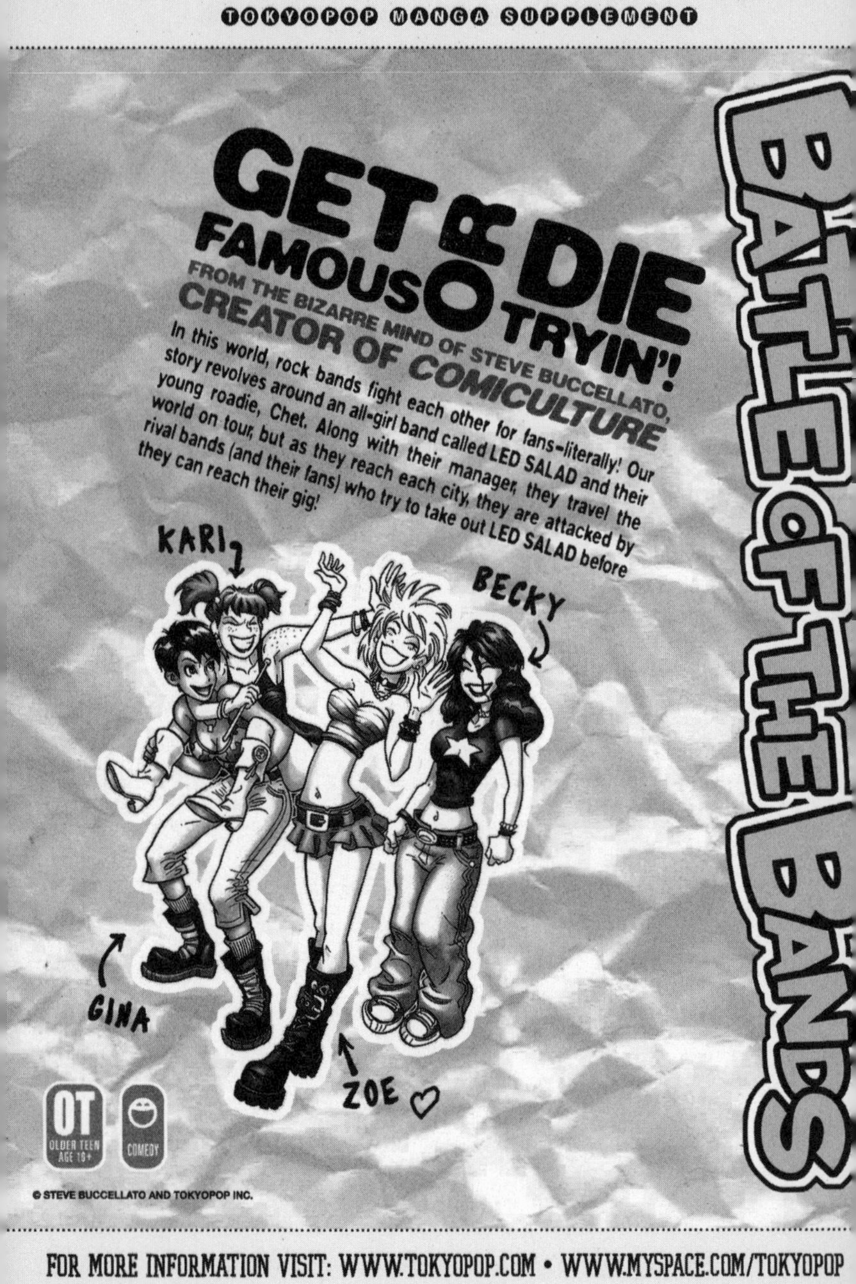
KARI
BECKY
GINA
ZOE

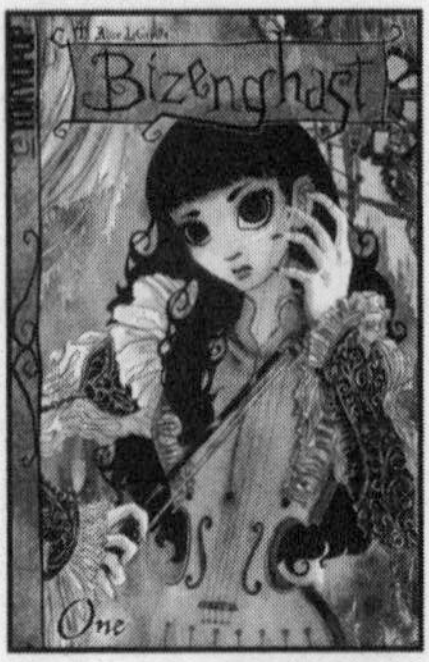
Bizenghast
One

FANTASY TEEN AGE 13+

BIZENGHAST:

BY M. ALICE LEGROW

I enjoy a good scare every now and then, and Bizenghast just has a way of getting under your skin. The best moments in M. Alice LeGrow's tale of tormented souls are the quieter ones: a prince dancing with his lover with a knife at her back, a witch quietly casting a spell on a young girl, then slowly strangling her to death. The book isn't over the top. It's just very, very creepy. It entrances you with its intricate, beautiful art, only to shock you with something unexpected and disturbing. And I, for one, can't wait for more.

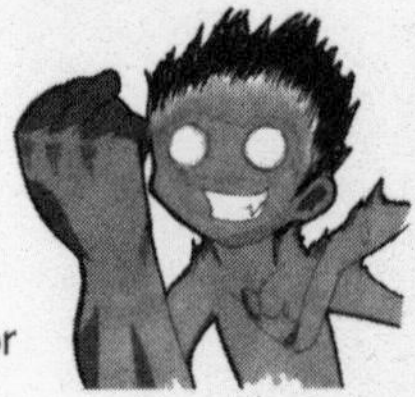

~Tim Beedle, Editor

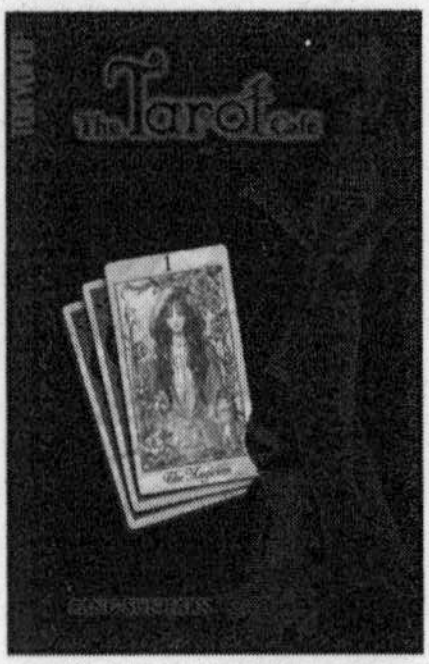

FANTASY TEEN AGE 13+

THE TAROT CAFÉ

BY SANG-SUN PARK

I was always kind of fond of Petshop of Horrors, and then along comes Tarot Cafe and blows me away. It's like Petshop, but with a bishonen factor that goes through the roof and into the stratosphere! Sang-Sung Park's art is just unreal. It's beautifully detailed, all the characters are stunning and unique, and while at first the story seems to be yet another gothy episodic piece of fluff, there is a dark side to Pamela and her powers that I can't wait to read more about. I'm a sucker for teenage werewolves, too.

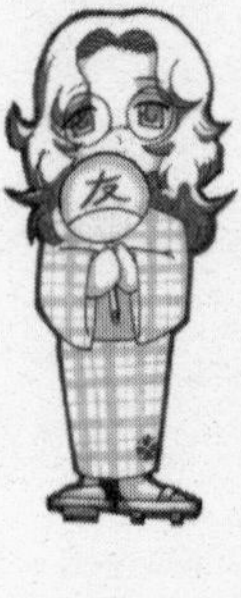

~ Lillian Diaz-Przybyl, Editor

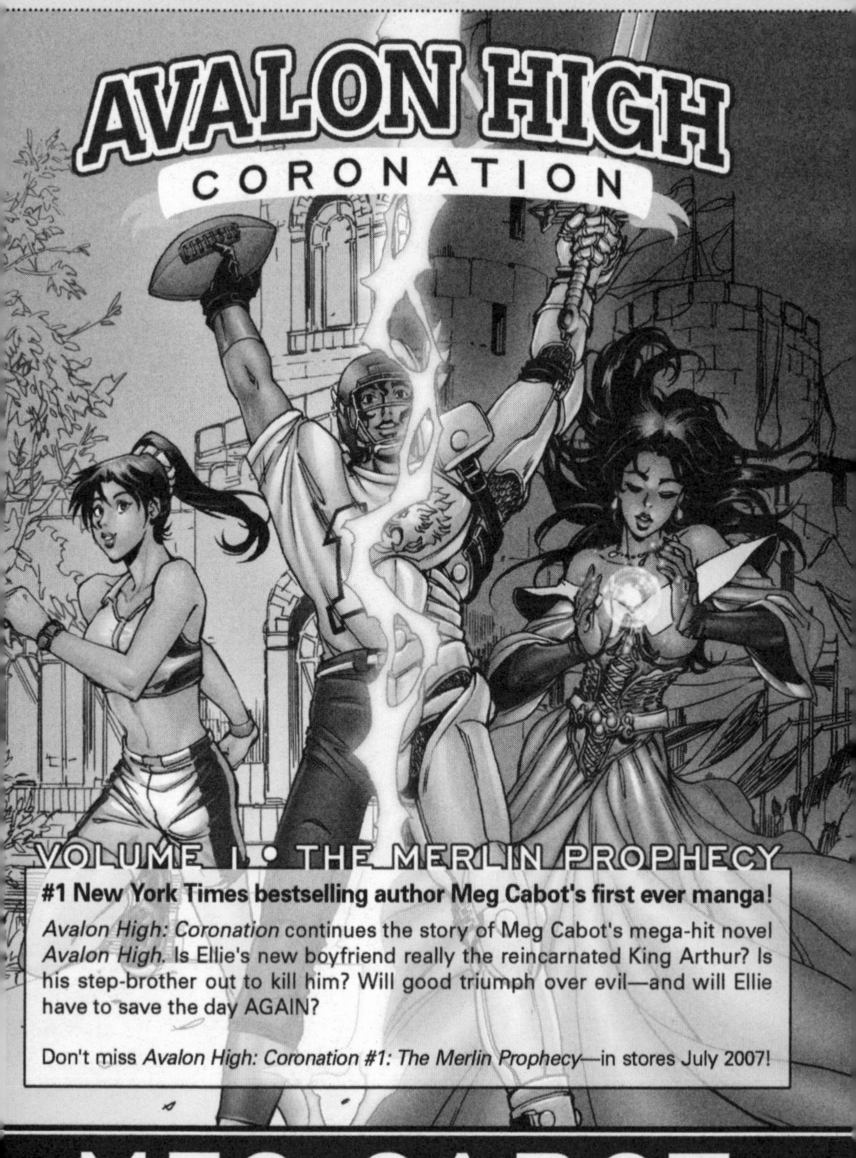
AVALON HIGH
CORONATION
VOLUME 1: THE MERLIN PROPHECY
#1 New York Times bestselling author Meg Cabot's first ever manga!
Avalon High: Coronation continues the story of Meg Cabot's mega-hit novel *Avalon High*. Is Ellie's new boyfriend really the reincarnated King Arthur? Is his step-brother out to kill him? Will good triumph over evil—and will Ellie have to save the day AGAIN?
Don't miss *Avalon High: Coronation #1: The Merlin Prophecy*—in stores July 2007!

KING OF THORN

™

YUJI
IWAHARA

ACTION

OT
OLDER TEEN
AGE 16+

WARNING:
Virus outbreak!

Kasumi and her
sister, Shizuku
are infected with
the fatal Medusa
virus. There is no
cure, but Kasumi
is selected to go
into a cryogenic
freezer until a
cure is found.
But when
Kasumi awakens,
she must struggle
to survive in a
treacherous
world if she
hopes to
discover what
happened to
her sister.

From Yuji Iwahara,
the creator of
the popular
Chikyu Misaki
and *Koudelka*

© YUJI IWAHARA